THE EMERGENCE AND EVOLUTION OF RELIGION

Written by leading theorists and empirical researchers, this book presents new ways of addressing the old question: Why did religion first emerge and then continue to evolve in all human societies? The authors of the book—each with a different background across the social sciences and humanities—assimilate conceptual leads and empirical findings from anthropology, evolutionary biology, evolutionary sociology, neurology, primate behavioral studies, explanations of human interaction and group dynamics, and a wide range of religious scholarship to construct a deeper and more powerful explanation of the origins and subsequent evolutionary development of religions than can currently be found in what is now vast literature. While explaining religion has been a central question in many disciplines for a long time, this book draws upon a much wider array of literature to develop a robust and cross-disciplinary analysis of religion. The book remains true to its subtitle by emphasizing an array of both biological and sociocultural forms of *selection dynamics* that are fundamental to explaining religion as a universal institution in human societies. In addition to Darwinian selection, which can explain the biology and neurology of religion, the book outlines a set of four additional types of sociocultural natural selection that can fill out the explanation of why religion first emerged as an institutional system in human societies, and why it has continued to evolve over the last 300,000 years of societal evolution. These sociocultural forms of natural selection are labeled by the names of the early sociologists who first emphasized them, and they can be seen as a necessary supplement to the type of natural selection theorized by Charles Darwin. Explanations of religion that remain in the shadow cast by Darwin's great insights will, it is argued, remain narrow and incomplete when explaining a robust sociocultural phenomenon like religion.

Jonathan H. Turner is 38th University Professor, University of California System, Research Professor, University of California, Santa Barbara, and Distinguished Professor of the Graduate Division, University of California, Riverside. He is also Director of the Institute for Theoretical Social Science, Santa Barbara, CA, USA.

Alexandra Maryanski is Professor of Sociology at the University of California, Riverside, USA.

Anders Klostergaard Petersen is Professor at the Department for the Study of Religion, School of Culture and Society, Aarhus University, Denmark.

Armin W. Geertz is Professor in the History of Religions at the Department for the Study of Religion, School of Culture and Society, and Jens Christian Skou Fellow at the Aarhus Institute of Advanced Studies, Aarhus University, Denmark.

Evolutionary Analysis in the Social Sciences
A series edited by Jonathan Turner and Kevin J. McCaffree

This new series is devoted to capturing the full range of scholarship and debate over how best to conduct evolutionary analyses on human behavior, interaction, and social organization. The series will range across social science disciplines and offer new cutting-edge theorizing in sociobiology, evolutionary psychology, stage-modeling, co-evolution, cliodynamics, and evolutionary biology.

The Emergence and Evolution of Religion

By Means of Natural Selection

Jonathan H. Turner

Alexandra Maryanski

Anders Klostergaard Petersen

Armin W. Geertz

Routledge
Taylor & Francis Group

NEW YORK AND LONDON

First published 2018
by Routledge
711 Third Avenue, New York, NY 10017

and by Routledge
2 Park Square, Milton Park, Abingdon, Oxon, OX14 4RN

Routledge is an imprint of the Taylor & Francis Group, an informa business

Library of Congress Cataloging-in-Publication Data
Names: Turner, Jonathan H., author.
Title: The emergence and evolution of religion by means of natural selection / Jonathan H. Turner, Alexandra Maryanski, Anders Klostergaard Petersen, Armin W. Geertz.
Description: 1 [edition]. | New York : Routledge-Taylor & Francis, 2017. | Series: Evolutionary analysis in the social sciences | Includes bibliographical references. | Description based on print version record and CIP data provided by publisher; resource not viewed.
Identifiers: LCCN 2017008446 (print) | LCCN 2017028200 (ebook) | ISBN 9781315111995 (Ebook) | ISBN 9781138080904 (hardback) | ISBN 9781138080928 (pbk.)
Subjects: LCSH: Religion—Philosophy. | Evolution. | Natural selection—Miscellanea.
Classification: LCC BL51 (ebook) | LCC BL51 .E493 2017 (print) | DDC 200.1—dc23
LC record available at https://lccn.loc.gov/2017008446

ISBN: 978-1-138-08090-4 (hbk)
ISBN: 978-1-138-08092-8 (pbk)
ISBN: 978-1-315-11199-5 (ebk)

Typeset in Minion
by Apex CoVantage, LLC

To the legacy of Robert Bellah,
who inspired the evolutionary analysis of religion in sociology.

Contents

Figures

Tables

About the Authors

Jonathan H. Turner is 38th University Professor, University of California System, Research Professor, University of California, Santa Barbara, and Distinguished Professor of the Graduate Division, University of California, Riverside. He is also Director of the Institute for Theoretical Social Science, Santa Barbara, CA, USA. He is primarily a general sociological theorist who has developed theoretical models and abstract principles explaining social processes operating at the macro, meso, and micro levels of social organization. He has a number of substantive interests, including: neurosociology, evolutionary sociology, sociology of emotions and interpersonal behaviors, stratification systems, dynamics of ethnic discrimination, institutional change analysis over long-term historical periods, philosophy of science, and theory construction in the social sciences. He is the author or coauthor of 41 books, editor or coeditor of nine books and handbooks, and author or coauthor of well over 200 research articles and chapters. He has been editor of two sociological journals, and on the editorial board of over 20 journals. His books are translated into 14 languages around the world.

Alexandra Maryanski is Professor of Sociology at the University of California, Riverside. She is also the Co-Director of the Institute for Theoretical Social Science, Santa Barbara, CA, USA. Trained in biological and cultural anthropology, as well as in primatology, she has devoted much of her career to bringing biological and evolutionary methods and substance, especially data on primates, into the social sciences. She has a number of additional specializations including: theoretical anthropology and sociology, sociology of religion, institutional analysis more broadly, evolution of human societies, hunter–gatherer social systems, and neurosociology. She was the founding Chair of the American Sociological Association's section on *Evolution, Biology, and Society*. She was the recent winner of the Best Book Award from the section in 2016. She has published four books and has in press a new book, *Emile Durkheim's Search for the Origins of Society in Religion*.

Anders Klostergaard Petersen is Professor at the Department for the Study of Religion, School of Culture and Society, Aarhus University, Denmark. His expertise is focused on late Second Temple Judaism, formative Christianity, and Graeco-Roman philosophy and religion, but he is also a regular participant in the media (national television, radio, and major newspapers) on matters pertaining to contemporary forms of religion. Additionally, he has a strong interest in matters relating to method and theory in the humanities and social sciences and overall questions pertaining to philosophy of science. Currently, he is working on a trilogy focused on the relationship between ritual, religion, and culture from Axial Age religion until today, in which he tries to combine his three major competencies in the history of religions, semiotics, and biocultural evolution. He is the author of 500 publications. Among his recent publications is the first edited volume in a newly launched series with Brill together with series-founder George van Kooten on *Religio-Philosophical Discourses in the Mediterranean World: From Plato, through Jesus, to Late Antiquity.* He is book review editor of *Journal for the Study of Judaism* and editor of the Danish journal *Religionsvidenskabeligt Tidsskrift.* In addition, he is a member of several editorial boards of leading book series and journals in the study of religion.

Armin W. Geertz is Professor in the History of Religions at the Department for the Study of Religion, School of Culture and Society, and Jens Christian Skou Fellow at the Aarhus Institute of Advanced Studies, Aarhus University, Denmark. He is co-founder of the Religion, Cognition and Culture Research Unit at Aarhus. His main expertise is in the history of religions; cognitive theory in the study of religion; neurobiology of religion, cognition and culture; biocultural approaches; extreme religiosity; evolutionary theories of religion; religions of indigenous peoples, especially North American Indians; contemporary religiosity; religion and law; and method and theory in comparative religions. He is the author of four books, editor or coeditor of 17 books and the author or coauthor of several hundred articles and book chapters. His publications in the cognitive science of religion range from religious narrative and evolutionary theory to the neurobiology of religion. His recent publications include *Religious Narrative, Cognition and Culture* (coeditor, 2011) and *Origins of Religion, Cognition and Culture* (editor, 2014). He has served on the editorial boards of many journals in the study of religion and is currently coeditor of *Journal for the Cognitive Science of Religion.* He has also served as coeditor of several book series in the study of religion and is currently coeditor of *Advances in the Cognitive Science of Religion* series at Equinox Publishers.

Preface

The authors represent a multidisciplinary expertise. Jonathan Turner is not an expert in religion but, rather, is a general sociological theorist who has sought to bring more biology and neurology into the social sciences, while theorizing about the dynamics of sociocultural systems more generally. Alexandra Maryanski is widely trained in both sociological and anthropological theory, as well as physical anthropology and primatology, but unlike Turner, she has considerable expertise on religions. Anders Klostergaard Petersen is a scholar of the history of religions with a primary expertise in late Second Temple Judaism, formative Christianity, Graeco-Roman philosophy and religion, and method and theory pertaining to the overall study of the humanities. Armin W. Geertz is also a historian of religions with a primary focus on indigenous religions, the anthropology of religion, the cognitive science of religion, and method and theory in the study of religion. Both Petersen and Geertz have been active in editing books series and journals as well as being members of the leading societies for the study of religion. The common thread in many of the works of these authors is an interest in evolution, particularly the evolution of religions—from their very origins in incipient religious behaviors to the present day and their various patterns of institutionalization.

The seeds for this project were planted in an interdisciplinary conference some years ago at Aarhus University where Turner and Maryanski met Petersen and Geertz. Their common interests were reinforced by a several months-long visit by Turner and Maryanski that Anders Petersen arranged at the Department for the Study of Religion in the summer/fall of 2014. During this time, a very rough draft of ideas about different types of selection, and how they affect the origins and subsequent evolution of religions was prepared and circulated among the authors. The ensuing period involved constant editing of and changes in the manuscript at a theoretical level, and then over the last year, materials on a wide variety of religions at various times and places were prepared to illustrate the utility of the different types of natural selection that are outlined in the chapters of this book. These illustrations are not meant to be definitive "tests" of the theoretical

ideas presented but, instead, they are intended to demonstrate the plausibility and utility of the theoretical models that we have outlined.

Thus, this book is a true collaborative effort of very different kinds of
scholars, with varying expertise that is blended in these pages to offer not
only a new way to theorize about religion but also sociocultural evolution
more generally. All institutional systems can, we think, be analyzed by
the models we offer. The underlying theoretical theme is that Darwinian
natural selection can only take the analysis of sociocultural systems so far;
understanding the biology and neurology of human behavior is critical,
and we document this conclusion in detail in the first chapters. At the same
time, once analysis moves to sociocultural systems, the nature of selection
changes, primarily because the actors in what we see as *superorganisms* have
capacities for agency and, indeed, are inherently teleological by virtue of
their neurological wiring. As a result they can use their capacities for agency
to generate new variants on which selection works, and moreover, they can
reconstruct the very environments to which they must adapt. Selection is
no longer "blind" but often purposive; and as a result, the dynamics of
natural selection on superorganisms is very different than that evident for
organisms. Selection is still a driving force of evolution, but its fundamental
nature changes, as do the specific dynamics involved in this evolutionary
process. In this manner, the book seeks to demonstrate that there is both
continuity in the evolution of organisms and superorganisms, but at the
same time, there is discontinuity that must be theorized.

Superorganisms reveal embedded layers of structure and culture, each
one composed of teleological actors adapting to a variety of environments.
Evolution and, hence, selection are multilevel; and moreover, the nature
of selection varies depending upon the level of analysis, from the human
organism through institutional systems and societies to even inter-societal
systems. We are quite sure that there are and will be many skeptics to this
conclusion, but we hope to demonstrate its plausibility by focusing on one
institutional system—religion—from its very beginnings as a genetically
driven behavioral propensity honed by Darwinian natural selection on
hominins to its subsequent evolution over the last 15,000 years into a wide
variety of religious formations.

Finally, the book is dedicated to Robert Bellah for the very simple reason that he would have understood what we have done as necessary. As
the most important sociologist *ever* to theorize about religion—and we
include even Max Weber here—this is a book that we think he would have
liked. Turner and Maryanski never met Bellah personally, but Turner had
considerable correspondence with him in the year before his death as he
was thinking through the theoretical ideas. He was most encouraging and

helpful. Similarly, Anders Petersen was in close contact with Robert Bellah until his death in late July 2013. At the previously mentioned conference on "Biological and Cultural Evolution and Their Interactions: Rethinking the Darwinian and Durkheimian Legacy in the Study of Religion," held at Aarhus University at the end of June 2012, Bellah was a keynote speaker. Given his advanced age and declining health, Bellah was not able to make it to Aarhus, but he generously gave a keynote lecture on "Religion in Human Evolution" skyped from his home at Berkeley. Subsequently, Bellah and Petersen remained in e-mail contact, and Petersen understands his current research on matters relating to Axial Age religion as deeply inspired by Bellah.

Current advances in all of the sciences have made this book possible. New insights have allowed us to once again raise grand questions and to provide possible ways of answering them. At the same time, the book testifies to an incipient development to move beyond the "two cultures." We show how scholars in the humanities and social sciences—strongly influenced by work in the natural sciences—can collaborate in a truly interdisciplinary manner that leads to new insights. As authors we are convinced that we have moved further in accounting for the selection mechanisms at play in human evolution. We have aspired to demonstrate how a multifarious phenomenon like religion and religious evolution can only be understood in terms of several selection mechanisms. Darwinian natural selection alone will not suffice. Nor will traditional studies founded on cultural evolutionary approaches alone. What is needed is a combination of different selection mechanisms. Only on the basis of such a theoretical approach, can we come closer to a fuller understanding of human beings as *homines duplices*, double-natured biological and cultural beings, as Émile Durkheim astutely acknowledged.

Jonathan H. Turner
Alexandra Maryanski
Anders Klostergaard Petersen
Armin W. Geertz

1
Explaining the Origins and Evolution of Religions

The belief in God has often been advanced as not only the greatest, but the most complete of all the distinctions between man and the lower animals. It is however impossible . . . to maintain that this belief is innate or instinctive in man. On the other hand a belief in all-pervading spiritual agencies seems to be universal.

Charles Darwin ([1871]1875)

Evolution and Religion

Religion emerged early in the first human societies. The structural core of these first societies was something rare for a primate: *nuclear families* of parents and offspring. As we shall see, the closest relatives of humans, the great apes, who are a good proxy for the last common ancestor to the earliest ancestors of humans, do not (and in the past, did not) form nuclear families, despite early romanticism by many social thinkers that the family is "the most natural of human" social forms. In fact, the opposite is the case; the evolution of the nuclear family is a remarkable feat for an animal whose ancestors, like the great apes today, are characterized by transient sexual relations and where even mother–offspring relations cease to exist for most offspring after leaving the natal unit after puberty. There is, then, little possibility among great apes and, hence, not much opportunity for humans' earliest relatives to form anything resembling a permanent nuclear family where kinship ties could be reckoned across generations.

Yet, biologically-based natural selection or a combination of the various types of natural selection to be examined in this book somehow produced *Homo sapiens*, along with the most unlikely social structure of all: nuclear families. Such families were organized into small bands of hunter–gatherers, and thus, there were two basic structures organizing the first human societies—nuclear families and bands—for as much as 95 percent of the time that *Homo sapiens* have existed on Earth.

As these structural forms organizing human ancestors—termed *hominins*—were evolving in the transition from the last hominins, *Homo erectus* to *Homo sapiens*, something else was also evolving in human societies; namely, religion![1] As we will document, the very forces that pushed hominins to become more social, more group oriented, and eventually more capable of forming enduring ties among males and females to form the nuclear family *are the very same forces* that would make religion inevitable in human societies. For, it was the push for capacity for more sociality and group formation among hominins over millions of years of evolution that made religion part of all human societies.

Religion and Society

This early arrival of the precursor to the institution of religion in human societies requires an explanation. Thus, in the chapters to follow, we seek to explain both the origins of religion under biological and non-biological modes of selection, as well as the subsequent evolution of religion over the last 300,000 years under mostly non-Darwinian modes of selection.[2] What the early arrival of religion signals is that there must have been biologically-based propensities for human reliance on religion at the beginnings of human societies; and the persistence of religion over the millennia signals that selection dynamics have favored religion as a core institutional system, even as post-industrial human societies became ever-more secular (McCaffree 2017).

Religion offers us a chance to explore how biological or what we will term *Darwinian selection* and other modes of more purely sociocultural selection operated simultaneously at the very beginnings of human society to produce the first religious behaviors among humans; and because of this fact, we may be able to understand some of the dynamics of several types of selection working in concert. Moreover, since religion continued to evolve as a core human social institution, we will also be able to understand *when* sociocultural forms of selection as it drives societal evolution become more critical to explanations of religious evolution than Darwinian natural selection. Hominins, whose descendants would become humans (see note 1), eventually began to create ever-larger societies only rivaled by insect societies, but in contrast to insects, the evolution of human megasocieties was driven mostly by non-Darwinian selection. Still, Darwinian selection was very much responsible for the cognitive, emotional, and behavioral propensities among humans that have made large-scale societies organized by culture and social structures possible. How did such large-bodied mammals as humans create societies of millions, if not billions, of people? Selection of various types and forms is part of the answer, and by following the evolution of religion as a way to illustrate the power of "selectionist" analysis, we can see and compare the biologically-based and socioculturally-based selection forces that allowed humans to construct macrosocieties. The analysis of religion, then, provides a segue into what is sometimes termed "ultrasociality" more generally because, without religion, societies on a human scale could not have evolved.

Many of the dynamics of sociocultural selection are similar to those in Darwinian selection, especially in some forms, but there are also fundamental differences in how biological organisms in ecosystems and how sociocultural forms in ecosystems "select"; and the result is that we *need new models* of selection that outline the dynamics of at least four additional types of sociocultural selection beyond strictly biologically-based natural selection. Our goal in this volume is thus to explicate these additional types of selection, using religion as a very useful exemplar for understanding their operation. The reason for this is that religion is only possible because Darwinian selection along the hominin line leading to humans was increasingly supplanted by other forms of selection, especially as societies grew and became more complex.

What Is Religion?

Let us begin with a composite definition of religious elements (Turner 1972, 1997a, 2003), saving preliminary types of non-Darwinian selection for the next chapter. At a fundamental and basic level, religion consists of (1) a community of individuals, (2) who share representations, ideas, and perhaps beliefs about a supernatural realm and the forces or beings inhabiting this realm, (3) who practice both individual and collective rituals addressing supernatural beings and forces inhabiting a sacred realm, and (4) who are often organized into small or big *cult structures* (religious corporate units) with specific practitioners charged with organizing the community and their ritual practices (cf. Geertz 2013). There are, of course, many different attempts at defining religion, none of which have gained general consensus (see Smith 1998; Geertz 1999, 2016; Platvoet and Molendijk 1999; Jensen 2014). The religions in nomadic hunting and gathering societies evidenced elements (1), (2), and (3), while element (4) was often only implicit in food-collecting or band societies. Once societies became more complex as human populations began to establish more permanent settlements, *cult structures* organizing community members and their ritual practices became clearly evident [i.e., element (4)].

In laying out this preliminary definition, however, qualifications and elaborations will be necessary as we move to the analysis on the origins and subsequent development of religion by various means of selection processes.

The sense of community so necessary for religion and the cult structures organizing worshipers of supernatural forces was, as we shall see, a hard-wired behavioral capacity and propensity found among both the great apes and humans' early hominin ancestors (Maryanski 2013). As such, a sense of community as a critical form of social organization (beyond kinship and band) *preceded* the evolution of religion and was one of the critical conditions necessary for religion to emerge and evolve. The conception of a sacred and supernatural realm of forces, beings, and entities will also need refinement, along two lines. The sacred has not always been attached to the supernatural although, in more modern analyses, the holy, sacred, and supernatural tend to be blended together conceptually. But, the original root term for "the sacred" denoted the fact that objects, ideas, relations, structures, or any social phenomena can be sacred when their importance and significance is paramount and charged with intense emotions. The first sacred objects were the new types of social formations among hominins as they became more organized in a struggle for survival in a new and hostile environment. Later, as selection pushed on these capacities to impute sacredness to these new types of social relations and social structures, and their cultures, a cognitive and emotional threshold was passed in either later hominins or, perhaps, only early *Homo sapiens* that allowed for the emergence of true religions. The capacity to impute sacredness could now denote the supernatural realm for members of even the earliest hunting and gathering societies.

Like the capacity to impute sacredness, we believe that the ability to use rituals—a critical property of all religions—surely preceded religion by hundreds of thousands of years, if not millions of years if we count early hominins. Rituals must have been critical to building up solidarities in the new social structures and cultural systems that would typify hominins and early human hominins. Indeed, as we will argue, rituals are a central part of *everyday* interactions and, as such, build up and sustain micro solidarities for the duration of any interaction or its repetition later in time. There is nothing necessarily sacred about rituals, *per se*, but they constituted, once again, one of the conditions necessary for religion to emerge and evolve. The ability of hominins to enact emotion-arousing rituals directed at objects symbolizing the sacred was thus a necessary precondition for religious behavior among the first humans.

Thus, many of the features necessary for religion to emerge—save for a notion of the supernatural—*already existed* in the behavioral repertory of comparatively big-brained hominoids (the ancestors and descendants of great apes and hominins on the human clade), as we will document later. Hence, as early hominins evolved and were replaced by *Homo sapiens* around 300,000 years ago, a number of preconditions for religion—a sense of community and a sense of self *vis-à-vis* other members of this community—were all present among early humans, just as they are now present in humans' closest relative, the chimpanzee. They had evolved in hominins beyond what is evident among chimpanzees and, hence, the last common ancestor to humans and present-day chimpanzees. (For discussions of self and community in chimpanzees, see Whiten et al. 1999; Herbinger et al. 2001; Hare 2011; Kaminski, Call, and Tomasello 2008; Matsuzawa 2009; Kaneko and Tomonaga 2011; Call and Tomasello 2008.) We will argue that evolution was driven by two related selection pressures on hominins to (1) *increase social solidarities among conspecifics* and (2) *increase capacities for more permanent groups organizing conspecifics.* Indeed, the fossil record documents that during the Miocene, Pliocene, and Pleistocene epochs, many hominoid species left the forest to take up a semi-terrestrial or terrestrial lifestyle but *no* species of apes survived. Even the giant Asian ape, *Gigantopithecus*, who had adapted to a ground-living lifestyle by sheer bulk, with speculation that it weighted at least 600 pounds and was 9 feet tall, went extinct about 100,000 years ago, and it is not clear if *Gigantopithecus* lived outside the forests in open-country savanna conditions (Andrews and Kelly 2007; Pilbeam and Young 2004; Fleagle 2013). Yet, natural selection hit upon a behavioral and organizational strategy that allowed *early Homo genera* to survive by favoring novel types of social bonds and more stable grouping patterns for an evolved, upright ape. Once in place, these evolutionary novelties were utilized by later hominins— but possibly only early humans—to forge the first religions that began to add a *notion of the supernatural* to the critical pre-existing capacities of humans' hominin ancestors.

As we will come to see, the notion of a supernatural is not just a cognitive leap "of faith," as it were, from a bigger brained evolved great ape like humans, but that some elements of this cognitive capacity were already in chimpanzees and, thus, present in humans' hominin ancestors and thereby subject to further selection. This underlying set of elements that would eventually allow for the conception of a supernatural realm to emerge among *Homo sapiens* is related to selection on what we will term the *community complex*, following Alexandra Maryanski's recent work (2018). This complex served, as will become evident in subsequent chapters, as the *sine qua non* for the emergence of religion. This complex in rudimentary form is present in the great apes today, notably chimpanzees, and hence was part of the behavioral and cognitive phenotype of the last common ancestor we shared with the great apes. Indeed, great apes and hence hominins evidence a cognitive conception of a larger community beyond the horizons of daily life; they can (and could in the distant past) see themselves as objects, or possess a sense of self and identity (a very rare capacity among only a few species of animals).[3] As Suddendorf and Collier-Baker (2009: 1676) put it, among primates it is "only the descendants of a hominoid that probably lived between 13.8 and 18 myr ago [that] have so far reliably demonstrated that they know who it is that . . . looks back at them when they look in the mirror."

In relation to a larger community force, hominins could impute something like sacred (or at least, emotionally special) qualities to this community; they could engage in emotion-arousing rituals directed at their sense of community with conspecifics, and perhaps they could even create totems marking the significance of relations and social structures inside their communities. It is this cluster of capacities revolving around animals that organize at the community *rather than group level* that is important in understanding the evolution of religion.

In this book we will also examine other behavioral capacities that are part of humans' primate ancestry—capacities to use linguistic symbols, to read the minds of conspecifics, to rhythmically interact, to mimic behaviors of others, to engage in play, and to calculate justice and reciprocities that form the beginnings of a proto-morality. Some of these capacities are already part of prominent theories on the origins of religion, but we will view them as *a bundle of inherited behavioral capacities.* This bundle of inherited traits, coupled with a sense of community, with the capacity to see self in relation to community, with reliance on emotionally charged rituals, with proto-conceptions of the sacred, with representations of the sacred with what might be totems, made the emergence of religion almost inevitable in human societies. This was especially so as the hominin neocortex began to grow with the appearance of *early Homo species.* Indeed, our goal in this monograph is to document that the behavioral capacities to be religious are only a short extension of the cognitive, emotional, and behavioral capacities of the great apes today. Hence, these capacities have long been present in the ancestors of present-day great apes over the last 10 million years and in all hominins that evolved along the human clade. Religion *was not a great leap forward* but, rather, a small but crucial step perhaps made by late hominins but certainly by the first human hominins, *Homo sapiens.*

Selection Dynamics and the Evolution of Religion

Too often, we believe, religion is considered to be something special and unlike anything else in the sociocultural universe. Perhaps this orientation is inevitable, given the power of religious beliefs and rituals to move individuals and, at times, whole societies or even systems of societies. From a neurosociological and evolutionary perspective, however, religion is like any other institutional system; it evolved by *Darwinian* "natural selection" that first operated on primate, hominoid, hominin, and human phenotypes and their underlying genetic basis and, then, by *new forms of selection* that operate on sociocultural formations that humans created.

Darwninian dynamics are most relevant for understanding the evolution of *organisms*, including humans, but it becomes necessary to explore new types of selection processes once analysis shifts to the dynamics of *superorganisms*, or the "organization of organisms" into societies (Spencer 1874–96; Turner and Maryanksi 2008, 2015; Richerson and Boyd 2005; Dunn 2016). As will become increasingly evident, the goal of this book is to offer a five-fold account of how religion has evolved by *different types of selection* during its early origins as a behavioral capacity and, later, during its institutionalization as a basic social formation in all human societies. Once institutionalized, religion has continued to evolve by new forms of natural selection up to the very present and probably long into the future, even as societies secularize many activities (McCaffree 2017).

A Basic Critique of Some of the Existing Approaches

As we begin to extend the conception of selection to explain the origins and subsequent evolution of religion, we will introduce ideas from many of the current explanations on the evolution of religion. Our approach begins with a more sociological form of analysis from what can be termed "the *new* evolutionary sociology" (Turner and Machalek 2018; Turner, Machalek and Maryanski 2015), which seeks to move beyond conceptions of institutional systems as outcomes of behavioral propensities of humans and, instead, to isolate the additional mechanisms and processes by which culture and social structure are built up from interpersonal behaviors. Sociology takes a very different approach than some of the most prominent explanations for religion; and, while these more cognitive and behavioral approaches are critical to *any* explanation of religion, they are nonetheless incomplete—at least from a sociological viewpoint. Of course, most approaches would not just assume that a behavioral propensity assures that an institutional system will be built up from this propensity. And yet, so many explanations do not take the additional theoretical steps needed to explain *why* and *how* institutional systems in societies evolve from simple behavioral propensities. To delineate these needed theoretical steps, it is necessary to turn to sociology more than biology and psychology. Thus, evolutionary biology and psychology get us so far, but sociology is needed in order to have a fuller, more robust explanation of emergent sociocultural formations like religion (or economy, polity, science, medicine, education, law, or any of the emergent institutional domains of more complex human societies).

From a sociological perspective, a good many of the explanatory efforts of distinguished scholars do not contain enough sociology, even though the intent is to explain a phenomenon that is as much sociological as psychological or even biological in nature. From the evolved biology and psychology of hominins and eventually humans, religion is more than a capacity or propensity to behave in certain ways. Religion is *institutionalized as a basic type of sociocultural formation* in all known human societies; and thus, it is necessary to leave biology and psychology at some point to address the dynamics of religion in more purely sociological and historical terms. It is, of course, entirely reasonable to try to examine religion at the biological level, even the genetic level if particular gene clusters are seen as generating neurological structures and propensities that lead to religious behavior. Thus, it is not the nature of non-sociological efforts, *per se*, that represents a problem but *the narrowness* of the biological (even genetic) and the psychological explanations, which often rely upon "just so" stories to connect biologically driven cognitive, emotional, and behavioral capacities that are seen as critical to the full institutionalization of religion in society. However, such explanations of the cognitive, emotional, and behavioral capacities and propensities of individuals *will always be a part of the explanation* on the origins of religion, but in our view, particularly in the analysis of religion, scholars often over-reach. They seek to explain social structures and culture without enough attention to the necessary sociological forces that institutionalized behavioral capacities and propensities installed by Darwinian natural selection. Our aim in this book, therefore, is to offer a more robust biological and neurological explanation than currently exists in theorizing on religion and, then, to add to this explanation *more sociological ideas* that are able to explain not only the early institutionalization of religion but also its continued development as societies have evolved.

Another shortcoming of many current explanations of religion is the emphasis on one or a small set of behavioral capacities. In our view, however, religion emerges from *many* cognitive, emotional, and behavioral capacities and/or propensities that were hard-wired *for millions of years* in the neurology of higher mammals, higher primates, great apes, and hominins. Thus, even at the level of specifying behavioral, cognitive, and emotional capacities, many biologically and psychologically oriented explanations are limited in their explanatory power. Particular genetic, neuro-structural, and behavioral or (cognitive, emotional) capacities may be important in explaining some aspects of religion, but these typically will not provide a very robust explanation of either the origin or the subsequent evolution of religions without recognizing two things: first, the biology and psychology of religion is very old and was not created *de novo* in the late Pleistocene by Darwinian natural selection; and second, the institutionalization of religion was inevitable given the kinds of selection pressures generated by humans' evolved psychology but, even more importantly, by the pressures on human populations generated from population growth, settlements, and differentiated institutional systems. Thus, we find current explanations couched mostly at the cognitive, emotional, and behavioral level important and valuable, to be sure, and very interesting, *per se*. But we also find them incomplete. They take us part of the way, but our goal is to visualize the rather robust set of behavioral capacities of humans as evolved great apes. Moreover, it is equally important to explain how these capacities became *institutionalized* in religious sociocultural formations in societies in the first place and, then, how these formations have evolved since their first emergence in early hunter–gatherer populations.

Figure 1.1 illustrates our muted and respectful criticism of existing biological and psychological explanations by using sociobiology and evolutionary psychology as exemplars of the basic problem. In sociobiology, it is argued that there are basic fitness-enhancing behaviors that evolved like any other trait in humans; and these behavioral propensities—e.g., kin selection, altruism, exchange, and reciprocity—have caused the emergence of basic institutional structures, such as kinship and economy (e.g., see: Alcock 2001; Axelrod 1984; Dawkins 1976; Hamilton 1964; Trivers 1971, 2005; Williams 1966; Wilson 1975, 1978). The problem with these types of explanations is denoted by the arrow on the far right of the figure, where the arrow to institutionalization represents a "gloss" on the sociocultural dynamics involved in institutionalization, and then subsequent evolution. Of course, biology and psychology are not obligated to explain institutionalization, but to the extent that theorists in these fields attempt to do so, *they need to use some sociology*. It is just assumed—often illustrated with a speculative though often fascinating "just so" story—that a behavioral propensity becomes institutionalized, without explaining how or why such institutionalization *actually occurred*. Moreover, even when sophisticated agent-based modeling and simulations are used (e.g., Skyrms 2004), these only demonstrate that it is possible to have a particular outcome starting with a behavioral propensity of interest. But these simulations do not explain *the processes by which a behavioral inclination becomes fully institutionalized* in corporate units organizing individuals' activities and in the culture of these units and the more inclusive institutional domain in which they are embedded. Simulations tend to gloss over these details.

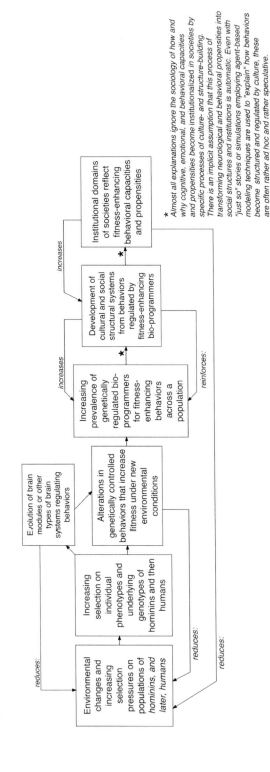

Figure 1.1 Limitations in the Models of Sociobiology and Evolutionary Psychology

Evolutionary psychology accepts many of the assumptions of sociobiology but adds the notion—at least in earlier versions (e.g., Cosmides and Tooby 1992)—that the behavioral propensities that lead to institutionalization are driven by "brain modules" that evolved during hominin evolution in the late Pleistocene epoch. There is little evidence from comparative neurology on great ape and human brains for the emergence of such new modules during the late Pleistocene, as we will outline in detail in subsequent chapters, but whether or not these modules exist is less important than, once again, the assumption that the existence of a "special-function" module or some other evolved neurological system explains the institutionalization and evolution of something as complicated as religion.

Other approaches, from cognitive psychology through psychoanalysis to evolutionary psychology and perhaps even general psychology make the same assumptions: a capacity or propensity for a given type of cognitive functioning, emotional response, or behavioral propensity goes a long way in explaining the evolution of institutional systems in societies. From a sociological perspective, the task is to explain *how* such capacities, propensities, and regularities in cognitions, emotions, and behaviors set into motion more structural and cultural dynamics by which behaviors became enshrined in institutional systems. This is where sociology is needed because it is the one discipline that studies organizational and institutional systems, often from an evolutionary perspective. Some approaches, however, adopt a more sociological stance, even though the authors often are unaware of the relevant sociological literatures. For example, Ara Norenzayan's fascinating book, *Big Gods: How Religion Transformed Cooperation and Conflict* (2013) offers a sociological explanation, one which revolves around what we will term *Type-1 Spencerian selection* for new types of social structures when existing structures are not capable of regulating, coordinating, and controlling a population. While there has been much criticism of this project (see, for example, the book symposium in *Religion, Brain and Behavior* 2015), it is a giant step in the right direction for understanding how new types of religion become institutionalized under sociocultural selection pressures. And while the book reintroduces sociological analyses (e.g., Swanson 1964), it also underemphasizes earlier sociological inquiries along these same lines (e.g., Spencer 1874–96 in his *Ecclesiastical Institutions*) as well as more contemporary theories in sociology. Norenzayan's book, on the other hand, is at an analytical level that allows more sociology to be added to biological and psychological explanations.

There is also a converse problem. Many sociologists reject biological and psychological explanations as relevant to *any* analysis of institutionalization. But this all too common stance ignores the fact that the biology of humans as evolved great apes is critical to any sociological explanation of universal behaviors that have become institutionalized in all societies. To ignore biology and psychology reduces the power of sociological explanation. And so, while many sociologists dismiss biological explanations of *anything* social, we do not; we embrace biology as making sociological explanations more robust, but we also recognize that one cannot take the short cut denoted in Figure 1.1. Existing explanations thus cry out for some sociology which, with a few notable exceptions (e.g., Bellah 2011a), is rarely found.

Darwinian natural selection as it installed the biology of humans as evolved great apes is critical to understanding how religion or any institutional system evolved in human societies, but explanation cannot stop at this point. What is needed is more detail on how and why the institutionalization of religion first occurred, and then how it has evolved, and why. As the title of this book emphasizes, we are focusing on selection but with what is not a too often repeated caveat: there are *other types of natural selection* beyond biological that help explain what most current theories cannot. How and why did religion become institutionalized, and how and why has it evolved as societies have become ever-larger and more complex? To answer such questions, we require explanations involving more than one type of selection. Thus, this book is dedicated to *expanding the scope of what is viewed as natural selection* beyond that evident for the evolution of organisms. Our goal is to explain the operation of selection forces of a different type than Darwinian natural selection.

These non-Darwinian forces are, we assert, *selection* but selection that works on *superorganisms* composed of humans and the corporate units organizing their activities. If all that is available to us is Darwinian natural selection, its limitations become very evident when addressing teleological systems like human superorganisms. Humans have capacities for agency, goal directness, innovation, and other processes of human will. And, these force us to extend the conceptualization of selection to take account of teleological actors and systems that can create variants of sociocultural phenotypes and that, in turn, can engage in new forms of competition and conflict for resources with each other and existing variants of corporate units in institutional domains. If non-teleological, blind Darwinian selection is the only legitimate mode of explanation, then this level of explanation can never explain the operation of religion in human superorganisms—despite dogmatic assertions, "just so stories," and simulations. Darwinian selection can, however, explain how these human capacities for agency evolved and, hence, the emotional, cognitive, and behavioral foundations on which non-Darwinian selection became possible in human superorganisms.

For, in the end, Darwinian natural selection worked on the basic great-ape anatomy and neuroanatomy to produce behavioral capacities and propensities among hominins and humans over the last 5 to 6 million years that made human societies possible and fitness-enhancing. But, once these capacities are part of the phenotype of organisms and hence are in play in the creation and evolution of sociocultural superorganisms, Darwinian selection loses much of its explanatory traction.

Other types of selection need to be considered; and while these bear some continuity with Darwinian selection, they take account of a universe filled with teleological creatures—i.e., humans—and teleological corporate units organizing into coordinated divisions of labor regulated by culture rather than genes. Selection is no longer blindly working only on phenotypes and underlying genotypes of organisms. Selection is now often *intentional*; and most importantly, variants on which selection work are no longer only tied to genetically driven phenotypical features of organisms (or other forces such as mutations, gene flow, and genetic drift). Rather, variations on which selection works are now *created* as features of corporate units organizing human activities.

Conclusion

In closing this short introduction, we should note that Darwin himself realized the limitations of his conception of natural selection on humans in later editions of his *The Descent of Man* (1871). He had not, of course, conceptualized the notion of genes as these became the units subject to variation by mutations, drift, flow, and selection on phenotypes; and in some ways, biology today resists what Darwin saw: humans are teleological, and they have the capacity (by their genetic endowment, of course) to change the very nature of the environments—physical, biological, and sociocultural—to which they must adapt. Superorganisms among humans (unlike insects; see Machalek 1992; Turner and Machalek 2018) are not locked into their genes because they are built up by the use of cultural information to create complex social morphologies that are subject to human direction and, hence, to change by innovation.

The social universe created by humans involves *multilevel selection* at the genetic level, to be sure, but equally important at various sociocultural levels as well. Variations can be created; they can be acted upon; and they can be used to build new cultural and social systems. We will focus on the dynamics of selection, as the subtitle of this book underscores. It is important to emphasize that an expanded view of selection dynamics can explain a lot but certainly *not everything*; but, by combining Darwinian natural selection with four types of sociocultural selection, we can develop a theory on the origins of religion and its subsequent evolution. We have labeled these sociocultural types of selection after historical figures in sociology who, both explicitly and implicitly, employed them: *Spencerian selection*, Type-1 and Type-2, *Durkheimian selection*, and *Marxian selection*. We will generally refer to biological natural selection as *Darwinian selection*. Perhaps it is misleading to label selection by historical figures, but we have chosen to do so in order to emphasize that sociology *as much as biology* in the 19th century was an explicitly evolutionary science.

Some of the existing theories on the evolution of religion have thus failed to fully appreciate Darwin's own insights into the problems that teleology imposes on biological explanations that try to explain complex sociocultural formations. Indeed, the social universe has a heavy dose of Lamarckian forces—that is acquired characteristics that are created by human agency and that, once created and institutionalized, can be passed down over time. We have not included Lamarck's efforts because his emphasis on acquired characteristics, which helps explain sources of sociocultural variations, does not fully capture the nature of the selection dynamics that we will emphasize in this book (see also Jablonka and Lamb 2005 for a very interesting effort to explain sources of variation in the history of life).

Efforts to explain institutional systems by behaviors installed by Darwinian natural selection alone are inevitably going to be limited because of the capacities of humans to innovate; and one of the most important innovations, occurring very early in human evolution, was the creation of religion by adding a seemingly small, but critical idea that only an animal with a big brain wired to be highly emotional could do: conceive of another plane or realm of existence inhabited by supernatural forces, beings, and objects that affect the profane and mundane world of human existence. Why would humans do this to themselves? That is the question that we seek to answer by extending the conceptualization of one of the key dynamics driving all organic and superorganic evolution: selection.

In the next chapter, we offer a preliminary overview of the five types of selection driving not only the biotic universe but also the sociocultural universe. Later chapters will elaborate on each of these five types of selection as they relate to the evolution of religion. The sociocultural universe created and altered by human agency executed in the structures and cultures of the corporate units organizing human activities in superorganisms is, to some extent, driven by all five types of selection. And the explanation of religion is incomplete without explaining the non-Darwinian selection processes that institutionalized religion in the first human societies and then the selection processes that have continued to drive the evolution of religion up to the present and, no doubt, into the future. Again, we should emphasize that even an expanded conceptualization of selection *does not explain everything*. Rather, our conceptualization of types of selection is simply another set of conceptual tools to explain important dynamics that occur in the evolution of human societies and its institutional systems, including religion.

Notes

1 Hominoid taxonomy is currently in flux with potential confusion on what the terms mean. We are using the widely accepted cladistic classification. Hominoids (or Hominoidea) who make up about 5 percent of primate species are the lesser apes (siamangs and gibbons); the great apes (orangutans, gorillas, and chimpanzees) and the human evolved ape. A *hominid* formerly used to denote only humans and near ancestors now includes the great apes as well. A *hominin* is now used to denote only humans and their ancestors or near ancestors, or any hominoid that habitually walks upright.

2 Just as the final editing on page proofs of this book was completed, startling new data on the emergence of *Homo* sapiens emerged. More accurate dating of fossils scattered about Africa now pushes back the emergence of humans another 100,000 years to at least 300,000 years ago. The size of the skulls is in the human measure but the shape is somewhat different and perhaps "primitive." What is clear is the fact that humans were more widely spread across Africa at a much earlier time. What is not clear is whether or not these early humans had traits like the finely attuned capacity for oral speech production, since the genetic data indicate the genes regulating the structures for articulated speech in the human measure have been under selection for 200,000 years (Enard et al. 2002a, 2002b). For the preliminary reports on this amazing set of finds on the origins of *Homo* sapiens, see: Stringer and Galway-Witham (2017); Richter, Grun, Joannes-Boyau, et al. (2017); Jacques Hublin, Ben-Ncer, Baily, et al. (2017); and Gallaway, Nature/News (online), June 7, 2017.

3 There are three evolved types of identities in mammalian evolution: one is a species identity (common to all mammals), another is a social identity (common to all social mammals), and, third, a rare self-identity. To date, a self-identify has only been documented in dolphins (and probably whales that belong to the same family), elephants, great apes, and humans (see Maryanski 2017).

2

Types of Natural Selection Driving Religious Evolution

A Preliminary Review

The question of questions for mankind—the Problem which underlies all others, and is more deeply interesting than any other—is the ascertainment of the place which Man occupies in nature and of his relations to the universe of things.

Thomas Huxley (1863: 71)

Darwinian Natural Selection

In the Modern Synthesis in biology, the "forces of evolution" include (1) natural selection, (2) mutations, (3) gene flow, and (4) genetic drift, with each affecting the distribution of genes in a population's "gene pool" (cf. Mayr 2001). Darwinian natural selection is a process that acts on the genetic variation in living populations of organisms whereby individual phenotypes (and hence the underlying genotypes generating these phenotypes) are selected by environments in which life forms seek to survive and reproduce. If the environment changes, selection acts as a sieve by working on phenotypes that reveal features that enable organisms to survive and reproduce, while removing or selecting out those phenotypes (and underlying genes) less compatible with a new environment. Thus, by *non-teleological* selection, the "fitness" of variations in phenotypes among members of a population is sorted; and from this process the population of life forms evolves (or changes), with evolution defined as "descent with modification." Table 2.1 highlights the key processes involved in Darwinian selection, while Figure 2.1 lays out Darwinian selection as a process.

The central force driving natural selection is environmental changes that lead to intensified competition among conspecifics over resources, a competition that favors those phenotypic variations in members of a population that increase fitness or the probability of survival and reproduction. While selection works on individual phenotypes, the emphasis of biology is on the evolution of *the population* as a distribution of phenotypes (and underlying distribution of genes generating variations in phenotypes)

16

TABLE 2.1 Key Elements of Darwinian Selection among Organisms

1. Species of organisms (and other organic forms) survive by securing resources from their environments, with those organisms able to secure sufficient resources to reproduce themselves being the most fit.

2. Fitness is thus determined by the degree to which the phenotypes (and underlying genotypes producing these phenotypes) of organisms allow individual organisms to secure resources and reproduce.

3. When the environment of organisms changes, for any reason, competition for resources in a niche will generally increase, thereby also increasing selection on *variants* of the phenotypes of organisms.

4. The most likely environmental changes stem from:

   a. ecological alterations in the distribution of physical and biotic resources in an environment

   b. growth in the population of organisms of a given type of resource niche

   c. migrations of other types of organisms into a resource niche.

5. There will always be a distribution of variations of phenotypes (and underlying genotypes) in a population of organisms, with variations potentially increasing from mutations and gene flow.

6. As competition for available resources among variants of a given type of organism or between different organisms increases, Darwinian selection increases and changes the distribution of phenotypes and genes in the gene pool of a population.

7. Thus, evolution revolves around descent with modification in the distribution of variations in phenotypes and the distribution of genotypes in a gene pool as selection favors those variations in phenotypes that allow organisms to secure resources, survive, and reproduce.

within a given resource niche in the environment. This last point is important because the unit of evolution in Darwinian theory, and the Modern Synthesis, is *the population* defined as a distribution of (a) phenotypes among members of the population and, as noted previously, (b) their genes in a "gene pool" (Ridley, 1996).

For the last 70 years or longer if we go back to early sociologists such as Herbert Spencer (1898[1874–96]) and Émile Durkheim (1947[1893]), social scientific research has shown that cultural transmission simply does not work like genetic transmission (Steward 1955 [1972]; Runciman 1983–97, 2009; Richerson and Boyd 2005; Turner and Maryanski 2008; Turner 1995, 2010a). Additionally, the unit of evolution is not the population of phenotypes (and underlying genotypes) but, instead, various

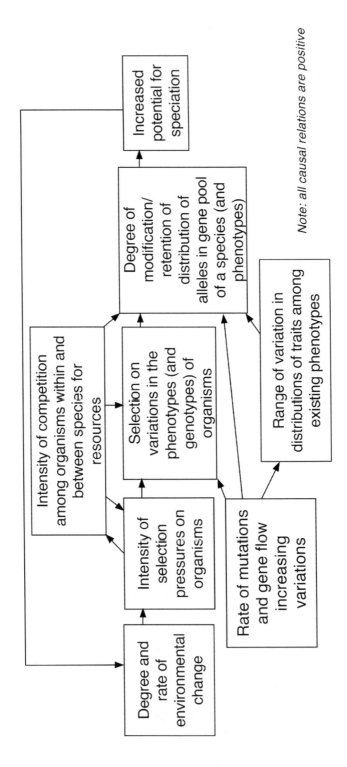

Figure 2.1 Darwinian Selection as Conceived by the Modern Synthesis

levels of sociocultural formation (e.g., corporate units that are organized by divisions of labor to pursue goals and thus become the building blocks of diverse institutional domains such as kinship, economy, polity, law, medicine, education, and of course, religion). Hence, fitness—which is perhaps an ill-fitting word—is defined *not* by passing on genes or even something as fanciful as "memes" (Dawkins 1976), but by the capacity of a sociocultural formation *to survive over time in an environment* (Turner and Maryanski 2008b, 2015). Evolution for sociocultural systems involves changes in the nature, type, number, distribution, and integration of corporate units (revealing divisions of labor in pursuit of goals) at various levels of social organization and the cultural systems (ideologies, beliefs, norms, technologies, texts, etc.) attached to these integrated systems of corporate units. Furthermore, the systems of information regulating behavior in social structures (i.e., culture) are not tightly integrated; and indeed, each can be subject to different selection pressures at the same time. Darwinian natural selection affects genetic codes via alterations in variations of phenotypes of individual organisms, and therefore, the information stored in genes. As a result, alterations in phenotypes and genotypes of organisms' genes have greater effects on subsequent generations of organisms than do the cultural systems that provide loose instructions for actors in superorganisms. Indeed, culture and social structure can be dramatically changed by what transpires as individuals and the corporate units organizing their activities react and interact with each other.

And, most importantly, selection in human *superorganisms* involves not only Darwinian selection on the phenotypes of individuals (and their genotypes), but also the structures and their cultures that make up each organizational level of human superorganisms in which individuals occupy status positions and play out roles in accordance with cultural codes of various sorts. Figure 2.2 illustrates the key levels of social organization on which selection can work, beginning with Darwinian selection at the bottom of the figure and, then, with *new types* of selection working at various levels of social organization. As one moves to higher levels of social organization, Darwinian selection loses explanatory power, while what we will term *Spencerian*, *Durkheimian*, and *Marxian* selection dynamics become increasingly more important to understanding the evolution of sociocultural systems, or superorganisms, and the institutional systems such as religion that evolve as part of human superorganisms. Yet, the effects of Darwinian selection never disappear because this type of selection has produced humans, as evolved great apes, with unique cognitive, motivational, and behavioral capacities. Indeed, if these capacities are loosely defined as "human nature" (extensions, basically, of great ape nature), they can be analyzed as *always*

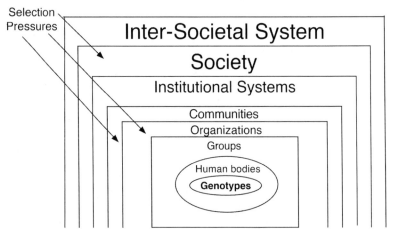

Note: While selection pressures can come from many sources, they must almost always have to pass through the sociocultural epidermis of communities, organizations, and groups. And indeed, they may emerge inside these structures. But the image of the genome as being only protected by the body is quite misleading, and increasingly so in a complex and highly differentiated societal and inter-societal systems with many layers of embedding and interdependencies that are also under selection. The precious cargo of the human body is inside a series of boxes that have boundaries, and more importantly, the capacity to be agents of change on their structure, culture, and operation to defend the precious cargo of the human body.

Figure 2.2 Sociocultural Survival Machines Beyond the Human Body and Multi-level Selection

exerting subtle selection pressures on patterns of social organization to meet these need-states inhering in this nature, but at the same time, the dynamics of these patterns can generate and sustain sociocultural systems harmful to human well being—as should be evident with just a casual look around the world (Turner 2015).

The human capacity for religion evolved under Darwinian selection pressures working on the phenotypes and underlying genotypes of humans' hominin ancestors. These selection pressures were not geared to religion, *per se*, but to making hominins (i.e., those ancestors on the human clade of evolution) *more social* than the last common ancestor that they shared with present-day great apes—humans' closest primate relatives who, as cladistic analysis reveals (see Chapter 3), *are not highly social*. It will be necessary, therefore, to know something about extant great apes and how they can provide critical information about the common ancestor that we humans shared with them some 13 million years ago. It is not possible to understand the evolution of humans, much less their propensities for certain types of behaviors that can be labeled "religious," unless we go back in deep time and examine the Darwinian selection pressures that worked to create primates in the first place and, then, their evolution into early hominins and, eventually, fully-modern human hominins. We will have to pay attention to very specific aspects of how these selection pressures rewired the neurology of hominins to produce the capacities for religion, as it was defined in Chapter 1.

As we will outline in Chapters 3 and 4, natural selection first acted upon the *subcortical areas* of the primate brain of hominins to make them more emotional and capable of forming stronger bonds of solidarity (Turner 2000, 2014, 2015, 2017a; Turner and Maryanski 2017); and then, only relatively late in hominin evolution, did natural selection begin to grow the size of the *neocortex* of hominins. Thus, the story on the origins of humans' capacity for religion does not begin with language, the larger neocortex, or even spoken culture because these are *not* what allowed hominins to survive. It was initially the alterations to the subcortical portions of the brain that are most critical for understanding why humans are religious. The neocortex, which gets far too much attention in most evolutionary analysis, could not ever grow to the human measure without Darwinian selection first increasing the size of subcortical areas of the brain, thereby giving hominins the capacity to be more emotional. Once we realize that cognitions to be adequately formed, remembered, or used in making decisions must also be tagged and laced with emotional valences (Damasio 1994), a very different picture of the evolution of the brain emerges (Turner 2000, 2014).

Early vertebrate brains did not have a neocortex but they did have other key neurological structures. Many of these *amniotes* (in which the *synapsids* line would evolve into mammals) evidenced structures that became part of what are now termed subcortical areas of the mammalian brain; and these subcortical structures were often organized around two basic emotional responses to the world—*fear* in the face of danger and defensive aggression (*anger*) when cornered by danger; and thus, the only "memories," if they can be called that, were about events that aroused anger or fear. Early reptiles and pre-mammals appear to have had an amygdala where fear and anger are generated along with the precursor to the hippocampus (see Figure 4.2 on p. 80) where cognitions could be tagged with emotions during memory formation, but the mechanisms are not as clear as they are today. Remembering situations of danger would be fitness-enhancing as would the evolution of a neocortex that could "store" memories, but it is important to emphasize that the origins of the neocortex among mammals are not clear (Dugas-Ford and Ragsdale 2015) and thus we are only speculating here (see, however, Karten 1997, Butler 1994, and Kemp 2005 for efforts to trace the origins of the neocortex in mammals).

Once the neocortex evolved over and around ancient subcortical areas, however, the nature of the brain changed; and emotions became a means for tagging experiences in ways that would allow them to become memories, originally stored in the hippocampus where the emotional tagging would occur and later moved to the frontal lobes to be retained as longer-term memories.

Still, complex memories are more typical of later mammals; and so, memories and other complex cognitions had to evolve over a long period of time along the mammalian line. Merlin Donald (1999, 2001) refers to these realities in his account of the origins of culture with his concept of "episodic culture" where even larger brained animals like great apes and most likely early hominins lived in the "here and now," but like all animals on Earth, memories that affect decisions and behaviors must be tagged with emotions. Therefore, from our perspective, only those animals with expanded emotional capacities beyond the raw fear and anger of early vertebrates could have mythic cultures, but even with considerable enhancement to the emotional palette, mammals continue to live in the here and now and, at best, revealed only episodic culture.

We see great apes, however, as having very sophisticated and nuanced palettes of emotions that arm their cognitive powers in ways that enable them to think, decide, and remember in ways far exceeding most mammals (aside from whales, elephants, and dolphins). Indeed, they clearly have entry-level culture and some arbitrary call signals as well as eye/facial gestures that carry meanings, a capacity that is greatly expanded when they are exposed to human language (Rumbaugh 2013, 2015; Rumbaugh and Washburn 2003). Great apes are not restricted to the here and now, but they are limited by their neocortex, which is one-third the size of the human neocortex, but their ancestors provided hominins with what was necessary to move out of states of episodic memory: variations in their palettes of emotions that could be subject to Darwinian selection, and thereby make hominins even more emotional. And, with an expanded palette of emotions, hominins could become more intelligent and fully liberated from the here and now and generate "mythic culture" in Donald's words and, eventually, religion.

To create "mythic culture" and, hence, religion requires other evolved capacities besides a larger brain capable of tagging cognitions. For example, Donald (2001) and others argue that ritual was essential to focusing thinking; and we too will argue along these lines, but like so much that allowed religion to emerge, a capacity for proto-rituals was *already a part* of great ape societies and, hence, the hominin behavioral repertoire. Rituals, to be sure, became more emotionally charged, but this basic capacity did not have to be "invented" by mutations; it only had to be enhanced by directional selection on *existing* capacities to use rituals and on other capacities such as rhythmic interactions. For example, as we will document, elements of what we will define as rituals are present, in very incipient form, among chimpanzee societies today, and hence, the society of the last common ancestor to chimpanzees and humans. These elements include rhythmic intonations of verbalizations and actions, as well as mimicry and collective emotional arousal, such as drumming on logs to intensify the acoustics of what appear to be at least quasi-rituals (Kühl et al. 2016). These propensities might be selected during hominin evolution if rituals toward totem-like objects had fitness-enhancing effects on group solidarities. What is true of rituals is evident in so much else about chimpanzees; virtually all key human behaviors responsible for religion—except the capacity to conceive of a supernatural realm—were already present in hominins. And, this will be a constant theme: much of the heavy lifting by natural selection *had been done* very early in great ape and, hence, hominin evolution because of the selection pressures to make evolving apes, who are highly individualistic and *not* group oriented, more social and more capable of forming stable groups. Much of the neurology for religion was thus "pre-installed," so to speak, by natural selection and could be easily enhanced without the need for mutations but, instead, by *directional selection* on the favored tails of the bell curves distributing traits such as emotional range and propensities for rituals.

As mammals and reptiles/birds evolved from amniotes, those with high levels of intelligence are more emotional than those with less intelligence, and they are more likely to engage in rituals, although a very large portion of life forms, even those such as snakes and other reptiles, can engage in hard-wired rituals. The key to greater intelligence leading to religion was the capacity to create new rituals to focus new cognitions tagged with new variants of emotions. The reason for this is not mysterious; it is lodged in a biological "founders effect" of intelligent life forms by early vertebrate amphibian ancestors to both mammals and birds. To be intelligent, a larger palette of emotions is required to tag cognitions so that they can be remembered and used in fitness-enhancing ways.

Once natural selection had significantly expanded the emotional palette of hominins beyond that of the ancestors of extant great apes, selection could grow the brain with fitness-enhancing consequences. It became possible for later hominins or perhaps only early modern humans to develop and use arbitrary symbols in an oral language and, as a consequence, to develop more complex cultures compared to their primate cousins. This combination of (1) a dramatically heightened set of emotional capacities, coupled with (2) a suddenly larger neocortex, (3) a dramatically enhanced capacity for nuanced emotional states to drive interpersonal processes promoting group solidarities, and (4) a sense of self as subject to moral evaluations by others, groups, and larger community formations is what ultimately drove the emergence of religious behaviors.

Without this sequence in the growth of hominin and then human brains, as it affects existing interpersonal propensities among hominins and existing capacities to see self *vis-à-vis* others and collectivities, *Homo sapiens* would not have been able to conceive of a world of the sacred and supernatural, to be capable of attributing causal powers to the beings and forces that inhabited this realm, to engage in ritualistic appeals to these powers to intervene and help people in the mundane world, and to form more permanent communities of fellow worshipers. Nor could they have begun to construct social structures—or what we will, following Wallace (1966), term *cult structures*—organized to make ritual appeals to the supernatural which, in turn, led to the institutionalization of religion as an early institutional domain in human societies.

But, to have the capacity to engage in such cognitive, emotional, behavioral, and organizational activities would not necessarily lead to the institutionalization of these activities. Capacities of the human brain only get institutionalized and evolve under forms of selection that are very different from that outlined by Darwin. And so, at this point we need to leave Darwinian natural selection and, instead, proceed to examine various types of sociocultural selection, which, from our view, are just as "natural" for human *superorganisms* as is Darwinian natural selection for human organisms and all other life forms.

Spencerian Selection

The famous phrase "survival of the fittest" was written by Herbert Spencer eight years before the publication of Darwin's *On the Origin of Species* (1859) and fifteen years before Spencer's *The Principles of Biology*. The phrase was developed in his first major work, which was a philosophical treatise (Spencer 1851), but it applied the image before Darwin began to do so publically as the conception of *natural selection*. Thus, in some ways, the provenance of the basic idea behind natural selection belongs with Spencer, who subsequently wrote multivolume treatises on psychology, biology, sociology, and ethics, with a short but useful volume on the application of the physics of his time to evolutionary analysis. So, if we usurp Darwin's ideas in ways that some in biology or psychology might find disturbing, if not offensive, it should be remembered that the *first to publish the idea of survival of the fit* was Spencer, who eventually became a sociologist. We are, therefore, simply extending a long sociological as much as biological tradition.

About the same time that Darwin (i.e., 1872) turned to the evolution of humans, Spencer (1873, 1874–96) made his move into a sociological analysis of societal evolution from simple to more complex forms. He began to apply his now over 20-year-old phrase, "survival of the fittest," to the analysis of warfare as a driving force in the movement of societies from simple to ever-more complex formations. In this analysis, Spencer also developed a general theory about the evolution of religion, and in many ways he anticipated Guy Swanson's (1964) analysis on *The Birth of the Gods* and, more recently, Ara Norenzayan's (2013) analysis of *Big Gods*. This strain in Spencer's theorizing represents what we will term *Spencerian selection, Type-2*. It is basically a conflict approach that emphasizes the connection between the rise of polity, its legitimation by religion, and the use of polity in the geopolitical arena in which the emerging state of one society conquers that of another, thereby increasing the scale of society and also of religion that is imported into the new societal formations and used to legitimate polity. We will address this view of selection dynamics after we examine *Spencerian selection, Type-1*, which is more foundational for understanding how religion originally became institutionalized in the first human societies.

Spencerian Selection, Type-1

Societal and Population-level Selection Pressures

Spencer formulated another view of selection that is essential in the sociological analysis of the evolution of sociocultural systems. Many of his ideas were converted to functionalism in the mid-to-late 20th century, but if we go back to Spencer's actual writings in *The Principles of Sociology* ([1898]1874–96), we can see an important type of selection that is critical to understanding human superorganisms. More than any of the founders of sociology, Herbert Spencer was an evolutionary theorist who argued that, as societies evolve, they become more complex by elaborating different types of social structures along four fundamental axes: (1) *production* of resources needed for humans to survive and to build social structures; (2) *reproduction* of individuals and the sociocultural formations organizing their activities; (3) *regulation* through the [a] consolidation of power, [b] codification of belief systems, and [c] formation of structural interdependencies through markets; and (4) *distribution* through the expansion of [a] infrastructures of moving resources, information, and people across territories and [b] markets facilitating exchanges of resources, information, and even people (e.g., slave markets, labor markets). Even though Spencer's coinage of the phrase "survival of the fittest" came before Darwin published his great work, this emphasis on axes of differentiation is a far more important contribution for conceptualizing a new, more teleological type of selection. In fact, Spencer emphasized that some very important types of selection pressures increase under conditions that would inevitably lead to a "species' death" if only Darwinian selection was operative: *an absence of variant sociocultural phenotypes capable of dealing with adaptive problems facing a population.* Under these conditions, selection does not sort among existing variants but, in human superorganisms, pushes individuals and the corporate units organizing their activities to create *new variants* that can then be selected upon to deal with an adaptive problem. Table 2.2 and Figure 2.3 outline the essentials of Spencer's argument.

Thus, *Spencerian selection, Type-1* occurs when populations of persons confront adaptive problems for which there are *no existing variants of social structures or cultural codings* that can deal with one or more of these adaptive problems. Spencer's axes or what later functionalists posited as "system requisites" and "need-states" (Durkheim 1893; Parsons 1951; Radcliffe-Brown 1952; Goldschmidt 1966; Luhmann 1982) are better visualized as basic "fault lines" where adaptive problems build up in human superorganisms and increase the pressure on actors to create, through their capacities for agency, new structural or cultural variants in the sociocultural morphology of a population. In Darwinian evolution, there is little room for such agency because selection is non-teleological, whereas Spencer's model accounts for the creation of new variants on which selection can go to work. On the one hand, Spencer always saw the possibility of disintegration or collapse as very real ("death of a superorganism," or sociocultural system), and yet, on the other hand, he recognized that humans have the unique ability to find organizational, technological, normative, and symbolic solutions that expand the structural and cultural repertoire of a superorganism. Spencerian selection, therefore, is driven by needs, motives, interests, and power-relations to "acquire" somehow, perhaps anyhow, new sociocultural phenotypes (Eisenstadt 1964; Rueschemeyer 1986;

TABLE 2.2 Spencerian Selection, Type-1, in the Absence of Fitness Enhancing Variants of Corporate Units

1. Adaptive problems for which there are no fitness-enhancing variants in the sociocultural morphology (social phenotype) organizing members of a population are often generated by:

   a. ecological changes (both biophysical and sociocultural) in a population's environment

   b. population growth and diversification

   c. internal pressures from existing sociocultural phenotypes, typically revolving around complexity of social morphology

   d. inequalities/stratification, intense Durkheimian selection, and Marxian selection pressures.

2. These adaptive problems can be viewed as four basic fault lines that all superorganic systems reveal and that, inevitably, generate selection pressures for new variants in sociocultural systems. These fault lines can be defined as:

   a. *production*, or securing sufficient resources to support people and the corporate units organizing their activities

   b. *reproduction*, or the capacity to generate new members of a society and fitness-enhancing corporate units organizing their activities

   c. *regulation*, or coordination and control by means of the (i) consolidation and use of power, (ii) structural interdependencies, and (iii) systems of culture

   d. *distribution*, or the movement of resources, information, and people by creating new types of (i) distributive infrastructures and (ii) market mechanisms for the exchange.

3. These kinds of adaptive problems, or fault lines, generate selection pressures that, in the absence of existing fitness-enhancing corporate units, push on individual and collective actors to mobilize capacities for agency in order to develop new types of fitness-enhancing corporate units and modes of their integration into new or existing institutional systems.

4. All institutional systems in human societies have evolved under Spencerian more than Darwinian selection pressures.

Turner 1995; Abrutyn 2014a; Turner and Abrutyn 2017). Individual and collective actors see, sense, and feel "selection pressures" and begin to innovate structurally and culturally in ways that can qualitatively transform the total superorganism, or some part of it. Indeed, it resembles what is now called "Lamarckism," or the hypothesis that changes in species occur because of the striving of conspecifics to change their own body structures and behaviors and these modified characters then get passed on

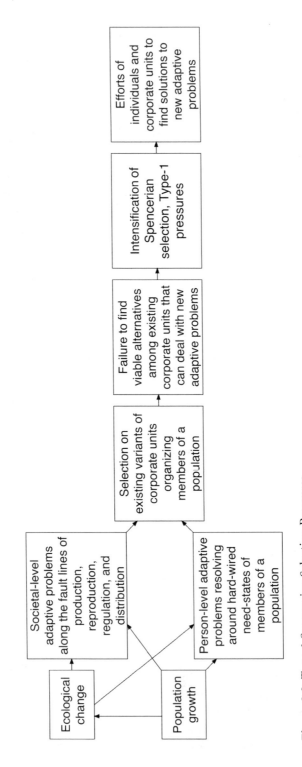

Figure 2.3 Type-1 Spencerian Selection Pressures

spontaneously to the next generation as a new adaptation (see Ridley 1996 for a discussion). Lamarckian inheritance of acquired characters has long been refuted because it did not work well as an explanation for the evolution of biological organisms, but it works much better in the analysis of human sociocultural systems, or superorganisms.

Indeed, in applying evolutionary ideas to human superorganisms, Lamarckian inheritance seems more current because human actors can spontaneously create new variations of social structures and culture that are retained in societies over time. And so, while Lamarck's speculations thus do not explain organismic evolution, they highlight what is typical when addressing Type-1 Spencerian selection: the creation of new forms of sociocultural variation that, if they resolve adaptive problems of a population, will be selected and passed on until they are no longer adaptive.

Yet, evolution by Spencerian selection, Type-1 pressures is neither inevitable nor uni-linear because, as the respective literatures on entrepreneurship (Eisenstadt 1964; Abrutyn 2014b) and social movements (Snow and Soule 2010) demonstrate, agents rarely achieve their stated goals as articulated. Instead, adjustments and accommodations are typically incomplete or partially but not fully adaptive (Colomy 1998). In fact, societies are almost always in at least a mild problematic state where Spencerian selection pushes on actors to fill in gaps in social structures arising from problems of production, reproduction, regulation, and distribution.

Institutional systems—that is, kinship, religion, economy, polity, law, education, etc.—thus develop among human populations from new types of non-Darwinian selection. Unlike Darwinian selection, it is not density of conspecifics that sets off competition and selection, but a situation that is much different, almost the opposite of what drives Darwinian selection. Human populations have often faced adaptive problems for which there are *no viable alternative organizational formations* that can deal with these problems, thereby putting enormous selection pressure on members of a population to find *new* organizational forms that can resolve these problems, or face the disintegrative consequences (Turner 1995, 2008, 2010a; Turner and Abrutyn 2017). All institutional domains in a society are, in essence, evolved outcomes of adaptive problems facing societies where existing variants of sociocultural formations were, at some point, not viable solutions to adaptive problems. These problems tend to accumulate along several fundamental axes or fault lines and begin to exert pressures on human populations. These fault lines where pressure builds up are thus much like fault lines that produce earthquakes that "shake" a population to "do something" about the adaptive problems that they face.

Indeed, large leaps in the evolutionary history of human societies have come when existing corporate units organizing people's activities in a society become less capable of dealing with adaptive problems that, perhaps, at one time in the past they could resolve. The consequence is that both individual and corporate actors are under pressure—not Darwinian but Spencerian—to invent a *new type of corporate unit* that, if proven effective in dealing with the adaptive problem, begets more such units, which eventually replace older types of ineffective corporate units. The result is institutional change initiated by Spencerian Type-1 selection and, as we will see shortly, filled out by more Durkheimian selection processes in which new corporate-unit templates outcompete older, less effective corporate-unit templates in subpopulations of corporate units seeking resources in a given niche. However, if no new corporate units can be founded and built up to deal with an adaptive problem, the entire society can face internal disintegration or conquest from another, more-fit society (by what we term Spencerian selection Type-2). In fact, every society that has ever existed has perished through disintegration or conquest by a society with a more fit set of institutional systems.

Person-level Selection Pressures

While Spencer emphasized the fault lines of production, reproduction, regulation and distribution, there is another source of adaptive problems arising from Darwinian selection on individuals: *need-states and behavioral propensities*. Humans are not passive vessels but active agents who are the outcome of Darwinian selection as it worked on the primate and hominin lines. Darwinian selection has hard-wired a surprisingly large set of behavioral capacities, action tendencies, and need-states in all humans; and when viewed collectively, these can been seen as a powerful set of selection pressures on sociocultural formations. As is evident in the lower portion of Figure 2.3 and elaborated upon in Figure 7.1 on p. 151, these represent a subtle but persistent pressure on sociocultural formations to be structured in ways that all these behavioral capacities and action tendencies, along with associated needs, can be realized. It is clear that many sociocultural formations for almost all of human history after hunting and gathering societies have repressed, violated, and otherwise worked against these selection pressures, but it can also be argued that, over time, these pressures force changes in societies. They become at strategic moments in the history of a population a force that, like the fault lines emphasized by Spencer, push actors to create new types of social structures and cultures. Indeed, when these more person-level, but really population-level when viewed collectively, pressures increase, they exert selection pressures that force changes in existing sociocultural formations and often lead to new formations. They can often drive conflict that moves beyond Spencerian selection and morph into more Marxian selection in which individuals collectively mobilize to tear down oppressive formations and work to create new, less restrictive formations.

The evolved psychology of humans thus operates very much like the fault lines of human superorganisms to push actors to innovate and to create new kinds of structures and cultures; and from these efforts, societies evolve. Indeed, as will become evident, religion evolved to some degree under both the fault lines emphasized by Spencer and the evolved cognitions, emotions, and behavioral propensities instilled and/or intensified by millions of years of Darwinian selection on primates and then hominins as they evolved into *Homo sapiens*. In Chapter 7, we will take up these processes as they led to the initial emergence of religion and as they have continued to exert pressure on the subsequent evolution of religion in human societies.

Spencerian Selection, Type-2

Even though the phrase "survival of the fittest" is often associated with Darwin and, sadly, with Social Darwinism, Darwin would not have phrased the matter in quite this way. He would emphasize "survival of the fit," or even "minimally fit"—an argument that connotes a very different view of how selection works. Survival occurs when the phenotypes of organisms have "just enough" of the traits needed to enable them to survive and reproduce.[1] Much modern-day analysis in biology emphasizes "maximization of fitness" in its models, but these models are borrowed from the mathematics of neo-classical economics, as applied by early founders of sociobiology such as Hamilton (1964). As a result, they over-state the case. Indeed, actors in economic systems rarely truly maximize their utilities, and such is even the case for the fitness of organisms in the biotic universe.

Fortunately, Spencer appears to have recognized his own overstatement and toned down the usage of the phrase "survival of the fittest" in his sociology. Spencer's entry into sociology began some 23 years after this phrase was first used, but he increasingly began to use the notion of fitness in a somewhat different way. Most significantly, he shifted its referent from individuals to more societal-level morphologies to explain the evolution of human societies from simple, homogeneous "masses" (hunting and gathering) to ever-more complex, and differentiated superorganisms. This evolution had been driven, to a high degree, by warfare, with the "more fit" society generally winning wars and, in some way, incorporating the conquered population into a larger and more complex superorganism.

Thus, through successive waves of warfare over the long-term of human history, societies had become ever-more complex. As an aside, Spencer argued that with industrial capitalisms, warfare was a less efficient way for societies to evolve, which is why he opposed British colonialism because it had biased productive activity to control and regulation by government of its far-flung colonies. In this line of thinking, he was perhaps the first to present an argument against the modern "military-industrial complex" where preparation for warfare deprives the broader domestic economy of productive capital, biases decision-making to military as opposed to diplomatic solutions to inter-societal conflict, undermines incentives for domestic production, and destroys the dynamism of markets in distribution of new productive outputs. It is better, Spencer argued, to unleash the incentive system inhering in free markets than to impose military rule on populations.

More important for our purposes here is the recognition that Spencer viewed the evolution of religion as very much tied to geopolitics among societies. Societies win wars under a number of critical conditions: their size, their level of technology, their resulting level of productivity, their level of political organization around administrative and coercive bases, their legitimation of consolidated and centralized power by religion and the forces of the supernatural. Thus, religion often has evolved in association with inter-societal conflict and with the winning side in this conflict imposing, to varying degrees, their institutional systems and religious beliefs on the conquered population.

He argued that the more success enjoyed by a society in war and conquest, the greater are the problems of social control and the more likely will the evolving polity rely upon the influence of religion in resolving these problems of social control (as generated by Spencerian selection, Type-1). One is the problem to legitimate the objectives of the polity engaged in war, and the second is to reconcile diverse religions—which he viewed as the origins of polytheism (whether correctly or incorrectly). Spencer also recognized as societies mobilize for war, power is concentrated and inequalities increase, creating potential internal threats that always arise from inequality. He then argued that religion needed to expand as the priestly class created religious ideologies that reconciled conflicting beliefs and, thereby, legitimated these inequalities. Spencer felt that they did so by creating ranked pantheons of gods that more or less mirrored the basic structure of political rankings, thereby suggesting that the inequalities in power and wealth of society are reflections of how the supernatural universe is ordered (an idea that is very close to Swanson's in *Birth of the Gods* (1964) and, more recently, Norenzayan's portrayal of *Big Gods* (2015)).

As the priestly class performs these legitimating functions, they consolidate their own base of power—as the symbolic base of political power—and expand their bureaucratic structures and their control of economic resources and thus wealth in a society. Yet, Spencer believed that as religion evolved in this direction, it created the conditions for a revolt against the privilege and regulatory bureaucracy of religion and its principle client, the bureaucratic state.

Thus, political conquest is very much responsible for the evolution of religion, but there is an implicit dialectic in this process: increased inequalities that generate internal threats and moreover that increase the potential for mobilization by class or by religious sects against the power of the state and its religious apologists. This is as far as Spencer went, and for this reason, we will need to label another type of selection—mobilization for conflict and violence—to pick up where Spencer leaves off. This type of selection will be termed Marxian selection (see below and Chapter 10).

For the present, let us formalize a bit our conception of Type-2 Spencerian selection. This is selection where, as the polity evolves as a regulatory mechanism in societies (in response to Type-1 Spencerian selection pressures), inequalities increase and lead to the use of an expanded religious system to legitimate polity and its usurpation of resources. Most importantly, religions often spread and evolve through geopolitical warfare, with religion becoming a key force in legitimating conquest and in maintaining control of the conquered population through a combination of imposing its religion on those conquered or, alternatively, by reconciling, co-opting, and even incorporating elements of the indigenous religions of conquered populations into the religion of their conquerors. Figure 2.4 outlines these dynamics of Spencerian selection Type-2, and Table 2.3 highlights the critical processes in this type of Spencerian selection, which to some degree overlaps with Spencerian selection, Type-1, but is still distinctive, especially in the context of religious evolution.

The evolution of societies has been driven by warfare because larger, more complex, and better organized societies are more likely to win wars, thereby conquering the less fit and typically incorporating them into their sociocultural formations (cf. the over-all argument in Turchin 2016). In this way, the size and complexity of the combined societies were successively increased. In his sociology, Spencer's use of his own image of evolution as driven by the "survival of the fittest" was generally used to explain the evolution of societies more than the distribution and death of individuals competing for resources within societies, although this latter usage does periodically appear in his arguments. So, an image of a kind of Darwinian-like struggle was early on part of sociology. This tradition continues in the works of scholars such as Peter Turchin (2003, 2007, 2016) who has made similar arguments (with much more sophistication than Spencer) about warfare and sociocultural evolution; and so, Spencer's early ideas live on in some contemporary work. Yet, as we emphasize in the next section, it is Durkheim who deserves more of the credit than Spencer for bringing the basic idea of competition for resources among

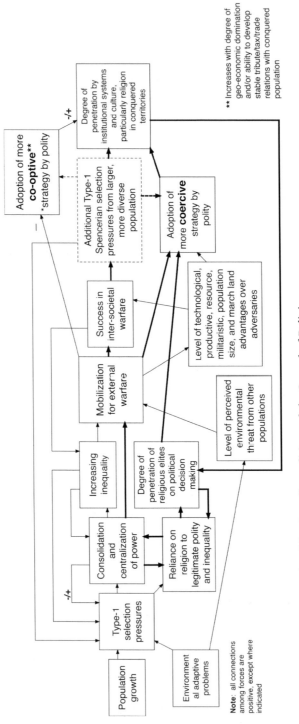

Figure 2.4 Type-2 Spencerian Selection: Geopolitics and the Spread of Religion

TABLE 2.3 Spencerian Selection, Type-2, on Geopolitics

1. As societies grow, the logistical loads for production, reproduction, regulation, and distribution all increase, setting into motion Spencerian selection Type-1 (see Table 2.2 and Figure 2.3 and 7.1 on p. 151).

2. As these Type-1 selection pressures mount, polity first emerges and then begins to grow as one response to Type-1 pressures for regulation.

3. Type-1 selection pressures also cause religion to emerge as one of the earliest institutional domains engaged in regulation in early human societies.

4. As polity grows and then, under external or internal threats, begins to consolidate its bases of power and to centralize control, the growing and centralizing political systems increasingly depend upon religious beliefs, rituals, and leaders for legitimation.

5. As polity continues to grow, inequalities in a society increase, setting into motion additional Type-1 selection pressures that are addressed by further expansion of religion.

6. As a response to external threats and internal threats (from inequality), polities often engage in geopolitical expansion, which requires further efforts by religion to legitimate warfare, to regulate the larger population that is created with conquest, and to reconcile diverse religious beliefs.

7. The more polity depends upon religion to provide solutions to 4, 5, and 6 above, the more religion itself becomes bureaucratized as an authority system and the more the pantheon of forces and beings becomes hierarchical; both of these hierarchies provide legitimation because of their equivalent form to a centralized political system engaged in coercive geopolitical activities.

8. Equally often, however, a conquering polity uses its coercive advantage to impose its culture, especially religion but also language and other institutional systems on a conquered population. In so doing, it hopes to gain better control of the population, under Type-1 Spencerian selection pressures, but whatever pushes polity to use coercive force almost always involves imposing its religion, which changes the culture of the conquered population, on the one hand, while providing a religious legitimation for the hegemonist controlling conquered territories.

actors in societies as the internal mechanism of evolution or "social speciation" leading to the division of labor and, hence, societal complexity.

Durkheimian Selection

Once institutionalized, the cult structures organizing communities of worshipers holding to a particular conception of the supernatural become the units under selection by more Darwinian-sounding mechanisms: growth in the number of cult structures, increased density within resource niches of those seeking religion that, in turn, escalate competition among cult structures for resources; and as such competition increases, selection ensues among corporate units able to secure resources and sustain themselves in a niche. Figure 2.5 outlines these Darwinian-like processes among corporate units in a more abstract way.

Organizational ecology changed the way complex organizations were analyzed in the social sciences. Originally framed to analyze the patterns of life and death among economic organizations in contemporary societies (Hannan and Freeman 1977, 1989; Hannan, Polos and Carroll 2007), the program has been adopted to the study of non-economic organizations in what can be seen as quasi-markets exchanging, for example, memberships for benefits that organizational membership can bring. While money may be exchanged in these quasi-markets, it is secondary to the exchange of memberships from various demographic categories for the non-monetary resources that organizations often provide. Ecological dynamics are thus seen to be useful in analyzing voluntary organizations in general in various resource niches (McPherson 1981, 1983b, 1983c; McPherson and Ranger-Moore 1991; McPherson and Rotolo 1996) and, more particularly, in analyzing religious organizations as they compete for adherents and members in various resource niches (e.g., Wuthnow 1987; Stark and Bainbridge 1996; Iannoccone and Brainbridge 2009; Turner and Abrutyn 2016).

Once religion is institutionalized in societies, its subsequent revolution has often revolved around the dynamics outlined in Figure 2.5. In particular, where markets in general and quasi-markets in particular are allowed by polity and law to operate, these Durkheimian dynamics are almost always present, not only in the economy but in other institutional domains as well, and especially so, in religion as an institutional domain. Indeed, because religion is always moralized, the competition can sometimes take on a moral character and, as a result, move beyond competition in quasi-markets and evolve into more violent conflict. As long as the conflict stays within the realm of religious conflict, it can be considered Durkheimian. But, because of the moral quality of religion, such is often not the case, and the conflict spills over into other institutional domains and often seeks much broader institutional change in a society or system of societies. At this point, Durkheimian selection morphs into Marxian selection, to be discussed shortly. Thus, religious evolution can be viewed as a kind of ecological process operating on sociocultural formations that organize human populations into superorganisms. While the evolution of religion is not wholly an ecological process of selection working on sociocultural phenotypes of cult structures, this emphasis on the ecology of cult structures can be useful in

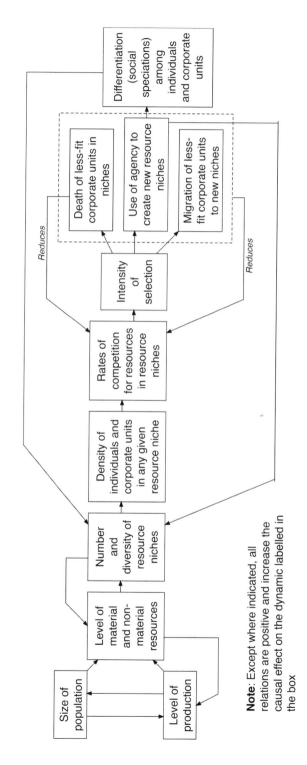

Note: Except where indicated, all relations are positive and increase the causal effect on the dynamic labelled in the box

Figure 2.5 Darwinian Imagery in Émile Durkheim's Theory of Societal Differentiation

explaining the ways in which religion becomes institutionalized in a society, and often re-institutionalized from the competition and conflict between existing religious cult structures. Table 2.4 outlines the basic elements of Durkheimian selection.

We are labeling the dynamics in Table 2.4 "Durkheimian" because Darwin's ideas were explicitly adopted into sociology in Émile Durkheim's *The Division of Labor in Society* (1947[1893]) to explain how competition and selection lead to "social speciation" or the division of labor within and between corporate units of various kinds. Durkheim emphasized that such competition is, to some degree, regulated by markets, law, and political authority; and so, we are limiting the scope of Durkheimian selection in ways consistent with Durkheimian goals: to explain how differentiation of more specialized ("social speciation") corporate units organizing divisions of labor evolve as societies grow and as corporate units within resource niches come into competition.

Durkheim tended to view the competition between individuals and corporate units as benign in this sense: those actors that cannot compete in one resource niche have the ability to move to other resource niches, or even to create a niche. No one appears to die in Durkheim's scheme, but organizational ecology was created to study the life and death of economic organizations as niches become dense and competition increases. And, while religious cults may have more staying power than economic units in intense market competition, we would be wise to recognize that Durkheimian selection, like all forms of selection, can select out types of corporate units from a societal morphology.

Moreover, Durkheim's emphasis on the agency of actors in competition for resources implies other important considerations. Durkheimian selection can often lead, as he emphasized, to the creation of new resource niches; and thus, it is often through Durkheimian competition (as well as Spencerian and Marxian selection) that new environments are created to which individuals and corporate units must now adapt. Thus, much of the environmental change that Darwinian selection emphasizes as a cause for selection on variants of phenotypes is created by the very processes of selection that occur within sociocultural systems, or human superorganisms.

Thus, there are extended implications of Durkheim's argument that force us to recognize that, while some of the dynamics of Durkheimian selection parallel those of Darwinian selection, the nature and effects of these dynamics are still quite distinctive and cannot be considered Darwinian because the units under selection are goal seeking corporate units and because of the capacity of all selection dynamics in human superorganisms to remake environments to which humans and units organizing their activities and other life forms must adapt. Indeed, as is clearly evident

TABLE 2.4 Durkheimian Selection on Corporate Units

1. As populations grow, they differentiate institutional systems and types of corporate units within these systems; this differentiation, in turn, can be seen as creating ever-more resource niches for the evolution of corporate units that organize individual members of a population.

2. Once some corporate units prove fit in securing resources in a niche, additional corporate units will enter this niche.

3. As the population of corporate units seeking resources in a niche increases, so does the level of density of these units.

4. As density increases, competition among corporate units (multi-level or group selection) intensifies, causing:

   a. some organizations to die

   b. other organizations to move to another existing niche

   c. still other organizations to create a new resource niche.

5. As density is reduced by competition, new corporate units can often enter or re-enter this niche and survive, as long as density remains below the carrying capacity of the niche.

6. Such Darwinian-like selection processes generally occur within an existing regulatory system that institutionalizes competition, typically through sociocultural formations that have evolved under Spencerian selection pressures (see Table 2.2 and 2.3):

   a. markets

   b. political authority

   c. legal regulation.

7. Both the units subject to selection and the regulatory systems regulating competition have capacities for agency, innovation, and other teleological capacities for creating new variants in the morphology and culture of corporate units seeking resources or regulating resource-seeking activities of corporate units in a population.

today, the environmental changes to which all life forms on Earth must adapt and re-adapt are generated by human superorganisms revealing high rates of Durkheimian selection made possible by markets and by a legal system capable of generating rules to guide contracts and market exchanges.

It should not be surprising that competition often turns violent under these conditions, but Durkheim himself had little to say about more violent conflict in human societies, primarily because he was always searching for the mechanisms that can integrate societies. As we will see in later chapters, his analysis of rituals, totems, cultural beliefs, and solidarity will be very much part of the explanation for how religion evolved. In fact, Durkheim abandoned many of the key ideas in *The Division of Labor in Society*, including the ecological model that we are emphasizing here. He turned to the intensive study of religion after 1895 because he thought that the organization of religion provides key insights in how to integrate secular societies; and these insights live on in modern sociological theory, including theories of how the first human societies evolved.

Yet, as Spencer recognized, competition can become unregulated and evolve into more intense forms of conflict, as is connoted by Spencer's phrase, "survival of the fittest." This phrase described not only external warfare among societies but internal conflicts stemming from inequalities within societies. But, his insights on the latter were not nearly as profound as those articulated by Marx, and so, we should posit a fourth type of selection—what we term *Marxian selection*—to explain conflict in which the existing institutional order is being challenged and defended by various actors. Indeed, this kind of conflict between religious cult structures can turn especially violent but, moreover, can spill over into inter-societal systems as, for example, is evident with ISIS today or the Christian Crusades centuries ago. Here is conflict that is not regulated by markets, law, or external political authority, but it is nonetheless a form of selection in superorganisms built up by humans. Indeed, without this more conflict-based and violent form of selection, one of the driving forces of selection operating in all human superorganisms more generally, and in religious evolution more specifically, will be missing from our analysis.

Marxian Selection

Though Marx's (1845–6) analysis of revolutionary class conflict is flawed (Turner 1975), it contains all of the key elements of conflict processes arising from institutional domains, particularly the economy and polity as they, in turn, generate inequalities in the distribution of resources. Those in subordinate sectors of this distribution experience a variety of deprivations that accumulate into a set of grievances that arouse intense negative emotions. The conflict process begins here and, under a number of conditions, leads subordinates to develop counter-ideologies against not only the legitimating ideologies of the political economy but also the institutional structure of a society more generally. As leaders articulate what are often a number of somewhat divergent counter-ideologies, they eventually begin to coalesce into a more coherent ideology for revolution in which a class "in itself" becomes organized as a class "for itself," willing to engage in conflict against the organizational structures and the ideologies imposed by elites to legitimate these structures. In Marx's view, this conflict will often be violent at some point and lead to an overthrow of the existing political regime, with a new regime imposing the counter-ideology emphasizing equality of economic relations among individuals, after a brief "dictatorship" by former subordinates who are now superordinates. Marx goes wrong in some of his predictions here, but the key point is that certain conditions lead to conflict that fall outside the bounds of Durkheimian selection because the conflict is over the very institutional systems—economy, markets, polity, law, and religion—that often regulate Durkheimian competition over resources. His ideas also go beyond Spencer because, as noted earlier, Spencer tended to emphasize warfare between societies rather than conflict within societies, whereas Marx allows for the analysis of both internal conflicts within a society, as well as external conflicts across societies. Indeed, it was Marx's hope that, once started, the predicted revolution by the proletariat would radiate across capitalist societies.

Among the early founders of sociology, then, Marx went the furthest along in conceiving of class conflict as arising from the internal dynamics of societies and then spreading across similarly structured societies. It is, of course, ironical that religious conflict, often conflated with ethnic dynamics, has been far more frequent over the last 150 years than Marx's hoped-for class conflict—especially since he saw religion as only a tool and superstructure used by those who own the means of production in a society. Still, his ideas can easily be adapted to the evolutionary analysis of religion, where cult structures begin to secure and mobilize resources to engage in conflict with other cult structures and the institutional systems supporting them. The process is ecological in that those cult structures able to secure the most resources will be the most likely to prevail and, thereby, to structure or restructure new variants of institutional formations within a society and, potentially, across societies. Table 2.5 and Figure 2.6 outline the elements of this type of selection.

Marxian ideas can be blended with organizational ecology arguments in the literature on social movements, thus making it clear that Marxian theorizing is still a selectionist argument. The social movement literature emphasizes the formation of social movement organizations (SMOs) that begin to organize in response to grievances against the existing institutional systems in a society (Snow and Soule 2010). The grievances are typically much broader than those conceptualized by Marx and neo-Marxists today; and though they may include class subordination, they generally involve a conception of other disadvantaged categories of persons, such as members of persecuted religious sects or minorities (and sometimes majorities, as was the case in Hussein's Iraq with Sunni Muslims ruling over the Shiite Muslim majority), ethnic minorities (and, in some cases, majorities, as was evident in South Africa), or patterns of discrimination against sex-based categories like gender and sexuality. It is this consolidation of bases of

TABLE 2.5 Marxian Selection and Institutional Change

1. At times members of populations begin to create social movement organizations that seek to change the distribution of resources to individuals and families by corporate units within an institutional system or large sets of institutional systems. Such political mobilization often generates conflict among corporate units and individuals within or across institutional domains, and even across societies.

2. The starting point for such social movement organizations is almost always dissatisfaction with, and negative emotional arousal against, an existing institutional system or set of institutional domains, which are seen as unfairly distributing resources but also as not meeting basic human need-states.

3. Such selection is Marxian because it involves intense forms of conflict, but this conflict is still ecological because it involves competition among organizations to secure resources in resource niches, including:

   a. demographic (members and adherents to a cause)

   b. cultural (symbols organized into ideologies)

   c. network (other corporate units, networks to other corporate units)

   d. material (money)

   e. political (power and networks of power)

   f. organizational (models and templates for organizing people into action)

   g. emotional (arousal of negative emotions against existing arrangements/enemies and positive emotions around ideologies of SMOs)

   h. leadership (that can articulate ideologies, arouse emotions, and organize adherents to the goals of the SMO).

4. Because such movements can challenge existing distributions of resources within and across institutional systems, they often encounter intense resistance that, in turn, leads to conflict, often violent.

5. The sets of organizations that engaged in conflict (extreme competition) for resources determine the degree to which, if any, an institutional system will be restructured or a set of institutional systems will be restructured.

6. The more resources an SMO can generate *vis-à-vis* the existing system of organizations within and across institutional domains, the more conflict will change the institutional domains organizing a population.

7. The fewer resources available to SMOs, the less likely are they to change institutional domains by direct action but, instead, by the reactions of existing centers of power to their challenge. Thus, even when the corporate units organizing a domain prevail in a challenge to their hegemony, the culture and structure of the domain, and perhaps several domains, changes as a result of the conflict and the effort to mobilize for potential conflict in the future.

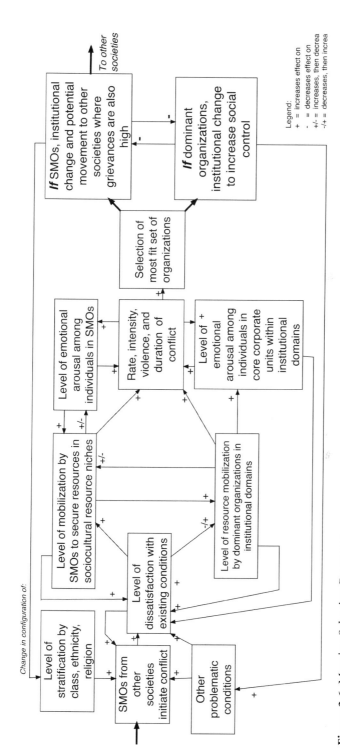

Figure 2.6 Marxian Selection Processes

inequality—say, class with ethnicity or religious affiliation—that makes grievances more intense and, as a result, drives up negative emotional arousal against the existing institutional systems in a society. Such emotions become yet one more resource niche to be exploited by SMOs, and when coupled with positive emotions toward the movement addressing grievances, this polarity intensifies both negative emotions against institutional systems and positive emotions fueling activism and the willingness to take risks (Goodwin and Jasper 2006; Jasper and Owens 2014; Turner 2010, Summers-Effler 2010). Furthermore, SMOs are often more focused on specific issues, such as those relating to environmental degradation and poverty, *per se*, rather than the entire stratification system; and SMOs often focus on such hot button issues as abortion and religion in schools in societies such as the United States.

Yet, the dynamics of mobilization are similar to those in both Marx and organizational ecology. Social movement organizations are responding to generalized beliefs articulating grievances (Smelser 1963) over some condition in a society. Over time, leadership of various organizations is sorted out (itself a selection process), while generalized beliefs are refined and "framed" in more coherent sets of grievances and, at the same time, moralized in terms of fairness, justice, equity, and other moral considerations (Snow and Soule 2010).

Emerging SMOs seek cultural or symbolic resources, often by framing their quest as an effort to realize the general values and moral codes in a society that have not been equally applied or in some way have been abrogated to narrow interests sustained by the existing institutional systems. Along with these ideological efforts that draw upon cultural resources, SMOs begin to seek a variety of additional resources, including members and volunteers willing to act, material resources such as money, organizational resources such as existing organizations (like churches or unions) and/or their templates for mobilizing individuals, networks or liaisons with other organizations or with kinship, occupational, and community structures as potential conduits for recruits and money, and as noted above, younger recruits who are more likely to take risks. They may also seek technological resources that can be employed to recruit members, sustain networks, and broadcast their cause to the larger population. The success of an SMO is a function of (1) their success in securing sufficient resources and in co-opting or eliminating other SMOs focusing on the same or similar issues, (2) their capacity to reach a large proportion of the population and neutralize potential resistance, (3) their ability to draw resources outside a society, and (4) their capacity to mobilize more resources than those actors within institutional domains resisting change in institutional structures. If polity is weak in terms of fiscal, organizational, and coercive and ideological resources to legitimate their goals, and if key actors in polity (e.g., military) and in the legal system (police and judges) are ambivalent about supporting polity, then SMOs can often prevail in conflict. Yet, a well-organized state with a loyal military is very difficult to overthrow, without mobilization for longer-term conflicts that move beyond initial phases of violence in the street to full mobilization of SMO members as a military force that can engage in more prolonged fighting that can become a full-blown civil war.

Many of the dynamics of SMOs involve Durkheimian selection as potential SMOs in the same niche compete for resources, typically with one winning out and forming a coalition with other organizations. If we combine the more Marxian view with the social movement literature—which is not a great stretch because various historians use resource mobilization theory to study revolutions (e.g., Tilly, Tilly, and Tilly 1975)—we can retain the organizational-ecological portions of the argument (or Durkheimian selection) and combine it with what often occurs as social movements expand into true revolutionary movements mobilized for warfare and willing to engage in more prolonged civil warfare with full military engagement. As SMOs assume this profile, they generally become intent on much more expansive change in the institutional domains of society—political, legal, economic, religious, educational, and potentially other domains—that Marx advocated. The goal is to fundamentally change existing institutional arrangements rather than to compete with other organizations; indeed, the goal is often to eliminate through violence organizational systems seen as supporting and/or causing patterns of perceived oppression.

A number of conditions make this violent form of selection (e.g., the fit win the war, the less fit are killed off or flee) more likely: intensity and duration of grievances over perceived inequalities; the proportion of the population that experiences grievances; the intensity of the negative emotions that are aroused, especially emotions such as vengeance and retribution; the focus of attributions for the cause of grievances on clearly definable targets; and the degree to which emotion-arousing rituals can focus emotions and attributions, while making movement members more willing to take risks. Other factors include the degree to which grievances are moralized in framing activities, giving them the quality of absolute rights and wrongs that make people more likely to be violent and not compromise through negotiations; the degree to which social movement mobilization involves identities of its members with respect to class, ethnicity, and religion; the extent to which members of movement organizations begin to define their sense of self in terms of the goals of the movement; the availability of resources of all types within and outside of a society; the ability to recruit younger age cohorts who are generally more willing to take risks and to be violent; and the weakness of oppositional forces in targeted institutional domains.

If the opposition of such movements is the state-level polity in a society, and the state has many of the same resources as the SMO, then the conflict will be violent and often prolonged, moving from a more revolutionary movement into a longer-term civil war. All of these diverse processes are, nonetheless, a form of selection dynamics within and often between superorganisms because they have been a chronic part of human social organization since leaving the comparative peace of hunting and gathering and because there is typically a winner and loser in such conflicts. Even if there is no clear winner, selection may still be operating as third parties from inside or outside the weakened sociocultural formation are able to become the winners of the conflict.

Religious cult structures have often been at the center of these more Marxian-type processes because they already have achieved what evolving SMOs always seek: (1) a highly moralized belief system that can be used to charge up emotions against non-members and institutional systems, (2) a collective memory that roots social ties and obligations in a sacred time, (3) emotion arousal rituals directed at totems symbolizing sacred beliefs, (4) an existing organizational structure with leaders and a division of labor ready to act and recruit further resources, and (5) individuals whose identity is tied to the success of a particular cult structure. Indeed, religious organizations have advantages over other types of organizations in that their rewards are intangible and long-term and, thus, commitment is intensified, especially where a singular, transcendental deity comprises the supernatural. Thus, many types of conflict often draw upon the resource mobilization capacities of religious cult structures, thereby converting what may have started out as a secular movement into a religious movement that changes not only the relative distribution of religious cult structures but also the broader institutional systems in a society. Indeed, it would not be possible to understand fully the dynamics, for example, in the Middle East today without this more conflictual form of Marxian selection dynamics that has been piggy-backed onto religious organizational structures and ideology.

Conclusion

We are seeking to develop a more comprehensive and robust approach to understanding religious evolution. Our goal is to expand and extend the power of evolutionary theorizing rather than remain confined within the limitations of evolutionary theorizing in biology, strictly speaking. We need not apologize for this because evolutionary thinking in sociology has as long a pedigree as it does in biology—despite the differences in the relative prestige of sociology and biology.

To expand inquiry and yet maintain some continuity with biology, we focus on the main mechanism of evolution—selection. We do this for several important reasons. First, the Darwinian portion of our analysis focuses on how the brain became rewired; hence, the other forces of the Modern Synthesis on evolution—that is, mutations, gene flow, and genetic drift—are less important than directional natural selection, which selects on *existing traits* in the phenotype of individuals and thereby moves distributions of phenotypes and underlying genotypes of the population of individuals. Over successive generations, as selection favors one side of the bell curve arraying the distribution of traits, evolution can become highly punctuated by simple direction selection, if one tail has large fitness-enhancing consequences. For example, let us assume that the size of a particular brain structure enhances fitness. This structure will be likely to array itself on a *bell curve* with respect to relative size across a population. Thus, one side of the bell curve will contain the smaller manifestations of this brain structure, while the other side or tail will array the larger manifestations of this structure. The middle portions of the bell curve, distributed around its mean size for this structure, will fill out the bell curve. Selection will thus favor those individuals with a larger manifestation of this brain structure on the right side of the bell curve, with the extreme right representing the largest manifestations of this brain structure. Let us assume that the smaller structures on the left side and tail of the curve reduce fitness significantly; selection will thus remove a large proportion of these phenotypes and genotypes from the population. The result is that the bell curve for subsequent generations shifts significantly, revealing a population with the larger brain structure. Let us assume that the right side is still very favored, while those brain structures on the left tail of the new, biased-toward-the-right-side of bell curve still inhibit fitness; the latter will be selected out of the population, with the result that the next bell curve will be even more biased to members whose brain structure promoting fitness was on the right. After many generations, selection will have eliminated those with a small size in this critical brain structure; and the population will be disproportionately persons with large manifestations of this brain structure. Here, then, the brain can evolve rapidly in evolutionary terms *without* mutations just by virtue of directional selection working on the favored side of the distribution of this particular trait, and the underlying genes generating this trait. Since so much of what makes humans a unique primate is the size and connectivity of the brain—traits that would naturally distribute on a bell curve—it is not unreasonable to see directional selection as the dominant force in human evolution from a biological perspective. Since the capacity to conceptualize a sacred and supernatural realm of forces and beings is the defining characteristic of religion and since this capacity is highly dependent upon the increasing size and connectivity of brain structures, directional selection[2] is what gave humans, and perhaps late hominins, the neurological capacity to be religious.

Second, we need to explain why mutations could not also do the same thing as directional selection, if they are sufficiently frequent with respect to particular brain structures. The problem with mutations is that they are generally harmful to organisms and do not promote fitness (Fisher 1930), and this could be even more the case for mutations on complex, highly interconnected neuro-structures (Stebbins 1969). So, while mutations may sometimes enhance fitness by creating new fitness-enhancing variants, they are less likely to have done so for the brain. Since the human brain does not reveal fundamentally new structures or "modules" as evolutionary psychologists once termed the matter, the evidence points toward directional selection on the relative size and connectivity of *existing* "modules" evolved millions of years before the Pleistocene. Change in the hominin brain has occurred, but the change was by directional natural selection more than any of the other forces of evolution in the current Modern Synthesis.

Once we leave Darwinian natural selection on individual organisms and shift analysis to what Herbert Spencer termed *superorganisms*—that is, organization of organisms into societies—the nature of selection changes. It is still "natural" in the general sense of being endemic to patterns of social organization among animals, including humans (Turner and Machalek 2017). Therefore, third, we need to understand the distinction among the types of selection that are not Darwinian—i.e., Spencerian (Type-1 and Type-2), Durkheimian, and Marxian selection—to take account of the fundamental differences in evolution between human superorganisms and individual organisms.

Notes

1 A case in point is upright walking. Habitual bipedalism was under directional selection for hominins but at some point selection was relaxed, leaving this adaptation rather makeshift and far from any kind of perfection. While monkeys and apes evidence few back problems, humans as they age can be often heard in the doctor's office voicing "Oh my aching back." As Krogman (1951: 54) pointed out in *The Scars of Human Evolution*, we walk on two legs but our "skeleton was originally designed for four. The result is some ingenious adaptations, not all of them successful."

2 Directional selection may seem to imply teleology, but such is not the case here. Blind natural selection moves in a given direction, once a particular trait selected upon increases fitness. Once fitness is increased, then selection will continue to select on the trait, moving its distribution in a "direction" that increases fitness.

3

In the Beginning
The Evolution of Primates

Descended from apes! My dear, let us hope that is not true, but if it is, let us pray that it will not become generally known.
Bishop of Worchester's wife (1860) on Darwin's theory of evolution

Most explanations on the origin of religion do not include humans' closest living relatives, the great apes, for information about the nature of our hominin ancestors where the basis of religion ultimately originates. This is unfortunate because we now have nearly 70 years of field data on the behavioral propensities, social structures, and life-ways of present-day great apes and their societies. We also possess a method to see millions of years back in time to the last common ancestor (LCA) of humans and present-day apes. And, if we know how this LCA organized, we are in a better position to understand how the human descendants of this ancestor developed the capacity for religion.

So, given that the evolution of religion has underlying biological components, it is important to know something about the evolution of those hominoid primates (i.e., apes and hominins) that became the ancestors of humans. For, in reality, humans are primates and certified members of the hominoid family tree. Indeed, this is confirmed by the fact that humans share 99 percent of our genes with living chimpanzees (*Pan*), 98 percent with lowland and highland gorillas (*Gorilla*), and 97 percent with orangutans (*Pongo*), albeit distributed on one extra pair of chromosomes (Varki and Nelson 2007; Chatterjee et al. 2009; Prado-Martinez et al. 2013; Prüfer et al. 2012). As will become evident, the emergence of religion among humans is the outcome of selection on the basic great-ape anatomy and neuroanatomy over millions of years of evolution. If we are to understand religion, then, it is instrumental to know how an anatomy and neuroanatomy that originated in the primate order was then reconfigured by Darwinian selection to create the hominoid lineage and, eventually, to give one hominoid—*Homo sapiens*—the capacity for religion.

The forces that led to religion did not, however, produce religion, *per se*, but as we will document, Darwinian selection worked on the neurobiology of human ancestors to make them much more social and group-oriented than other members of the hominoid lineage. Essentially, we will argue that selection pressures for increased sociality and more permanent group formations dramatically increased once hominins (those hominoids on the human evolutionary clade) were forced away from wooded regions; and, then, as the Earth grew colder with repeated glaciers, early *Homo* ancestors gradually abandoned their natal habitat of forest niches and, increasingly, were pushed toward more open woodlands and grasslands. Before they permanently left, however, atmospheric changes to a cooler, dryer climate surely led early *Homo* genera to spend longer and longer stretches of time foraging on the edges of woodland belts and then retreating to the safety of trees at night to sleep as a few chimpanzees populations living on the fringes of the African forests in Senegal do today (Baldwin 1979; Baldwin, McGrew, and Tutin 1982; McGrew 1981, 1992, 2010; McGrew, Baldwin, and Tutin 1981).[1] Then, at the onset of the Pleistocene epoch about 1.7 million years ago, the fossil record and archaeological sites document the appearance of a more advanced hominoid, *Homo erectus*, who made a major adaptive shift by permanently moving out to the bushlands and dry, open land-scapes (see Fleagle 2013 and Stanford et al. 2013 for discussions).

While the *Homo* lineage flourished and later went on to dominate the planet, the rest of the hominoid line floundered and are seen today as "atypical relict forms" (Corruccini and Ciochon 1983: 14) or, in fitness terms, as "evolutionary failures" (Andrews 1981: 25). Indeed, our closest ape relatives now live only in small populations inside narrow and restricted habitats and make up only a handful of species compared to the many dozens of species of monkeys (our distant cousins) or even prosimians (descendants of the first primates) (Temerin and Cant 1983). In Figure 3.1 is a histogram of the relative numbers of present-day apes, monkeys, and prosimians. As is clear, species of apes constitute a very small portion of the primate order, although one evolved ape—*Homo sapiens*—dominates the biotic world with their vast numbers of conspecifics.

Yet, strangely enough, a primate histogram drawn in deep time would reflect just the opposite of what is seen in Figure 3.1: "a land of the apes," where apes dominated the primate landscape both in numbers and spe-cies, until their downfall of apocalyptic proportions about 10 million years ago. The handful of great apes that exist today are simply the "leftovers" of a bygone golden age. Yet, it is abundantly evident that one evolved ape—*Homo sapiens*—appears adapted to all habitats and, indeed, is so reproductively successful that it becomes ever-more likely that humans, at a minimum, might cause the extinction of their ape cousins in their few remaining habitats or, at a maximum, that a Malthusian correction on a global scale will kill off many humans and other species of animals and

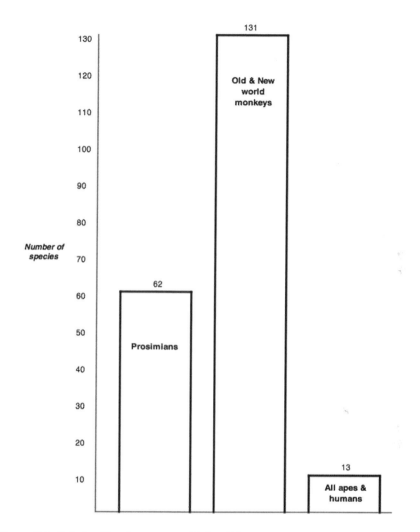

Figure 3.1 Relative Numbers among Living Primates

life forms more generally. Add to these problems the ecological destruction wrought by humans around the globe, and the future on Earth does not look very bright. How did such a creative but potentially destructive animal as *Homo sapiens sapiens* evolve and, of all things, become a religious hominoid?

To get answers, we need to start by going back to the beginnings of the primate order and work our way forward. In this way, we can come to understand why most apes went extinct and why humans were able to evolve out of those hominins that were able to adapt to the vicissitudes of open-country conditions where predators were far bigger and far more abundant than they are today.

On the Origin of Primates

Ascension to the Arboreal Habitat and Natural Selection

The primate order is very old; it originated during the Paleocene epoch about 65 million years ago when small shrew-like mammals climbed or clawed their way into the arboreal habitat (Gebo 2004; Sargis 2004; Fleagle 2013; Maryanski and Turner 1992; Turner and Maryanski 2005, 2008). This movement of terrestrial shrew-sized mammals who would evolve into committed arborealists came about with the demise of the dinosaurs. Suddenly, a wide range of new niches opened up in a wide variety of habitats such as the forests of Africa; and with intense directional selection for changes in proto-primate anatomy and neuroanatomy, the primate order was initiated, with proto-primates thriving for many millions of years.[2] In appearance proto-primates were little furry creatures with eyes to the sides of their faces, quadrupedal gaits, bushy tails, elongated snouts, and dentition that reflected a diet of fruits and plants. Of consequence is a small reduction in their olfactory bulbs and the uptick in their neocortical tissue over other Paleocene mammals.

During the early Eocene, about 55 million years ago, the first true primates, or the prosimians (i.e., pre-monkeys and apes) appeared in the forest habitat.[3] While early prosimians comprise a huge and eclectic assortment of different shapes and sizes, they all shared noticeable changes over their proto-primate ancestors by evolving larger brain cases and, in particular, neocortical enhancements in their parietal lobes (i.e., general somatic for more precise muscular movement), and in their occipital lobes (visual regions), with a concomitant reduction in their olfactory bulbs. Prosimian eyes had also shifted to forward positions, with this overlap signaling an increasing dependence on the visual cortex for moving about in a three-dimensional world, often far off the ground.

By the late Eocene wholly new types of primates appeared—the anthropoids or higher primates. One family of anthropoids is particularly important for hominin evolution because it contains *Aegyptopithecus*, a quadrupedal, generalized anthropoid that lived about 30 million years ago in an arboreal niche and that may be ancestral to Old World monkeys, apes, and humans. In looks, *Aegytopithecus* was a jumble of prosimian traits and innovative monkey-ape traits. Of consequence is an expansion in the parietal region of the neocortex, a large reduction in its subcortical olfactory bulb, and a definitive shift to more reliance on its visual modality located in the neocortex (Fleagle 2013: 275ff; Simons 1993). Thus, *Aegytopithecus* represents the beginning of an evolutionary trend towards *visual dominance*, a neocortically-centered trend that would lead to a capacity for all great apes and hominins to represent the world symbolically and, in the case of humans alone, a trend that would culminate in the origin of religion.

So the first step towards an understanding of the origin of religion is an appreciation of the revolutionary shift that took place from an olfactory dominant shrew-sized mammal to a visually dominant anthropoid mammal. In sensory biology, nearly all mammals are olfactory dominant, a few are auditory dominant (e.g., bats, dolphins, whales), and only a very few use vision as their primary sense modality.[4] All mammals, of course, have the same sensory fields; what differs is the relative amount of cortical tissue and how much of this tissue is devoted to each sense modality. It is clearly fitness-enhancing for an arboreal animal that must make its way in a precarious three-dimensional world to evolve ever-more neocortical tissue and to be visually dominant. Foraging for food by smelling, bouncing sounds off tree limbs (acoustic location), or feeling with body parts one's way about in the swaying branches of treetops is obviously a huge disadvantage; and so, natural selection worked to shift the balance among the sensory modalities in primates to a heavy reliance on sight with the other senses subordinated to the visual sensory mode (for discussions on the mammalian neocortices and on primate evolution, see Krubitzer and Kaas 2005; Hoover 2010; Rakic and Kormack 2007; Fleagle 2013; Maryanski 2013; Conroy and Pontzer 2012).

The importance of this qualitative sensory change from olfaction to vision cannot be overstated when it comes to laying the groundwork for the origin of religion. For this momentous transition essentially rewired the primate brain away from (a) a mammal with dominant olfactory receptors that project primarily to subcortical regions of the brain and geared mostly to the internal well being of an organism for preservative and protective responses to (b) a mammal with dominant visual receptors that project primarily to neocortical regions of the brain and that are geared mostly to the reception and understanding of the external world (Geschwind 1965a, 1965b, 1965c, 1985; Geschwind and Damasio 1984; Maryanski 2013).

Thus, for over 30 million years after the first appearance of primates, selection honed the anatomy and neuroanatomy of members of the primate order for survival and reproduction in a rainforest habitat. During extensive and large primate radiations during the Eocene, Oligocene, and Miocene epochs, primates became differentiated into two major groups or what today are two suborders: (1) *Prosimii*: the lemurs and lorises who are the descendants of the early primates; and (2) *Anthropoidea*: the monkeys, apes, and human hominins who are considered the highly intelligent, neocortical-centered higher primates. For our purposes, it is the differentiation of apes from Old World monkeys and the rise and demise of the apes that is essential in understanding how religion could ever have evolved among humans, and, perhaps, late hominins.

Trials and Tribulations of Miocene Monkeys and Apes

Old World monkeys, apes, and humans share a host of sophisticated traits that include large brains for mammals, prehensile hands, and virtually the same sensory system because they once shared a common ancestor.[5] The molecular data and the fossil record indicate that the branching away of the monkey daughter lineage and the hominoid daughter lineage (of apes and hominins) from its anthropoid mother population took place between 28 and 24 million years ago during the late Oligocene or early Miocene epoch (Stevens et al. 2013; Zalmout et al. 2010; Glazko and Nei 2003).

After the split, monkeys and apes settled in the densely forested African landscape. While the remains of both taxa are found in early Miocene fossil beds, the fossil record tells us that early monkeys were small (about 10 pounds) and so rare at this time that early monkeys are all of the genera *Victoriapithecidae*, a small monkey family (Dean and Leakey 2004). In comparison, it was a "milk and honey" time for apes, a glorious "Golden Age" when a great diversity and abundance of apes occupied most niches in the primeval forests. Apes held this large advantage seemingly because of their large body size (many were chimpanzee size) and a lifeway of living in trees with few predators (Maclatchy 2004). Their staple diet of high-energy fruits and their sheer size relative to monkeys also points to a stable habitat with little competition where they evolved *life history traits* for slow reproduction and a prolonged maturation.

Then, starting about 17 million years ago in the Middle Miocene, when the Earth began to cool, hominoid numbers dramatically declined. Fortunately, for apes, a land bridge opened up between Africa and Eurasia, with ape species migrating to more balmy climates in parts of Eurasia, resulting in such a wide diversity of ape species that some took up a semi-terrestrial lifestyle in the wetlands and woodlands. But in a cruel twist of fate, the ill-winds returned about 11 million years ago, fueled by a world-wide global cooling trend that is associated with a gradual extinction of nearly all hominoids in both Eurasia and Africa (Andrews and Kelley 2007; Andrews 2007; Potts 2004).

What caused the great ape extinction? While a detailed account is not necessary here (but see Turner and Maryanski 2008; Maryanski 2013), the cooling trend that depleted many forest habitats and, thereby, concentrated the remaining forests is surely one reason for the great ape die-offs. Yet, the picture is far more complicated and mysterious. Nearly all ape species perished but all the forests did not dry up and disappear and, oddly enough, the then rare monkeys did not die off with the apes. In fact, monkeys did the exact opposite by proliferating and moving into now vacated ape niches. So during the late Miocene the "planet of the apes" transitioned into the "land of the monkeys." Old World monkeys still reign supreme in the forests of Africa and Asia, as Figure 3.1 so clearly underscores. Indeed, Old World monkeys are so fit in an evolutionary sense and are such a great success story that they now inhabit forests, woodlands, snow-capped terrains, parklands, and deserts in Africa, Asia, and even Europe (for discussions, see Keller and Barron 1987; Fortelius and Hokkanen 2001).

Did Miocene monkeys get favored over apes because of their smaller bodies compared to the larger bodies of apes whose calorie needs were far greater? Lower nutritional requirements would certainly give monkeys a competitive edge. Dentition differences also indicate that Miocene apes relied on soft, ripe fruits, whereas monkeys could subsist on less nutritious and fallback foods. In addition, the dentition of juvenile apes of the early Miocene who died when their molar cusps were first surfacing indicate that young apes matured very slowly. And, this slow pace of life history traits corresponds with the juvenile stage of development among present-day apes. Given that molar morphology is entirely under genetic control and is a reliable yardstick for other bundled life history traits, Miocene apes seemingly had a slower rate of reproduction and gestation, a longer socialization phase, and a longer life span than Miocene monkeys. These findings led Kelley and Smith (2002: 326) to conclude "there was a shift to the prolonged life histories that characterize extant apes [and humans] early in the evolution of the *Hominoidea*" (see Maclatchy 2004 and Kelley 2002).

In contrast, Old World monkeys matured at a fast pace compared to apes; this wide disparity in life history traits between Miocene monkeys and apes probably also accounts for why early Miocene apes had larger brain volumes with more neocortical tissue than monkeys (controlling for body size). Other scholars have also proposed that the expansion of visual receptors in the Miocene ape visual cortex was a key factor in hominoid brain evolution, and notably for enhanced cognition (Barton 1998; Kirk 2006). Once these extended life history traits exist, they can serve as pre-adaptations for directional selection to work on for further encephalization of the neocortex (Potts 2004). All these hypotheses ring true but they do not fully explain why monkeys not only survived but also thrived in a receding rain forest by greatly multiplying their absolute numbers and the number of species.

A second long-standing hypothesis is that monkeys, in their competition for resources with apes, evolved a cut-throat arsenal weapon—a capacity among monkeys to neutralize the deadly toxins found in raw fruits (Andrews 1989; Kay and Ungar 1997; Temerin and Cant 1983). What makes this hypothesis plausible is that some present-day monkeys, the colobines (*Colobinae*) who inhabit the rainforests of both Africa and Asia, have multi-chambered stomachs that can effectively neutralize the toxic compounds found in certain plants, seeds, and unripe fruits, compounds that are poisonous for apes (and humans).

Did Miocene monkeys evolve stomachs to detoxify and digest raw fruits, the dietary staple of apes, before apes could eat these fruits? If so, it would sound the death knell for apes who must wait for fruits to ripen before consumption. Soft tissue rarely fossilizes but the timing of this happening is in agreement with the molecular clock and the fossil record that present-day Colobines first appear in the middle Miocene fossil beds between 16.2 and 14.7 million years ago, with a split between Eurasian and African colobines in the late Miocene about 11.5 million years ago (for discussions, see Raaum et al. 2005; Sterck 2012; Fashing 2011; Fleagle 2013).

Another platform of support for the unripe-fruit hypothesis is the nature of the few ape lineages that survived the general extinction and lived on to carry forth the hominoid lineage. To appreciate the after-effect and repercussions of this catastrophic event requires that we first provide a brief account of how some ape lineages were selectively swept away, while others were given a reprieve and survived. Above all, it is this dramatic transition in relative numbers of ape and monkey species that not only altered the ancestral line of Miocene hominoids and drove the future course of hominoid evolution, but also eventually set the stage for the origin of religion.

In brief, during the early Miocene, the two key players in this drama can be distinguished on the basis of skeletal elements and sorted into two hominoid types: (1) *Proconsulidae* or *Proconsul* and (2) *Morotopithecus*. The *Proconsuls* represent the prototype of Miocene apes. Highly successful and evidencing many diverse species of varying size, *Proconsuls* lived in exceptionally vast numbers in the preferred central zones of the African forest canopy where they reigned supreme for millions of years. In features, *Proconsul* had an ape dentition and some contemporary ape characteristics but its fossilized limb bones indicate a pronograde posture or a skeletal anatomy with limb proportions that rely on the hands and feet for locomotion. That is, *Proconsul* lacked the skeletal anatomy of all living apes and humans. Instead it had a skeletal structure and a locomotor anatomy that resembles present-day monkeys' mode of locomotion or a primate with limbs built for traveling about on the tops of tree limbs (Kagaya et al. 2010; Gebo et al. 1997).

In contrast, *Morotopithecus*, a rare early Miocene ape, had a skeletal anatomy more similar to present-day apes and humans. *Morotopithecus* had limb bones adapted for locomotor suspension, that is using the arms for hanging and a more orthograde posture for vertical climbing. Using the arms and shoulders for hanging or to propel the body through space is unique among mammals, requiring major evolutionary changes in skeletal and neurological features (e.g., in shoulders, finger bones, wrist joint stability, feet and cross-modal associations for hand–eye coordination), and is a very complex adaptation compared to the rather stereotyped movement of the four-footed *Proconsul*. Such novel traits signal that *Morotopithecus* did not occupy a conventional early ape niche but, rather, one that required to some degree an under-the-branch foraging strategy. Thus, limb bones in primates reflect their mode of locomotion. *Proconsul* limb bones point to a monkey-like adaptation dependent upon a quadrupedal progression with emphasis on the hind-limbs for propulsion, whereas *Morotopithecus* bones point to a dependence upon limbs that can act independently by using the forelimbs for support and for propulsion of the body through space (for discussions, see Conroy and Pontzer 2012; Maclatchy 2004; Gebo, Maclatchy, and Kityo 1997).

The skeletal features distinguishing *Proconsul* and *Morotopithecus* are illuminating for the clues that they provide into the cataclysmic extinction of most Miocene apes. The losses during the late Miocene were catastrophic because it was the dominant, superabundant, and successful *Proconsul*-like apes with their pronograde posture that natural selection targeted for extinction, leaving the *Morotopithecus*-like apes with their orthograde posture swinging on the hominoid family tree. Why target *Proconsul*-like apes? The answer takes us back to the unripe fruit hypothesis. A four-footed *Proconsul* foraging for ripe fruits travels step-by-step on the tops of sturdy tree limbs just as arboreal monkeys do today. If Miocene monkeys evolved a specialized digestive tract for consuming unripe fruits toxic to apes, the *Proconsul*-types could not compete for the bounty of fruits concentrated in the central zones of the forest canopy. Yet, no matter how agile a monkey or a *Proconsul*-type ape, neither one could step on the thin, swaying branches at the terminal ends of the forest canopy. A *Morotopithecus*-type ape, however, could accomplish this gymnastic feat by using its prehensile hands and feet differentially, spreading each limb wide apart and using multiple branches for support, or one hand could be used for hanging from a higher branch while the other could be deployed to grasp a soft, ripe fruit on a slim terminal branch.[6]

We do not know whether the last common ancestor of great apes and humans is a direct descendent of the *Morotopithecus* lineage, as some suggest, but we can take it for granted that the ancestors of present-day apes and humans inherited this orthograde morphology with a suspensory capacity because it is embodied in *all* present-day apes and humans.[7] Moreover, with regard to the hominin line, as Young et al. (2015) expressed it,

> the modern human shoulder evolved from an African ape-like LCA via long-term directional selection on a single but integrated trait: a longer and more lateralized configuration of the spine and glenoid mapped onto a shared African ape blade shape.

The Last Common Ancestor: Locomotion and Social Structure

Most paleoanthropologists agree that little gibbon/siamang apes (hylobates) and great apes—orangutans, gorillas, chimpanzees, and humans—make up a monophyletic clade. According to the molecular clock, the last common ancestor of all apes (including the gibbon here) lived about 19 million years ago (around the time of *Morotopithecus*). As shown in the cladogram in Figure 3.2 on p. 65, the orangutan line branched away from the last ancestor of great apes and humans between 13 and 16 million years ago; the gorilla line branched away between 8 and 9 million years ago; and the common chimpanzee and hominin line branched away between as early as 7 but, more likely, 5 million years ago (Conroy and Pontzer 2012; Chatterjee et al. 2009; Israfil et al. 2011; Bradley 2008).

During the late Miocene when the forested paleo-environment continued to get dryer and more seasonal, monkeys continued to proliferate and *Proconsul*-type apes continued to decline. The dentition (e.g., thick-enameled molars) and the thick-set jaws of some of these apes reflect a change in dietary habits from a staple of soft fruits to more plants and the consumption of hard-object foods such as roots and tubers, while post-cranial remains indicate an adaptation to a semi-terrestrial existence. Yet, the carnage of apes went on unabated and continued to pile up. By 5 million years ago in Eurasia, all ape species had gone extinct except for the leftovers of today—Asian gibbons/siamangs and orangutans.[8]

In Africa, the fossil record is sketchy because the number of hominoid fossils that date to the late Miocene is scant, although a few old ape fossils have been recovered dating to about 10 million years ago. Otherwise, the African fossil record is deadly silent. So, despite the high piles of ape remains recovered during the long heyday of the apes, as the Miocene epoch drew to a close, the ape fossil record is so bleak that not one confirmed extinct ancestor of present-day chimpanzees and gorillas has ever been recovered (Harrison 2010; Conroy and Pontzer 2012).

How did the last ancestor of great apes and humans manage to survive the ominous wipeout? We need to know because who lived and who died during the Miocene had enormous consequences for later hominoid and human evolution. The silent fossil record cannot help us, but we can still learn a great deal by turning to the skeletal anatomy and life-ways of our extant great ape cousins.

Primate Anatomy and Locomotion

If we begin with the skeletal structure of living apes (and humans), they reflect a past adaptation to a locomotor pattern that included suspensory hanging where the arms are held directly overhead and used to travel about (Pilbeam and Young 2004). Such a torso and limb morphology makes it possible to support the body using only the arms and shoulders. It also called for a strong finger flexion to enable the arms to suspend the body like a piece of hanging fruit. The hand (rather than the foot in quadrupedal locomotion) also required modifications to pitch the body through space, and it required an extreme range of supination so that apes (and humans) have also inherited a distinctive wrist joint. These modifications enable an ape or human to use their prehensile hands to pivot at the necessary half circle for suspension (Young 2003; Gregory 1916; Napier 1963).

To successfully move about in an environment where a fall to the forest floor would be fatal also required neocortical-centered expansions for precise hand–eye coordination (requiring cross-modal associations among sense modalities), finer motor control for the delicate movements (unlike the four-footed stereotyped monkey locomotion), abilities to navigate and calculate egocentric distances, and expanded memory banks for learning and mastering secondary depth cues. The tactile modality would also require a more refined sensitivity given that the visual modality can only detect the character appearance of objects. In a suspensory adaptation, a secure "hand-hold" is essential and, in turn, requires the ability to discern texture, as well as its smoothness or roughness and, above all, to determine the support capacity of an overhanging branch or limb to support the weight of an ape. While monkeys and apes are both visually dominant, suspensory apes would require expanded association cortices for cross-modal associations among vision, sound, and touch because the visual modality is not self-alerting; it cannot detect what lies under the surface of objects and it is virtually useless for night traveling. To react quickly would require assistance from the self-alerting haptic and auditory modalities and their corresponding sensory receptors, with sensors working together efficiently to complement the visual sense in a precarious three-dimensional habitat.

Thus, strong directional selection would be needed to satisfy the requirements of what is nothing less than a *sui generis* suspensory and vertical climbing adaptation. What potent selection pressures could force such a peculiar and novel lifeway?

The answer lies, we believe, in the particulars of an adaptation to a narrow and marginal foraging area at the endpoints of the hominoid tree niche. The last common ancestor of orangutans, gorillas, apes, and humans not only passed on these suspensory capacities to its descendants, it passed on many other traits entailed to a suspensory pattern of location. For primate locomotion also interfaces with organizational and social patterns in complex and reciprocal interdependencies that are reflected not only in hominoid physiology but, in the case of the last ancestor, is indicative of *an atypical form of social organization* for a primate that required an equally atypical neurobiology. To reconstruct these evolutionary entailments, we need to apply a scientific procedure known as *cladistic analysis*, coupled with *network theory*, to understand the atypical patterns of social organization among the last common ancestor to great apes and hominins, as well as their atypical neurological structures that, as we will come to see, are critical to the emergence and evolution of *Homo sapiens*.

Cladistics: A Mirror to the Distant Past

What is traditionally known as the historical comparative method is a powerful scientific tool with a long history of general use in historical linguistics and textual criticism and, more recently, in biogeography and comparative biology, where it is called *cladistics*. The first step in using this procedure is to identify and assemble a group of entities known to be descendants or end points of an evolutionary or developmental process. Like any comparative method cladistics searches for similarities not by analogy but, instead, by isolating out entities by homology or ancestor-descent relationships. For example, in historical linguistics the logic of cladistics or the method of historical comparison is used to compare words in related languages in search of "sound correspondences." Once these cognates are identified from daughter languages, they are then used to reconstruct the proto-language or speech forms of an extinct mother language. Alternatively, it is used in textual criticism by assembling alternate forms of a handwritten document that are then used to recreate the original document (e.g., the Bible) from which all others were derived. In biology the related entities are assembled in the same way—on the basis of shared diagnostic characters.

Cladistic analysis also incorporates a control group, usually a closely related sister lineage or "outgroup population" to precisely identify measurable "evolutionary novelties" or unique "derived characters" retained by related descendants after they branched away from a last common ancestor population. While the relationships themselves are not always testable, this scientific tool builds in two testable assumptions: (1) a "relatedness hypothesis," that holds that a class of derived characters or evolutionary novelties are the result of descent from a stem LCA and not by chance, and (2) a "regularity hypothesis," that holds that the modifications from the ancestral to descendant entities are systematically biased by evidencing a "founders effect" (see Jeffers and Lehiste 1979: 6; Forey et al. 1994; Maas 1958). It is also assumed that the more novelties or derived characters held in common among entities, the more closely related are the entities. This straightforward methodology offers a means to reconstruct ancestral patterns for a proto-language, an ancient text, an ancient social structure, or any set of related entities (for detailed applications of this type of analysis, see Maryanski and Turner 1992; Turner and Maryanski 2005, 2008).

Great Ape Cognition: A Cladistic Analysis

We need to start by conveying some of the sweeping changes in the hominoid brain from the early Miocene to the late Miocene. The early Miocene apes, *Proconsul* and *Morotopithecus* (circa 20 million years ago), had brain volumes of about 150 cc's (about the size of the biggest monkey brains today). After most apes had gone extinct, two well-preserved hominoids were unearthed that lived about 10 million years ago: *Sivapithecus* (who is thought to be ancestral to orangutans) and *Dryopithecus* (who is thought to be ancestral to gorillas and chimpanzees). By the late Miocene, *Dryopithecus* had a brain volume that had expanded to about 350 cc's with enhanced association areas in the range of the three great apes today. Both *Sivapithecus* and *Dryopithecus* were orthograde suspensory apes (no surprise there) with a life history profile of a long gestation and a slow maturation much like the living apes and humans today (for discussions, see Conroy and Pontzer 2012; Begun 2002).

We can learn a great deal about brain size and shape from fossilized endocasts but they cannot tell us much about brain neuroanatomy. To learn more, we have to turn to living apes. Although hominins and apes are the end products of their own equally long lineages, present-day apes never ventured away from forest zones during the last 20 million years, even the ones who took up a semi-terrestrial habitat. As a result, ape neuroanatomy did not undergo the sweeping changes of hominins who had to adapt to more open-country ecologies. So, orangutans, gorillas, and chimpanzees make a rather good approximation of the brain of the last common ancestor to humans and present-day great apes (Sherwood et al. 2008). In applying cladistic analysis, we can start by asking: what cognitive traits or evolutionary novelties have the great apes acquired since their separation from the last common ancestor they shared with the Old World monkeys?

A comparison of present-day Old World monkey and ape brains using the strict procedures of cladistics makes it immediately obvious that both brains are constructed from the same genetic blueprint, an expected finding given their shared ancestry. The difference is that the ape's brain is far larger and more sophisticated when compared to the monkey brain. The ape brain's outside layers of neocortical tissues have a very wrinkled or ruffled appearance as the uppermost cortical surface is rolled, and folds in and upon itself, thereby creating deep fissures or grooves. This folding serves to maximize the neocortical surface area for higher neuron densities, abundant and highly specific connections, and a higher capacity for processing in a limited space. In the crumpled ape brain, the neurological wiring is also cognitively advanced for more complex interconnections. On top of that, selection fostered in apes an augmentation of neocortical tissue in specialized association zones for integrating diverse information for higher perceptual functioning. Environmental demands also selected for a much greater diversity of nerve cells, with changes in neurochemistry for precise interconnections between classes of neurons to enhance memory, learning, and other cognitive functions (Semendeferi and Damasio 2000; Clowry 2014: 223).

One key finding of this cladistic analysis is the validation that, when the Old World monkeys line and hominoid line branched away from their common ancestor (between 28 and 25 million years ago), the monkey lineage and ape/hominin lineage took very different evolutionary paths. The outcome of these stepped up neocortical refinements over millions of years of hominoid evolution was the acquisition of some "avant-garde" endowments courtesy of the last common ancestor of great apes and humans that laid the foundations for further brain elaborations. One was a cognitive leap to a mind with revolutionary facets that included the appearance of a personal *self*, a trait that is activated by early and ongoing exposure to conspecifics. Among the 200-plus primates, only the great apes and humans evolved the complex neural circuits for perceiving a sense of self in which they can see themselves as an object in their environments. A self-identity is a truly liberating force that increases cognitive flexibility and opens the door to self-awareness, self-reliance, self-centeredness, and self-agency. As Kaneko and Tomonaga (2011: 3701) concluded, "chimpanzees and humans share fundamental cognitive processes underlying the sense of being an independent agent; that is self-agency" (for discussions of self in great apes, see Gallup 1980; Beran et al. 2016; Gallup, Platek, and Spaulding 2014; Suddendorf and Collier-Baker 2009).

Another emergent property of this cognitive leap was a higher-order ability to represent concrete physical objects in the mind using visual receptors and to represent physical objects or abstractions symbolically. Great apes routinely use symbolic gestures to communicate with conspecifics by channeling them through their visual-tactile modalities. Following Tomasello and Call (2007: 226), the

> apes are learning or inventing many of their gestures, and they are choosing particular gestures for particular contexts, following up with other gestures if the first one does not work. Apes have social/communicative goals, and in their gestural communications . . . [T]hey are pursuing them flexibly.

Great apes also have the cognitive equipment to use many facets of human language although in simpler forms. Indeed, chimpanzees have neurological structures that are actually primed to accept symbolic communications, using the visual–gestural communication system in the chimpanzee world or in the human world using American sign language or an invented computer language of abstract lexigrams in language-research centers. One astonishing discovery was the ability of chimpanzees to spontaneously comprehend human speech. While apes cannot vocally "speak," they do have an innate capacity to learn American English by isolating phonemes, applying the rules of English grammar, and then stringing words together for understanding complete sentences (Tomasello et al. 1994: 381). Following Lieberman (2006), the key finding in ape-language research is that apes have the biological capacity to acquire and use human words and syntax at about the level of a 3-year-old normal human child. As all three great apes (and humans) share these emergent cognitive properties, they represent a host of pre-adaptations inherited from their last common hominoid ancestor.

The Social Structures of the Last Hominoid Ancestor of the Great Apes: A Cladistic Analysis

Cladistic analysis can also be used to look back in time at social structures which, of course, are not preserved in the fossil record. However, by examining the behaviors of present-day apes and monkeys that forge social ties among conspecifics, we can then employ network analysis to determine the likely social structures of the distant ancestors of contemporary primates. In network theory, the unit of analysis is the social tie, or lack of ties, in any social network. A network approach is especially valuable for highlighting the fundamental *forms of relations* and, in doing so, for uncovering the underlying relational structure that is not easily seen when the focus is on individual attributes or classes of individuals, and on behaviors *per se*. By examining the social bonds and social structures that emerge from the social behaviors among conspecifics, it becomes possible to make reasonable inferences about the nature of the social structures organizing the common ancestors of present-day primates. A comparative network analysis of the social ties among our closest living relatives can, therefore, provide some essential clues into the relational ties of the last common ancestor of apes and hominins (for discussions of social networks, see Wellman and Berkowitz 1988; Borgatti, Everett, and Johnson 2013).

Alexandra Maryanski (1986, 1987, 1992, 1993, 1995) performed such an exercise on the social structures of present-day ape societies, using cladistics, social network theory, and a control sample of representative species of monkeys. As discussed earlier, cladistics uses the basic logic of historical linguistics, which applies this procedure to reconstruct a mother root language by isolating out what is shared by a set of related daughter languages that are thought to have evolved from a common origin. What a present-day set of related languages have in common is very likely to be the derived set of characteristics of the mother language of these current languages. In the case of primates, the derived characteristics of the last common ancestor to a set of extant species are examined. So, for example, if different species of present-day great apes living in different habitats universally have female transfer from their natal communities at puberty (which is a rare trait for Old World monkeys), this behavioral propensity was also likely to have been present in the last common ancestor of extant great apes and those hominins who would later form the human clade. Or, if most social ties among conspecifics are weak, adult sexual promiscuity is high, and permanent groups are not typical of present-day species of great apes, then the common ancestor to these apes and hominins is also likely to have had these characteristics.

Using these scientific procedures, Maryanski reconstructed the likely social structure of the last common ancestor to present-day great apes and hominin ancestors. One finding is that the ancestral social structure was probably very much like the very weakly-tied structure of semi-solitary orangutans, who are genetically more distant from humans than either chimpanzees or gorillas, but whose social structure is probably a good prototype for the mother population (of apes and humans) that lived some 16–13 million years ago. Like orangutans, this last ancestor revealed no strong ties among conspecifics, except the basic mammalian tie of mother to her young offspring, a tie that is broken when both sons and daughters at puberty disperse from their mother's ranging area. Most other ties among adults and between adults are weak in orangutan societies. Indeed, orangutans live a near hermit's life, with males pursuing females when receptive for courting and mating for a few weeks and then leaving her alone to give birth and raise her offspring to puberty (Russon 2009; Setia et al. 2009; Knott et al. 2008; Atmoko et al. 2008).

As the cladogram in Figure 3.2 outlines, the last common ancestor for all present-day great apes and humans lived many millions of years ago, but with each spin-off of the ancestors of extant apes, the *final* last common ancestor of apes and hominins was shared with chimpanzees, which is why chimpanzees are so closely related genetically to humans; and in fact, chimpanzees are genetically more closely related to humans than they are to either gorillas or orangutans.

Chimpanzees and gorillas reveal newer layers of sociality and structure not evident with orangutans, but these have probably evolved since the split with the last common ancestor of all extant great apes and humans. Among these additional ties among gorillas are the lead-silverback's attachment to females with offspring, with the female using the lead male as a babysitter, at times, in order to pursue other activities (including having sex with other males). Should a mother die before her offspring reaches puberty, the lead male usually takes over the care of the dependent offspring until they reach puberty. Other gorilla ties, however, are null to weak. For example, some researchers have literally classified gorilla females as "non-female bonded" and "dispersal egalitarian" (quoted in Robbins 2011: 335). Another structural form is the dominance of the leader silverback in

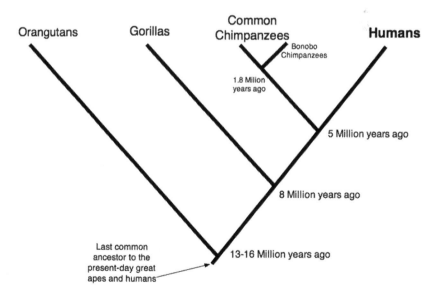

Figure 3.2 Approximate Dates of Last Common Ancestors of Humans and Present-day Species of Great Apes

a gorilla grouping—called a band—that lasts longer than is evident among other apes.

Among chimpanzees, males do not leave their natal community at puberty as do all chimpanzee females at puberty. In chimpanzee communities, adult males retain moderate-to-strong ties with their mothers whom they frequently visit (fathers are unknown because of great ape promiscuity). Chimpanzee males have strong ties with their brothers, but the strongest ties are often with a few preferred male friends.[9] Even with these stronger ties, *none lead to permanent groupings* among either kin or friends. In chimpanzee society, the only enduring quasi-group structure is the mother–preadolescent offspring tie that, at puberty, is broken when male orangutans and gorillas and female gorillas, orangutans, and chimpanzees *all* leave their natal unit. As emphasized, male chimpanzees remain lifetime locals in their natal community but move about independently during the day or join a mixed variety of community members in fleeting short-term gatherings or "parties" for sociality. In chimpanzee society, stable adult groupings are non-existent whether with mothers, brothers, or preferred friends. Ties among adult females are mostly weak. Indeed, Jane Goodall refers to adult female–female ties as "neutral relationships" or ones that can be characterized as neither friendly nor unfriendly. Moreover, while members of a chimpanzees community can number up to 150 individuals, they rarely, if ever, assemble together into one concentrated space (for discussions of gorilla and chimpanzee societies, see Harcourt and Stewart 2007; Bradley et al. 2005; Rosenbaum, Maldonado-Chapparo, and Stoinski 2016; Lukas et al. 2005; Watts and Mitani 2002; Goodall 1986, 1990; Nishida 1990; Stumpf et al. 2009; Boesch and Boesch-Achermann 2000).

In Table 3.1, Maryanki's cladistic analysis of contemporary apes' social structure is reported, with a blueprint of the hypothesized social structure of the last common ancestor presented in the column on the far right.[10] Based on the shared great ape social ties, the common ancestor evidenced no permanent social ties, and the only longer-term tie was that between females and their offspring—a strong tie that is, however, broken at puberty when offspring depart from the natal unit never to return. There appears to be no other strong ties among this last common ancestor; and thus, humans are ultimately descendants of ancestral hominoids that reveal mostly *weak social ties and no permanent group structures.*

In cladistic analysis, a control population discussed previously is often used to assure that the characteristics of the focal population are unique to that population and not part of a more extensive heritage from ancestors of related but still distant populations within the same order. The procedure then is designed to exclusively cordon off only "evolutionary novelties" or the derived traits from a last common ancestor before each

TABLE 3.1 Strength of Social Ties[1] among Extant Species of Great Apes

Species of Apes

	Gorillas (Gorilla)	Chimpanzees (Pan)	Orangutans (Pongo)	Last Common Ancestor
Adult-to-Adult Ties:				
Male–Male	0	0/+	0	0*
Female–Female	0	0	0	0*
Male–Female	0/+	0	0	0*
Adult-to-Adult Offspring Procreation Ties:				
Mother–Daughter	0	0	0	0*
Father–Daughter	0	0	0	0*
Mother–Son	0	+	0	0*
Father–Son	0	0	0	0*
Adult-to-Pre-Adolescent Offspring Ties:				
Mother–Daughter	+	+	+	+*
Father–Daughter	0	0	0	0*
Mother–Son	+	+	+	+*
Father–Son	0	0	0	0*

0 = no or very weak ties
0/+ = weak to moderate ties
+ = strong tie
* = is used to denote a reconstructed social structure, in this case the likely structure, of the last common ancestor to humans and extant great apes. As is evident, this structure is most like that of contemporary orangutans.
1. All primates have preferential relationships within and between age and sex categories (Cheney, Seyfarth, and Smuts 1986; Hinde 1983). For primates, the strength of social bonds is assessed on the basis of social grooming, food sharing, aiding and protecting, continual close proximity, embracing (excluding sexual contact), and the length and intensity of social relationships. The table summarizes the emergent properties—network ties of varying strength—that result from these kinds of behaviors.

lineage branched away. Thus, if Old World monkeys with whom we shared a common ancestor before the split in the Miocene revealed many of the same structural patterns as great apes, then it must be assumed that it was the shared ancestor of apes *and* monkeys that passed on these traits. So, by using monkey societies as a control, it is possible to gain confidence that the cluster of behavioral propensities and social ties among apes are *unique to great apes*; and indeed, such is seemingly the case. In fact, the social structures of monkey societies are almost the exact opposite of those organizing apes. Monkey females rarely leave their natal group. Instead, adolescent females remain life-long members of matrilines composed of (using common western kinship terminology) mothers, maternal grandmothers, aunts, and cousins. In contrast, all adolescent males depart their natal group and then, depending on the species, become solitary for a time, attempt to become a leader of a harem group composed of several matrilines, or more commonly, join large mixed troops in neighboring ranges, slowly gaining acceptance and then competing for dominance in these adopted groups. In turn, in large mixed groups (e.g., baboons and macaques), departing males are replaced by immigrating males. As Thierry (2011: 229) summed up the organization of macaque monkeys (*Macaca*), who are arguably the most successful Old World monkeys in terms of species, population numbers, and sheer variety of habitats in which they can live:

> Their social organization is characterized by both a profound unity and a great diversity, which may be best described as variations on the same theme . . . [M]acaques share the same basic patterns of organization. They form multimale/multifemale groups . . . [F]emales are philopatric—consequently forming kin-bonded sub-groups within their natal group, and most males disperse and periodically transfer from one group to another.

Thus, structurally, a general characteristic of all Old World monkey societies is that they are organized at the group level where male hierarchy and permanent female matrilines assure a stable intergenerational social structure at the level of the group rather than the larger community or regional population (for discussions of Old World monkey societies, see Campbell et al. 2011 and Cords 2012).

In great ape societies, the organizational arrangements are far more flexible because they usually incorporate a larger community or regional population as the more permanent structure. Among apes, most social formations among conspecifics are temporary. Even gorillas who organize into bands at one time actually reflect a shifting collection of individuals over time. In all ape societies, adolescent females leave the natal community at puberty, thereby short-circuiting the formation of matrifocal units so evident among monkeys; and in orangutan and gorilla communities, adolescent males leave as well, with the noted exception of chimpanzee males who remain in their natal community. In chimpanzee society, gatherings will form but soon disband within a few minutes, a few hours, or perhaps as long as a day. Community members frequently wander about the communal range alone or in small foraging parties where individuals can socialize or leave at will. While permanent adult groups never form, the larger community or home range is relatively permanent, with ongoing patrols by males along the community's boundaries to prevent incursions by males from other communities. Neighboring females are, of course, welcomed because they replace the emigrating females of the community. But neighboring males are threatened or killed (this behavior may be the result of males in a chimpanzee community being homegrown and not immigrants). As we will see, this orientation to community rather than to a group is part of a complex of behavioral propensities and capacities that, we argue, led to the evolution of the propensity for religious behaviors among humans and for the institutionalization of religion in even early band societies.

Cladistic analysis is much like the Hubble telescope; it allows us to look back in time and see a blueprint of the social structure of the last common ancestor of the great apes and humans. Yet, in looking back, the most startling feature of this ancestral social formation is the weak ties and the seeming absence of any permanent social relations or groupings beyond the mother–dependent offspring bonds. What selection forces might account for such a weakly connected social formation composed mostly of an aggregate of individuals without stable groupings or permanent kinship ties? And, what source of integration is possible with such inadequate ties?

A social structure built from mostly weak ties is intuitively viewed as tenuous and fragile. There is, however, a positive side to a weakly-tied social structure: it fosters independence by placing few constraints or obligations on individuals because they are not locked into strong-tied cliques. We do not know when a weakly-tied social structure originally evolved, but the handy-work of natural selection is still evident in present-day ape societies. Along with the fossil record and molecular data, we can reconstruct how the weak-tie system of organization was accomplished and probably why it was an effective lifeline for suspensory apes. As discussed previously, the fossil and molecular data tell us that about 28 million years ago the *first* monkeys and apes split from a last common ancestor.[11] As species typically build on the social structure that they inherit, we can assume that after branching away from their common ancestor, early Miocene monkeys and apes started out with a matri-focal system with male dispersal at puberty because this arrangement is common to most social mammals and Old World monkeys.

As discussed earlier, the *vanishing* Miocene apes had a body type and gait of four-footed monkeys, an adaptation for *above* branch foraging in the thick, central parts of the forest where the *Proconsul*-types dominated the forests for millions of years and could easily feast on plentiful soft-ripe fruits. In contrast, the *surviving* Miocene apes had a body type and gait built for suspensory and vertical climbing, an adaptation for *below* branch foraging in the thin, borderline edges of the rainforest.

In the case of the last common ancestor of apes and humans, a weakly-tied social structure would have fostered the necessary self-reliance for foraging alone; for, how many big apes can forage together for widely scattered and seasonal fruits at the terminal ends of branches? A collective foraging strategy would have also spurred intense competition for a handful of ripe fruits in suspensory niches. Given these conditions, pressures for change would have operated and as natural selection is a parsimonious force it would start with the most efficient pathway—disrupting the matrilineal networks by dispersing all the ape females along with the already departing males at puberty.

When tight-knit social formations are advantageous, strong ties are best. When loose social formations are advantageous, weaker ties are best because they generate an open-ended flexibility that is not possible in strong-tied formations. In the case of a marginal feeding niche, weak ties would allow individuals the freedom to forage with others or alone, depending on available resources. Yet, as individuals can maintain many more weak ties than strong ties on average, this means that residents can be in contact and interact with many more individuals even in a widely scattered "fission-fusion" population. The end result is an alternative type of structural integrity built on a few kinship ties but mostly on weak, non-kinship ties—a social formation that is not possible on the basis of strong ties alone.

Still, the problem of integration would surely remain of how to counter the fragmenting effects of such a widely scattered conglomeration of individualistic apes with mostly weak voluntary ties. Drawing on the cladistic analysis of contemporary ape cognition outlined earlier, all three apes (and humans) share a rare mosaic of cognitive properties consisting of (a) a self-identity, (b) a capacity for symbolic "linguistic-like" communication, and (c) awareness of a relational field that transcends transient, weak-tie social relations. For chimpanzees, a *community spirit* is the touchstone for integrating a social structure erected mostly on voluntary associations. While it is now very well documented that chimpanzees have a strong sense of community as do humans, of course, evidence is now accumulating that gorillas and, surprisingly, even the semi-solitary orang-utans are also organized around macro-regional populations that form a very loosely coupled community type of organization.[12] As Anne Russon (2009: 295) summed up:

> Orangutans have long been stereotyped as solitary apes. . . . Recent studies, however, have revealed a distinct social life within loosely organized, dispersed communities. . . . Orangutans also show chimpanzee-like traditions, so they too sustain cultures. Given their dispersed sociality, how they do so is unclear.

If hominoids all have a notion of something greater than self and if these characteristics are truly rare among mammals, this bundle of derived characteristics was likely passed down by the last common ancestor of apes and humans. Supposedly, under the right conditions the great apes and humans are primed to experience an emotionally driven, extra-mundane entity.

Thus, as ape descendants branched away from the LCA and adapted to new ecologies, some strengthening of ties was needed for survival and reproductive success. Selection can only act, however, to modify traits present in a species' repertoire. Random mutations do occur, but as the "principle of conservation" states, following Stebbins (1969: 105):

> Once a unit of action has been assembled at a lower level of the hierarchy of organization . . . mutations that might interfere with the activity of this unit are so strongly disadvantaged that they are rejected at the cellular level and never appear in the adult individual in which they occur.

So, the probability of favorable large mutations at this late stage of hominoid evolution is remote. Fortunately for apes and humans, their last common ancestor bequeathed to its descendants a suite of neurological pre-adaptations (or *exaptations*) that were surely originally entailed with a weak-tie social structure (see Maryanski 2017). But once in place, these pre-adaptations would be available for selection to work on, even though they originally had nothing to do with a future adaptation. Our focus in the next two chapters will be on those pre-adaptations as well as the in-place behavioral capacities and propensities of weak-tie primates that when passed down to *Homo sapiens* enabled them to become religious. Of special importance is how selection worked on hominin emotion centers, which intensified all of these pre-adaptations and behavioral propensities;

and in so doing, emotions worked to forge stronger bonds. As these same emotional enhancements worked to forge strong bonds, they also allow enlargement of the neocortex to be fitness-enhancing; and with this larger neocortex came a new capacity: to begin conceptualizing a sacred universe beyond the profane and mundane activities of community-based social life.

Conclusion

It did not look promising for apes as the forests shrank and the great savannas of Africa began to expand. Eventually, some would have to leave the protection of the forests and adapt to an entirely new and dangerous terrestrial habitat. How could a weak-tie, non-kin oriented, and non-group forming animal possibly survive the dangers of the savanna? The answer, of course, was that virtually all apes went extinct, except those few great apes that never left the primary or secondary forests in Africa and Asia. In contrast to apes, monkeys were well organized and could thus adapt to just about any new habitat—indeed monkeys now prosper where most apes were doomed to extinction. It is for this reason that there are so few species of apes left in the primate order, as is made clear in Figure 3.1 on p. 51. But, somehow, natural selection, working blindly on the neuroanatomy of those great apes that evolved into hominins, hit upon a strategy that worked. For, as hominins evolved, they became ever-more capable of forming stronger social ties and more permanent groups, but this new capability was not achieved by re-installing bioprogrammers for group and kin formation. Rather, an alternative set of mechanisms in the neurology of the subcortical areas of the brain were to be responsible for our ancestors' increasing ability to sustain groups and hence survive in the niches of the savanna habitat. It is in the story of how these mechanisms evolved that, ultimately, the origins of religion are to be discovered. These origins were driven by means of Darwinian natural selection, as we will see in the next two chapters.

Notes

1 Two early hominins—the robust australopithecines A. (Paranthropus) robustus and A. boisei, lived during the Late Pliocene/early Pleistocene and co-existed with Homo genera until the australopiths went extinct a million years ago. They are associated with early Homo in slightly open and wetland habitats. Homo taxa later moved out to much drier bushlands and open landscapes (Conroy and Pontzer 2012; Fleagle 2013).

2 In geological time, the primates originated in association with the opening of vacant tree niches and new sources of foods. In particular, angiosperms (flowering plants) and

ripe, soft fruits became rich, dietary sources for the nascent primate order (for discussions, see Bloch et al. 2007 and Harwig 2007).

3 For convenience, we are using the traditional nomenclature in lieu of the Strepsirhini and Haplorhini taxonomy. Tarsiers, of course, sit astride both suborders and defy classification. The adaptive radiation of a particular grouping of primates is associated with each epoch of the Cenozoic Era although depending on the lines, there is overlap.

4 The essential task of the mammalian senses is to signal the different properties of objects in space. So the core modalities—smell, sight, hearing, and touch—are all specialized and sensitive to particular forms of physical stimulation. All sensory equipment is obviously important for survival but the organ that is dominant is the one used primarily to locate objects in space.

5 Other joint traits include living in year-round societies composed of adult males and females, adolescents, juveniles and infants, a long period of socialization, single births for infants, menstrual cycles for females, and long life expectancies for mammals. Monkeys can live over 30 years and apes can live for more than 55 years.

6 A paper was presented at an American Anthropological Association meeting in 2015 where the authors proposed an alternative hypothesis for the origin of the suspensory adaptation of the 20 million year old *Morotopithecus*. They suggested that it evolved so this ape could travel between gaps in a broken forest canopy. While this contrasts with the long-standing unripe fruit hypothesis, the new explanation still depicts a marginal niche for *Morotopithecus*, and it remains supportive of the weak-tie hypothesis and its evolutionary consequences. The broken canopy explanation does not, however, help to explain the massive wipeout of *Proconsul* apes (see Maclatchy et al. 2015).

7 A hominoid body plan with an orthograde adaptation during the middle Miocene is unequivocally evident in a 13 million year old partial skeleton of the Spanish ape, *Pierolapithecus* (see Conroy and Pontzer 2012: 112ff for a detailed discussion of Miocene hominoids).

8 The only exception is the great hulking Asian *Gigantopithecus* discussed earlier. This ape went extinct about 500,000 years ago. However, only jaws and teeth have been recovered. Such a huge ape, estimated to weigh at least 600 pounds, was surely not a tree-dweller but one of the semi-terrestrial Asian apes during the late Miocene.

9 Mothers nurse a single offspring for at least 4 years before getting pregnant again, with gestation close to 9 months. So male siblings are at least 5 years apart. If a female is born between male pregnancies, the age difference between brothers would be closer to 10 years. Orangutan females are at the extreme end of this scale. A female has her first "child" between 15 and 16 years, with 6 to 9 years between births. The offspring then remain dependent for 7 to 10 years (Russon 2009).

10 These findings come from a comprehensive analysis of field data on the social bonds of apes and Old World monkeys. As these patterns reflect nearly 70 years of field observations by different researchers, we used a simple scale of tie strength: null or weak ties, weak or moderate ties, and strong ties. Assembling tie strength is an uncomplicated procedure as most researchers can easily see "who likes to be with whom." In this analysis, only the core social ties are assembled, but distinctive bonding patterns exist for all age and sex classes (e.g., infant–adolescent; juvenile–adolescent). In Table 3.1 we included only the widespread common chimpanzee.

11 The last common ancestor of Old World monkeys, apes, and humans is still elusive, but a recent unearthed anthropoid, *Saadanius hijazensis* who lived between 28 and 30 million years ago, is a fossil of interest. This specimen supports the evidence from the molecular

clock that the split between monkeys and apes/hominins occurred between 24 and 28 million years ago (Zalmout et al. 2010).

12 The notion that orangutans live in loose communities has been a source of serious speculation for a long time (see Mackinnon 1974). In the past few years, evidence has been accumulating that this is the case. In the case of gorillas, Goodall and Grover (1977) separated a number of gorilla bands over a wide area of home ranges. They discovered that bands that interacted with each other were also the ones that shared a home ranging area with weak ties also connecting particular bands with particular lone males. For one regional population, they suggested the existence of a residential population in the range of 68 members and in other communities at least 77 members.

4
Darwinian Selection on the Hominin Brain I
Directional Selection on Pre-adaptations

*Nothing in biology makes sense except
in the light of evolution*

Theodosius Dobzhansky (1973: 125)

As hominins gradually split off from their last common ancestor with chimpanzees, they remained mostly in wooded habitats. Yet, at some point, as the forests continued to recede, they would venture out into more open ecosystems returning to forests and woodlands at night for protection from predators. As glacial cycles intensified, the forests continued to recede; and thus, with the successive appearance of *Australopithecines* around 4.2 million years and later *Homo erectus* at 1.8 million years, ever more time was spent by hominins in semi-terrestrial environments (Cerling et al. 2011; Quinn et al. 2007; Fleagle 2013). As a result, selection pressures would have increased dramatically for hominins to become more group-oriented in order to defend themselves against predation and to coordinate foraging (and perhaps hunting). The hominin descendants of arboreal apes would thus increasingly be forced to overcome their behavioral propensities for weak social ties and unstable group formations, or die.

The very interpersonal skills that had allowed great apes and then hom-inins to sustain their communities and maintain their self-autonomy in the forests and semi-forests would be enhanced by emotions and, thereby, pull ever-more terrestrial[1] *Homo habilis* and *Homo erectus* into tighter-knit groups and more enduring social relations. As Jane Goodall famously put it, "chimpanzees have a sense of community" (Goodall 1986), but, the hom-inin descendants of great apes began to fill their communities with more cohesive and stable group-level formations. In so doing, they used these same interpersonal skills inhering in the great ape and hominin lines, but these skills were now charged with more emotions and thus had more power to generate social bonds and group solidarities. In the next chapter, we will examine how Darwinian selection worked on the brains of hominins to increase the power of these interpersonal skills to forge stronger social bonds and group solidarities among hominins as they spent ever-more time in open-country conditions. In this chapter, our focus will be on the pre-adaptations that hominins inherited from their great ape ancestors and how Darwinian natural selection rewired the hominin brain to take advantage of these pre-adaptations to make hominins more social and more group oriented.

A *pre-adaptation* (or *exaptation*) is an earlier trait installed by natural selection or is a byproduct of selection entailed to an earlier trait. Using the telescope provided by cladistics analysis, we can look back 4 to 7 million years ago and see what anatomical and neuro-anatomical structures were available for natural selection.

Figure 4.1 provides a time frame by listing the approximate dates given to various hominins along or near the clade that led to the emergence of *Homo sapiens*. Such diagrams are, however, subject to constant change as new fossils are discovered or old ones given new interpretations; and so, at best, this figure represents a rough timeline. The key developments, we argue, are after chimpanzees and hominins split from their last common hominoid ancestor some 5–7 million years ago. While *Australopithecines* ventured out from closed forests to semi-terrestrial landscapes, they also spent a great deal of time in the forests, as is revealed by the size and density of their bones (Rugg et al. 1916). Thus, it is with late *Homo habilis*

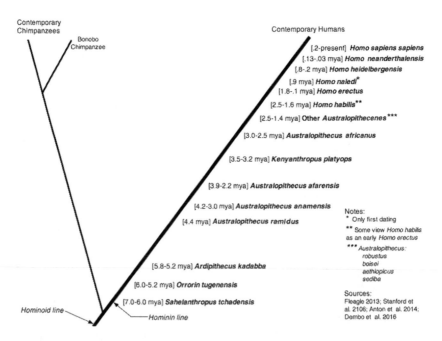

Figure 4.1 Cladogram of Hominins

and, then, during the long run of *Homo erectus* that such activity greatly increased and eventually led to a hominin that could spend large amounts of time in open country and, later, in diverse habitats in most parts of the globe. Once the metabolic demands of sustaining stronger bones lessened, some of the metabolic activity required to do so could be redirected to enlarging the brain of various species of Homo such as *Homo habilis* and *Homo erectus*.

While the transition to more open landscapes probably began with early hominins like the *Austrapithecines* whose brain size was only a little larger than living chimpanzees, it is also linked in time with another adaptive change: a postcranial anatomy designed for an upright walking gait. The hominin shift to habitual bipedalism was probably as great as the radical differences between *Proconsul* apes that walked like quadrupedal monkeys on the tops of branches and *Morotopithecus* apes that swung like a pendulum suspended on branches (see previous chapter).

Such a novel pattern of mobility surely signaled that hominin taxa were pursuing a new adaptive strategy and, in our view, the adoption of bipedalism as a habitual mode of movement is linked to foraging in more open habitats. Thus, it was not a dramatic increase in the size of hominin brains that initially mattered but, rather, the change to bipedal locomotion perhaps in response to the periodic cooling cycles that lead to a decline in African rainforests and an expansion of closed woodland and terrestrial ecologies.[2] Indeed, the timing of the gradual movement of hominins to more open landscapes fits nicely with evidence that, about 2.5 million years ago, a new cycle of lower temperatures with advancing glaciers began (after a period of warmer temperatures during the middle Pliocene). These glacial cycles had a far-reaching impact on climate around the globe (for discussions see Conroy and Pontzer 2012: 28ff and Shackleton 1987).[3]

These short forays by taxa of Australopiths to open terrain likely represented new adaptations outside the forests but, as noted, were not accompanied by changes in the size of hominin brains. Not until *Homo erectus* and what are now sometimes considered early forms of *Homo erectus*—*Homo habilis*—did the size of the neocortex begin to grow significantly judging by endocasts of early skulls. Put in comparative terms, Australopithecines (e.g., *afarensis*) have a cranial capacity of about 450cc's; early specimens of *Homo habilis* (designated ER 1470) have a capacity of 775cc's, which is still very short of the human measure of 1400cc's (Stanford et al. 2013: 322, 342). The first *Homo erectus* fossil find exhibited a cranial capacity of over 800 to 850cc's, although other finds show wide variation in cranial capacity below this large size with some earlier fossils and above this capacity with late *Homo erectus* (Zolikoffer and Ponce de

Leon 2013; Gibbons 2013). Some of this variation may be the result of genetic drift because populations that reveal relatively smaller brains were nonetheless able to migrate out of Africa, become somewhat isolated and subject to selection in a variety of habitats and niches. The result would be more variations among populations that had become dispersed (for a recent review of movements of out of Africa, see Gibbons 2016).

Yet, despite the small brain size of *Australopithecus,* we believe that subcortical changes were well underway to make Australopithecines more emotional and hence more able to form stronger bonds and social ties, but these dramatic changes would not be reflected in endocasts because the latter can only capture the external surface impressions made by neocortical tissue as it pressed on skull walls, whereas subcortical areas of the brain reside, to a great degree, inside the neocortex that wraps around the older structures of the mammalian brain. Indeed, the first proto-mammals did not have much, if any, neocortex (Kemp 2005), but when the neocortex began to evolve, it was piled on top and around much of the subcortex, although it is not known when and how the necortex evolved. As the subcortex grew during hominin evolution and thereby increased the capacity of hominins to experience and express a larger palette of emotions, this expanded emotionality would also allow for growth in the size of the neocortex from late *Homo habilis* through *Homo erectus* to *Homo sapiens* (and including Neanderthals).

Natural Selection on the Hominin Brain

Selection on such a complex structure as the hominin brain presents a challenging problem. Large mutations would be universally harmful to brain structures of advanced mammals because of their complex interdependencies; indeed, large mutations would be much like throwing a grenade into the brain. This fact has always posed a problem in earlier versions of evolutionary psychology in its one-time emphasis on the evolution of function-specific modules during the Pleistocene on hominins. In fact, as Fisher (1930) and later Stebbins (1969) emphasized, mutations of any sort in the hominin brain would have faced the challenge of successfully integrating with an already precise and programmed pattern of genes and gene products directing the organization of such a complex neurological system as a large primate brain.

The alternative route for natural selection is *directional selection* on *existing* brain structures (or modules) that vary, on a bell curve, by two key properties: (1) their relative size and (2) their degree of connectivity (Rilling 2014). Thus, if increasing or decreasing the size of a brain structure is fitness-enhancing, then selection would work on the tail or side of the bell curve where smaller or larger versions of a structure are distributed. As we will see for the hominin brain, directional selection was working on the tail of the bell curve distributing larger-sized structures during much of hominin evolution. Thus, selection was pushing to increase the size of specific brain components as well as the overall size of the brain. As the growing size of endocasts of hominins enumerated earlier suggest, selection initially increased the size of the brain with *Australopithecines* (4.2 million years ago) by about 100cc's over that of contemporary chimpanzees; the brain increased in size even more with later *Homo habilis*; and then with *Homo erectus* 1.8 million years ago, the rate of growth in the size of the brain accelerated all the way to the emergence of *Homo sapiens*. Almost all of this growth was surely by directional selection on existing modules and neurological systems in the brain and on increasing the connectivity among these larger brain structures to create larger and more complex structural assemblages across the brain.

In this way, directional selection on hominin populations in somewhat different habitats and niches could work on existing structures in the brain where pre-adaptations and behavioral capacities/propensities are activated. In particular, natural selection was operating on one underlying imperative—strengthening hominin social bonds—so that they could live in group-like structures which, as we outlined in the last chapter, were not and are not typical of great apes today, especially compared to the tight-knit group structures of monkey societies. In Figure 4.2, the particular brain systems that we will reference are delineated so that it is possible to see where selection was working during hominin evolution.

As Figure 4.2 highlights, the mammalian brain is divided between a *subcortex* and a *neocortex*, with the latter wrapped over and around the subcortex, some of which was inherited from the two lines of early amphibious vertebrates from which, respectively, the reptile/birds and the mammalian lines of terrestrial animals evolved. We can adopt the logic of cladistic analysis used in the previous chapter to determine what selection was doing to hominin brains over the last 5 to 7 million years. The brains of the three extant great apes—i.e., chimpanzees, gorillas, and orangutans—can give us a rough sense for what the brains of the last common ancestor to apes and hominins were like. Then, if we compare these ape brains with human brains, the differences become a "smoking gun" revealing what Darwinian natural selection did to the brain as successive species of hominins evolved along the human clade. Our approach is simply an adaptation of the large literature comparing ape and human brains (e.g., Rilling et al. 2013; Taglialetela et al. 2008), but our focus is ultimately on how changes

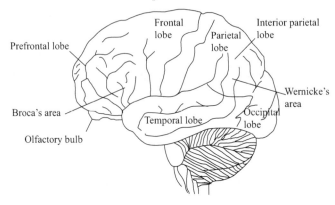

Left Hemisphere of Neocortex

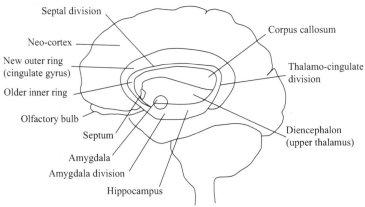

Cross-Sectional Analysis of Neocortex and Subcortical Limbic System

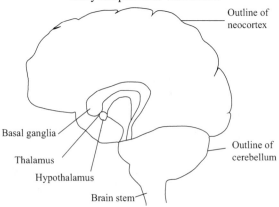

Ancient Subcortial Areas Inherited from Early Amphibious Vertebrates

Figure 4.2 Key Areas of the Brain under Directional Selection

in the brain working on pre-adaptations and behavioral propensities made *Homo sapiens* religious.

Natural Selection on Pre-adaptations among Hominins

Comparatively Large Brains

To repeat the obvious, we should simply re-emphasize that hominins had large brains for a mammal, just as great apes today have large brains.[4] The brain of hominins also had most of the existing structures, or modules (if this term is appropriate) that humans have, although some, such as Broca's for speech production, were only incipient, but their existence allowed for directional selection to grow the brain's size to increase functionality (see later discussion). The fact that large random mutations would be harmful to the brain means that existing variations among structures of the brain would need to be selected upon. Indeed, directional selection on tails of bell curves describing *existing variations of structures* in the brain could do most of the work; moreover, such directional selection can move very rapidly when enlargement of a brain structure or increases in its connectivity are fitness-enhancing, as was evident with the acceleration of neocortical growth with later *Homo erectus*.

Thus, transformation and rewiring of the brain did not have to overcome the obstacles that selection would have faced with a more primitive, early mammal because there were existing brain modules and assemblages that could be subject to directional selection revolving around increasing the size and connectivity of *existing* brain structures.

Selection on the Expanded Palette of Primary Emotions

Virtually all mammals possess at least the four primary emotions of *assertion-anger*, *aversion-fear*, *disappointment-sadness*, and most importantly, *satisfaction-happiness* (Turner 2000). *Anger* and *fear* were inherited from the two early amphibious vertebrae that initiated, respectively, the bird/reptilian and mammalian lines of evolution millions upon millions of years ago. The addition of *sadness* and *happiness* may be unique to mammals, although highly intelligent birds also seem to possess analogies or perhaps even homologies to these emotional capacities in their more reptilian-looking brains.

Social solidarity in the absence of dedicated bioprogrammers for group formation *can only be generated by positive emotions*, and so, if natural selection was to enhance hominin sociality, bonding, and group formation, the power of the three negative emotions—i.e., *anger*, *fear*, and *sadness*—had to be mitigated to some degree, while the salience and power of the *satisfaction-happiness* continuum had to be expanded. Most mammals reveal bioprogrammers for forming herds, packs, pods, troops, and other group structures, and therefore, even when negative emotional states arise in these groupings, these proclivities keep members together. But, with evolving apes, these biologically-driven proclivities had been lost or at least greatly attenuated; and thus, other forces were needed to promote social bonding. Yet, unlike many other mammals, great apes and particularly chimpanzees (and hence, their common ancestor with hominins) already possess (possessed) a rather sophisticated emotional communication system (Parr, Waller, and Fugate 2005), and so there was something already present on which selection could go to work. Since solidarity is achieved in humans by interactions signaling positive emotions, this was clearly one route that selection took; once more emotions and nonverbal emotional gestures proved fitness-enhancing, selection would continue to enhance and expand the palette of emotions and the gestures signaling these emotions.

Since positive emotional arousal is what gives human groups solidarity today, selection obviously hit upon this "solution" at some point during hominin evolution. So the emotional basis of solidarity is not a matter of supposition but, rather, a factual matter that requires us to learn how and, if possible, when hominins became more emotional, especially with respect to positive sentiments that facilitate social bonding. To enhance emotions, selection had to begin with the subcortex where emotions are generated in all mammals. Thus, while the neocortex is given much attention in evolutionary analysis, it is important to emphasize that selection on the subcortex for increased emotionality also enlarged key structures of the subcortex and their patterns of connectivity within the subcortex and between the subcortex and neocortex. Indeed, without this prior selection on older portions of the brain, growth of the neocortex could not have occurred.

Growth of Emotion Centers in the Hominin Subcortex

Careful measurements on the relative size of brain components in human and great ape brains reveal that the subcortical areas of the human brain are, on average, *twice as large* controlling for differences in body size, as the same areas in the great-ape brain. We believe that this selection on emotion centers of the subcortex started with those early hominins that began to venture periodically out into more open terrestrial habitats, perhaps as early as 7 million years ago but clearly with *Australopithecines* some 4 to 3 million years ago. The measurements in Table 4.1 are old, but for a long time, they were the best available. More recently, studies on the amygdaloid

TABLE 4.1 Relative Size of Brain Components of Apes and Humans, Compared to *Tenrecinae*

Brain Component	Apes (Pongids)	Humans (Homo)
Neocortex	61.88	196.41
Diencephalon thalamus hypothalamus	8.57	14.76
Amygdala	1.85	4.48
centromedial	1.06	2.52
basolateral	2.45	6.02
Septum	2.16	5.48
Hippocampus	2.99	4.87
Transition cortices	2.38	4.43

Sources: Data from Stephan 1983; Stephan and Andy 1969, 1977; and Eccles 1989.
Note: Numbers represent how many times larger than *Tenrecinae* each area of the brain is, with *Tenrecinae* representing a base of 1.

complex have added new, more refined insights on what natural selection was doing to the brain. But first, let us review briefly the implications of the measurement reported in Table 4.1. As is evident, the neocortex of humans is about three times that of great apes and early hominins, controlling for body size. But, looking down the next rows in the table reveals that the thalamus, hypothalamus, amygdala, septum, hippocampus, and transition cortices are, as just noted, about twice the size in the human subcortex compared to the subcortex of great apes. These structures are involved in the production of emotions; and so, selection was surely enhancing emotions. We argue that this enhancement was under way certainly with *Australopithicines* long before the neocortex began to grow toward the human measure.

The *amygdala* has been given special attention in the literature because it is the ancient area for anger and fear inherited by early descendants of the amphibious vertebrates who apparently initiated the mammalian line (and reptilian line as well[5]). It also appears that the amygdala has additional functions in some higher mammals revolving around appraising the social environment and assessing the likely courses of actions of others (a critical capacity in role-taking and coordinating interpersonal behaviors). If this area could be further selected upon, which appears certain given the size difference between human and great ape amygdaloid complexes, understanding how the amygdaloid complex works in humans can provide further insights into what was occurring along the hominin line as natural selection was working on the subcortex.

Selection was working to increase sociality and bonding by mitigating negative emotions, while increasing capacities for the arousal of more positive emotions. The interpretation of the authors whose measurements appear in Table 4.1 suggest that new areas for pleasure were slapped onto the basolateral areas of the amygdala complex (see Stephen et al. 1987; Eccles 1989), thus accounting for most of the size difference between great apes and humans, although some of their interpretations also point toward the path that more recent literature has taken (Marger et al. 2012: 30–35). Moreover, new neuronets travelling from the prefrontal cortex, where decision making occurs in the neocortex (see Figure 4.2), are thicker than in great apes, and they travel through the upper portion of the amygdala that appears to serve as a switching station routing the flow of neurons back and forth among subcortical areas of the brain *and* between these subcortical neuronets and the prefrontal cortex. Of course, the *thalamus* is still very much the key structure in moving sensory inputs to neocortical lobes and subcortical emotion centers, but the emotions used in situational appraisals and in making decisions travel through the amygdala to the prefrontal cortex.

Turning to other subcortical structures that grew during hominin evolution, the *septum* in humans is well over twice as large as in the highly-sexed and promiscuous great apes; perhaps this growth is an indication that new emotions for bonding, above and beyond the pleasure associated with sex, were being installed—a necessary emotional precursor for the eventual evolution of the nuclear family. The *hippocampus* and *transition cortices* that feed into this key structure are responsible for short-term memory and tagging cognitive experiences with varying degrees and valences of emotions so that they can be remembered. The expanded activity of the amygdaloid complex in assessing social context and the growth of the septum as a center of sexual pleasure caused new emotions to emerge between sexual partners; these new emotions would push the hippocampus to cognitions about social–sexual relations with more nuanced valences. Those experiences that are tagged with emotions are logged into the hippocampus for shorter-term storage as memories. If memories of experiences stored in the hippocampus are revisited by individuals, they fire off the original emotions by activating the relevant areas of the subcortex that were in play when the original memory was formed (Damasio 1994). If these cognitions are consistently revisited by individuals, thereby arousing the emotions associated with them, they are shipped up to the frontal lobe for longer-term storage as memories that can be used in making decisions (by the prefrontal cortex).

The hippocampus had to grow, then, because it was working with a much more expanded palette of emotions to tag cognitions, especially with respect to social experiences. This is, we think, the best interpretation for the data in Figure 4.1. More recent data on the amygdala offer additional insights into what natural selection was doing.

The amygdaloid complex in humans now operates to facilitate learning, to mark salient stimuli, to consolidate memory formation (Phelps 2005), to appraise the social environment with respect to gaze monitoring, to process meanings of vocal, facial, and body gestures (Yang et al. 2002), and to evaluate trustworthiness of others (Singer et al. 2004). Thus, the nuclei of the complex do much more than generate fear and anger, and while primate amygdala also serves some of these functions, the amygdaloid complex in humans is considerably larger than it is in great apes. For example, in a series of studies focusing on the basolateral nuclei of the amygdaloid complex, findings indicate that the *lateral nucleus* contains "59% more neurons than predicted by allometric regressions on nonhuman primate data" (Marger et al. 2012: 30–35), leading the authors of this comprehensive study to argue that "the lateral nucleus is the main characteristic of amygdala specialization over the course of human evolution" because most of the size differences between great ape and human amygdala are located in this nucleus (a finding similar to that reported in Table 4.1 but eliminates the basal nuclei). Given the integrative functions of the amygdala, it is "strategically positioned to bridge higher-order sensory information from the neocortex with brainstem and subcortical structures that facilitate the production of adaptive motor responses" (Marger et al. 2012: 35–36), as well as detecting threat, value, ambiguity, and salience, while also being associated with social behaviors and affiliation (Brothers 1990; Adophs 2003).

Thus, it is not surprising that selection was so intense on the lateral nucleus of the amygdala because, if natural selection was working to increase sociality and bonding, this would be a key subcortical structure to target given its centrality in the neuronets of the subcortex. In fact, Barger, Semendeferi, and colleagues (2014), in a later study on specialization on the human limbic system, argue that regions of the brain involved in emotion processing "may have even been enhanced in recent human evolution."

The lateral nucleus of the amygdaloid complex appears to be related to two syndromes that help underscore its importance in generating increased sociality. Autism is one outcome of deformities in this nucleus, thereby dramatically reducing individuals' ability to role-take and read the emotions of others. In contrast, Williams' Syndrome is another outcome of deformities, leading to behaviors that are the opposite of autism: over-empathizing with others. Children with this syndrome will, for example, walk up and hug strangers if they sense any distress in them. What these two syndromes highlight is that natural selection was working on the lateral nucleus of the amygdala to sharpen role-taking, to enable individuals to assess context, and most importantly, to assess the emotional states of others. These are some of the "smoking gun" evidence left by natural selection on how the subcortical areas of the hominin brain were transformed in the evolution to *Homo sapiens*.

How Emotions Evolved

Chimpanzees have control of sensory inputs via Wernicke's area (see Figure 4.1), and they can control the emission of calls carrying meanings (Rauschecker and Scott 2016), even in emotion-arousing dangerous locates such as is the case when chimpanzee males on patrol of their community will dip into the territory of another. And so, great apes, whose Broca's hump is rather small compared to humans, can still regulate and control emotions—when necessary. Similarly, chimpanzees will control vocals and long-distance hoots to members of their community in order to stay in contact when coordinating actions (Fedurek et al. 2013), and thus, there was an existing mechanism for vocal control, perhaps the somewhat truncated Broca's area evident in the brains of great apes.

Still, without a fully developed Broca's area, they cannot entirely control emotionally charged auditory outputs, and the more emotional they become, the more likely are chimpanzees to become noisy. As we will note elsewhere, selection began to grow Broca's area—the structure in the human brain responsible for controlled speech production whereby the brain's gestalt-based thinking is downloaded and translated into sequential speech (Taglialatela et al. 2008). If natural selection could increase control of emotional outputs via expanded neuronets from the prefrontal cortex to subcortical areas, particularly the amygdala, then some of the neurology would be in place to expand the palette of primary emotions in early hominins. With more neuronets connecting subcortical areas, and then further linking subcortical areas to the prefrontal cortex, more variants of primary emotions evident in all mammals—*anger, fear, sadness*, and *happiness*—could be expanded. Table 4.2 illustrates some of the variants that probably emerged in this initial stage of expanding hominin emotional capacities.

If these variants allowed more nuance and variety to emotions that, in turn, could increase sociality and social bonds when piggy backed onto the existing gestural system of great apes and their hominin descendents, then selection would continue to increase the size of emotion centers and the neuronets connecting them together, and to the prefrontal cortex. The next step in this process, Turner (1997, 1999a, 1999b, 2000, 2007, 2014a, 2014b)

TABLE 4.2 Variants of Primary Emotions

Primary Emotions	Low Intensity	Moderate Intensity	High Intensity
SATISFACTION-HAPPINESS	content sanguine serene gratified	cheerful buoyant friendly amiable enjoyment	joy bliss rapture jubilant gaiety elation delight thrilled exhilarated love
AVERSION-FEAR	concern hesitancy reluctance shyness	misgivings trepidation anxiety fear alarmed unnerved panic	terror horror high anxiety
ASSERTION-ANGER	annoyed agitated irritated vexed perturbed nettled rankled piqued	displeased frustrated belligerent contentious hostile ired animosity offended consternated	dislike loathing disgust hate despise detest seething wrath furious inflamed incensed outrage
DISAPPOINTMENT-SADNESS	discouraged downcast dispirited	dismayed disheartened glum resigned gloomy woeful pained dejected	sorrow heartsick despondent anguished crestfallen

Source: Data from Turner 1999a, 1999b

has argued, was to combine variants of two primary emotions to produce what can be termed *first-order elaborations* (see alternative conceptualization by Plutchik 1980). These combinations are, by analogy, somewhat like a color wheel in which all other colors are mixes among a small palette of primary colors. Natural selection appears to have adopted a similar strategy in enlarging the palette of emotions by combining primary emotions together to produce a much large repertoire of more complex and nuanced emotions. First-order elaborations of emotions involve combining in some unknown (neurological) manner a greater amount of one primary emotion with a lesser amount of another, thereby producing a much more robust and varied set of emotions. Examples of these more nuanced emotional combinations are listed in Table 4.3.

TABLE 4.3 Combinations of Primary Emotions

Primary Emotions		*First-Order Elaborations*
SATISFACTION-HAPPINESS		
satisfaction-happiness + aversion-fear	*generate*	wonder, hope, relief, gratitude, pride, reverence
satisfaction-happiness + assertion-anger	*generate*	vengeance, appeasement, calm, soothment, relish, triumph, bemusement
satisfaction-happiness + disappointment-sadness	*generate*	nostalgia, yearning, hope
AVERSION-FEAR		
aversion-fear + satisfaction-happiness	*generate*	awe, reverence, veneration
aversion-fear + assertion-anger	*generate*	revulsion, repulsion, antagonism, dislike, envy
aversion-fear + disappointment-sadness	*generate*	dread, wariness
ASSERTION-ANGER		
assertion-anger + satisfaction-happiness	*generate*	condescension, mollification, rudeness, placation, righteousness
assertion-anger + aversion-fear	*generate*	abhorrence, jealousy, suspiciousness
assertion-anger + disappointment-sadness	*generate*	bitterness, depression, sense of betrayal

Primary Emotions		First-Order Elaborations
DISAPPOINTMENT-SADNESS		
disappointment-sadness + satisfaction-happiness	*generate*	acceptance, moroseness, solace, melancholy
disappointment-sadness + aversion-fear	*generate*	regret, forlornness, remorse, misery
disappointment-sadness + assertion-anger	*generate*	aggrieved, discontent, dissatisfaction, unfulfilled, boredom, grief, envy, sullenness

One problem with using emotions to enhance sociality is that three of the four primary emotions are negative—i.e., anger, fear, and sadness—while only one is positive—i.e., variants of happiness. If other primary emotions are added to the list, such as *disgust, surprise, embarrassment, shame,* or *expectancy,* the ratio of positive to negative emotions does not change (see Turner 2000; Turner and Stets 2005: 14–16 for lists of various hypothesized primary emotions from diverse scholars). Thus, emotions are biased toward negative valences, and negative emotions do not promote solidarity. As noted earlier, having this negative bias is not a problem when mammals also have bioprogammers that, in essence, force affiliation because, even with episodes of negative emotional arousal, the bioprogrammers sustain kin and group relations.

For hominins, however, the very lack of these bioprogrammers would make any group structures built from interactions precarious, given the negative bias of emotions that are easily aroused during the course of interaction. To some extent, the first-order elaborations among primary emotions reduce some of the negative bias; and even elaborations that have fear, sadness, and anger in them are mitigated in their negative power and potentially could be used in mild sanctioning that would not be so disruptive as raw fear and anger alone. Still, some very deadly first-order elaborations are generated in this process of construction. For instance, the emotion of *vengeance,* which is a combination of anger and happiness, is one of the most disruptive emotions possible because it gives individuals happiness as they vent their aggression on others. It is, indeed, the emotion of terrorism and genocide in the modern world. Yet, we can also see emotions that might be relevant to the conceptualization in the human mind of a supernatural and sacred realm—emotions such as *veneration, awe, wonder, reverence,* and *righteousness*—that come by mixing smaller amounts of fear and anger with happiness. It would be difficult to view religion as possible without at least the capacity to experience these kinds of emotions made possible by expanding and mixing primary emotions and their variants in some unknown manner.

Very late in hominin evolution or perhaps exclusively in the transition from *Homo erectus* to *Homo sapiens*, natural selection worked to create what have been termed by Turner (2000) as *second-order elaborations* combining the three negative primary emotions—anger, fear, and sadness—into such emotions as *shame* and *guilt*. Two of these second-order elaborations—*shame* and *guilt*—are seen by many other commentators as the emotions of social control. With these two emotions, individuals monitor and sanction *themselves* for failing to live up to situational expectations and the dictates of moral codes. These emotions are almost certainly unique to humans (because other primates do not reveal them; Boehm 2013), and so, they evolved *only after* variants of primary and first-order elaborations had evolved (enumerated Tables 4.2 and 4.3). But these emotions solved an important problem: creating powerful emotions that forge bonds and commitments out of the three negative emotions.

In Table 4.4, the structure of the two most important second-order elaborations is outlined. The dominant emotion in both shame and guilt is a variant of *sadness*, the least volatile of the negative primary emotions. It is the order of intensity of the other two additional negative primary emotions—anger and fear—that determines whether a person will experience shame or guilt. Shame is an emotion that people experience when they have not lived up to expectations, and its underlying structure in order of magnitude of the three negative emotions is: sadness, anger (at self), and fear (of the consequences to self). Guilt is the emotion that people experience when they have violated moral codes, and its structure reverses the order of anger and fear to: sadness, fear (about the consequences to self) and anger (at self).

These "moral emotions" also relieve others from the constant burden of monitoring and then imposing negative sanctions on people who fail to meet expectations or violate moral codes (Turner 1997, 2006a, 2006b,

TABLE 4.4 The Structure of Shame and Guilt

Emotion	Rank–ordering of Constituent Primary Emotions		
	1	*2*	*3*
Shame	disappointment–sadness (at self)	assertion–anger (at self)	aversion–fear (at consequences for self)
Guilt	disappointment–sadness (at self)	aversion–fear (at consequences for self)	assertion–anger (at self)

2007, 2010, 2014). For constant negative sanctioning will arouse counter-anger against those who have meted out negative sanctions, which is a spiraling negative emotional dynamic that is hardly conducive to strong social ties and group solidarity. As long as animals have genetically-based drives to form group bonds, negative emotions can be activated and *not* destroy the group, but for animals without such bioprogrammers, breaches during episodes of interpersonal contact disrupt fragile group solidarity—as is all too evident with contemporary humans. Thus, with the evolution of shame and guilt, which appear unique to humans (Boehm 2013), social control can become self-control rather than imposed control by conspecifics that might arouse negative emotions and breach the interaction. Moreover, these two emotions of self-control are also the emotions of conscience and morality that ultimately undergird commitments to moral codes of any kind, including those provided by religion.

Guilt and shame are emotions that depend upon the behavioral capacity to see *self* as a complex object, with many levels and variations. Reciprocally, using moral emotions to evaluate self increases the salience of self and its importance in social relations. Great apes can also see self, and hence so could early hominins, but not in the highly complex way that humans can. For, among humans with their larger neocortex and expanded emotions, self revolves around codification of various levels and types of identities that humans seek to validate in interaction with each other; and shame and guilt can only be viable if they make persons see that they might fail to validate or verify their sense of self with respect to key identities. Indeed, humans are the only primate and probably mammal to blush, which is indicative of mild forms of shame in the evaluation of self *vis-à-vis* others and the larger community of others (de Waal 2013). Indeed, conscience and morality in the strong sense are not possible unless an animal evaluates self *vis-à-vis* others' expectations and moral codes. And, just as strong morality is not possible without self, so religion is not viable without people evaluating various types and levels of self from the perceived expectations of supernatural beings and forces, and then experiencing *pride* when these expectations are met or either *shame* or *guilt*, and perhaps both, when they are not.

Visual Dominance and the Neurology of Proto-Languages

During the adaptive shift of early primates to visual dominance in the arboreal habitat, the primate brain was significantly rewired around the *inferior parietal lobe* (Geschwind 1965a, 1965b, 1965c, 1985; Geschwind and Damasio 1984; Maryanski and Turner 1992; Turner 2000; Jarvis and Ettlinger 1977; and Passingham 1973, 1975, 1982: 51–55). This sensory shift from olfactory dominance (typical of most mammals) to visual dominance (comparatively rare), set the stage for using arbitrary linguistic symbols to represent something that is not physically present in space or time—but only among primates who had *reached a certain threshold of intelligence.* Among all non-human primates of today, only great apes exceeded this threshold and, so, it is likely that hominins also had the neurological capacity for linguistic-based symbolization. Chimpanzees, gorillas, and orangutans can use hand-based signs or computer-based pictograms to communicate meanings albeit at about the level of a 3-year-old normal human child (Rumbaugh and Savage-Rumbaugh 1990; Savage-Rumbaugh and Lewin 1994; Savage-Rumbaugh et al. 1988, 1993; Bickerton 2003; Lieberman 2006). This ability probably emerged as a pre-adaptation to the ancestors of these extant great apes and, of course, hominins.

It is important to re-emphasize that great apes have a rather sophisticated gestural system of communication outside of the laboratories (where they spontaneously learn the spoken languages of humans and "speak back" through hand signs or computer pictograms). The wiring for using linguistic codes resulting from the shift to visual dominance may have been used early in ape societies because they have the capacity to communicate with face and eyes very complex meanings, allowing them to coordinate actions. Indeed, early researchers were often mystified over how they communicated in such quiet and subtle ways (Menzel 1971); and over the last 50 years of field research, it is now clear that chimpanzees have a large repertoire of symbolic gestures revolving around vocal calls, body movements, and facial expressions (Gillespie-Lynch et al. 2013; Savage-Rumbaugh, Rumbaugh, and Boysen 1978). The result is a highly efficient symbolic system for intentional, flexible, meaningful, and goal-oriented communication that can transmit information from simple requests (e.g., "follow me," "groom me," "stop that") to commands (e.g., "start play," "change play," "climb on me"). Gesturing is also used to denote objects and/or their location, to negotiate exchanges, and to coordinate social relations. Moreover, different sex and age classes often have their own idiosyncratic gesturing systems. Juveniles in a community, for example, prefer to use gestures not used by adults (perhaps like human teenagers everywhere). As Jane Goodall (1986) emphasized, both adults and their offspring "invent signals as needed." The neurology for a language-based system of communication was thus *already wired* into the great ape and hominin lines, and eventually, articulated speech could be integrated with the visual language of emotions that evolved first. An interesting comparison with monkeys reveals the importance of neurology; monkeys are more "speech ready" than great apes, but they cannot talk because they do not possess the necessary intelligence to take advantage of the wiring that was installed early in primate evolution in the transition from olfactory to visual dominance (Fitch et al. 2016). But great apes have a language facility as a pre-adaptation and can "speak" in sentences if they can use American Sign Language (ASL) for the deaf or pictograms ordered by typing on a keyboard; and so, when speech became fitness-enhancing, selection had an existing neurological capacity to select on.

Yet, fine-grained oral speech using the vocal-auditory channel appears to be a recent trait (Enard 1978; Enard et al. 2002a, 2002b) and is probably unique to human primates. The first linguistic-based communication probably revolved around a simple system of discrete verbal calls, coupled with a more robust system of non-verbal gestural communicated by gestures of face, body, and prehensile hands under the watchful eye of the visual modality (see Maryanski 1996). Yet, with bipedalism that began with Australopiths, the vocal tract was opened up; and the stretching of this tract can be seen as another pre-adaptation that would dramatically facilitate vocalizations of later hominins—a key ingredient of auditory language—and, equally important, to rituals and rhythmic synchronization of interactions that probably began to evolve before the finely grained speech of humans that seemingly emerged some 300,000 years ago with *Homo sapiens* (Enard et al. 2002a, 2002b).[6]

Unlike the capacity for the production of vocalizations via a poorly developed Broca's "hump," the area of the brain responsible for uploading sensory inputs—i.e., Wernicke's area (see Figure 4.2 on p. 80)—into the brain's way of processing sensory information was fully developed in hominins, because it exists in chimpanzees today as a fully functional, neocortical-based system as it is among humans. Therefore, vocal comprehension of non-verbal gestural signals could be uploaded into the brains of even early hominins through Wernicke's area. With such a critical neocortical area for language comprehension—indeed a module-like structure—*already present* in the hominin line, it did not have to be created by later mutations or even directional selection.

The presence of Wernicke's area in great apes (and hence hominins) explains how young great apes can spontaneously decode spoken human languages (Savage-Rumbaugh and Lewin 1994; Savage-Rumbaugh et al. 1993). Moreover, like humans, great apes can recognize individuals by their vocalizations (Belin 2006), presumably because auditory inputs are routed through Wernicke's area and remembered in relation to the physical characteristics of the individual "speaking." As noted above, in contrast to Wernicke's area, however, the reciprocal area for language *production*—termed Broca's area (see Figure 4.2)—was not enhanced among early hominins for a language because it does not exist in fully developed form in great apes (Schenker et al. 2007; Taglialatela et al. 2009; Lieberman 2006; and Jackendoff 2002). There is an asymmetry, as noted earlier, on the left side of the great-ape brain in the approximate location where Broca's area sits along the frontal lobe in humans (around the Sylvian fissure of the parietal cortex) and is sometimes termed Broca's "hump" (see Falk 2007, for a detailed analysis; see also Schenker et al. 2007). So, even if hominins had the same physical modification as humans in lips, tongue, and larynx to produce finely-tuned and articulated speech, rapid and complex speech would not be easy without the human-level of functioning of a full Broca's area, in which the brain's mode of more gestalt thinking is downloaded as sequential speech by a fully developed Broca's area. Nonetheless, the existence of the "hump" meant that there was something to select on; and the end result is that Broca's speech area was reconfigured to facilitate control of speech production (Falk 2011: 27)—a critical necessity if true spoken language was ever to evolve along the hominin line.

Thus, while apes and their early hominin descendants cannot speak in the same fine-grained manner as humans, they do have the neurological wiring in place for linguistic activity (Savage-Rumbaugh et al. 1978; Gillespie-Lynch et al. 2013). This means that much of what is considered unique to humans—the neurological capacity for culture and language—did not have to be wholly created by later mutations for new brain modules among hominins; rather, existing modules only needed to be selected upon to produce hominins revealing a combination of vocalizations and visual signals carrying intentional meanings. Indeed, one of the biggest obstacles to language in the human measure was not so much the size of the neocortex, but the necessary reworking of muscles and structures in and around the lips, mouth, tongue, and throat in ways allowing for fine-tuned and rapid speech production.

However, long before a developed spoken language system evolved, a more gestural system was evolving among hominins. Spoken language was thus not the first linguistic system in hominin evolution; rather, a system of visually-based systems evolved on the neurological platform evident among great apes today and, over time, increasingly allowed for the communication of emotionally charged meanings with conspecifics. We see this fully operational system *today* in the human capacity to read complex and emotionally-charged meanings communicated via eyes, face, and body countenance—as can be quickly tested by simply turning off the sound on the television or computer as a story unfolds. When doing so, reading visual gestures, while having some sense of the context, allows a viewer to follow the story line without the benefit of spoken language. This human ability to follow the story line today was surely preceded by a growing capacity of hominins to communicate rather robust meanings through emotionally-balanced eye, face, and body gestures, coupled with perhaps an increasing vocabulary of calls to supplement the gestural system of communication. Indeed, it could be argued (see Turner 2000, 2007) that this gestural system is still the primary language system when humans communicate emotions.

Thus, by relying upon the dominant visual modality, coupling non-verbal gestures with discrete vocal calls, the enhancement of emotions would be the easiest and quickest way to generate a force capable of forging stronger social ties among hominins and, at the same time, committing hominins to a path of ever-greater linguistic use because of its fitness-enhancing value. Moreover, once there is a well-developed visual–gestural system interfaced by a colorful mixing and variety of emotions, this system would provide a neurological base upon which an oral language can slowly evolve. Then, once selection acted to place the vocal-auditory channel under cortical or voluntary control through enlargement of Broca's area, a tonal palette of spoken sounds could shift the heavy reliance on gestural communication to a spoken communication. Indeed, that appears to be what occurred, beginning with *Homo habilis*. Recent data suggest that Broca's hump was being rapidly selected upon, increasing in size and connectivity to other brain systems with *Homo habilis* 2.2–0.2 million years ago, when the brain grew significantly from 600cc's to over 700cc's. This sudden growth was occurring at about the same time that hominins had to spend more time in open-country habitats. It is likely that the initial growth of Broca's area was to gain control over emotions that, if uttered vocally in open-country, would invite predators and reduce fitness; and as noted earlier, control of emotions was also the neurological key to creating first- and second-order elaborations of primary emotions. But, as Broca's area continued to grow in the transition to *Homo erectus* (1.8 million years ago), it would dramatically expand the capacity to use calls for communication, especially as the larynx had dropped down the vocal tract and, thereby, increased the ability to make diverse calls; and so, by the time selection began to work on the facial and vocal tracts of later hominins and early humans, it is likely that *Homo erectus* used a sophisticated emotional grammar and an increasingly complex vocal system of calls carrying common meanings.

Piggy-backing onto this evolving capacity to articulate increasingly fine-grained vocalization of symbols carrying meanings onto *an already in place* neurological wiring of an emotional grammar of visual gestures and select vocal calls immediately makes the meanings of spoken words and sentences compelling, especially since visual–gestural language revolved around signaling emotional states still accompanies whatever emotional inflections are given to spoken words. Words ordered into sentences now have power because they can be (1) laced with emotions and (2) accompanied by the more primal gestural communication produced by face and body. Words can become moral because they are connected to emotional states in general and *moral* emotional states made possible by the evolution of shame and guilt as second-order emotions.

Without this coordination with the emotional gestural symbolic system, a vocal language would be like citing an instruction manual for a cell phone; it can be highly instrumental and focused, and this can have fitness-enhancing consequences, but for hominins in open habitats, selection was surely focused on enhancing social bonds and for building up more stable relations in groups rather than for following instructions. Words alone, no matter how eloquently spoken, cannot do this unless they *carry emotional overtones*; and without the prior wiring for a complex range and variety of emotionality, auditory language probably would never have evolved, and open-country hominins would likely be one more evolutionary dead-end for taxa who sought to adapt to open-country conditions. With auditory language being built on the subcortical base of fine-tuned emotions fused with a cortically based visual-gestural system, speech *automatically* becomes moral; and if speech is moral, religion and all that it implies cannot be far behind.

Mother–Infant Bonding

All mammals evidence mother–offspring attachments, sometimes for a lifetime but always in infancy. A discrete area of the mammalian brain—the *anterior cingulate gyrus* (see Figure 4.2)—is where playfulness, mother–offspring bonds, and the separation cry of infants when separated from mothers are generated (Turner 2000); and so, this area could be subject to additional selection to increase mother–infant bonds. But the question is: could natural selection have extended this same propensity for emotional attachments to adult males? There is no clear answer to this question, but if mother–offspring bonds could be enhanced and, then, if more enduring mother–father relations (or relations with at least another adult male) could somehow be forged, then something like a nuclear family could begin to evolve, even if the anterior cingulate of males was not subject to further selection to match the behavioral propensities of females.

Another and perhaps more likely route to creating male–female attachments was through directional selection on the *septum* of hominins (see Figure 4.2), thereby enhancing the pleasure associated with sexual relations. Given that females and their offspring are already attached by genetically-controlled bioprogrammers (generated in the *anterior cingulate cortex*), the key was to increase emotional attachments between mothers and male partners. It is much easier to select on an existing and discrete subcortical structure such as the septum to enhance the pleasure of sexual relations than to rewire among males a complex neurological system, such as anterior cingulate gyrus, to match its female counterpart.

As noted earlier and documented in Table 4.1, the evidence for what occurred is clear in the subcortical areas of the human brain where the *septum* in humans—the organ responsible for the pleasure of sex among mammals—is over twice as large in humans as in chimpanzees. Since chimpanzees are already highly sexual, promiscuous, and pleasure-seeking, this enlargement cannot be solely devoted to enhancing the sexual experience, *per se*, which apes already find highly pleasurable (and, hence, the same would have been surely true of hominins).

Once selection went down this path of using emotions as an alternative means for generating social attachments, this directional selection would find discrete locations such as the septum dedicated to specific types of relationships. And, if indeed the septum was one target of selection, it helped to establish relationships that would be critical to hominin and eventually human survival through the evolution of such a critical structure as the nuclear family. Yet, as fitness-enhancing as a nuclear family-based foraging strategy might be, it bears repeating that it is *not a natural unit for evolved apes* like hominins. But, the pre-adaptation for mother–infant bonding could still have served as an initial, although capacious, platform on which natural selection could push for the evolution of nuclear kinship ties. Selection on the septum could have completed what was necessary for a relatively stable nuclear family.

The Lack of Matrilines and Weak Female–Female Ties

While Old World monkeys vary in the particulars of their organizational arrangements, they have with a few exceptions two basic mating plans: (1) an arrangement of one male and a number of females who are embedded in matrilines and (2) a multi-male-multi-female plan of numerous males and females who are embedded in matrilines. Monkey groups are very stable, with members moving in a synchronized fashion across many terrestrial habitats, whereas the many tree-living monkeys move within a concentrated arboreal space in close proximity. Matrilines[7] among genetically related females are generally the anchors for Old World monkey groups, which is why Old World monkey societies are called "female bonded societies" (Campbell et al. 2011; Bernard 2011). In fact, a female will usually form a strong tie with an adult male only when she lacks matriline relatives in the group and troop.

As discussed in Chapter 3, great apes have dramatically different organizational arrangements that defy easy classification. Orangutans are nearly solitary with an elusive community structure of weak ties. Male and female orangutans have relatively brief hookups (at most several weeks), with a male after mating leaving the female alone to raise their offspring. A gorilla band superficially resembles a monkey "harem" group in that there is usually one lead male and a number of females. However, up to four other adult males may be present in a gorilla band. More importantly, gorilla females tolerate but rarely interact with each other (as they are immigrants from other bands); they are attached more to the lead male than to other females (and this male–female bond is dependent in part on whether or not the leader male is willing to provide parental care for her dependents). In addition, gorilla females are highly individualistic and can abruptly leave a gorilla band at any time to join a lone male or a nearby band (in monkey matrifocal units, females never abandon their matrilines). Chimpanzees evidence rather open promiscuity, and at times, males literally stand in line and peacefully wait their turn to enjoy the sexual favors of a receptive female.

Yet, an ability to build up family—even a polygamous one—was unlikely to be programmed in any direct way into the genome of hominins. Indeed, female great apes are mobile across communities and somewhat individualistic and promiscuous, while being strangers to each other, exhibiting a kind of neutral relationship.[8] While female (and male) promiscuity can be viewed as a roadblock to stable nuclear families, it does not represent the same barrier that matrilines would represent forming nuclear families, if selection favored them as a basic organizing unit (which it did). So, the *lack* of matrilines as anchors in great ape societies and surely in early hominins allows for *the possibility* that a nuclear family pattern built from male–female bonding could potentially evolve, if selection could find an alternative route to overcome the hominin proclivity for free sexual liaisons and to forge more emotional ties and thereby allow for more permanent bonds among adult males and females with offspring.

Moreover, among great apes, it is possible to observe at times that males and females develop friendships; and so, this propensity probably also existed among hominins. While friendships do not translate into monogamy, *per se*, if this behavioral propensity for male-female friendships could be selected upon, it could further attach males to females. Thus, if selection focused on a structure like the septum to increase the emotions aroused in sex to something more than the pleasure involved and, instead, produced emotions like "love" between sexual partners, friendships between adult males and females could become more permanent, and perhaps the promiscuity rate would decrease. Without matrilines, these changes to the septum would open the door to the possibility of nuclear families forming.

Life History Pre-adaptations

As we outlined in Chapter 3, apes are very different from monkeys in terms of what are called "life-history characteristics" (Turner and Maryanski 2008: 34; Nargolwalla et al. 2005; Kelley and Smith 2003; Kelley 2004; Guatelli-Steinber, et al. 2005; Dean and Leakey 2004). Great apes are not only much bigger than monkeys (a trait built into their genome), but they also take longer to develop at all phases of the life cycle—gestation, infancy, juvenile, adolescent, and adult—and they live longer and space their births much further apart than monkeys (Falk 2000; Wolpoff 1999).

The great ape (and human) prolonged life-history pattern, which reaches back to the early Miocene, can be viewed as a pre-adaptation for what was to occur for hominins: increases in brain size, thus requiring more time for the brain to develop inside and *then* outside the womb. In this way, the brain after reaching the maximum size possible without preventing the head of a newborn to pass through the cervix (and killing the mother) can then have adequate parental care. Indeed, hominin mothers in open-country would be especially vulnerable to predation, much like gorilla mothers but unlike "single moms" in chimpanzee and orangutan societies who can rely on the relative safety of a closed canopy forest.[9] Longer periods of nursing, infant care, and even juvenile care (7 years for chimps, and only 4.4 years for baboons) could be selected upon, as could the average year of spacing offspring (for example, 1.7 years for baboons and monkeys and 5.6 years for chimpanzees), to allow biologically and neurologically immature apes and hominins to complete what could not be accomplished in the womb. Monkeys, of course, are favored with much longer life history profiles than most mammals but when it comes to comparing monkeys and great apes, monkeys are in the fast lane and apes are in the slow lane.

Only mammals with such long life history characteristics programmed into their genome could support larger-brained offspring. Without this pre-adaptation in the hominoid lineage, further expansion in the hominin brain probably could not have occurred because prematurely born infants (to get through the female cervix) would be too vulnerable to survive. The hominoid life history characteristics that foster long-term parental care were a crucial adaptation for the growth and dramatic expansion of the neocortex among later hominins; and, the expansion of the neocortex, in turn, was essential for the evolution of religious behavior among humans.

Moreover, prolonged parental care involves kissing (licking) and other expressions of "love," which, in turn, increase the emotional energy of offspring. Energetic offspring can become bored, leading to another important pre-adaptation for sociality: active play, which was already built into the mammalian line. Thus, many of the behaviors associated with higher solidarity can be found in hominoid parental care (Eibl-Eibesfieldt 1996[1971]), which ends with offspring dispersing from their natal community at puberty. Still, in the case of chimpanzee males, who remain in their natal community, their forming life-long bonds with their mothers indicates that they are capable of forming stronger and more enduring attachments *if* both remain in the same community. To the extent that this chimpanzee pattern was part of the genome of evolving hominins, the kinship link between mothers and sons could be selected upon as part of a general movement toward more cohesive inter-generational kinship structures (see Chapter 6).

In addition, there is strong evidence of sexual avoidance between chimpanzee mothers and sons to prevent inbreeding depression. This biologically-based "incest taboo" is so ancient and deep-seated that it is also well documented in Old World monkeys. As Jolly (1985) highlighted, "adult sons seem to specifically avoid mating with their own mothers." This taboo is so hard-wired in the primate line that even mothers and sons who are caged together for years refrain from any sexual activity whatsoever (Rhine and Maryanski, 1996; see Pusey 1980, 2005 for a review). If a mother–son bond of strong ties exists among chimpanzees, it represented something that Darwinian natural selection could select on to forge even more stable bonds between mothers and sons in early efforts for hominins to form more permanent groups.

Play

Young mammals almost universally play, which involves some rather complex activities (Burghardt 2005): to assume a role (say, as aggressor or pursued), to initiate role-playing, to coordinate switches in roles, to be aggressive without hurting play partners, to know the rules of the game, and other behaviors that must be coordinated. This play, as noted, is programmed into the genome and is wired in the *anterior cingulate gyrus*. Play is probably very much like training to participate in roles for various forms of groupings among mammals; and, although apes do not form stable groups, play probably is essential to developing and honing many of the interactive techniques that hominin descendants of great apes used to communicate and, when necessary, to coordinate activities. For some time, scholars have viewed play as a necessary precursor to behaviors that are more human-like, such as role-taking, ritual, mimicry, and interpersonal attunement (Mead 1934; Huizinga [1949] 1955; Beckoff and Pierce, 2009; Bellah 2011). Still others have argued that play and ritual are necessary precursors to the evolution of mind and cultural beliefs (Donald 1991, 2001; Bellah 2011).

Yet, all mammals possess the capacity to play and, hence, so did all hominins for behaviors such as role-taking and empathizing. More extended play among later hominins may have been more of a means to increase the skills of hominins at role-taking, minded behaviors, and empathy with conspecifics; or as George Herbert Mead argued (1934), role-taking at the level of the "play," "game," and "generalized other" are reciprocally related, and mutually intensifying, to the development of *mind* (the capacity to make decisions facilitating cooperation) and to produce and reproduce *society* (stable ongoing patterns of social organization) among humans. Once forces began to keep parents and offspring together in early quasi-kinship systems that were to become the backbone of early human societies, the behaviors among young mammals for play among the young could also work to forge stronger bonds not only with each other but parents or parent surrogates. Play could thus become an adaptive strategy for more enduring social relations in the gradual transition to a nuclear family (Bellah 2011: 74–91; Huizinga 1950[1938]; Burghardt 2005; Deacon 2009; see also Chapter 6).

Low Levels of Grooming and Reliance on Cognitive Mapping

Great apes do not groom nearly as much as monkeys; instead, they sustain relations with conspecifics by virtue of a process of cognitive mapping of the boundaries of their communities, especially who belongs and does not belong in this community (Maryanski 1995, 1997). Moreover, even with a comparatively small great ape brain, community members can easily keep track of 100 members, recalling when they last met up and what transpired. This capacity would be enhanced among larger-brain hominins and it was, no doubt, useful in sustaining a sense of community, even as subgroups such as nuclear families and band formations began to emerge within communities. So, while hominins were like great apes and did not groom extensively, they had well-honed interpersonal skills to maintain the weak social ties of great ape communities.[10]

Community as the Basic Social Unit

By reckoning the more macro-level community over local groups, a great deal of *potential* flexibility was built into great apes for building up more complex social structures *if* selection could work to make hominins and then humans capable of forming stronger but still versatile and flexible forms of group structures. A key characteristic of communities is that conspecifics "know" *of* each other, even if they do not interact on a regular basis, as is always the case with species organized only in compact face-to-face groups and troops. Among great apes, particularly chimpanzees but also among orangutans and gorillas as well, a large number of interpersonal skills (to be examined in the next chapter) exist to sustain weakly-tied great-ape communities. Chimpanzees, for example, can pick up social relations with relative ease on the basis of their interpersonal skills and cognitive capacities for mapping conspecifics within communities. Other highly intelligent mammals such as elephants (Plotnik et al. 2006) and dolphins (Hart et al. 2008; Reiss 2001) also possess considerable skill in interpersonal hookups with a great many others in their community.

Another feature of intelligent animals organized at a community level of social organization is the capacity to see self as an object in the environment; and as Maryanski (2018) has recently argued, there is a fundamental relationship between self, interpersonal skills, fission–fusion groups within community, and the capacity to see and evaluate self as an object *vis-à-vis* others (Kaneko and Tomonaga 2011; Suddendorf and Collier-Baker 2009; Westergaard and Hyatt 1994; Whitten and Suddendorf 2007). Moreover, they not only appear to perceive and evaluate self from the perceived perspective of others in face-to-face interaction but also from what Mead termed the "generalized other" or "community of attitudes." This community complex, as we have termed it, was to be important not only in the formation of the first hominin societies but also in the emergence of religious behavior among humans. Religion is about cognitions and beliefs about another realm of reality, inhabited by supernatural beings and forces. As emotional solidarities in groups within communities were built up through animated interactions and ritualized forms of greeting and address, the larger community as an (important) orientation becomes ever-more salient; and not only salient, it is a "thing" to be reinforced and protected from incursions. Further growth of the hominin neocortex was perhaps all that was needed neurologically for an even more distant and asbstract "thing"—the supernatural realm—to be recognized or sensed among hominins who were now smarter and more emotional.

Conclusion

The pre-adaptations outlined in this chapter were present in hominins because they are present in all great apes today and, hence, the common ancestors of extant great apes and hominins. These are genetically-regulated traits of great apes and hominins that are mostly regulated by neurostructures in the subcortex and neocortex of the hominin brain. As a result they were always available for selection to enhance. Natural selection hit upon a very efficient solution to the low-sociality and non-group organization of great apes: first enhance emotions among early hominins because, by doing so, the larger palette of emotional valences gives *all* genetically controlled structural formations and interpersonal propensities extra power. We have outlined this super-charging effect on pre-adaptations in this chapter; in the next chapter, we turn to behavioral capacities and propensities, beginning with the recognition that emotions gave these capacities and propensities new powers to overcome weak-tie sociality among hominins forced into open-country conditions.

While emotions had this broad effect on all pre-adaptations, selection was still working on specific neurosystems, and we have tried to outline these selection dynamics as well. The hominin brain was, to a degree, rewired but no really new modules were created; rather, existing modules and neuro-systems were altered by directional selection working on the tails of bell curves of trait distribution. Thus, by growing many key structures, like almost all subcortical neurosystems and then later the neocortex and important structures like Broca's area and the vocal tract, the 2 million years of evolution through late *Homo habilis* and then *Homo erectus* produced the human brain.

This transformation alone is an interesting and important story to tell, but our concern is with the emergence of religion as an outcome of the selection processes pushing for increased sociality and capacities to form more stable groups. As we will see in Chapter 6, some of these pre-adaptations were important in the formation of the first stable groupings that would lead to the nuclear family and band (e.g., mother–offspring bonding and individualistic females, lack of strong matrilines, low levels of grooming, cognitive mapping of communities, and perhaps somewhat surprisingly, female and male promiscuity) that would be the first structural home for religion. Some of these pre-adaptations, plus the rest (larger brains, hard-wired linguistic capacities, comparatively large palette of primary emotions, play, cognitive mapping, and community as the basic social unit), were to be more directly involved in generating the capacity of hominins to become religious. Yet, until we review the work of natural selection on the behavioral propensities wired into the hominin brain in the next chapter, we will not be in a position to see how humans' ability to generate the collective emotions of religious experience could evolve by means of Darwinian natural selection.

Notes

1 Predation pressure has long been viewed as a major catalyst for shaping primate behaviors and organizational arrangements. While forest primates are subjected to predation pressures mostly from birds of prey, snakes, and some felines, the vulnerability of terrestrial primates—Old World monkeys—is especially severe. Forest primates have the natural protection of trees, whereas, as the saying goes, a single primate on the savanna is a dead primate. This is one reason why ground-living primates often live in much larger groups than forest-living primates (for a review of primate predation see Miller and Treves 2011).

2 For other analyses of bipedalism, see Fleagle (2013: 375ff), Ruff et al. (2016).

3 During the Pleistocene, there is evidence of 12 glacial advances and retreats, marking this epoch as one of profound climatic flux (for discussions, see Conroy and Pontzer 2012 and Shackleton 1987).

4 In general, brain and body size are related, but direct analogies of scaling between the bodies and brains of great apes and humans do not hold precisely. Human brains are quite large, as are the brains of great apes, but those of great apes such as orangutans and gorillas are smaller relative to body size than are the brains of humans. Selection may have favored brawn over brain during primate evolution for some great apes, whereas clearly for humans, selection began to enlarge the brain, creating a different scaling effect between body size and brain size for humans compared to at least some great apes. See Herculano-Houzel (2012) and Herculano-Houzel and Kaas (2011) for discussion and analyses.

5 For a long time, researchers on emotions followed Paul McClean's view that the mammalian brain was built over the reptilian brain, but it now appears that such is not the case. Rather, reptiles/birds evolved from a different, but related, line of vertebrate amphibians, but there probably was not much difference between the respective cortices of mammals and reptiles at these beginning stages of evolution. Mammals did not have a neocortex and, in all likelihood, neither did reptiles at the very beginning of terrestrial life on the planet. They both probably had somewhat truncated versions of a primitive subcortex evident in both reptiles and mammals today. For a review, see Dugas-Ford and Ragsdale (2015).

6 Human speech, of course, required elaborations in the larynx, pharynx, lips, tongue, vocal tract, and muscles controlling these and, of course, related neurological structures in order to modify sounds and to rapidly produce and sequence phonemes. The recent finding that *Homo sapiens* existed across Africa 300,000 years ago puts into conflict the date of 200,000 for the structures responsible for finely-grained speech to be under selection. It may be that the first *Homo sapiens* might not have been fully capable of speech production. Indeed, perhaps there was a much less finely-tuned speech among the very first humans that over the first 100,000 years of their evolution led to the changes that Enard (2002a, 2002b) and his colleagues document in their analysis of selection on the genes responsible for articulated human speech.

7 Among Old World Monkeys (*Cercopithecoidea*), matrilines play the crucial role as organizational anchors with male dispersal at puberty in *Cercopithecinae* (with Hamadryas baboons the single exception). Their cousins, the *Colobinae*, also anchor their groups with matriliny and with male dispersal, but occasionally for some colobines both males and females disperse, although females after migration often join a group with related individuals. To account for this deviance from the normative Old World monkey pattern in these cases, it is hypothesized that females leave for inbreeding avoidance and

to prevent infanticide (when outside males challenge inside males) (see Newton and Dunbar 1994; Sterck 2012; Pusey and Packer 1987; Cords 2012).

8 One odd exception are bonobos (*Pan paniscus*), a small population of chimpanzees who inhabit the Zaire River Basin having branched off from the widespread common chimpanzee about 1.8 million years ago. Like the regular chimp, they live in a fission–fusion community with female dispersal. But, unlike common chimpanzee females, bonobo females elicit an erotic behavior unique to primates: when two adult females meet up they practice a genito-genital (or GG) rubbing by grabbing each other and rapidly rubbing their genitals together. White (1989) noted that it was an adaptation "to reduce tensions among unrelated females" (also see Stevens et al. 2006). As their habitat is one with concentrated resources, females must often feed in propinquity and this peculiar genital rubbing seemingly promotes sociality. It is not, however, a natural affect tie (such as found in matrilines) but an adaptation to foster female tolerance of each other. We agree with Rice and Moloney (2005) that "this kind of sexuality was not found in the LCA either" but is a clear evolutionary novelty unique to bonobo females.

9 Gorillas inhabit secondary forests (i.e. re-generating semi-open forests), spending their days on the forest floor. As discussed in Chapter 3, gorilla moms are very vulnerable to predation (especially from felines) so they rely on the leader silverback male for protection but only *if* he provides adequate "parental" care for her dependent offspring (see Harcourt and Stewart 2007: 187ff).

10 Robin Dunbar (1996) has proposed that the brain of hominins grew to compensate for the inability to groom as communities became larger. This thesis has two problems. One is that apes do not groom very much; and so, the initial assumption is more true of monkeys than great apes. Second, great apes can easily remember the 100 or so in great ape communities, and this number does not exceed what human hunting and gathering bands and even systems of bands revealed. So, the brain grew for other reasons that we have tried to document here.

5

Darwinian Selection on the Hominin Brain II

Selection on Behavioral Propensities and Capacities

The capacity of the ape to be part of different types of social groupings and . . .
ability to recognize relationships with other individuals over time and space . . .
[is] a behavioral tendency which we have inherited from our common stock,
and may be responsible for preadapting the human line for its successful
colonization of the savannas.
          Vernon Reynolds (1967: 270) in *The Apes: The Gorilla, Chimpanzee,*
                    Orangutan and Gibbon—Their History and Their World

Great apes are predisposed toward a number of behavioral propensities, but these are rather flexible and are not regulated by powerful bioprogrammers that limit and delimit the range of behaviors. Instead, *they expand the potential range of behaviors* that can be emitted; and during hominin evolution, it was the interpersonal proclivities of hominins that eventually allowed for the construction of quasi-kin groupings. Yet, at the same time, these group-level constructions did not lock hominins into monkey-like structures driven by bioprogrammers. Instead, these proclivities allowed hominins considerable freedom, mobility, and individualism afforded by constructing social ties less regulated by their genomes than is the case with most mammals and primates in the monkey line.

In what may seem like a contradiction, weakly-tied animals that must periodically meet up can often have sophisticated interpersonal skills, as is the case for present-day great apes (and, hence, hominins). These skills were surely used by hominins to service face-to-face relations in ways that sustained the larger community—the basic structure organizing great apes—and, at the same time, allowed for considerable individual autonomy. If enhanced with more emotions, however, these same interpersonal skills can forge stronger social bonds and solidarity. This is what natural selection apparently did: by enhancing emotions and integrating them with basic modes of communication by vocal calls and non-verbal gestures organized by a grammar, the very same interpersonal capacities that maintained weak-ties *could be used to build up stronger-tie relations.*[1]

It is not clear to what extent these behavioral capacities, especially evident among chimpanzees (and, hence, early hominins), required any additional selection beyond the boost that enhancing emotions gave to the all interpersonal behaviors and capacities among hominins. Moreover, the expanded emotional palette and a quasi-language of non-verbal gestures made enlargement of the neocortex potentially fitness-enhancing. In fact, it may be that simply enlarging the neocortex also made the interpersonal capacities and propensities described in this chapter more robust, particularly as the call systems of early hominins began to evolve into a kind of quasi-spoken language accompanied by non-verbal cues of eyes, face, and body. Thus, directional selection was initially more on the subcortical areas of the brain and, only later, on neocortical areas of the brain. During this sequence of directional selection on the subcortex where emotions are generated and, then, on the necortex where memories are stored and retrieved in decision making, the late hominin brain became dramatically larger and more connected than it is among great apes and early hominins. This enlargement of the neocortex alone probably accounts for much of the increased power and facility of interpersonal behaviors. Again, as is typically the case, selection was taking the easiest route by growing the size of the neocortex rather than selecting on specific neuro-structures responsible for particular behaviors.

Behavioral Capacities and Propensities of Apes

Reading of Face and Eyes

Apes are disposed to read gestures in the face and eyes of conspecifics (Osgood 1966; Menzel 1971; Stanford 1999; Mitani and Watts 2000; Turner and Maryanski 2008). In fact, they will follow the gaze and eye movements of conspecifics to determine what another is observing and thinking (Hare, Call, and Tomassello 2001; Hare, Call, and Tomasello 2006; Povinelli 2000; Povinelli and Eddy 1997; Itakura 1996; Baizer et al. 2007; Tomasello, Hare, and Fogelman 2001; Okomoto et al. 2002). Since humans do much the same when trying to determine the emotional states of others, this behavioral propensity was surely enhanced when selection worked to expand the emotional capacities of hominins and, later, the size of the neocortex.

The early rewiring of the primate brain for visual dominance was one contributing factor to this propensity to read face and eyes. Lacking a vocal language and a powerful olfactory modality dictating the emotional and dispositional states of others, apes use, by default, their dominant sense modality—their eyes—to role-take with conspecifics. Moreover, face and eyes are the place where emotions can be readily seen; and, as is outlined in the next section, great apes (and hence hominins) are (and were) from birth genetically predisposed to read emotions in the faces of conspecifics—just as humans are today.

Imitation of Facial Gestures Revealing Emotions

The natural ability of both human and ape infants to imitate oral–facial movements of caregivers indicates that they are predisposed to learn non-verbal gestures carrying meanings at a very early age (Emde 1962; Ekman 1984; Sherwood et al. 2008; Tomonaga 1999; Subiaul 2007; Horowitz 2003; Gergely and Csibra 2006). Newborn human infants can mimic with facial gestures signaling the four primary emotions emitted by caregivers within weeks of birth. Thus, human infants have a natural bent to read emotions *years before* they can read, understand, and emit vocal gestures, indicating that this developmental sequence provides indirect evidence that the evolution of the gestural and vision-based quasi-language of emotions developed long before speech among hominins. Moreover, these data suggest that spoken language among *Homo sapiens* was piggy-backed onto the neurological platform of the more primal gestural/emotional language. At the very least, this is a hypothesis worth considering, especially since evolutionary stages are often manifest in developmental stages, creating a homology that also suggests that the primal basis for language in humans is still visual signals that reveal a grammar organizing emotional valences (for a more general argument, see Clark 2012).

Capacities for Empathy and Role-taking

The great apes evidence the capacity for empathy by reading the gestures of conspecifics to determine others' emotional states and, then, to respond to them appropriately (de Waal 1996, 2009, 2016). Thus, the behavioral capacity for what George Herbert Mead (1934) termed "role-taking" is evident among all great apes and, hence, must have been a part of the behavioral repertoire of our hominin ancestors. More recent conceptualizations of what is also called "Theory of Mind" are very similar to Mead's (1934) concept of "role-taking," and demonstrate that, while rare, a few other mammals (e.g., elephants, whales, and dolphins) besides humans and great apes have this capacity (Premack and Woodruff 1978; Hare, Call, and Tomasello 2001; Povinelli and Vonk 2003; Povinelli, Nelson, and Boysen 1990; Mitchell 2011a, 2011b; Meltzoff 2002; Parr et al. 2005). Moreover, given that the hominoid capacity for role-taking runs deep, early hominins must have possessed this same capacity to determine the emotional states driving the actions of others. Much of this capacity is made possible by mirror neurons, but great apes and hominins probably have (had) additional neurological capacities, such as the ability to experience a sense of self, that allow for the reading of gestures emitted by others to determine their emotional states.

The capacity to role-take at this level of precision thus signals that an animal has a sense of self *vis-à-vis* others; and this capacity for self is seemingly a precondition for societies organized at a weak-tie community level but integrated by the ability to cognitively reckon community and who belongs, and then, to interact in ways that sustain the sense of community while maintaining weak social ties and a sense of individual autonomy. Only highly intelligent animals with a sense of self that is evaluated by others can become religious because, in the end, religious behavior involves role-taking with the inhabitants (sacred and transcendent "others") in the supernatural realm and with, using Mead's terms, the "generalized others" embodying the beliefs and moral codes that are part of virtually all religions.

Rhythmic Interaction

The discovery of mirror neurons in monkeys and, later, apes and humans indicates that there is a neurological basis for role-taking, empathy, and mimicry (Rizzolatti and Gorrado 2008). Equally important, mirror neurons facilitate the rhythmic character of body and verbal sounds among humans (Rizzolatti et al. 2002), which is a critical part of normal human interaction as well as religious rituals. Even though apes and humans have a similar system of mirror neurons, great apes do not have the human-levels of rhythmic synchronization of talk, body, and even neurological systems. As sociological theorists such as Randall Collins (2004; see also McNeill 1997) and empirical psychologists (Obhi and Sebanz 2011; Tsai, Sebanz, and Knoblich 2011) have documented, human interactions consistently fall into a synchronization of talk and body movements. In fact, without this rhythmic synchronization, the emission of rituals and arousal of emotions is difficult. Indeed, greeting rituals kick-start the synchronization and, coupled with synchronization of vocalizations and body language, rituals increase the flow of positive emotions, not only for humans but apes and, hence, our hominin ancestors in the distant past (see Figure 6.1 on p. 132 for a preview of these ritual dynamics in humans).

Thus, rituals and rhythmic synchronization are neurologically hardwired in humans, but can the same be said for great apes and, hence, hominins? Here the data are sketchy. Great apes will fall into a kind of rhythmic pace in interaction, with one vocalizing or acting out in a particular way, followed by a conspecific doing similar actions. Moreover, the play activities of juveniles reveal a considerable amount of rhythmic synchrony and coordination of movements, suggesting that rhythmic interactions begin early in the young. Yet, while these interactions among both the young and adults evidence a propensity to learn how to engage in rhythmic interactions, these are not so tightly woven nor are they synchronized as are human interactions. And while emotional arousal will increase mimicry of actions and vocalizations, they do not always seem fully synchronized in a highly rhythmic fashion. Religion involves emotional arousal and rhythmic synchronizations during the emission of more collectively enacted rituals; and *if* great apes could combine these together as humans do, then we could assert that early hominins were on the verge of quasi-religious behavior—*sans* a clear articulation of the supernatural. However, it appears that great apes are not quite capable of combining all of these emotional/cognitive/behavioral capacities into full synchronization of voices and bodies, except perhaps the "rain dance" to be discussed in this chapter, but the fundamentals for doing so are present for further selection on emotion and cognitive centers in the brain, which means that they were also present for hominins. Perhaps the closest that chimpanzees come to rhythmic synchronization is during episodes of carnival, examined below, which appear very much like Émile Durkheim's portrayal of "emotional effervescence" that he found in Spencer and Gillen's analysis in *The Native Tribes of Central Australia* (1899).

Collective Emotional Effervescence

Studies of free-ranging chimpanzees have documented that, on some occasions when larger numbers of chimpanzees assemble in propinquity, a kind of "carnival" takes place, with these accounts going back to the 19th century. For example, in 1844, Thomas Savage described a collective gathering of chimpanzees noting that: "[t]hey occasionally assemble in large numbers in gambols . . . not less than 50 engaged in hooting, screaming and drumming with sticks on old logs" (quoted in Reynolds 1965: 157).

In 1896, R.L. Gardner, a self-trained zoologist observing free-ranging chimpanzees in Gabor, described a sequence of events where chimpanzees made a drum-like object out of clay obtained from a riverbank of a stream. To intensify the sound, the clay object was put on a peat bed that served as a resonance cavity. When the drum was ready, Garner then described what in native tongue is called *Kanjo*, a kind of riotous gambol or a *carnival* (1896: 59–60):

After the drum is quite dry, the chimpanzees assemble by night in great numbers, and the carnival begins. One or two will beat violently on this dry clay, while others jump up and down in a wild and grotesque manner. Some of them utter long, rolling sounds, as if trying to sing. When one tires of beating the drum, another relieves him, and the festivities continue in this fashion for hours.

In 1965, Vernon Reynolds, a well-regarded anthropologist studying wild chimpanzees in Uganda, witnessed something rather similar to what Garner had seen—chimpanzees using tree planks to create a "big bass-drum" sound by beating their hands and feet on specific tree planks. Reynolds also observed social "carnivals" of drumming with calling, hooting, and screaming, sometimes during the day and night. With all the carnival antics observed, he noticed an important regularity: "groups which had moved closer to each other slowly and noisily over a long period beforehand got into this wildly excited state when they finally met" (Reynolds 1965: 156–59). Reynolds also noted that

> there exists a very complex system of communication in chimpanzees, the most exceptional feature of which is the fact that a whole group of chimpanzees will combine time after time each day to produce a communal din which will carry up to two miles and which is answered by any other groups in the vicinity.

As noted earlier, chimpanzee carnival depictions of high emotions closely resemble Durkheim's description of clan assemblies in his account on the origin of religion (also see Allen 1998). Drawing upon Spencer and Gillen's (1899) account of Australian Aborigines, Émile Durkheim (1912) emphasized this "collective effervescence" as the primal source of all social solidarity (and, hence, as the origins of religion), leading individuals to represent with totems their sense of "sacred" and supernatural powers that, in turn, led to developing beliefs about the nature of this power. Thus, there was an existing hard-wired behavioral propensity in early hominins to be emotionally aroused in collective interaction that could be selected upon and, thereby, lay the groundwork for humans to become religious.

Ritual Behaviors

As we eluded to previously, chimpanzees engage in what we will distinguish in Chapter 6 as "rituals with a small 'r'" and "rituals with a big 'R.'" Small "r" rituals can be seen in the greetings that are emitted when conspecifics meet up and engage in interaction—vocalizations of apparent "delight" and perhaps a quick hug—that are very similar to what humans do when initiating an interaction after not seeing each other for a time. This is also a time when chimpanzees may groom, normally an infrequent behavior. There sometimes is a corresponding departure ritual—hugs and touching, with vocalization—when chimpanzees depart after an episode of interaction. Thus, the propensity of humans to engage in these kinds of rituals with a small "r" (see Turner 2002: 160 for a classification) should not be surprising since they are an essential part of the weak-tie relations among chimpanzees and, hence, were surely also part of the interpersonal repertoire of species on the hominin line.

The propensities of chimpanzees to engage in what is sometimes termed "carnival" by primatologists suggest that there is a behavioral capacity for chimps to engage in at least some elements of rituals with a big "R" (consult Figure 6.1 on p. 132 for a preview of what big "R" rituals involve), especially emotional animation, an entrainment generating feelings of solidarity. When chimpanzees engage in carnival, we cannot say that such behaviors are rituals, *per se*, but we can suggest that they are a critical behavioral propensity for human rituals with a big "R". Among these are rituals that are highly infused with emotions, loud pant-hooting, beating on hollow logs to amplify the sounds, animated behaviors, emotional entrainment, and a high sense of collective solidarity. Moreover, something like rituals with a small "r" are directed toward what can only be described as totems marking the almost "sacred qualities" of groups with high solidarity. Figure 6.1 outlines Randall Collins' (1975, 2004) theory of rituals, which begin with small "r" greeting and focusing rituals, followed by a series of events that leads to high group solidarity that, in turn, becomes symbolized as an object worthy of celebrating, if not "worshiping."

Let us quote from Durkheim's interpretation of the collective effervescence of Australian aboriginals, comparing it to that of the researchers who had observed chimpanzee "effervescence" with an eye to noting a hard-wired capacity in the hominin line for entrained emotional effervescence that, ultimately, is the underlying behavioral propensity of big "R" rituals and of the solidarities generated by religious rituals. Here is Durkheim's ([1912] 1995: 217) description of someone getting important news in a collective situation:

> There are transports of enthusiasm. If the opposite happens, he is seen running hither and yon like a madman, giving way to all sorts of chaotic movements: shouting, screaming, gathering dust and throwing it in all directions, biting himself, brandishing his weapons furiously, and so on. The very act of congregating is an exceptionally powerful stimulant. Once the individuals are gathered together, a sort

of electricity is generated from their closeness and quickly launches them to an extraordinary height of exaltation.

It is tempting to say that these humans were "going ape" which, decades ago, was once a popular phrase used in the United States to describe such out of control activity by people who had never heard of Durkheim, nor even known that apes engaged in similar carnivals. Moreover, the phrase was an inter-species slur on the dignity of great apes. Still, the phrase is revealing. The question is, however: are these actions by chimpanzees rituals or just emotional outbursts? They seem to have a ritual-like character because they are celebrations about something that almost appears to be "sacred": the collective community. Chimps, like Durkheim's description of humans, are seemingly celebrating, if not "worshiping," their community and their sense of collective being. There is no supernatural in the celebrations of chimpanzees in carnival, but they are celebrating some transcendent and powerful force beyond the individual. For evolved human great apes, with a brain three times the size of that evident in great apes and charged up by more emotions, carnival-like behavioral propensities (which are still manifest in raves, and collective celebrations in places as diverse as New Orleans in the U.S. and Rio de Janeiro in Brazil) could rather easily be converted into more focused rituals directed at totems marking powerful forces of kind. Chimpanzees are not religious in our full definition of religion, but there is a propensity for carnival that can be converted to religion by human primates that have larger brains, that can rhythmically synchronize talk and body, and that can engage in both small "r" and big "R" rituals. Still, from where did the emotional underpinnings of solidarity rituals, whether small "r" or big "R", come? Rituals among humans possess a cognitive element, especially when religious and directed at beliefs about the sacred and supernatural, but what drives rituals are emotions that, potentially, can become entrained and focused on a sense of solidarity with conspecifics. The data on chimpanzees tell us that these emotional capacities and propensities already existed among chimpanzees and, thus surely among their common ancestors with hominins.

In the pages following the quote from Durkheim, he moves the argument further toward our emphasis (Durkheim [1995] 1912: 217–18):

The very act of congregating is an exceptionally powerful stimulant. Once the individuals are gathered together, a sort of electricity is generated from their closeness and quickly launches them into an extraordinary height of exaltation. . . . The initial impulse is thereby amplified each time it is echoed, like an avalanche that grows as it goes along.

Durkheim goes on to emphasize that these calls of exaltation fall into a rhythmic harmony and unison; and while these additional features of human carnival or rituals with a bigger "R" are beyond what chimpanzees do, it is not difficult to see their foundation in acts of carnival among chimpanzees.

It is interesting that Jane Goodall, who spent 44 years studying the social behaviors of free-ranging chimpanzees, answered the question of whether chimpanzees engage in spiritual-like rituals in the following way:

> They (chimps) are capable of intellectual performances that we once thought unique to ourselves, such as recognition of self, abstraction and generalization, cross modal transfer of information, and theory of mind. They have a sense of humor. . . . Perhaps, after all, it is not so ridiculous to speculate as to whether chimpanzees might show precursors of religious behaviors. In fact, it seems quite possible that they do.
> (Goodall 2005: 275)

Goodall then reports an example of the emotional "waterfall dance" where chimpanzees stand near an ethereal, roaring waterfall, seemingly transfixed by its power and beauty, swaying with rhythmic movements and otherwise behaving with human-like wonder. Here, then, is a time when there is a quiet rhythmic synchronization of bodies at perhaps somewhat less animated emotional intensity; and so, great apes and hominins must have (had) some capacity to engage in synchronized rituals when, apparently, something inspires awe worthy of "worship." Is this spirituality in an almost religious sense? Goodall suggests that it is; and even if it is not, it reveals underlying emotional and cognitive capacities that hominins inherited from ancestral great apes and that, to some degree, undergird religious behavior. In a sense, an evolved ape in the human measure, or even close to this measure with late hominins like *Homo erectus*, is seemingly "primed" to be religious. In fact, some relatively recent data indicate that a loss of selfness (attention to self) and an increase in "spiritual transcendence" occurs with decreased functioning of the *right parietal lobe*; such transcendence is best achieved by meditation, prayer, and quiet synchronization of voice and body. Thus, the "rain dance," which is really a quiet synchronization of bodies, represents the very conditions that would reduce right parietal lobe activity, thus giving chimpanzees what researchers assume is a transcendent spirituality. The key point is that this capacity was already *wired into the great ape and human lines*, even with comparatively smaller brains. Hence, this capacity would be intensified and expanded with the enlargement of the subcortex and neocortex, or perhaps be directly selected upon (see Johnstone et al. 2012).

Similar actions have been described as rhythmic dances among chimpanzees during rainfalls, and another study reports slow-motion displays of more terrestrial chimpanzees in Senegal during brush fires.[2] Are these dances and displays of respect and awe to a larger power? If so, they are close to being rituals directed at something that has strange powers to a chimpanzee.

Researchers have also observed that male chimpanzees often engage in "hoot-chorusing" during gatherings. These hoots can be heard as far away as 2 miles, and researchers view them as bonding mechanisms among males (Fedurek et al. 2013; Mitani and Brandt 1994; Mitani and Gros-Louis 1998; Mitani and Nishida 1993; Mitani and Watts 2005) But, could they also be celebrating in a ritual manner the existing bonds among males? If so, they are evidence of more synchronized ritual activities among chimpanzees, suggesting that hominins would have had this same propensity. With a larger neocortex, made possible by much stronger emotional capacities, humans later used these same behavioral propensities to create religions.

Another recent discovery about chimpanzees adds more data to whether or not chimpanzees engage in rituals with a big "R." The researchers (Hjalmar et al. 2016) document seemingly ritualized displays of stone throwing. In West Africa during a 34-month period (using remote video cameras), researchers filmed stone throwing events by mostly males who would approach specific trees and throw rocks through holes and gaps in the trees, thereby creating piles of rocks in the trees that resemble human cairns found around the globe. These episodes of stone throwing involve a very stereotypical and apparently ritualized sequence of behaviors—swaying, vocalizing, screaming, and drumming—as rocks were picked up and thrown toward the trees.[3]

It is difficult to know if this is just a game of some sort among mostly males, or if it portends to something more that could be a precursor to religious behaviors. There is no answer here, but it is clear that these are ritual-like displays; and even if not actual rituals, they reveal many of the underlying behaviors typical of rituals. It is not difficult to see the basic foundation for something that is like religious rituals, although chimpanzees probably do not have sufficiently large brains or the capacity to communicate about a supernatural realm. Still, these ritual-like behavioral propensities suggest that some of what is needed for religious behavior is part of the genome of chimpanzees and, hence, hominins. Even if it is pushing it somewhat to see these as rituals, it is nonetheless reasonable to see capacities for carnival, rock throwing, and even swaying with quiet awe at waterfalls as underlying behavioral tendencies that could have been selected upon, or that simply were expanded as the neocortex among late hominins began to grow.

Reciprocity

Higher primates, including monkeys, possess a sense of reciprocity (Cosmides 1989; de Waal 1989, 1991, 1996; de Waal and Brosnan 2006), as do higher mammals in general. Exchange is one of the essential properties of strong social bonds in groups; and one form of exchange critical to sustaining longer-term social relations is *reciprocal exchange* where resources given at one point in time will, at a later point in time, be reciprocated—thereby strengthening social bonds over time between givers and receivers of resources. Reciprocal exchanges, where resources such as positive emotions flow back and forth during an interaction, also charge up local solidarity and, if repeated over time, can lead to the strengthening of bonds. In fact, as is noted by many sociologists, exchanges of material resources, when reciprocated, lead to the arousal of positive emotions (Lawler, Thye, and Yoon 2009) that, in turn, become one more highly valued resource—positive emotions. As positive emotions are exchanged, commitments to social relations and, potentially, more remote social structures increase. It is a relatively short step, then, to an even more remote arena: the supernatural.

Calculations of Justice

Anthropoids have a sense of justice, as do many other mammals. Thus, both monkeys and apes calculate justice and perceived fairness in exchange relations. For example, a New World capuchin monkey will stop exchanging with a caregiver if another capuchin is seen as getting more rewards for emitting the same behaviors (Brosnan et al. 2005; Brosnan 2006). Such calculations involve a comparison of the reward payoffs of others and their respective behaviors to get these rewards, which can be seen as not only a behavioral capacity that gives exchanges a moral character but also as a precursor to morality itself. A recent study of chimpanzees indicates a step toward an altruistic sense of morality when a chimpanzee ceased exchanging with its caregiver because a relative (e.g., mother, sister, brother) was not receiving the same reward level from the caregiver. It is not a great step to see this behavior as invoking a moral code of fairness not just for self but also for others, and for the collectivity or community in which they live (Lents 2016).

In more naturalistic settings, male chimpanzees have been discovered to hunt meat (Fahy et al. 2013), and what is interesting is that when the kill is divided up, the male most responsible for making the kill is given the most amount of meat. Others are given meat apparently in proportion to their perceived contribution to the successful kill. Clearly, chimpanzees are defining justice in terms of relative contributions to outcomes, which is a rather sophisticated form of conceptualizing justice. It is also invoking an attribution dynamic that, as we argue, is central to any capacity to see self as an object, to evaluate self, and eventually to see and evaluate self from the perspective of generalized others.

Indeed, some of the power behind moral codes that are articulated with language are extensions of this capacity of apes and certainly our hominin ancestors to develop a *proto-morality* that generates positive emotions when expectations for rewards are met, while generating negative emotions and negative sanctions when expectations are not realized. The emotions and even cognitions necessary for morality exist and had somewhat of a linguistic character in the simple vocal calls and the more robust gestural grammar of emotions of hominins; thus, with the late growth of the neocortex along the hominin line, it was but only a short step to speech and articulated moral codes. However, the "teeth" of these codes still resided *in the emotions* aroused when calculating the fairness and justice in the distribution of resources. Thus, the basic neurology for justice has probably been in the primate line for millions of years, and as the range and intensity of emotions built up over time on the hominin line, morality close to the human measure could be found. Religious morality is only a special case of this more generalized capacity to experience emotions when fairness and justice prevail, or fail to do so, among still comparatively small-brained animals compared to humans.

Seeing Self as Object

Along with other highly intelligent mammals (Gallup 1970, 1979, 1982, 2014), such as dolphins (Whithead and Rendell 2015; Keenan et al. 2003; Caldwell and Caldwell 1966) and elephants (Elephant Voices 2016; Plotnik et al. 2006; Benjamin et al. 2008), great apes can recognize themselves in a mirror.[4] For example, not only do chimpanzees clearly develop a sense of self *vis-á vis* others; but, when young chimpanzees have been raised by humans, they also view themselves as "human" (Hays 1951). For example, Vickie, a chimp raised by the Hays, was asked to stack animal pictures into one pile, and human pictures into another. She stacked other chimps, dogs, cats, horses into one pile and humans into the other, and when coming to a picture of herself, she put it on top of the human pile. Moreover, as Vickie became an adolescent, she was not interested in male chimpanzees as sexual partners; she was attracted to human males, which made for some interesting interactions.

The capacity to see oneself as an object in its environment is both the consequence of other cognitive processes as well as a causal force behind these same cognitive processes. For instance, the capacity to assess reciprocity and calculate justice depends, to a high degree, on seeing oneself as separate from others with whom an exchange occurs, while on the other hand, acts of assessing reciprocities and justice (to self) not only encourage the further development of self but also further exchanges. The ability to make attributions about who or what has caused feelings and experience of self depends again on the ability to separate self as an object from other objects in the environment, and then to attribute experiences to either self or another object. As this process occurs, both self and attributions become ever-more part of the cognitive structure of an animal and its behavioral propensities. All these processes would be fitness-enhancing to the degree that selection is trying to forge strong bonds and emotional/cognitive mechanisms for forming groups. Because of these fitness-enhancing effects, they would push selection for further emotional and cognitive development (Matsuzawa, Humle, and Sugiyama 2011) and, with such a development, all other self-related processes would be enhanced.

Once an animal has one or several identities of itself, as do humans, it is in the position to not only see itself from the perspective of others but to evaluate itself from the perspective of a community of others—a key condition for the emergence of religion. Given the push for further expansion of the subcortex that then allowed the neocortex of hominins to begin to grow, hominins would increasingly be very much orientated to the evaluation of others and, eventually, to the evaluation of self by Mead's "generalized other" or "community of attitudes," thereby creating the cognitive and emotional neurology for eventually being monitored and evaluated by even more remote others, such as deities in a supernatural realm.

Capacities to Make Attributions

Related to self and calculations of justice is the capacity of chimpanzees, and hence, hominins, to make attributions for their experiences, particularly experiences that arouse emotions. When an animal can distinguish its sense of self from others, it generally has a brain large enough to reckon the causes for the experiences of self. In a more sociological adaptation of attribution theory (for the psychological version, see Weiner 1986), emphasis is on seeing attributions as either self-related or external. In self-related attributions, individuals see themselves as responsible for their actions and experiences, whereas when external attributions are made, these individuals see others with a sense of self and capacities for agency or even situations and social structures as causally responsible for their experiences. Since chimpanzees have this rudimentary capacity to distinguish between their acts of agency (self attributions) and those acts of others (external attributions) that have consequences for self (Kaneko and

Tomonaga 2011), this behavioral capacity to make attributions was also evident with hominins. It may directly have been selected upon, but more likely, we think, the ability to make internal and external attributions was simply enhanced by selection for a larger neocortex, thereby allowing late hominins to sort out their varied emotional experiences, and who or what was responsible for them.

Attributions depend upon ever-more complex cognitive capacities to classify and denote objects and others in the environment. For example, Haun and Call (2009) emphasize the ability to understand relation similarities among classes of objects and others—something chimpanzees can do. With more cognitive development as a result of larger, more emotionally infused brains, this capacity can increase, and the attributions that later hominins could make moved beyond just self and others to other types of others and objects, eventually including a notion of others in another realm, the supernatural.

Thus, religious behaviors always involve an attribution dynamic in that forces and entities in a supernatural realm are seen as responsible for certain outcomes to a person, group of persons, or particular categories of persons. Humans are constantly making attributions, typically around self-attributions and external attributions, for their experiences and even the experiences of others. Once the cognitive capacity exists to conceptualize a supernatural world beyond the mundane, attributions are made to the forces in this supernatural realm, and eventually the supernatural is assumed to have causal effects on profane experiences—the ultimate external attribution. As we will see in the next chapter, the capacity to make external attributions may also be, itself, a cause of how and why humans are able to conceptualize a supernatural realm.

Edward Lawler and colleagues (2009) have developed a theory, backed by controlled experiments, of commitments to larger, more remote social structures that follows from a particular type of exchange: *productive exchange*. Productive exchanges are those where individuals engaged in coordinated efforts to realize a goal are not able to separate their respective individual contributions to the outcome, whether positive or negative. The consequence of such productive exchanges is that participants in coordinated actions develop commitments to the larger social structure in which they are engaged ("we are in this together"); moreover, they experience a "sense of efficacy," which itself is a highly rewarding resource. Thus, flowing out of exchanges are emotions that can move outward, as individuals make external attributions to social structures; and the more they are successful in their productive efforts, the more likely are positive emotions to flow out to more macro structures, including an entire societal structure. They thus make an external attribution to the positive effects of more remote social objects, and from here, it is not a dramatic leap to see the same attributions being made to a supernatural realm and its inhabitants.

Weaker Hierarchies and the Reckoning of Status and Roles

Many species of monkeys form linear hierarchies of dominance among males, and sometimes among females in the ranked matrilines of lineal and collateral female kin (Cords 2012). As emphasized earlier, such hierarchies impose a limit on the kinds of social structures that can exist in monkey societies; and, indeed, they close off the perspective of conspecifics who remained attuned only to the local troop. In contrast, apes vary considerably in the strength and linearity of their hierarchies. Gibbons and siamangs, who are little Asian apes distant from the human and even great ape lines, reveal equality between males and females; orangutans do not seem to possess much in the way of hierarchies because they are semi-solitary and do not need them; gorillas form a laid-back hierarchy around lead silverbacks who at times try to control their foraging groups, with varying degrees of success; and chimpanzees, at times, compete for dominance and form somewhat loose hierarchies, especially if they find themselves forced to remain in close proximity.

Even in normally more dispersed communities, there is some behavioral propensity among our close primate relatives to reckon status differences and status hierarchies, and so, this weak propensity for hierarchy was probably evident in the last common ancestor to extant chimpanzees and our hominin ancestors. This propensity would, if selected upon, increase the propensity of all hominins to reckon the relative status of self; assessing relative status would, in turn, allow a more flexible integration of groupings by status but not necessarily by rigid or fully linear hierarchies. If such had been the case, this capacity to reckon status, *per se*, could be seen as a pre-adaptation because it kept hominins from trying to get organized *only through hierarchy*, which is built on negative rather than positive emotions and, thus, is accompanied by strong bioprogrammers for group organization in the face of negative emotions aroused by hierarchy and negative sanctions meted out by those high in the hierarchy (as is the case of many group-organizing animals). Yet, weaker hierarchies still made hominins aware of status differences in general and forced them to adjust their respective lines of conduct in terms of relative status—something that humans do constantly.[5] Thus, role-taking in G.H. Mead's sense (1994) or in the sense of those emphasizing Theory of Mind in the neuropsychological literature was not just about understanding internal states; this capacity could easily be adapted for understanding status in a process of "status-taking" of not only differences by age and sex classes but also status distinctions built around power and perhaps abilities at various tasks (Turner 2018).

The data documenting systematic hunting by male chimpanzees in Senegal suggest an even more sophisticated manner of determining status, which corresponds to the huge literature (see note 5 for references) on status processes in humans. Humans make status distinctions on the basis of performance, and apparently, this capacity was inherited from humans' great ape and hominin ancestors. By agreeing on the respective contributions of individuals to particular outcomes, status distinctions could be made; these become a means for organizing collective efforts, such as hunting. Thus, while hierarchy is also reckoned at times among great apes, far more important for the evolution of the first human societies was the capacity to bestow honor and prestige for the relative skill and talents among conspecifics and to use these differential evaluations as a basis of social organization. This capacity feeds into the ability to make attributions, to differentiate selves in terms of particular skill sets, and to make more complex assessment of reciprocity and justice—all of which becomes part of the moral codes in religion. Since primates with 400cc brains can make all of these cognitive assessments, the more than tripling in size of the human brain assures that, when hominins became religious, their moral codes would include all of these cognitive elements for self and other evaluations, attributions, bestowing of status and prestige, assessing reciprocities, and calculating justice.

Hunting and Gathering Behavioral Propensities

Chimpanzee males often coordinate hunting for meat, which is often right around them in forest habitats. But more contemporary chimpanzees of West Senegal (Pruetz and LaDuke 2010; Pruetz and Bertolani 2009) now spend a considerable time on the savanna; and they too hunt, but more effectively than forest dwellers because they have invented spears. In fact, they hunt so frequently that isotope evidence of male meat-eating distinguishes them from females, who gather plant life and, as a result, eat much less meat (Fahy et al. 2013).

Through visual gestures not fully understood by scientists, male chimpanzees in the forest can silently collaborate and communicate with only non-vocal gestures so as to flush out a prey, such as a baby baboon, and catch it when it runs, and then share in eating the carcass (Menzel 1971). More recently, it has become clear that forest-based chimpanzees engage in hunting on a regular basis to supplement their foraging activity. Chimpanzee communities today that have adapted to daytime activities on the outskirts of forests consistently engage in hunting activities (Fahy et al. 2013)—as surely as their hominin and then human descendants over the last 2 million years. These behavioral propensities in chimpanzees can perhaps be seen as a pre-adaptation for forming hunting and gathering bands, but they can also be viewed as behavioral capacities that allowed for survival in ever-more open landscapes. Perhaps by combining male groups that were used to patrol community boundaries of chimpanzees to coordinate hunting and scavenger activities, the shift to a hunting and gathering mode of adaptation occurred during late hominin evolution. In turn, hunting not only provided a fulcrum around which new kinds of group bonds could be built, it also allowed for apes on the edges of the forest in more open woodland conditions to get more protein than is possible in the forest alone. In this way, the behavioral propensity to hunt can be seen as a pre-adaptation for growth of the brain when the expansion of the emotion centers of the brain were sufficient to make such growth of the neocortex fitness-enhancing. Once this process began, later hominins could secure more protein through hunting groups that, in turn, would begin the process of converting communities of hominins into bands, with subgroups forming around new kin relations and economic divisions of labor within kin groups. Such evolutionary developments could be built upon the propensity of great apes to reckon community, groups of bands now constituting a new type of home range and community. When thrust out onto more open-country conditions (just like their ancestral hominin cousins some 2 million years ago) great apes of the past and today, as is illustrated in Senegal, begin to develop economic specialization around hunting and gathering. Such differentiated activities, in turn, encourage tool use and differentiation between males who hunt and females who gather. It is therefore not so surprising that late hominins continued this propensity to divide food collection and, as more structure was required, created the nuclear family.

Male Friendships and Fellowships

It appears that all of the great apes develop a sense of community and that, to varying degrees, some who are born into these communities do not all transfer to other communities. A few orangutan females may stay in their natal community but they remain semi-solitary. Some male gorillas may stay in their natal community as "loners" moving about and remaining on the fringes of groups controlled by lead silverbacks. Most consistently, chimpanzee males remain in their natal community for a lifetime. Thus, while female and male dispersal is the modal pattern among orangutans and gorillas (and among chimpanzee females), there are exceptions that can be seen as a target for selection *if* remaining in a community would be fitness-enhancing.

Of particular importance are male chimpanzees, who, unlike orangutans and gorillas, never leave their natal community. Their patterns of ties give us a sense for what probably occurred during late hominin evolution, as will be explored in the next chapter. Chimpanzee males form strong ties with their mothers, brothers, and close friends; and while these social ties do not result in the formation of stable groups, they allow for kin relations with brothers and mothers, while allowing for strong ties with preferred male friends. Thus, one route that selection probably took was to enhance the bonds among males since there was already present such a behavioral propensity of chimpanzee males. Coupled with the genetically based avoidance of sexual relations between chimpanzee males and their mothers (Turner and Maryanski 2005), early efforts to structure more permanent groups probably began with stronger ties among males in a community, and between males and their mothers. Female ties could remain weaker, as long as ties among males, their mothers, and immigrant females could develop.

The voluntary friendships of chimpanzee males are especially important behaviors that can lead to more stable groupings. Male chimpanzee siblings have strong ties and support each other, but they often prefer to form stronger ties with male friends (Mitani et al. 2000; Lukas et al. 2005). Thus, male friends will gather and perhaps coordinate hunts together or engage in community defense patrols. They do not form stable groups, but chimpanzees are not quite the loners that orangutans are, nor are they involved like silverbacks in more structured band activities. The good fellowship among male chimpanzees is something that could be worked upon by Darwinian natural selection because it is clearly a male proclivity and, thus, represents one route to forging stronger group bonds when such bonds were necessary and critical to fitness in wide-open habitats.

Conclusion

The behavioral propensities outlined in this chapter would seem, at first glance, to be sufficient for increasing social bonds and group solidarity if subject to selection. However, comparative neuroanatomy suggests that they were not; otherwise, selection would not have so dramatically rewired subcortical areas of the brain and the connections between neocortical and subcortical areas, especially between the prefrontal cortex and the enlarged emotion centers in the subcortical part of mammalian brains. Clearly, something more was needed as later hominins began to adapt to more open-country habitats; and that "something" was a larger, more nuanced palette of emotions that could charge up pre-adaptations and existing behavioral propensities to make hominins more socially oriented.

In fact, as emphasized earlier, initially selecting only on emotions would be the simplest route to take because, once emotions are charged up, the expanded range and palette of emotional valences would have direct affects *on all behavioral propensities* without a need for selecting on each one individually. Emotions, as they simultaneously enhanced *all* behavioral capacities and pre-adaptations, were used to make hominins more social. These fitness-enhancing effects of increased sociality would feed back and select for more diverse and nuanced emotions; and out of this reciprocal and self-escalating process, hominins developed a quasi-language of emotions revolving around gestalts of non-verbal gestures. Like non-verbal language today among humans, these emotional displays among hominins communicated *shared meanings*. Once this use of what we term today as "body language" was in place, the stage was set for selection to make the growth of the hominin neocortex fitness-enhancing. It is this last phase of neurological development among hominins that would eventually allow for the conception of a supernatural realm and, thereby, make religious behavior possible in human hunting and gathering populations.

One point that we should interject here is that chimpanzees and hence early hominins can (and could) create unique cultures, but in any case, these are not nearly as important as the dynamics that we have described in the last two chapters. Still, even a small 400cc brain can develop call systems that are unique to communities and that carry common meanings and, moreover, that are passed down from generation to generation. They may also develop different tool kits across communities, even different traditions and patterns of food collection. At times, these can be transmitted by females immigrating between chimpanzee communities. Yet, without a spoken language, culture is quite limited but still impressive among animals that communicate primarily by non-verbal gestures. This behavioral capacity to communicate common meanings through a gestural language documents the potential for the evolution of more complex cultural systems built on speech. In some ways, the "search for culture" has gotten in the way of the more important neurological capacities made available by pre-adaptations and the remarkably robust behavioral and interpersonal capacities of great apes and the earliest of hominins.[6]

The next chapter continues what has only been periodically emphasized thus far: the changes in the brain as natural selection took advantage of the pre-adaptations and hard-wired behavioral propensities that hominins inherited from their great-ape ancestors. Here, we have just summarized as briefly as possible *what was present for natural selection to work on*; in Chapter 6, we will outline how these pre-adaptations and behavioral capacities/ propensities affected group formation and interpersonal behaviors of late hominins, including human hominins, that in turn led to the emergence of religious behaviors. By the end of Chapter 6, we will have almost completed our use of Darwinian selection dynamics to explain the emergence of religion. In Chapters 7 through 10, we will increasingly shift to non-Darwinian selection forces as religion was institutionalized in the first human societies and, then, how religion developed and evolved to the present era.

Notes

1 Mark Granovetter (1973) emphasized that strong and weak ties can both be used to create structural coherence but they offer different bases of integration. Granovetter's theory is consistent with the following proposition: the higher the level of density (or strong ties) at the micro-group level, the less is the integration level at the macro-community level; the lower the level of density (weak ties) at the micro-group organizational level, the greater is the level of integration at the macro-community level.
2 See Pruetz and LaDuke (2010).
3 Kühl et al. (2016) Nature.com/Scientific Reports. See also: www.npr.org/sections/13.7/why-do-wild-chimpanzees-throw-stones-at-trees.
4 See, for example, Gallup (1970, 1979, 1982, 2014), Anderson and Gallup (1995), Heyes (1994), Kitchen et al. (1996), Povinelli et al. (1993).
5 See, for example: Berger (1988); Berger, Cohen, and Zelditch (1972); Berger et al. (1977); Berger and Zelditch (1985). See also Turner (2002, 2007).
6 For examples of diverse reports summarizing great ape culture, see Whiten et al. (1999), Luncz et al. (2012), and Arbib (2011).

6

The Profane Origins of the Sacred and Supernatural

Darwinian and Type-1 Spencerian Natural Selection

The smallscale, the here-and-now of face-to-face interaction, is the scene of social action . . . If we are going to find the agency of social life, it will be here. Here reside the energy of movement and change, the glue of solidarity, and the conservation of stasis . . . Here is where intentionality and consciousness find their places; here, too, is the site of emotional . . . aspects of human interaction.

Randall Collins (2004: 3) in *Interaction Ritual Chains*

Religious behavior revolves around the capacity to conceptualize a supernatural realm, beyond the mundane and temporal world of daily activities. It also involves the capacity and propensity to emit emotion-arousing rituals directed at the sacred forces and beings in this supernatural world and to make attributions about their power to affect happenings in the temporal world. Religion requires a sense of community of worshipers who also engage in these emotion-arousing rituals and, moreover, are willing to do so collectively. Finally, religion eventually involves the institutionalization of such behaviors in a cult structure that can potentially reveal a division of labor between worshipers and religious practitioners mediating contact with the supernatural.

All of these necessary behaviors for religion were surely evident among even early hominins, save for a conception of the supernatural. As the subcortex and emotion centers grew during the period of late *Homo habilis* and *Homo erectus*, from 2.2 to 0.2 million years ago, the prior growth of the emotion centers allowed for a very rapid and dram atic growth of the neocortex in late *Homo erectus* to well within the human measure of size, with brain size measures as high as 1,200cc's. Thus, in just over 2 million years, the brain of hominins doubled from around 600cc's with early *Homo habilis* to 1,200cc's in some cases with late *Homo erectus*. With *Homo sapiens*, the brain had grown yet another 200 to 300cc's. This growth in the brain enhanced most pre-adaptations and behavioral propensities analyzed in Chapters 4 and 5, as delineated in Tables 6.1 and 6.2. Moreover, the growth of the brain also allowed for the increasing development of auditory language; coupled with a larger neocortex that can ponder more remote domains of the universe, it became possible at some point for later hominins to have the capacity to conceptualize a supernatural universe and to articulate the nature of this realm, not only with self but with conspecifics as well.

For the last ingredient of religion to fall into place—cult structures—it was necessary for hominins to begin forging more stable bonds and group formations; we already know that these societal units would be nomadic hunting and gathering bands. This adaptation is the longest lasting societal form in human history, lasting into the present day, but more importantly, it was the dominant societal form for at least 95 percent of humans' time on earth. These first societies were built from two universal structural units: (1) *nuclear families* of mothers, fathers, and offspring organized in (2) *bands* composed of five or six nuclear families. These bands wandered delimited territories with males primarily responsible for hunting and females (often with help of older offspring) gathering edible plant foods. Thus, the organization structure of the first human societies (and likely the later societies of *Homo erectus*) was not a religious-based unit but rather a productive-, reproductive-, regulatory-, and distributive-unit that emerged not so much under Darwinian selection as much as Spencerian selection, Type-1, as we will see later in this chapter. Still, even as more sociocultural types of selection began to direct societal evolution, Darwinian selection persisted in the transition from less well-organized productive- and reproductive-units in the transition to the nuclear family. Religion was likely embedded in nuclear families and bands; and while the conception of a supernatural realm was not highly developed, hunter-gatherers still made some attributions to the powers of non-worldly forces on the temporal world of their daily lives. Even when worldly forces were totemized, such as the "wind" and "earth," they were seen to have special power over human daily life.

The lists of pre-adaptations and behavioral capacities/propensities in Tables 6.1 and 6.2 indicate how these mundane but critical adaptations and behaviors—when emotionally intensified and attached to a much larger subcortex and neocortex—could produce religious behaviors because hominins were already close to being able to emit all of the necessary behaviors, except the ability to conceptualize a supernatural realm and to articulate its nature. Let us first outline how interpersonal capacities and propensities, when charged up by emotions and by dramatically increased cognitive capacities and language facility, would make human beings religious.

TABLE 6.1 Pre-adaptations Available for Selection among Hominins

1.	*Comparatively large brain*, with large and complex subcortical areas producing emotions and a very large and complex neocortex relative to body size.
2.	*Hard-wired potential for language* (a) production (via auditory sense modality but more significantly, via non-verbal sense modalities, particularly gestures of face, body, body countenance, and hands) and for (b) full language comprehension via all sense modalities.
3.	*Comparatively large palette of basic primary emotions* and variants of primary emotions for a mammal generated by subcortical areas of the brain but used by the neocortex to assess self and others in communities.
4.	*Mother–offspring bonding until puberty*, typically broken at puberty, thereby eliminating linear generational ties among conspecifics.
5.	*Lack of matrilines and strong ties among females*, thereby assuring no permanent intergenerational ties among female members of the community.
6.	*Protracted life history characteristics at all stages of reproduction* (gestation in womb, infancy, childhood, juvenile, adolescent, and adulthood).
7.	*Low levels of physical grooming among adult conspecifics*, except in greeting rituals and in interaction with dependent young.
8.	*High levels of play among young*, revolving around role-switching, mimicry, and ritual.
9.	*Cognitive mapping of community and its members* (up to at least 150 different individuals), despite long periods where there is little or no interaction with conspecifics in a community.
10.	*Community as the only stable unit of organization* generating a "community complex" consisting of such interrelated behaviors as (a) cognitive mapping of community boundaries and community members, (b) ritualized interpersonal greeting among conspecifics when meeting up, (c) presentations of self to others and evaluations of responses to self, and (d) viewing self from the perspective of the community.

TABLE 6.2 Behavioral Propensities and Capacities among Hominins

1.	*Propensity to focus on eyes and face* for determining emotions of conspecifics during episodes of interaction.
2.	*Capacity and propensity to focus on facial gestures revealing emotions* and to mimic these gestures during infancy.

3. ***Capacity to role-take (Theory of Mind)*** to determine likely courses of action of conspecifics.

4. ***Capacity and propensity during role-taking for empathy*** with conspecifics by mutually reading emotional states so as to respond appropriately to others.

5. ***Capacity to make causal attributions*** by individuals as to whether self or others are causally responsible for experiences associated with behavioral outcomes.

6. ***Propensity to mimic responses*** of conspecifics during play.

7. ***Propensity to emit ritualized behaviors*** when meeting up with, and departing from, interactions with conspecifics and at times ritual-like behavioral sequences that appear to affirm solidarity among conspecifics in a community.

8. ***Propensity to fall into rhythmic interaction with*** conspecifics, especially if emotions are aroused, with the result that mimicry and pacing of interpersonal exchanges occurs.

9. ***Propensity for collective emotional arousal*** during periodic gatherings of larger numbers of conspecifics in a community and to emit emotionally-charged, ritual-like behaviors collectively.

10. ***Propensity to assess reciprocities*** in exchanges of resources with conspecifics.

11. ***Propensity to calculate fairness and justice of exchanges*** with conspecifics and to sanction (positively or negatively, respectively) perceptions of fairness and unfairness with either positive or negative emotions.

12. ***Capacity to see self as an object during interactions with others*** and to emit gestures expressing conceptions of self and to evaluate self by role-taking with the gestures of others and, at times, with a sense of the larger community as a collective "other."

13. ***Capacity to reckon status of others*** and to respond appropriately to status differences, particularly those marking hierarchies but also those marking distinctive social categories, such as age, gender, and community membership.

14. ***Capacity of males to form friendships*** with male conspecifics and, occasionally, with female conspecifics among chimpanzees.

15. ***Propensities of males to hunt and females to gather resources,*** as is the case among chimpanzees.

Making *Homo Sapiens* Religious

One way to assess how *Homo sapiens*, as the last hominin, became religious is to review the definition of religion from Chapter 1 and re-stated above. By taking each element in this definition and then scanning Tables 6.1 and 6.2, we can immediately see how close hominins were well-along the path to becoming religious.

Community of Worshipers

This element was certainly the easiest for hominins to realize because they inherited the orientation to community as the only stable unit of social organization among great apes. Hominins could cognitively map the membership of their community, consisting of as many as 100 members spread out over potentially many square miles, and they had the interpersonal skills to hook up with conspecifics, even when they had not seen each other for a time. These skills included (from Table 6.2) the capacity to engage in opening and closing rituals, reading of gestures in face and body for emotions, role-taking and empathizing (Theory of Mind), rhythmically interacting, exchanging and reciprocating, and seeing self as an object *vis-à-vis* others and perhaps even the larger community. In this way, a sense of a larger community could be sustained.

Indeed, as we have mentioned, hominins inherited, like their great ape ancestors and cousins today, what we have termed "the community complex." This complex, which is evident in other highly intelligent animals such as dolphins, whales, and elephants involves a number of related elements: (a) organization into communities as much or more than local groups, (b) cognitive mapping of not only geographical space but also demographic space (what age and sex categories exist in the community), (c) capacity to see self as a distinctive object in their environment, (d) ritual behaviors for greeting and parting between conspecifics when they meet up, and (e) rhythmic interactions and emotionally charged carnivals where there appears to be a celebration of the community as a collective force.

Emotionally-Charged Rituals

As the brain grew, all elements of this community complex could increase in several ways: the number of conspecifics to be mapped and tracked could increase, the greeting and parting rituals could become more elaborate and emotional, the sense of self could become more complex, the self could become evaluated by the emotional reactions of conspecifics and perhaps even evaluated from a more "generalized other" representing the "communities of attitudes" or perspective of the community as a whole, and the rhythmic nature of interactions could become more synchronized. Rhythmic synchronization is critical to charging up rituals because it allows conspecifics to become fully entrained emotionally and able to synchronize body movements and verbalizations which, in turn, lead to new kinds of rituals with a big "R" and to more focused and coordinated collective carnivals.

The most complete conceptualization of human big "R" rituals is that done by Collins (1975, 2004). Figure 6.1 lays out our interpretation of his model. The hominin capacity for rhythmic interaction, for greeting and closing rituals (i.e., small "r" rituals), for mimicry, role-taking, empathy, and emotional effervescence eventually bestowed upon late hominins or *Homo sapiens* the capacities outlined in this model. These interaction rituals with a big "R" are essential in creating strong bonds and group solidarities. As can be seen, rituals with a little "r" open and focus the interaction, but the critical dynamics are those that flow from left to right in the model, revolving around rhythmic synchronization of talk and bodies, increasing emotional entrainment, feelings of group solidarity, building up particularized cultural capital (memories and feelings unique to the group), and increasing needs in conversations to represent this solidarity. Hominins could do some of these, but only with late hominins and *Homo sapiens* would the full big "R" rituals be enacted consistently. At this point rituals now have the potential to become truly religious. Indeed, groups often represent themselves with totemic symbols or badges, forms of dress, and virtually any object that communicates the quasi-"sacred" (important) character of the group. The more that these kinds of interaction rituals are iterated and strung together in chains of such rituals (Collins 2004), the greater will be the solidarity and group cohesion generated. As these kinds of big "R" rituals become the fundamental micro-basis of normal interactions, the basic template for religious rituals is not only laid down but constantly repeated. Thus, it is not a very long step to using this template to engage in religious behavior.

Like chimpanzees, hominins were always able to engage in greeting and parting rituals, and the data we briefly summarized in the last chapter suggests that they could engage in rituals directed at something more than just others who are physically co-present. With growth of the subcortex and neocortex, rituals could become even more emotionally charged in a wider variety of ways and perhaps eventually directed at the sense of power and awe of not just natural events such as rain or waterfalls, but also the power of the collective community when carnivals erupted. But now, the emotions would be more channeled and synchronized, revealing the emotional

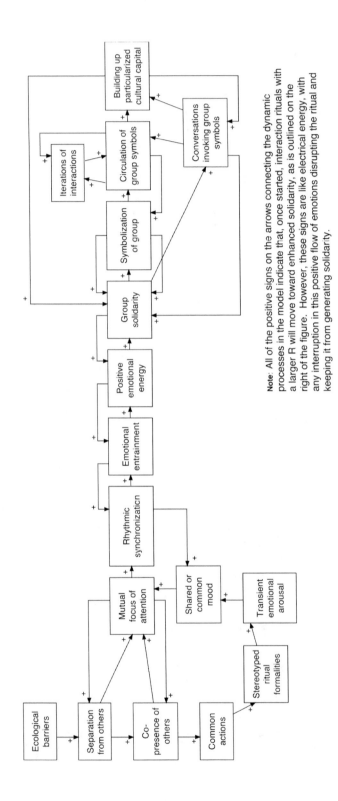

Note: All of the positive signs on the arrows connecting the dynamic processes in the model indicate that, once started, interaction rituals with a larger R will move toward enhanced solidarity, as is outlined on the right of the figure. However, these signs are like electrical energy, with any interruption in this positive flow of emotions disrupting the ritual and keeping it from generating solidarity.

Figure 6.1 Collins Elaborated Model of Interaction Rituals

entrainment of body and talk creating a sense of forces above and beyond the individual—in the sense originally outlined by Durkheim (1912).

In this transition to interaction rituals with a big "R," rituals became more than greetings; they now could be celebrations of this external force of the community, above and beyond the individual. Perhaps attributions could begin to be made about the "sacred" nature of this force, especially as talk began to be woven into language production. For, bipedalism had already lowered the larynx and expanded the pharynx by creating a curvature of the vocal tract, thereby increasing the range of sounds that could be produced. As a result, Broca's area or "hump" could come under selection for greater linguistic capacities.

With augmented vocalizatons, the emotional stakes could then increase that much more when evaluations of more complex senses of self evolved with the larger neocortex. At some point, a larger neocortex allowed for (a) more focus, rhythm, and synchronization of bodies during rituals, and particularly as vocal sounds could pace and synchronize the rhythm of rituals; (b) more focus on verifying more complex identities which, in turn, would raise the emotional stakes in the ritual; (c) more varied emotions that could become entrained and thus synchronize bodies and talk; and (d) more remote attributions to the powers that were being encountered, beyond the individual and community to, at some point, another more remote realm of forces having new powers to effect the profane world.

Conceptions of the Supernatural

The above elements of religion, we think, would inevitably push late hominins and certainly *Homo sapiens* to begin to perceive a special and sacred world beyond the community, and particularly if Spencerian Type-1 selection pressures (see Figures 2.3 on p. 28 and 7.1 on p. 151) were beginning to exert pressures on hunting and gathering populations. As the examples of religion among hunter-gatherers offered in the next chapter reveal, the conception of the supernatural realm is often rather unclear and, among many hunter-gatherers, not given the great powers that would come later as societies grew and became more complex. From ancestor worship and dreamtime through conceptions of the forces inhering in land, sea, and air to sacredness of particular animals that often became totems for a population or subpopulation, the supernatural was often vague and equally often not seen as "all that powerful." Indeed, the supernatural was real but was not constantly monitoring or throwing its weight around in mundane, daily affairs. Only when Spencerian Type-1 selection pressures increased did big, often angry, and always-monitoring gods begin to inhabit the supernatural and impose themselves on individuals.

Collective beliefs with some precision about the nature of the super-natural probably only came with speech, perhaps only the speech of *Homo sapiens* but also possibly the advancing speech facility of later *Homo erectus*. A sense of a larger power beyond can occur without speech, as chimpan-zees' emotional effervescence about their community or their seeming reverence for, and awe of, the powers of rain and waterfalls suggest. Yet, to have something more than this vague sense it is critical to be able to describe with words what the supernatural is, and what beings and forces inhabit this realm. Moreover, if religious-based morality is to evolve, it must be spoken and allow for the articulation of moral codes.[1] Thus, as soon as the hominin brain became large enough, and as soon as more articulate speech was possible (not necessarily in the full human measure, however), the supernatural realm and what it would represent to humans could evolve. A late *Homo erectus* brain over 1,100 to 1,200cc's and the capacity to do more than make just discrete vocal calls carrying common meanings (which chimpanzees can do) but, instead, to be able to string together calls that carry more complex common meanings might be the tipping point where even late hominins could have religion. Certainly, early *Homo sapi-ens* forms, including Neanderthals, probably had religion, at least in some very elemental form.

The Mundane Origins of Religion

All of the elements of religious behavior were made possible by the pre-adaptations and behavioral capacities/propensities enumerated in Tables 6.1 and 6.2. It is likely that the growth of the subcortex and then the neocortex worked (in the order that we have presented) on the basic elements of religion: heightened emotions and greater cognitive powers strengthened the community complex; then, ritual capacities for mimicry and rhythmic interactions, coupled with talk and heightened emotionality, could further emotional entrainment and synchronize interactions in ways that made rituals much more powerful and potentially focused; and, then, perhaps with a push from early Spencerian selection pressures on the first hunting and gathering bands, a supernatural realm could be conceptual-ized and, most importantly, talked about among later hominins or perhaps only *Homo sapiens*. But, none of these religious behaviors were selected for; rather, pressures for increasing social bonds and the stability of group structures were what drove selection.

Human social interaction is very complex; and, indeed, there is a vast liter-ature on its dynamics that many scholars on the origins of religious evolution often ignore (for illustrative reviews, see Turner 1988, 2002, 2007, 2010b; Collins 1975, 2004). Yet, the origins of religion ultimately are to be found in the interpersonal dynamics that guide each and every interaction among humans. In giving these more emotional valences and in dramatically augmenting the cognitive capacities of humans, religion could also evolve from the mundane, though complex, ways that humans interact. Thus, to get a better handle on how religious sentiments and behaviors evolved and why religious behavior reveals certain distinctive properties, it is best to go back to the behavioral capacities of great apes and then compare those with what humans do with their larger palette of emotions and dramatically expanded cognitive capacities. In many ways, *ritual worship of the supernatural is very much like regular interaction among individuals*; and the reason for this convergence, of course, is that religion emerges as a result of the neurological changes that made hominins more social. We have only focused on those interpersonal processes that had the greatest impact on the origins of religion. A more thorough review of all of the interpersonal dynamics of human interaction remains fertile ground for an even greater understanding of religion.

On the Origins of Human Societies

The Emergence of the Horde

Many early theorists in anthropology and sociology posited a hypothetical conception of the "horde." Positing the existence of the horde was an effort to answer the question: what were the first, more stable patterns of organization among humans before the nuclear kinship unit and the hunting and gathering band evolved? Long ago, scholars such as Émile Durkheim (1893) recognized that the nuclear family *is not* the first or even most natural unit of social organization among humans. Something came before the nuclear family, and that something was the often hypothesized horde (e.g., Bachhofen 1861; McLennan 1865, 1896; Morgan 1871). As Durkheim ([1893] 1984: 119) emphasized: "nothing proceeds from nothing." A corollary of this sentiment is the epitome of Robert Bellah's work on cultural evolution: "Nothing is ever lost," that is, anything of great importance (Bellah 2005, 2011; Joas 2014). For us, the "something" (in Bellah's sense) that human social organization and religion ultimately come from is the pre-adaptations and behavioral propensities of ancestral great apes honed by Darwinian natural selection, as was outlined in earlier chapters. Since selection was pushing for more stable units of social organization among individualistic, weak-tie hominins, there were intermediate steps along the way; and one of these steps is "the horde." Durkheim felt that the horde was a promiscuous aggregation of early humans in which incest was common, whereas we will argue that Durkheim's image of the "horde" better suits the traits that hominins inherited from their great ape ancestors and that can still be seen in humans' great-ape cousins. Moreover, incest was not as widespread as Durkheim thought because a small grouping of individuals sharing 25 percent to 50 percent of their genes would not be reproductively fit.

Biasing Constraints

If we look at the list of pre-adaptations that hominins revealed, some of these biased the direction that natural selection took leading up to hunting and gathering bands composed of nuclear families. Thus, selection was biased by the community as the natural unit of organization of hominins, the existence of weak ties among females who have migrated into a community, the mother–offspring ties that are broken at puberty (except for chimpanzee males who remain in their natal community), the lack of strong matrilines among females, and the protracted life history characteristics allowing early birth of big-brained offspring with assured mother nurturance. These pre-adaptations would impose constraints on the nature of more stable group structures along the hominin line as forced adaptation to open-country habitats increased. As Hans Kummer (1971: 129), a world-renowned primate ethnologist, emphasized:

> The adaptive potential of a species is limited by phylogenetic dispositions. New behavioral adaptations are possible only if the necessary dispositions are within the scope of the behavioral heritage, and if they can be accommodated within the existing system.

Some behavioral propensities would do the same, and several would be particularly powerful bias forces, including: the propensity of adult males and females to have promiscuous sexual relations; the resulting lack of knowledge about the paternity of offspring and hence intergenerational relations between fathers and offspring; the propensity of males to live in their natal community (as was the case with chimpanzees and their ancestors) and, thereby, to form moderate-to-strong ties with their mothers, their brothers, and particularly their friends; and the incipient tendency for males to hunt and females to gather food resources.

Thus, as natural selection worked on pre-adaptations and behavioral propensities to enhance sociality that could lead to stronger bonds and, ultimately, to the emergence of religion, it was doing so in order to underpin more stable groups for survival and reproductive success in more open-country, terrestrial habitats. Large brains, more emotions, and dramatically enhanced capacities for ritual provide clues for how social bonds were strengthened and how solidarities could be generated by the nature of groups that would evolve—that is, groups held together by emotional attachments more than by bioprogrammers. This kind of bias has enabled humans to create many different types of corporate units revealing high degrees of flexibility. The other pre-adaptations and behavioral propensities, however, that we have listed—i.e., adult sexual promiscuity, weak ties among females, stronger ties among males if they remain in their natal community, offspring transfer of all females from natal community, and differentiation of male–female economic behaviors—have an even greater impact on how the first grouping evolved among hominins. Following an old speculative tradition (e.g., Bachhofen 1861; McLennan 1865, 1896; Morgan 1871), we will find "the horde" as the key transitional structure to evolve before the nuclear family. Moreover, the transition from horde to nuclear family can also be seen as a point where Spencerian selection began to supplement and supplant evolutionary dynamics driven by Darwinian natural selection. To be sure, the nuclear family is probably the first stable structural unit in which religion could survive; and while pre-adaptations and neurologically-driven behaviors were installed by Darwinian selection, the first nuclear families that emerged from the horde were very likely to have evolved in response to Type-1 Spencerian selection dynamics.

A Hypothetical Reconstruction

Religion cannot solely have come from Darwinian selection processes. Religion emerged in human social systems because of Type-1 Spencerian selection pressures revolving around production, reproduction, regulation, and distribution that pushed on late hominins and early *Homo sapiens* to develop more cohesive social structures within their more natural community structural formations.

Indirect evidence for these pressures can be observed, as noted in earlier chapters, among those chimpanzees that today spend a considerable amount of time on the savanna in West Senegal, retreating to their open canopy forest or gallery forest in order to sleep. What has emerged are somewhat more permanent groups, perhaps extending the propensity of male chimpanzees to move along the borders of the community to protect against incursion of males from other communities. On the savanna, of course, a discrete community boundary is more difficult to maintain because of the many predators that would hardly honor such boundaries and because of the openness of the grassland habitat itself. What emerges, however, is fellowships of chimpanzee males and sometimes even an occasional female engaged in hunting and scavenging activities, very much like males in human hunting and gathering societies who face the same selection pressures of late hominins and certainly early humans: to find a way to form more stable subgroup formations within the larger community. Moreover, these more savanna-dwelling chimpanzees develop more technologies and begin to form a division of labor between males and females over, respectively, hunting vs. gathering (for relevant data, see: Baldwin 1979; Baldwin et al. 1981; Baldwin et al. 1982; McGrew 1981, 1983, 1992, 2010; McGrew, Baldwin, and Tutin 1981; Tutin, McGrew, and Baldwin 1982, 1983; Pruetz and Bertolani 2007; Stanford 1999; Mitani and Watts 2001; Mitani and Rodman 1979; Hunt and McGrew 2002; Pruetz 2006; Moore, Langergraber, and Vigilant 2015; Hernandez-Aguilar, Moore, and Pickering 2007; Langergraber et al. 2011).

What was there to select on by either Darwinian or Spencerian selection? One answer is *male fellowships and friendships* that are evident among forest-dwelling chimpanzees. This would have to have been the core, and Darwinian selection could work to enhance this relationship, while Spencerian selection could force males to form more stable groups in order to survive as initially part-time hunters on the savanna. Another answer would be *the mother–adult son bond* on which both Darwinian and Spencerian selection could work, but it is more likely to be Spencerian selection because Darwinian selection had done the difficult part of keeping males in the community, programming sons and mothers to sustain relations throughout their adult lives, and producing bioprogrammers against sexual relations between mothers and sons. Under pressure to get organized or die, these existing ties are evident in chimpanzees today and, hence, the past hominin ancestors of humans were probably the basis for what Durkheim and others (e.g., Bachhofen 1861; McLennan 1865, 1896; Morgan 1871; Durkheim 1893; Turner and Maryanski 2008) termed the "horde," which was a rather speculative formulation by early scholars but, today, the speculation has some support with the advent of cladistic analysis (see Chapter 3). These early scholars recognized, however, as noted above, that nuclear kinship systems could not have evolved "from nothing"; there had to be some kind of pre-kinship basis of social organization among hominins. Figure 6.2 outlines the social structure of the horde, the first step in getting low-sociality evolving apes more group oriented.

The horde, then, consisted of the following features:

1. Community males, who built more permanent groups on the basis of friendships and attachments to brothers, both of which are clearly evident in forest-dwelling chimpanzees today.
2. Mothers and their sons, who form visiting relationships among contemporary chimpanzees, but our belief is that these became more permanent, especially because there was an existing bioprogrammer against incest and hence against the potential for inbreeding depression already wired into this dyad.

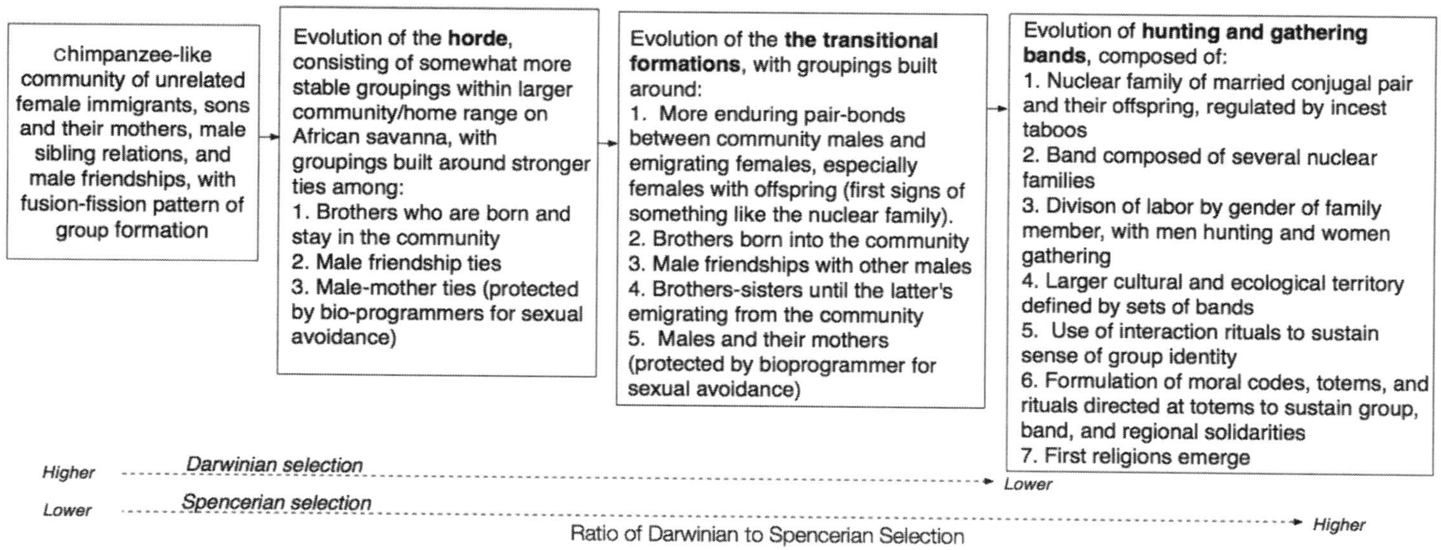

Chimpanzee-like community of unrelated female immigrants, sons and their mothers, male sibling relations, and male friendships, with fusion-fission pattern of group formation

Evolution of the **horde**, consisting of somewhat more stable groupings within larger community/home range on African savanna, with groupings built around stronger ties among:
1. Brothers who are born and stay in the community
2. Male friendship ties
3. Male-mother ties (protected by bio-programmers for sexual avoidance)

Evolution of the **the transitional formations**, with groupings built around:
1. More enduring pair-bonds between community males and emigrating females, especially females with offspring (first signs of something like the nuclear family).
2. Brothers born into the community
3. Male friendships with other males
4. Brothers-sisters until the latter's emigrating from the community
5. Males and their mothers (protected by bioprogrammer for sexual avoidance)

Evolution of **hunting and gathering bands**, composed of:
1. Nuclear family of married conjugal pair and their offspring, regulated by incest taboos
2. Band composed of several nuclear families
3. Divison of labor by gender of family member, with men hunting and women gathering
4. Larger cultural and ecological territory defined by sets of bands
5. Use of interaction rituals to sustain sense of group identity
6. Formulation of moral codes, totems, and rituals directed at totems to sustain group, band, and regional solidarities
7. First religions emerge

Higher .... *Darwinian selection*

Lower ------- *Spencerian selection*

Lower ------------→ Higher

Ratio of Darwinian to Spencerian Selection

Figure 6.2 The Organizational Transition to the Hunting and Gathering Band

3. Brothers and their female siblings, at least to the point where at puberty the females transfer out of the community, never to return. The maintenance of this transfer pattern would be essential for mixing genomes and, of course, potential sexual relations between brothers and sisters.

At first, these relationships may have been only enhanced slightly by Darwinian natural selection, with more periodic fusion in the face of danger. But, as Type-1 Spencerian selection pressures were pushing for more stable organization (in order to survive full time in open-country savanna conditions), conspecifics realized the advantages, just as chimpanzees on the savanna do today, of hanging together for protection from predation and for hunting and scavenging for protein provided by meat. Perhaps Darwinian selection was still working to add emotional enhancements to the relations, or working on the already existing propensities that lead extant chimpanzee males to form relationships with each other and their mothers. Yet, however enhanced, this horde is probably not as cohesive as it would need to be as hominins began to spend more time, including nighttime, out in open country niches and, increasingly, on the ground, even at night. Darwinian selection would have worked indirectly on hominins by enhancing emotional capacities to the point of forming the gestural languages with emotional grammar as well as more vocally-based language, ordering calls a proto-grammar. In so doing, selection would have made all of the interpersonal practices used by apes today more compelling and effective, with the result that the horde could become more cohesive and, equally significant, more stable and permanent.

The Evolution of More Stable Subgroupings

The concept of *sodalities* was invented by anthropologists to account for the propensity of humans to form a diverse variety of subgroups and networks around distinctive features, such as gendered, age-related, economic, political, class, religious, ethnic, and even secret associations (Lowie 1948). As Gestalt psychologists emphasized, with their concept of *contrast-conceptions*, humans recognize differences in what Peter Blau (1977, 1994) labeled as *parameters* marking differences, which can be *nominal* (gender, ethnic) or *graduated* (levels of income, years of education, amounts of prestige). In both traditional and modern societies, sodalities emerge around these parameters and become key organizing features. Early anthropologists, for example, observed "sodalities" emerging as men's houses and female-only groupings, along with age cohorts (Lowie 1948: 294–316). As Robert Lowie (1966: 309) emphasized:

Sodalities vary so greatly . . . that no single formula can do justice to all of the relevant phenomena. The concept is of some utility in bringing home the fact that individuals associate irrespective of whether they belong to the same family, clan, or territorial group; and that such associations play a dominant part in the social life of many people, rivaling and sporadically even overshadowing other ties.

We can faithfully adopt this idea to speculate on the transitional organizational form between the horde and the band composed of nuclear families, because something like the dynamics forming sodalities were operative. Also, the notion of sodalities emphasizes that there is some propensity for humans to join subgroups, despite their weak-tie and non-group origins as evolved primates. We have to be cautious and only label movement from the horde to more stable subgroups *the transitional form* between horde and hunting/gathering band.

To create the nuclear family, adult males and females need to form more permanent relationships, something that chimpanzees do not do. Lead silverback gorillas form a bond with females when they have young offspring, and thus there is some propensity for at least temporary relationships between males and females in the great ape lineage that Darwinian selection might have worked on. As emphasized in earlier chapters, some selection may have been Darwinian with directional selection on the *septum*—where the pleasure associated with sex is generated among mammals. The fact that human *septum* doubled in size over that of great apes and probably their hominin descendants suggests that selection was hard at work enhancing in some way the emotions associated with sex. As noted in other chapters, some companionship relations between males and females can at times also develop, offering a clear target on which Darwinian selection could have gone to work. The *transitional formation* between the horde and nuclear-family-based hunting and gathering band might have looked something like the middle portions of Figure 6.2:

1. subgroups formed around male and female partnerships when females have offspring (whether or not the male is the father of offspring)
2. a bias for the males in the sodality to be male siblings and male friends, much as is the case among contemporary chimpanzees, but the relationships are sustained on a more day–to-day basis than among chimpanzees
3. males and their mothers, plus siblings with male siblings destined to become part of the sodality, while female siblings being a part of the sodality until they transfer from their natal community at puberty.

This structure begins the process of attaching adult females and males together for at least the critical periods of infant and juvenile offspring vulnerabilities to predation; and, once it provided fitness enhancement, Darwinian selection could continue working on the *septum* and any other neurological centers for male–female attachments. Thus, this transitional form is built from a conjugal pair bond of some sort, male fellowships, male siblings, and mothers of all or at least some of the males. It is a kind of kin-dominated band within which the beginnings of the nuclear family can be found.

We believe that this transitional form was built from Darwinian selection coming close to completing the emotional enhancement of interpersonal processes used by humans today to form relationships and bonds of solidarity. We would argue that this phase of structural evolution accompanied Darwinian selection's push on the tails of the bell curves describing the distribution of varying-sized neocortical structures to complete the dramatic increase in the size of the neocortex of *Homo erectus* to the lower end of the brain size of modern humans at around 1,000 to 1,250cc's, or perhaps a bit larger. At this point near the transition to *Homo sapiens*, a larynx-based spoken language with a grammar has been emerging and the capacity to develop arbitrary symbols carrying meaning began to lay down cultural codes among late hominins and early humans. Indeed, spoken language would be necessary among early humans if religion containing an articulated supernatural realm in which forces and beings announce and/or impose moral codes on persons was to evolve. Without this conception of the supernatural realm, religion could not be fully born. The transition was built upon the community complex and the enhanced sets of interpersonal processes described in Chapters 4 and 5 to forge stronger bonds; moreover, these bonds began to be represented in moral codes at about the time that powerful emotions of social control such as *shame* and *guilt* were becoming part of the neurology of the brain.

Each interaction became a lower-key, mini-carnival of emotional arousal and interpersonal rituals that reinforced a sense of "groupness" within larger community configurations (Goffman 1967; Collins 1975, 2004) and, as moral codes began to evolve, some would denote the sanctity and sacredness of group and community. The transitional form was a sacred thing to which obligations were owed; these obligations may well have been played out in rituals with a big "R" in relation to totems marking the significance, if not sacredness, of the subgroup and the larger community structure to which these subgroups belonged.

As Durkheim emphasized, sacredness is a property of religion, even though people can feel the same emotional experience toward objects that are sacred only to a single individual. What makes an object sacred in a religious sense is when it is deemed sacred by the community at large because religion is always a collective phenomena. Thus, a totem is an object symbolizing a group formation, and it can have very special significance and importance to people, which is why they totemized the group in the first place. When it is seen to have sacred qualities separated from the profane and mundane, then the totem takes on religious significance. Thus, the sacred is an extension of powerful emotions that humans can experience about *any* aspect of their environment, including themselves as objects, and they often symbolize these strong sentiments in totems. It is not a great leap from this capacity to viewing totems as sacred, as somehow special from the profane; and once this step is taken, totems become religious because they symbolize a special realm of reality, above and beyond the profane.

It is at this point, then, that notions of a sacred and new supernatural realm—above and beyond, and yet attached, to the community and its now more stable subgroups—began to be conceptualized by late hominins or perhaps only subspecies of early *Homo*. As the brain began to grow from the capacity to tag cognitions with a more complex palette of emotions, the more mundane complex of interpersonal practices described in the last chapter became fully operational in emerging human-like communities. Religion in the terms that we have defined it represented a response to Type-1 Spencerian selection pressures to regulate emerging family, group, and community relations, to regularize and stabilize reproductive units, to organize productive activities around hunting and gathering, and to provide a basis for the distribution of resources within and perhaps across groups within a larger community. At the same time, religion would meet many of the person-level needs of individuals for anxiety reduction in the face of the dangers of open-country niches (see Chapter 2 and the next chapter, especially Figure 7.1 on p. 151), to provide a basis in solidarity and community for identity verification, to give persons a sense of control and efficacy over their actions, and perhaps to meet other needs of a big-brained primate, wired to be highly emotional.

The Evolution of the Hunting and Gathering Band

The hunting and gathering band is a marvel of adaptation; and indeed, for most of human existence, it was the basic mode of adaptation in a wide variety of habitats. It consists of four or five nuclear families in a band that wanders a delimited territory with males coordinating hunting and females (often with offspring) gathering vegetables, tubers, fruits, honey, and other non-meat sources of food. Bands view themselves as part of a larger system of bands or band complex in a region; this system is probably an extension of the propensity to reckon the larger community organization, encompassing all of the elements of what we have termed the community complex. Most hunter-gatherer populations have some sense of supernatural forces, entities, and beings with the power to affect profane activities, but as emphasized earlier, there is considerable variation in how clearly demarcated the supernatural is from the profane and how the supernatural forces operate and affect daily life. The most minimal conception of the supernatural might be something as simple as ancestor worship, where dead ancestors are seen to inhabit another realm beyond the profane and to provide guidance for how people should conduct themselves (Lee and Daly 1999). These are not Big Gods, as some have argued (Norenzayan 2013; Norenzayan and Shariff 2008; Shariff and Norenzayan 2007), but smaller, less-coherent supernatural entities. Yet, whether Big or small, they are critical to social control and to the maintenance of the very simple systems of hunter–gatherers (Johnson 2014; Johnson and Kruger 2004), and they provide a platform on which more discrete views of the supernatural and the forces therein can be developed, *if* Type-1 Spencerian selection pressures intensify, as they surely did once hunter-gatherers began to settle into more permanent communities. The neurology had been put in place by natural selection to rewire hominins to become more social and to form the horde, and then sodalities in the transition to the hunting and gathering band.

What was necessary to make the hunting and gathering band viable? The answer to this question resides in what had to occur to make the nuclear family viable,[2] since the great ape ancestors of hominins naturally reckon larger community formations. The key was to create a more stable nuclear family as the *basic building block of these larger formations* (Turner and Maryanski 2005). How was this done?

1. Darwininan selection completed its work on the *septum* and other biopro-grammers for male–female bonding, while Type-1 Spencerian selection created pressures to somehow moralize through ritual "marriages" and equally important "divorces" (for still very promiscuous animals) so that families with offspring can assure that the offspring are protected. Thus, marriage and dissolution of marriages had to become institutionalized in moralized cultural codes, reinforced by rituals, and perhaps even sanctioned by supernatural forces (Deacon 1997b: 398–410).

2. Incest and the effects of inbreeding depression would be mitigated by the mother–son bioprogrammer that appears to be part of the primate line, and transfer of female offspring their bands at puberty to another

band or even another system of bands would mitigate against sibling and father–daughter incest (Turner and Maryanski 2008; Maryanski and Turner 2018; Durham and Wolf 2004).

3. If, however, siblings stayed together past puberty, two new potentially incestuous dyads in the nuclear family emerge when offspring stay in the kin unit past puberty: sibling incest and father–daughter incest.

   a. The father–daughter potential for incest is the most problematic and certainly was subject to Spencerian selection. A daughter in a family past puberty is not regulated by a bioprogrammer against sexual relations, because throughout the history of all great apes and early hominins, paternity has not been known because of promiscuity and, in any case, daughters left the community before a chance sexual meeting between a daughter and her father was likely. But, another adult female in the nuclear family is potentially disruptive, as it is in dysfunctional contemporary families where such incest occurs. Incest not only disrupts the dyads of the nuclear family; individuals sharing 50 percent of their genes produce inbreeding depressions that can be very severe. No doubt, among early hunter-gatherers where incest occurred soon recognized all of these problems and created the incest taboo, which we believe was created for the father–daughter dyad and then spread as the moral backup to the other two dyads where there are existing bioprogrammers for sexual avoidance (see Turner and Maryanski 2005 for a more thorough discussion).

   b. Siblings appear to reveal a bioprogrammer, first described by Edward Westermarck and labeled the "Westermarck effect" by Robin Fox (1980). Children who play together and engage in physical contact through "roughhousing" and other activities where there is physical contact when young, do not develop sexual attractions to each other when reaching puberty. Chimpanzees seem to reveal this same effect between opposite-sexed siblings, and it may have been in the ape line all along but not evident because of female transfer. If it was not in the ape line, then the effect is the outcome of Darwinian selection during the movement to the nuclear family, although in most hunting and gathering families, females are nearly adults by puberty and thus often leave the community, but some may stay as hunter-gatherers settled down, if only temporarily. However the Westermarck effect evolved, it is powerful, although in modern families with all of their pathologies (abuse, drug misuse, etc.), sibling incest may be as common or even more common than father–daughter incest. Still, among early hunter-gatherers, transfer of females coupled with the Westermarck effect was probably sufficient to stem inbreeding.

Constructing taboos against incest were perhaps among the first legislative acts among early hunter-gathering populations (Turner and Maryanski 2005). Taboos add power to morality because they indicate that which is *forbidden*, and once something is forbidden, it is necessary to enforce the taboo. Moreover, the notion of taboo, *per se*, invokes a sense of a higher morality, potentially mandated by forces in a supernatural realm. Still, this enforcement can be done by people themselves, or it can even be self-enforcement to avoid experiencing the new, perhaps uniquely human emotions of shame and guilt. Of course, it is very useful to invoke the power of supernatural forces to monitor and enforce taboos. Indeed, the taboo always takes on more power when seen as a mandate from the supernatural realm.

It is difficult to know just when taboos were put into place, because many populations studied by early anthropologists did not seem to have them because it was believed to be ludicrous that parents would mate with their opposite-sexed offspring or that siblings would seek a sexual relationship. The near universality of the taboo (at least in the nuclear family), however, except for the few exceptions that are often cited (Maryanski and Turner 2017), suggests that the taboo was needed, either because people were worried about incest or because they had seen its effects on deformed offspring from inbreeding depression, which is high once large and complex mammals share 25 percent to 50 percent of their genes. Durkheim argued that religion is related to what is taboo, but at the very least, religion is a powerful way to moralize a taboo and force people to abide by its mandates. Therefore, to the extent that early nuclear families in emerging hunting and gathering societies needed to forbid sexual relations among parent–offspring dyads or sibling dyads, these Type-1 Spencerian selection pressures were often met by legislating an incest taboo that was enforced by the supernatural.

Cultural Control and Religion

Once humans began to use culture and moral codes to regulate actions of persons in societies—at first nuclear families and bands and later communities of settled hunter-gatherers, horticulturalists, and pastoralists—social control was no longer completely based upon interpersonal sanctioning. Rules were created and enforced to regulate all of the potential fault lines in human superorganisms—production, reproduction, regulation, distribution, and human need-states (see Chapters 2 and 7)—and once social control relied, to some degree, on cultural rules, self-enforcement came with the emotions unique to humans (shame and guilt), external enforcement continued to come by virtue of interaction rituals but, now, increasingly from those charged with maintaining political control, and increasingly from the powers of sacred forces in the supernatural. Once religion became institutionalized under these selection pressures, it was then available to reinforce other cultural and moral systems in new, emerging institutional domains such as polity and law. With sufficient economic productivity, surplus production could be used to support new kinds of religious corporate units within a distinct institutional domain. Yet, as will be outlined in Chapter 9, there is an additional type of selection—*Type-2 Spencerian*, and, coupled with *Marxian selection* outlined in Chapter 10, selection became increasingly violent, as societies settled down and grew, and then came into conflict over resources. The evolution of religion became increasingly interwoven in political conflicts within and between societies—a fact of human social life that persists to this day.

Conclusion

Religion evolved as a byproduct of Darwinian selection working on the pre-adaptations and behavioral propensities of hominins listed in Tables 6.1 and 6.2. Yet, as this Darwinian selection ramped up all of the elements defining religious behavior, selection for more stable groupings within communities increasingly had an element of Spencerian selection in the transition from horde to bands composed of nuclear families. We have speculated on these transition formations by recognizing the biasing effects of the traits outlined in Tables 6.1 and 6.2, but for the nuclear family to evolve, non-Darwinian types of selection began to kick in, particularly Type-1 Spencerian selection. Here selection worked on the potential fault lines of a society organized around bands and nuclear families, creating normative taboos and other cultural systems to regulate social relations within and between nuclear families, as well as relations within and between bands. Many of these relations involved institutionalizing not only religion to add moral imperatives but also exchange reciprocities and considerations of justice that are part of the hard-wired behavioral repertoire of almost all primates and a good many higher mammals.

In the next chapter, we will turn to the first of the non-Darwinian selection dynamics: Type-1 Spencerian selection. This is the selection that finalized the transition to hunting and gathering that remained the primary adaptation of humans for at least 190,000 years, or longer if we push back *Homo sapiens* another 100,000 years. Once humans began to settle down into more permanent communities, however, other types of natural selection began to supplement Darwinian and Type-1 Spencerian selection. In the next chapter we will see how religion became institution-alized in human societies under both Darwinian and Spencerian Type-1 selection; and then we will explore how religion continued to evolve under Type-2 Spencerian, Durkheimian, and Marxian selection.

Notes

1   A gestural language like that used by the deaf is a true language, and it is far beyond the gestural language of hominins. Indeed, for a gestural language to have the complexity and specificity of spoken language, it is probably necessary to base it on existing spoken languages. What emerged among hominins was a gestural language that is very much like what humans can do when they turn off the sound on a video presentation among actors. To describe gods, forces, beings, moral codes, and other features of religion requires a language that can denote complex sets of symbols, denoting and describing in more detail a reality not directly observable. Such would be difficult to do with a sign language, unless it was based on an existing auditory (speech) language.

2   It is important to emphasize that even when other people are added, such as additional wives or husbands, the core unit is still the nuclear family of parents and their offspring. For a discussion, see the early data presented by George P. Murdock (1949: 1–23).

7
Type-1 Spencerian Selection
The Early Institutionalization of Religion

The importance of the study of hunting–gathering society comes from the fact that it is the key, not only to the formation of human society from sub-human primate society, but also to the evolution to a higher level of complex human societies.

Jiro Tanaka (1969)

Religion as a Byproduct or Spandrel?

The capacity for religion is an outcome of Darwinian selection on the anatomy and neuroanatomy of hominins to make them more capable of forming social bonds and group-level solidarities. Whether we want to call religion a byproduct or an outcome of selection for emotion-generating interaction processes that would increase group solidarities makes little difference. The critical point is that religion is possible *by virtue of these* Darwinian selection processes that (a) infused even more emotion into the community complex, (b) supercharged interpersonal dynamics so as to increase sociality, bonding, and group formation, and (c) provided the necessary emotional platform that would make growth of the neocortex among hominins fitness-enhancing (Turner 1996, 1997, 2000, 2002, 2008, 2010b).

The nature of religion as it has evolved has always been constrained by the behavioral capacities installed by natural selection, and one of the most obvious features of these properties is the *human capacity for agency*. Human action is teleological, directed at goals; and the units organizing human activities are also teleological, geared to organize persons into divisions of labor to achieve goals. Thus, once late hominins and then humans gained a larger neocortex, especially a rapid-fire prefrontal cortex that could make decisions by virtue of capacities to tag alternatives with more complex and nuanced emotional valences, the evolution of the social universe of humans became ever-more Larmarckian in this sense: late hominins and certainly early humans could create or acquire *new sociocultural characteristics*, independent of their morphology and neuroanatomy. Darwinian selection is always operating and can be thrown into full operation if the social environment of humans changed rapidly, as would be the case if a pandemic rapidly spread across Earth. Selection at the biological level could be very punctuated—on tail ends of distributions of immune systems, for example—but selection would also be on sociocultural formations, such as medical care systems that determine how many members of a society survive infectious diseases. A medical care system is an acquired sociocultural characteristic, and it is the product of a very different kind of evolution. Humans can now create and acquire through their capacities for agency new variations of sociocultural morphologies that can then be subject to selection. Many in biology prefer to focus on only one type of selection—Darwinian—but to understand the social universe we need to recognize that additional types of selection operate on sociocultural formations.

New Types of Selection Dynamics

In trying to understand how the capacities for religious behaviors first emerged, we have emphasized Darwinian selection on pre-adaptations and the interpersonal skills of hominins as well as the behavioral and cognitive capacities inherent in the community complex. These hominin traits were honed by Darwinian selection working on organic phenotypes, especially neuroanatomy. However, when we move to the question of why religion became *institutionalized* so early in the evolution of human societies, focus must shift to what we began to address in the last chapter as *Type-1 Spencerian selection* pressures (see Figure 2.3 on p. 28 and Figure 7.1 below). Type-1 Spencerian selection pressures push on populations to resolve particular adaptive problems for which there are *no existing sociocultural variants* capable of managing these problems. The pressure is on members of a population and the units organizing their activities *to create a new variant*, or suffer the disintegrative consequences, including not only death to the superorganism but also death to the organisms making up this superorganism.

Selection is thus on the superorganism and its integration of corporate units organizing human activity (see Figure 2.2 on p. 20). People and corporate units are put under pressure to find or create new variants that will enhance societal fitness, or die. Religion may have appeared in late hominins before nuclear families were created because there were selection pressures to find a new form of organization, above and beyond what some early social scientists (Bachhofen 1861; Morgan 1871; McLennan 1896; and Durkheim 1893 [1997]) speculatively portrayed as the primal

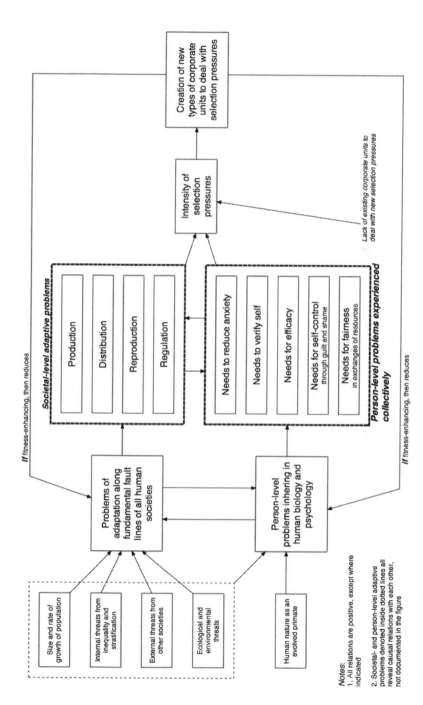

Figure 7.1 Spencer's Elaborated Model of Selection Dynamics, Type-1, as Affecting Evolution of Religion

"horde," which, as we outlined in Chapter 6, would be the *first new kind of structure* among evolving hominins beyond the weak-tie, fusion–fission groups within more stable communities.

The evolution of religion is seemingly tied to the first reorganization of the primal horde by Type-1 Spencerian selection pressures. Under these selection pressures, more stable and cohesive subgroups began to replace the purely fusion–fission pattern inherited by hominins from their great-ape ancestors. Then, from this more stable structural base, Type-1 Spencerian selection forged the most unlikely unit of all, the nuclear family (somehow derived from promiscuous ape-like hominins) that was then organized into bands of hunter–gatherers. These three stages of evolution of sociocultural formations were, in all likelihood, part of a co-evolutionary process (Durham 1991) revolving around Darwinian selection as it altered hominin and then human neuroanatomy and anatomy *and* Spencerian selection as it placed pressures on early social formations to become better organized. It is during this transformation of the horde to advanced hominins into bands of hunter–gatherers composed of nuclear family units that religion began to appear and, then, increasingly, became institutionalized as part of human superorganisms.

Our definition of religion as including the capacity to conceptualize a supernatural realm might disqualify some early bands of hunter–gatherers as not being religious, but if not, they were very close because ghosts, spirits, ancestor worship, and conceptions of dreamtime are, for us, the beginning of a conception of another realm beyond the human realm of day-to-day activities. As a consequence of diffusion or perhaps out of patterns of conflict and conquest among bands, religious-like sentiments were brought to those bands without a fully-realized institution of religion (as part of what we labeled in Chapter 2, *Type-2 Spencerian selection*). For, the pressure to create a more stable structure was thus realized among humans by the evolution of the nuclear family under Type-1 Spencerian selection; and as this structure was evolved, religion began to emerge among hunter–gatherer societies built from nuclear families in bands.

Once operating as a force, Type-1 Spencerian selection would continue to put pressures on human populations as they settled down into permanent communities and, as was often the case, began to grow the size of their populations. Such growth invited a new round of Type-1 Spencerian selection pressures to create new variants capable of organizing larger, settled populations. More permanent communities, political systems, law, and new technologies for economic activity all began to differentiate, with selection working to create new forms of religion that could manage each new level of complexity, as well as the fundamental human need-states to be outlined shortly. For those hunting and gathering populations that may not have had religion in their fully-institutionalized measure, their settled descendants soon created religion in response to intensifying Spencerian selection pressures. Religion thus became over time a universal across all human societies.

Spencerian Selection Dynamics

For the present, let us outline again the processes denoted by the label Type-1 Spencerian selection. By referencing Figure 7.1, it is evident that Spencerian selection pressures operate at two levels: (1) *person-level* pressures that, when viewed collectively, becomes population-level pressures generated by *the common needs* that all humans as evolved apes possess and (2) *corporate-unit level*, where selections for new types of corporate units to solve adaptive problems that all populations of humans confront: production, reproduction, regulation, and distribution. Let us begin with person-level pressures that, at the population level, exert constant pressure on the sociocultural formations that humans create.

Population-level Selection Pressures from Fundamental Human Needs

Darwinian selection over millions of years produced a more social and group-oriented ape through selection on subcortical and neocortical areas of the brain. In so doing, it produced new and complex capacities for forging social bonds through face-to-face interaction, while at the same time intensifying the power of the elements making up the community complex. By installing these neurological capacities, Darwinian selection did something else: it generated a new suite of selection pressures emanating from need-states generated by these new neurological capacities. For, when viewed collectively among all members of a population, these person-level needs become a subtle but *persistent* pressure on sociocultural survivor machines. A simple way to say this is that "human nature" or the capacities and behavioral propensities of evolved human neuroanatomy exert a *constant pressure on sociocultural formations* that, in turn, force actors to create new kinds of sociocultural formations to manage these pressures when existing formations are increasingly felt by people to be inadequate. What are some of these pressures? Below we enumerate some of the most important ones. These forces might be viewed as universal need-states of all humans (cf. Malinowski 1944) that are an outgrowth of what Darwinian selection accomplished in making humans more social (see also Turner 1987, 1988, 2002, 2007, 2010b).

Anxiety Reduction

One problem with dramatically increasing the capacities of hominins and then humans to be more emotional is the escalation of many types of anxiety, or general fear responses. Fear is an emotion inherited from the earliest mammalian descendants of the amphibious vertebrates that initiated the mammalian line. Fear is generated in the amygdala, which, as noted in Chapter 4, is twice as large in humans as in great apes, although most of this growth was devoted to increasing sociality, to assessing contexts, and to role taking. Nonetheless, the expansion of the emotional repertoire during hominin evolution assured that there were many ways to experience high levels of fear and anxiety. An emotionally charged, big-brained mammal with a large palette of emotions (see Tables 4.2, 4.3, 4.4 on pp. 87–90), coupled with a large neocortex that can store memories and download these into working consciousness, will be an anxious animal, especially given its acuity to role-take and assess context. Add to these sources of anxiety the fact that a large neocortex with a very fast processor in the prefrontal cortex can (a) remember the distant past where fear was generated and stored in memories and (b) ponder the distant future where fears about the unknown can easily be generated. Throw in the present, where at any moment interaction can be breached or new contingencies arise that force interpersonal adjustments that generate uncertainty and anxiety, and it is not difficult to see how big brains—already wired with a negative bias in humans' emotional makeup—could evolve to solve one set of problems about getting low-sociality apes more organized but, at the same time, generate a new set of problems revolving around fear responses.

Fear is primal and ancient, and it haunts humans constantly and exerts pressures to create new kinds of sociocultural formations to deal with it. One of these formations was religion, where ritual appeals to the power of sacred forces and beings in a supernatural realm could reduce fear responses because of beliefs in the capacity of these forces to intervene in the mundane, daily lives of humans. Rituals, per se, charge up positive emotions that push back on fear responses, and when rituals invoke beliefs in the powers of a sacred and supernatural realm to help persons deal with their negative emotions, the effect is calming. As easy as hunting and gathering lifeways appear to have been in increasing fitness of hominins and then humans, this early "garden of Eden" was not without fears. Therefore, it is not surprising that one response of early humans and perhaps late hominins was to begin to institutionalize religion or, at a minimum, three of its key elements: (1) a community that could organize (2) emotion-arousing ritual appeals to (3) the forces and beings of a supernatural realm. We should emphasize that while elements (1) and (2) were evident very early in hominin evolution, because they are clearly evident in chimpanzees today, element (3) depended upon the capacity for speech. It may be that there could be "sense" of another realm or something beyond the local community, but for there to be a true supernatural realm, individuals need to vocalize about it. Since finely articulated speech only appears to have emerged around 200,000 years ago, conceptions of a supernatural may have been unique to later *Homo sapiens* (Enard et al. 2002a, 2002b), who first evolved 300,000 years ago; and especially since *Homo sapiens* appear to have existed in Africa some 300,000 years ago. Thus all elements of religion have only come with the transition to *Homo sapiens*. Yet, it is certainly possible that late *Homo erectus* could have had a sense of another "realm" of reality and could have articulated this sense in a more primitive proto-language of some sort, since their brains were in the lower range of *Homo sapien* brains. More importantly, perhaps, late *Homo erectus* was probably in the process of acquiring enhanced oral capacities as the vocal track was in the process of being expanded, and Broca's hump was evolving into Broca's area, thereby allowing for cruder forms of speech production. Something very like religion may have already existed in the final transition of hominins to *Homo sapiens* (Geertz 2013).

A few hunting and gathering bands may also have had shamans or specialists to direct ritual appeals to the supernatural, but most religion among nomadic hunter–gatherers was likely practiced within kin and band structures without mediation by religious specialists. Cult structures with specialized religious practitioners did not fully emerge until hunting and gathering populations settled into communities[1] led by Big Men, or actual horticultural communities led by chiefs and paramount chiefs (Wallace 1966; Johnson and Earle 2000; Turner 1972, 1997, 2003; Turner and Maryanski 2008). In any case, by the time that settled hunter–gatherers appeared, all of the basic elements of religion—including the beginnings of cult structures revealing a division of specialized labor for religious practices—were either fully in place or falling into place by virtue of Type-1 Spencerian selection. Then, over the next millennia, as they became larger and more complex, religion became ever-more institutionalized as a differentiated and somewhat autonomous institutional domain from kinship, economy, polity, and other institutional domains.

Needs to Verify Self

Efficacy is always relevant to animals that have the capacity to see themselves as objects in the environment and to evaluate this sense of self. The number of distinctive identities among hunter–gatherers was probably much less than today in complex societies where identities can be tied to all-important roles that individuals play and all social categories to which they may belong (e.g., gender, ethnicity, age, religious affiliation). Still, the basic need to see self in a positive light and to experience verification of this sense of self by others is as old as humanity and perhaps as old as hominoids. Indeed, the basic capacity to see self in relation to others and, in all likelihood, also to evaluate self is probably as old as the great-ape line, certainly with the last common ancestor to hominins and orangutans some 13 to 16 million years ago, and probably even older. Few animals can see themselves *vis-à-vis* other objects in their environment (Gallup 1970, 1979, 1982, 2014), but the few that can do so—e.g., whales, dolphins, and elephants—probably also have needs to experience positive emotions about self (Whitehead and Rendell 2015). Religion can provide this sense by giving humans ritualized procedures for appealing to supernatural forces to, first of all, give individuals approval and, secondly, to allow others to see them in a positive light.

A very large neocortex can store many memories of how others have responded to self, and some of these memories can be negative and thus activate anxiety about self. Therefore, once an animal possesses the capacity to see and evaluate itself and to experience chronic anxiety, there is a focal point of this anxiety: the self. Indeed, when self is codified into a series of identities, humans can evaluate themselves as anxious or calm, which is a whole new level of reflexive cognitive ability that most mammals do not possess. Moreover, this reflexivity can be augmented by new layers of emotions revolving around the evaluation of self in terms of how anxious or calm the person is. People can be ashamed of being fearful or anxious, and ashamed of being ashamed, thereby adding to their woes and feelings about themselves (Scheff 1988). One antidote to this potential spiral of anxiety is to see self as fulfilling the moral mandates of religious beliefs and, thereby, pleasing the supernatural forces monitoring conformity to these beliefs. Approval from gods provides an increased sense of self-worth and self-control, while reducing anxiety.

Self-Control

Late in hominin evolution or, perhaps, only with the emergence of *Homo sapiens*, the emotions of *guilt* and *shame* evolved (Turner 2000). Great apes do not experience shame and guilt (Boehm 2013), and so these emotions emerged during late hominin evolution as the emotion centers and the neocortex began to grow toward the human measure. Such emotions can only have power with an animal capable of viewing and evaluating self as an object in relation to moral beliefs (guilt) and expectations of others (shame). These emotions evolved to reduce the need for external control and negative sanctions from others, which would arouse negative emotions of anger, fear, resentment, and sadness that, in turn, would disrupt social relations.

Shame arises from perceptions of not meeting the expectations of others, and guilt comes from a sense of violating moral codes, with these second-order elaborations of negative emotions (see Table 4.4 on p. 90) having even greater power when conformity to these expectations and moral codes is monitored as sanctioned by supernatural forces. When externalized control from others is shifted to self-control by persons themselves, negative emotions do not affect the collective whole but only the person who becomes highly motivated to reduce the pain associated with shame or guilt. Once humans possessed the capacity to experience these second-order elaborations of the three negative primary emotions (see Table 4.4), these emotions can generate selection pressures for religious beliefs and supernaturals who can evaluate individuals; in this way, the burden of sanctioning is shifted from conspecifics to supernatural others lodged in each person's religious beliefs about the supernatural. The result is that social control by conspecifics is reduced and given over to the powers of the supernatural, thereby converting social control to motivations of individuals to appease the supernatural. Even if others still directly sanction a person and invite negative emotional responses from this person, these others can also make reference to moral codes and expectations enshrined in beliefs about the sacred and supernatural, thus deflecting some of the negative reaction a person might have to these others to an evaluation of self by the beings inhabiting the supernatural realm. The burden of social control is thus increasingly placed on the person, and the relations of persons to supernatural forces.

Needs for Efficacy

Humans have the propensity to develop attributions for who and what is responsible for their experiences and, thereby, to make determinations as to whether self, immediate others, situational constraints, social structures, or supernatural realms are responsible for their experiences. Attributions may be part of what might be seen as a basic need for efficacy, where one can have some control over one's actions. Control of one's fate, however, is never easy; and so, this need for efficacy was probably much like anxiety and encouraged humans to use their powers to reconsider and think about causes of events and, then, to make use of beliefs in the powers of the supernatural to "manage" these events. By attributing to the supernatural the power to affect daily life, rituals directed at the supernatural could increase people's sense of control of their environment and their world.

Needs for Fairness/Justice in Exchanges of Resources

One of the most powerful forces, inherited from both monkeys and apes, is the propensity for primates to calculate justice in exchanges of resources (Brosnan and de Waal 2003, 2014; Brosnan et al. 2002; de Waal 1989, 1991, and 1996). In fact, it can be argued that this is one of the fundamental need-states driving human action and responses to others; and, as we will see in Marxian selection, it is one of the driving forces that makes individuals willing to initiate violent conflict against those who are perceived to deny them access to valued resources.

In some ways, religion re-balances the scales; and the world religions such as Islam and Christianity offer a fairer "new life" after death, which is of course why Marx saw religion as an opiate of the masses. Indeed, most of the religions that would become world religions offered a clear promise to re-balance the scales of justice in a "new life" *if* individuals followed the moral codes of religion in the present life; it is for this reason that they tended to out-compete polytheistic religions through Durkheimian selection.

Thus, these and perhaps additional need-states exert pressure on societal structures and their culture when large numbers of individuals are experiencing similar arousal of need-states and experiencing deprivations that stir intense emotions. These collectively experienced need-states become societal level need-states, putting pressure on societal-fault lines, particularly over the distribution of resources and regulation by centers of power. Indeed, it is the way that societies have organized along these societal-level fault lines that typically arouses or mollifies the negative emotions associated with failure to realize these fundamental human need-states. At first, religion operated within kin corporate units and bands to meet these need-states, but eventually as religion became more institutionalized, the new types of corporate units that were created to deal with all types of selection pressures, both those inhering in the human psyche and in larger, more complex sociocultural formations.

Selection pressures to institutionalize religion increased once humans developed the following triggers: the capacity to experience diffuse anxiety in the present and from the past into the future; the need to view themselves as in control of their fate (as excessively teleological creatures); a sense of self as an object elaborated into identities monitored by the gods; emotions such as shame and guilt evolved to dilute the raw power of sadness, fear, and anger and convert this power into the emotions of self control (i.e., guilt and shame). The concentration of power and expansion of inequalities violated humans' basic need to perceive fairness in exchanges. Religion reduces anxiety, even as it often increases the anxiety to be reduced by ritual appeals to the supernatural; it offers a platform by which to see and evaluate self, converting external control from conspecifics to supernatural forces that demand self-control by each individual. In so doing, individuals ironically gain some sense that they have control of their immediate world, even as the sacred world dominates their thoughts and actions. Religion offers the reality or, more likely, the hope of a fair and just existence in the future.

Religion could evolve quite naturally and easily in a mammal that already possessed the community complex, and then, as selection expanded older subcortical and neocortical regions of the hominin brain to be more emotional and more intelligent, conceptualizing a supernatural realm would eventually become possible. As interpersonal behaviors increasingly involved rhythmic synchronization and emotional entrainment to forge stronger social ties (see Figure 6.1 on p. 132), this animal would be on the verge of being religious. As a spoken language facility increased, conceptions of the supernatural, its inhabitants, and its morality could be articulated into beliefs about the powers of the supernatural. Thus, it is not much of a step for such a big-brained and emotional animal, whose neurology is already biased by the community complex, to use these same interpersonal processes to develop solidarities with powerful beings and forces in a sacred and supernatural realm. Ritual appeals to the supernatural would represent just *another form of interaction* that arouses emotions and that bonds persons to "others" but, in this case, the others are sacred and especially powerful. Therefore, if religion is not seen as a by-product of interpersonal dynamics, then it can be seen rather easily as a solution to adaptive problems created by individuals in societies as they sought some relief from the negative emotional states that they must experience by virtue of how their brains are wired.

Selection Pressures from Sociocultural Formations

There is a limited number of fault lines where selection pressures build up in human sociocultural formations—or, for that matter, in all super-organisms. As these pressures increase, they force members of a society to innovate and develop new kinds of corporate units and their attendant cultures, or face the disintegrative consequences. The rather minimal sociocultural formations of hunting and gathering—i.e., nuclear families in small bands—would not seem so complicated that they would generate selection pressures along these fault lines. However, we must remember that groups, *per se, are not easily forged among evolved apes.* They take constant monitoring and interpersonal work to be sustained and reproduced over time. True, the emotional and cognitive systems of humans make them possible, but almost any group forged by humans is rife with potential problems because of their ape ancestry as rather low-sociality animals with a proclivity for fluid social formations. To now expect an animal like an evolved great ape to live out its life in groups may not be as simple as it seems, especially an animal that has dramatically enhanced emotions. Indeed, we need only look at the problems that contemporary families have, or work groups, and in fact just about any group that we can imagine, to recognize how precarious most groups are. They are often rife with conflict and tensions because the emotions that bind people to each other and to the group have a dark side: negative emotional arousal that can drive people apart, often with considerable violence.

Moreover, even the most minimal social structures and cultures are only sustained by very complex interpersonal processes that are fraught with potential problems among big-brained, highly emotional animals. The result is that even small and simple sociocultural formations generate Type-1 Spencerian selection pressures from *regulation* as a fault line in all patterns of human social organization.

Furthermore, given that nomadic food collectors worked so hard to repress inequalities in power and prestige (presumably because of the tension and conflict that these can generate), regulation could not come from power and authority, as it would with the evolution of more complexity. Thus, the dilemma of how to regulate emotions and make culture more powerful may have been very real, thereby generating Type-1 Spencerian selection for increased regulation without giving other humans power. One path would be to give the beings and forces in the supernatural realm what they already possessed in the minds of individuals: the power to intervene in the mundane world. These are powers that require ritual observance and conformity to perceived moral demands; and so, even with a simple band social structure, selection pressures emanating from regulation may well have been rather intense—thus forcing the institutionalization of religion as the likely "next structure" to evolve as societies grew more complex but, among hunter–gatherers, as a structure whose sometimes vague pantheon of supernatural forces and beings, along with their moral codes, had to be obeyed, or else. Thus, unlike the Big Gods hypothesis (Norenzayan 2013), little gods or even forces not fully anthropomorphized can have commanded obedience and can be seen to monitor whether or not people have obeyed a moral directive (Johnson 2005, 2009, 2014; Johnson and Bering 2006; Johnson and Kruger 2004).

Giving Values Extra Power

Even a simple society like hunting and gathering has some abstract moral codes that individuals are expected to follow. In smaller groupings, it is relatively easy to monitor the conformity of others and even to sanction them negatively for non-conformity to moral codes. But monitoring and sanctioning are costly in terms of people's energy and the emotional costs when forced to administer negative sanctions, and a small grouping of persons can easily be disrupted by these efforts of external social control. This is, no doubt, why the emotions of shame and guilt evolved to convert external control by others to self-control by self. It is then but another short step to transfer more of these control functions over to the supernatural, especially in light of the fact that religion is already revolving around the person-level need-states summarized earlier. If moral codes are specified by the supernatural, if conformity to these codes is monitored by forces and beings in this supernatural realm, and if failure to abide by codes is sanctioned negatively by the "gods," then the power of cultural codes and the likelihood that they will be obeyed is increased.

Big-brained animals that live in communities rather than local groups can begin to see self in relation to the broader community, thereby liberating them from the immediate "here and now" of relations with conspecifics; some, like chimpanzees, appear to celebrate their sense of community in carnival-like behaviors. Selection on this community complex of late hominins like *Homo erectus*—now endowed with a larger neocortex and palette of emotions—might have allowed late hominins to have perhaps vague conceptions of a realm away from the mundane world and, possibly could even have led them to vague perceptions of a supernatural realm inhabited by forces with special powers. Such conceptions, whenever they first emerged, would reduce the social control burdens on conspecifics by creating an ethereal "police force" of "supernatural cops" that could monitor and sanction. With the late evolution of shame and guilt, the social control burden is further shifted away from conspecifics to ritualized interactions with the gods of the supernatural realm.

Social control in small bands would seem to be easier and not require intervention of the supernatural, but we must always remember that groups are jerry-rigged sociocultural constructions by evolved apes. They are not "natural," only "necessary" for survival. Negative sanctioning and the negative emotional reaction to such sanctions can immediately disrupt solidarity, at a moment's notice. For example, by examining the positive arrows in Randall Collins' views of the dynamics of interaction rituals in Figure 6.1 on p. 132, just one negative signed arrow can cascade across the positively signed arrows to blow apart the episode of interaction and reduce solidarity. All human sociocultural formations are vulnerable in that way because of the need to use emotions rather than hard-wired bioprogrammers to forge strong bonds, perhaps with the exception of the mother–offspring bond, which is as close to a social bioprogrammer as humans can get. To avoid blow-ups in interactions with conspecifics, then, sanctioning by outsiders like the supernatural forces of a sacred realm removes much of the burden of social control from conspecifics to control by gods. Self-control by those who fear the power of the gods and who experience shame and guilt when they disappoint the gods deflects negative emotions away from the fragile sociocultural constructions of humans. It is entirely possible that shame and guilt co-evolved with religion.

Reinforcing Norms

Much of the same argument above can be made for the power of religious beliefs and supernatural agents monitoring and potentially sanctioning individuals. Key norms of the kinship system composed of nuclear families must overcome ape promiscuity, while norms on band-level rights and responsibilities must overcome ape individualism. Such norms are more effective if imposed by supernatural forces, monitored by inhabitants of the supernatural realm or its agents in the secular world, and, if necessary, sanctioned by them. Indeed, if the supernatural is doing the monitoring, there is "no place to hide," as can persons in the mundane world. The forces of the supernatural can potentially be all-seeing, but equally important little gods or even vague forces can do the same. Furthermore, the supernatural can not only see all actions but can penetrate thoughts and motives as well. The beings of the supernatural realm know if a person has been sincere or cynical in conformity to key norms guiding kin, economic, and band activities. Thus, even as individuals may monitor and sanction, they have "backup" in the powers of the supernatural, thereby making less necessary the need to engage in potentially disruptive monitoring and sanctioning by mortals in the mundane world, especially since individuals are still always trying to see themselves in a positive light from the evaluations of the supernatural that are not only watching them but sensing what they think and feel. It should not be surprising, then, that shamans would emerge early in sociocultural evolution and with the first religions in some cases because the shaman is, at one and the same time, a diagnostician of the problems that a person faces and a clinician who can suggest ritual remedies to these problems. Still, among nomadic hunter–gatherers, other forces would have to be in play to invoke the big gods. For example, Inuit hunter–gatherers confront danger because of their ecological location, and they form larger semi-permanent settlements to ride out winters. We might expect their gods to have more powers in contrast to hunter–gatherers in more predictable and less extreme ecologies.

As members of nomadic food-collecting bands work very hard at minimizing inequalities and keeping any one person from gaining power over others, religion would not be necessary to legitimate inequalities and concentrations of power because much of the sanctioning in bands addresses this topic of keeping anyone from thinking that they are "better than others." Still, it is very likely that nomadic hunter–gatherers settled in communities for a time, initially only periodically but eventually more permanently. Once settlement occurs, bands often grow and begin to feel the pressures from regulation as a Type-1 Spencerian selection pressure. The result is for political leaders like the Big Man of settled hunter–gatherers to now own all of the productive outputs of the village, although this same leader is often required to redistribute these outputs in prestige-bestowing ritual ceremonies. Thus, inequalities in material things, power, and prestige that nomadic hunter–gatherers sought to avoid will quickly make their entrance into small-scale societies and become part of all societies that eventually evolved from this small sociocultural base. Religion itself can be seen as a pre-adaptation that can be quickly used to legitimate inequalities in material well-being, power, and prestige; or it can also be viewed as a force that allows it to occur without dramatically disrupting the society. Indeed, it is likely that, if religion did not already exist, it might well have had to be invented under Type-1 Spencerian selection pressures in order to keep settled populations from disintegrating from the pressures of increased regulation, production, and distribution. Religion, beliefs in supernatural powers, and rituals directed at these powers can all be quickly adjusted to deal with inequalities, making it seem as if leaders have the blessings of the supernatural while, at the same time, monitoring leaders, such as Big Men, by even Bigger Gods in the supernatural realm to assure that political leaders do what is best for society—whether or not this is factually the case.

Illustrative Data on the Institutionalization of Religion under Type-1 Spencerian Selection

Bushmen Hunter–Gatherers

Although the Bushmen are genetically among the oldest people on Earth (Wells 2002: 56f.), the details of their cultural evolution are complex because of a variety of factors during the past. There is disagreement on whether the prehistoric Bushmen were hunter–gatherers or pastoralists. The evidence seems to support the former (Biesele and Royal-/O/OO 1999: 205). The basic structure of their society is the family and the band; sometimes a group of families would reside near each other for a while, thus functioning at a level between the family and the band. Bands would get together, especially during drought periods, into larger groups around the more permanent water sources, thus forming band clusters or "big bands," such as the !Xō (Guenther 1999: 24). Because of changing circumstances, their society, according to anthropologist Mathias Guenther, was and is flexible, adaptable, diverse, fluid, amorphous, ambivalent, and ambiguous (Guenther 1999: 13). The mainstay of their society and religion, however, is the "foraging ethos" or "foraging ideology," by which the "fluidity of Bushman religion is an ideological counterpart to the fluidity of Bushman society" (Guenther 1999: 5). This fluidity is evident in relation to marauding outsiders. Thus, for instance, the Nharo in the Ghanzi District were organized during the late 18th and early 19th centuries in a centralized, feudal state-like system under the leadership of an autocratic war-chieftain who led hundreds of well-armed warriors against black African intruders. With the influx of Europeans during the latter half of the 19th century, they were again reduced to small groups due to "encroachment, encapsulation, enserfment, labor exploitation," and disease (Guenther 1999: 19). Depending on the fluctuations of the environment, Bushmen maintain their hunting ethos, but organize themselves in whatever way necessary under Type-1 Spencerian selection pressures.

The Ju/'hoansi of Botswana and Namibia are a hunter–gatherer people in the Kalahari who subsist on over 100 edible plant species including staples such as the mongongo nut. Two-thirds of their diet is vegetable foods collected by the women and one-third meat hunted by the men, who hunt some 55 animal species (Biesele and Royal-/O/OO 1999: 206; Biesele 1993). They live in small settlements of 15–50 persons and come together with other groups during the winter close to permanent water sources. Land is owned collectively by male and female kin, and they maintain gender egalitarianism (Biesele and Royal-/O/OO 1999: 207). There is a great deal of family group and band movement due to the vicissitudes of resources; thus, groups can enter the territories of other groups by permission and use their resources, which subsequently can be reciprocated as the environment changes (Guenther 1999: 26). Although men and women each have their own subsistence roles, there are no strict gender codes for men and women in relation to their roles. Women can help in the hunt just as they also can dance with the men if they so choose. Men can also help in gathering plant foods, housework, child-rearing, etc. In other words, contrary to most other parts of the world, women and men are not restricted by gender taboos (Guenther 1999: 27).

Politically, the accruement of wealth and status is abhorred. Anger, resentment, and jealousy are repressed, whereas sharing and equality are encouraged (Biesele and Royal-/O/OO 1999: 208). The Bushmen deliberately counteract any attempts at self-aggrandizement. Excessive hunter's pride, arrogance, and self-importance would immediately be reprimanded (Katz 1982b: 347; Guenther 1999: 34). Indeed, they practice the "exchange of arrows" based on the idea that the meat belongs to the owner of the arrow and not to the hunter who had actually killed the animal (Platvoet 1999: 23). Sharing is paramount: "The essence of this way of life is sharing. The hunting band or camp is a unit of sharing and if sharing breaks down, it ceases to be a camp" (Lee 1979: 118). Reciprocity is further emphasized by the gift-giving of food surpluses and handiwork, thus increasing social capital and strengthening bonds within wider social and trading networks (Platvoet 1999: 23). This sharing and foraging ethos can lead to tension and conflict; however, this often finds release in games, humor, moral exhortation, "complaint discourses," chants, and the all-night *n/om* dances (Guenther 1999: 36–37, 157). It would be a small step for these to take on a highly religious character, if tension or conflict became too great.

A number of writers have noted the role that discourse plays in alleviating tension and potential conflict. The forms taken are various but their function is clearly similar to the Inuit "song fights" or the Yanomami "war games." Africanists Jiro Tanaka and Kazuyoshi Sugawara note in their work on the /Gui and //Ghana of Botswana:

> Micro-political processes within a camp were closely articulated with the peculiar organization of everyday conversation. All sorts of conflict continue to be incessantly argued about and criticized in informal talk studded with unique interactional or rhetorical devices such as simultaneous discourse, redundant narrative, and direct quotation of past speech. Such openness of discussion is backed by the belief that hiding anything is an abominable vice which will extinguish the community.
>
> (Tanaka and Sugawara 2010: 197–198)

Guenther noted that "talking" between two or more people is engaged with "much zeal and zest, lustily and argumentatively, as a cherished pastime and as something of an art form" (1999: 34). He continues: "They may be subtle and discreet, consisting of spoken or sung monologues, or of dialogues—in earshot of the party at whom they are aimed, forcing him or her into such response-ploys as the 'forced eavesdrop' or 'auditory withdrawal'" (1999: 34–35). The backdrop of such discourse is humor and laughter, as between joking partners, but the underlying message is tense and sometimes leads to rage and occasional violence. Guenther described the exchange of raging insults between two Nharo men that attracted a large group of people. As the men exchanged insults, the crowd either repeated the insults even more exaggeratedly than the contestants or laughed inappropriately at them. After a while, the situation was so hilariously absurd that the two contestants rushed "toward each other, bent over and eyes streaming with laughter, to slap each other on the shoulder" (Guenther 1999: 36). If these various methods do not help, people just leave (Guenther 1999: 38).

The Ju/'hoansi speak of a creator god called ≠Gao N!a, a trickster deity called //Gauwa, and the spirits of deceased kin (//gauwasi). Interestingly, they believe that death and evil were created by ≠Gao N!a and that misfortune is sent by //Gauwa and sickness by deceased kin. Thus, in contrast to just about every other religion in the history of humanity, the Ju/'hoansi do not attribute death and misery to some fatal mistake made by humans in primordial times. Furthermore and, again strikingly, they do not share the common belief that evil and sickness are caused by human witches. There are examples, however, of Bushmen who upon becoming farmhands for their non-Khoisan neighbors, actually take on witchcraft ideas (Platvoet 1999: 32, n. 165). They do not normally use magic in hunting, healing, protection, or war. Nor are there cultic rituals to the dead or the gods (Platvoet 1999: 33). The only religious ceremony they perform has the sole purpose of healing members of the group by absorbing and casting out the pathogenic arrows and objects sent by the gods and deceased kin (Platvoet 1999: 39; Katz 1982b: 349).

Although capricious, ≠Gao N!a created everything including social institutions and cultural practices. The trickster, //Gauwa, however, is central to Bushman religion because he embodies the ambiguity in Bushman mythology and cosmology. Guenther claimed that the trance dancer is the ritual equivalent of this ambiguity as well (Guenther 1999: 4). The trickster is startlingly multifarious in name, appearance, identity, age, gender, and behavior. His ambiguity extends to ontological, moral, social, and physical domains. He creates, destroys, and subverts beings, things, rules, and categories (Guenther 1999: 101). He mostly transformed the flux of primordial chaos into present-day order; and besides, tales about him are enormously entertaining.

The trance-curing dance, Guenther noted, can be regarded "as a more or less overt device for ludic conflict resolution" (1999: 37). Psychologist Richard Katz noted that the dance's "'synergistic' performance has a Durkheimian, morally integrating effect that can soothe tempers and tension" (Gunther 1999: 37; Katz 1982a: 35, 54–55). Katz gives a precise description of the dance:

> The central event in the healing tradition is the all-night dance. Four times in a month, on the average, the women sit around the fire, singing and rhythmically clapping as night falls, signaling the start of a healing dance. The men, sometimes joined by the women, dance around the singers; the entire village participates. As the dance intensifies, *n/um*, or energy, is activated in those who are healers, most of whom are among the dancing men. As *n/um* intensifies in the healers, they experience an enhanced consciousness called *!kia*, during which they heal all those at the dance. The dance usually ends before the sun rises the next morning. Those who are at the dance confront the uncertainties and contradictions of their experience, attempting to resolve issues dividing the group, reaffirming the group's spiritual cohesion. They find it exciting, joyful, and powerful. "Being at a dance makes our hearts happy," the !Kung say.
>
> (Katz 1982b: 347–348)

The boiling of energy can be painful and dangerous. Furthermore it intensifies the emotions, whether positive or negative, not only of the dancer but also of the other participants, thus a clear example of Durkheimian effervescence. Novices must be carefully supervised because of fear and pain and changes of consciousness. Those who can control the *!kia* gain clairvoyance and can see not only the pathogens in people's bodies but also the spirits and gods with whom they argue, harangue, plead, and struggle (Katz 1982b: 349–350). This remarkable ritual of ecstatic experience is not directed at the supernatural world. Furthermore, although it may outwardly look like spirit possession, it is not. Gaining *!kia*, however, allows practitioners to counter the harmful deeds of the spirit world for the good of the social group. In a true egalitarian spirit, *!kia* is not restricted to a few specialists.

Despite the incredible diversity and history of the Bushmen, the seductively unavoidable impression we get is that Bushman religiosity reflects a primordial form of religiosity that existed before agriculture literally changed everything. Indeed, some argue that the ancient Bushman rock art with its elegant illustrations of the hunt and dance are graphic illustrations of the *n/um* dance and the *!kia* experience (Platvoet 1999: 9–11; Lewis-Williams 1990).

Iglulik Hunter–Gatherers

The Danish-Greenlandic scientist-adventurer Knud Rasmussen cited in his *Intellectual Culture of the Iglulik Eskimos* the following quote from one of his informants: "We do not believe, we fear." Anua, the local shaman near Cape Elisabeth in the northeasterly region of arctic Canada, after mentioning all of the things that they fear, concluded:

> Therefore it is that our fathers have inherited from their fathers all the old rules of life which are based on the experience and wisdom of generations. We do not know how, we cannot say why, but we keep those rules in order that we may live untroubled. And so ignorant are we in spite of all our shamans, that we fear everything unfamiliar. We fear what we see about us, and we fear all the invisible things that are likewise about us, all that we have heard of in our forefathers' stories and myths. Therefore we have our customs.
>
> (Rasmussen 1929: 56)

What is it that they fear? The forces that influence their everyday lives. "You see," Anua said, "All our customs come from life and turn towards life." But what forces have such power over their lives? The weather spirit, the Mother of the Sea animals, the evil spirits and spirits of the dead, and witches and evil shamans that cause sickness and death. They fear the souls of the dead and the souls of the animals that they kill. In order to pacify these creatures and forces, the Iglulik have developed very strict rules of behavior, taboos that regulate all aspects of life. Taboos regulate most significantly relations between men and women and between humans and animals. The rules are especially harsh concerning the relations between women and animals of the hunt, perhaps because men and women each have their own cycles—men protect and kill, women produce and give birth. These cycles must not come into contact with one another.

When taboos are broken, the spirits and forces become angry, the animals thus stay away and people starve. In order to placate the forces behind this, the shaman must perform séances during which he discerns the causes of the calamity—most often broken taboos—and then performs the rituals necessary to re-establish harmonious relations between humans and supernatural beings. Taboos are rules of personal norms that have very concrete social consequences. Menstruation, miscarriage, and childbirth are under very strict rules. While menstruating, the woman must remain in the house so that no animal of the hunt can see her. Miscarriage is surrounded by extreme measures: if a woman has had a miscarriage, everyone in the house must throw away all of the house contents. Thus, under such circumstances, women are not motivated to tell anyone. So, Iglulik society has developed special procedures when illness strikes or the animals of the hunt are scarce.

When game is scarce, the shaman must hold a séance for the whole village in order to travel in spirit to the Mother of the Sea, who out of anger keeps the animals at bay. It is a dangerous trip for the shaman and is filled with high drama in the darkness of the snow hut or in the house, during which the inhabitants clearly hear his helping spirits and strange noises from dreadful monsters that hang around the edge of their reality, held in check by the shaman's helping spirits but waiting to grab anyone foolish enough to come near them. The inhabitants are clearly frightened, and they sing songs to help the shaman on his way and to find his way back as well as to maintain their own sanity. When the shaman returns, accompanied by dramatic breathing and other fearful sounds, he tells about his dangerous journey and how he found the Mother of the Sea in her house, angered by the mess and stink of human misdeeds and offences littered in her house and her long, tousled hair filled with the foulness of broken taboos. The shaman had to clean her house and comb her hair and placate her so that she would release the animals.

Then the shaman initiates a ritual exchange with the inhabitants by saying, "I have something to say," and they reply in unison, "Let us hear, let us hear," after which he says, "Words will arise." Everyone knows that taboos have been broken, and the phrase "words will arise" signals that they must all confess individual breaches of taboo, real or imagined, one after the other. If anyone is not attending the séance, they are called in to come and confess. These confessions are accompanied by weeping, shameful tears, mournful exclamations, and abject posturings. Once the confessions have ceased, then the shaman announces that the game has been released, and everyone becomes filled with joy, and the men go confidently out to hunt (Rasmussen 1929: 124–129).

Thus, through fear and guilt, collective norms are enforced and rituals are performed that at the same time increase stress and guilt but also decrease fear and insecurity. The communal rituals of confession transform anxiety to joy, release, and common purpose, thus increasing the group's chances of survival in a harsh environment. But this emotionally stimulating ritual can also lead to negative results because the participants also reveal secrets that can easily lead to suspicion, jealousy, accusations of witchcraft, and violence that split the community with feuds only resolved by one of the parties leaving the area (Mary-Rousselière 1984). Weakened communities can in such circumstances simply die out.

If we compare the elements listed under societal and person-level selection pressures in Figure 7.1, it is clear that they are pushing on the Iglulik population, especially compared to the Bushmen who use ritual not always attached to a notion of the supernatural to meet Type-1 selection pressures. Part of the difference is the nature of the ecology between the two populations; another part may be the incredible flexibility of the Bushmen in adapting their sociocultural formations to changed environmental circumstances, including in-migrations from other regions. Their ability to stave off potential group disintegration through stereotyped speech-forms and, of course, the highly ritualized trance dance may have served as an anxiety-deflecting mechanism while at the same time reducing the need for more complex conceptualizations of the supernatural world. Although acknowledging the supernatural world, their rituals are used to counteract the harmful effects of supernatural creatures rather than placate them. More explicit religion comes with problems of regulation and with anxieties, with the result that the Iglulik reveal more elements of religion than Bushmen, and use religion in response to Type-1 Spencerian selection. In fact, a more complete comparison among hunter–gatherers living in diverse habitats, including sociocultural habitats, would probably reveal large differences in the degree to which these diverse populations evidence all of the elements of religion, including a vision of the supernatural inhabited by forces and beings. The more difficult the adaptation to their diverse ecology of various hunter–gatherers, the more evident is religion and the more explicit is the pantheon in the supernatural, and the greater are the powers contained in the forces and beings of the supernatural. The earliest hunter–gatherers in a world with, at best, six million humans would be under less pressure (although some have the figure as low as one million humans), unless adapting to a difficult habitat, and so, religion would be rudimentary much like that among the Bushman who probably are under far greater pressure today and in the recent past (with European contact and population growth) than they were several thousand years ago. Religion is beginning to become institutionalized, with a shaman intermediary, for the Iglulik, and probably much earlier because of a difficult ecology that generated more intense selection pressures on a less flexible band structure.

The Transition to Non-Ethnic Types of Religion

It may appear odd at this point to jump from Bushman and Iglulik hunter–gatherers to the sixth century BCE and onwards to the emergence of early Christ-religion (at this time and during the subsequent at least two centuries still an intrinsic part of Judaism). There are, however, two good reasons for this transition. First, we want to demonstrate a point that permeates all of Bellah's work on cultural evolution, namely that "Nothing is ever lost," at least nothing decisively (cf. Bellah 2005, 2011b). By making this maxim a fundamental tenet of his thinking, Bellah stressed the fact that every new formation in the history of religion is not only built upon but is unthinkable without the vestiges of previous forms of religion. Second, the emergence of Axial age types of religions and their subsequent dissemination to considerably larger segments of a population as, for example, in the spread of Buddhism under King Ashoka (268–239 BCE) and the formation and rapid expansion of early Christ-religion patently demonstrates the importance of Type-1 Spencerian selection.

We will return more thoroughly to the concept of Axial age religion in Chapters 8 and 9, but briefly the term refers to a religious transition around the sixth century BCE on the Eurasian continent. These changes occurred in China in the Far East, where religio-philosophical movements arose beginning with Laozi and subsequently with figures such as Confucius, Xunzi, and Mencius. On the southern part of the continent, a similar development took place with the transition from the Vedic literature to the Upanishads, the emergence of Siddhartha Gautama, the Buddha to be, and the rise of the three great trajectories of Indian religiosity, the two non-Brahmin religions Buddhism, Jainism, and that comprehensive and manifold phenomenon we traditionally name Hinduism. In Israel the emergence of the prophetic literature and not least the appearance of wisdom literature in such works as Job and Ecclesiastes testify to a parallel development. Furthest in the West, a comparable development took place with the pre-Socratic philosophers, Socrates, Plato, and Aristotle, and the subsequent development of the four major Hellenistic religio-philosophical schools, Stoicism, Skepticism, Epicureanism, and Cynicism. As a reaction to prior ethnic and archaic religions, these types of religions focused on individual salvation and were trans-ethnic as well as universalizing.

How does Axial age religion exemplify Type-1 Spencerian selection? This form of religion arose on the Eurasian continent during a time of never before seen large-scale groups, such as highly populous cities and mega-empires (cf. Henrich 2016; Turchin 2016). This population growth called for new forms of religion establishing norms and systems of reward and sanctioning that would enable considerably larger communities to endure without falling victim to social corrosion and cultural dissolution. The appearance of Axial age religions is a vivid example of how religion became available to reinforce other cultural and moral systems in new, emerging institutional domains such as polity and law. Early Christ-religion clearly evinced an axial religion belief system, but did not have the social complexity that would eventually characterize axiality. Although the first small Christ-religion communities that struggled for existence played out on the tail end of the Roman Empire, we can clearly see how Spencerian Type-1 selection put pressure on the first Christ-religion communities.

An obvious example comes from the earliest texts that we have from formative Christ-religion, the letters of Paul. His letters typically comprise two major parts that are closely interwoven. The first part expresses central elements of his religious worldview relating to the specific situation of his intended audience. The second part comprises earnest religious-moral advice as an admonishing example of the behavioral implications of the first part (Petersen 2005; 2012).

In chapter four of his earliest letter, 1 Thessalonians, Paul admonishes his recipients to excel in ideal behavior towards in-group members. At the same time, they should demonstrate their ethical superiority in the eyes of outsiders, thereby drawing the latter to Christ-religion:

> As for brotherly love, there is no need to write to you about that, since you have yourselves learnt from God to love one another, and in fact this is how you treat all the brothers throughout the whole of Macedonia. However, we do urge you, brothers, to go on making even greater progress and to make a point of living quietly, attending to your own business and earning your living, just as we told you to, so that you may earn the respect of outsiders and not be dependent on anyone.
> (4:9–18, Bible translation from The New Jerusalem Bible)

In the following chapter, Paul proceeds to emphasize how the day of the Lord will come as a thief in the night. The threat is obvious. There is a continuous balance between evoking emotions of fear, on the one hand, and happiness and a sense of progress, on the other, both intimately related to notions of divine retribution and reward:

> It is when people are saying, "How quiet and peaceful it is" that sudden destruction falls on them, as suddenly as labour pains come on a pregnant woman; and there is no escape. But you, brothers, do not live in the dark, that the Day should take you unawares like a thief. No, you are all children of light and children of the day: we do not belong to the night or to darkness, so we should not go on sleeping, as everyone else does, but stay wide awake and sober. Night is the time for sleepers to sleep and night the time for drunkards to be drunk, but we belong to the day and we should be sober; let us put on faith and love for a breastplate, and the hope of salvation for a helmet. God destined us not for his retribution, but to win salvation through our Lord Jesus Christ, who died for us so that, awake or asleep, we should still live united to him. So give encouragement to each other, and keep strengthening one another, as you do already.
>
> (5:3–11)

It is clear that Paul (as well as other promoters of early Christ-religion) was in the process of creating a new community, institutionalized with new rules instituted to enforce and regulate all of the potential fault lines in human superorganisms. Paul's letters exemplify how, once social control relies, to some degree, on cultural rules, self-enforcement comes with the human emotions of shame and guilt. They also demonstrate how external enforcement was performed by means of rituals charged with maintaining political control and involving representations of the sacred powers of the supernatural. Two examples will suffice to make the point.

In his First Letter to the Corinthians from around 50 AD, Paul publically castigates a member of the community for having had an illicit sexual relationship with his stepmother. The details of the case are unknown, but there is no doubt about the outcome of the incident. This sexual culprit was to be expelled from the community. In fact, the text is a case of ostracism in which Paul by means of a well-known ritual metaphor from the Hebrew Bible, and closely connected to the Easter festival, claims that if the community does not drive out the wrongdoer, they will themselves as well as the community become contaminated and impure. Although physically absent, Paul is, by means of the spirit, present in the community when they make their decision. Paul's spiritual presence together with the invocation of the power of the Lord and the presence of the Spirit at the event imbues the policing with strong representations of superhuman enforcement.

It is widely reported that there is sexual immorality among you, immorality of a kind that is not found even among gentiles: that one of you is living with his stepmother. And you so filled with your own self-importance! It would have been better if you had been grieving bitterly, so that the man who has done this thing were turned out of the community. For my part, however distant I am physically, I am present in spirit and have already condemned the man who behaved in this way, just as though I were present in person. When you have gathered together in the name of our Lord Jesus, with the presence of my spirit, and in the power of our Lord Jesus, hand such a man over to Satan, to be destroyed as far as natural life is concerned, so that on the Day of the Lord his spirit may be saved. Your self-satisfaction is ill founded. Do you not realize that only a little yeast leavens the whole batch of dough? Throw out the old yeast so that you can be the fresh dough, unleavened as you are. For our Passover has been sacrificed, that is, Christ; let us keep the feast, then, with none of the old yeast and no leavening of evil and wickedness, but only the unleavened bread of sincerity and truth.

(5:1–8)

Our last example of Spencerian Type-1 selection in the context of Axial age religion also comes from Paul. In another passage in 1 Corinthians, he condemns how social differences in the community had led to a division between the affluent and the poor during the communal ritual *par excellence*, the Lord's Supper. The wealthy in the community had turned the ritual into a demonstration of their superiority, thereby annihilating not only the meaning of the ritual but also the impact of Christ's death:

for when the eating begins, each one of you has his own supper first, and there is one going hungry while another is getting drunk. Surely you have homes for doing your eating and drinking in? Or have you such disregard for God's assembly that you can put to shame those who have nothing? What am I to say to you? Congratulate you? On this I cannot congratulate you.

(11:21f.)

Strengthening the rhetoric, Paul proceeds to recount the basic wording of the ritual and, then, moves on to claim that the many ill, weak, and number of dead in the community is an indication of their contempt for the ritual

(11:30). To the extent that they do not change behavior, they will eat and drink their own condemnation (11:29–34).

Paul's letters, as well as numerous other texts of early Christ-religion, take up the central issues relating to Spencerian Type-1 selection: social regulation with respect to production, reproduction, regulation, distribution, and human need-states. His letters patently demonstrate how shame and guilt as well as praise and recognition are used in order to obtain desired social effects. They vividly document how external enforcement is performed by means of rituals charged with maintaining political control and involving strong representations of supernatural powers involved in the rewarding and punishing of the community. Finally, they testify to a form of religion in which *askēsis* in the basic meaning of training has come to encompass all aspects of life. Parallel to Pierre Hadot's idea of ancient philosophy as a way of life (*une manière de vivre*), this form of religion made extreme demands on its followers.

Conclusion

In sum, while most of the points that we have made in this chapter have long been a part of sociological explanations for the origins and persistence of religion, we have extracted and recast them from their functionalist origins into a view of selection processes—thereby making them more compatible with modern evolutionary theorizing. In this way, the insights from functionalism are retained but they are now couched in the language of evolution that maintains the emphasis on selection but also recognizes that selection in sociocultural systems is different from Darwinian selection when examining the evolution of superorganisms rather than organisms. Much sociobiology and evolutionary psychology implicitly tries to sustain a Darwinian view when, in fact, superorganisms operate under different mechanisms than organisms. Superorganisms may have some of the same kinds of adaptive problems as organisms, as Herbert Spencer ([1998] 1874–94) emphasized in his organismic analogy or as living systems theory (Miller 1978) did more recently, but the selection dynamics involved are very different. These selection pressures do not blindly select existing variants of social structures but, instead, force actors to create new structures and cultures because existing variants of corporate units and their cultures cannot solve adaptive problems. Evolution thus becomes more Lamarckian-like than Darwinian. Still, it *is* selection to which human actors can respond by creating new sociocultural variants—like religion—that can manage these pressures; and the evolution of each institutional domain in human societies—kinship, economy, religion, polity, law, education, medicine, sport, art, etc.—evolved initially under such selection pressures.

In Darwinian selection, organisms are locked into a phenotype and underlying genotype, essentially waiting for mutations and gene flow to add new variants across generations that could then be selected upon. In contrast, humans and the corporate units organizing their activities have the capacity to innovate, borrow, or steal new cultural and structural phenotypes. While existing sociocultural formations can exhibit inertial tendencies that make it difficult to respond to these selection pressures, thereby decreasing sociocultural fitness, humans can still break through these inertial tendencies and create new types of sociocultural formations that evolve into the institutional domains that represent the strongest pillar on which societies—simple or complex—are built.

Yet, there is the third type of selection—*Durkheimian selection*—that has always driven the evolution of any institutional domain, once established under Type-1 Spencerian selection pressures. This type of selection is more Darwinian, although the objects of selection are not individuals and their underlying phenotypes and genotypes but, rather, "corporate units" and their cultures. But the dynamics of such "group selection" or, more diplomatically, multi-level selection are decidedly Darwinian in at least a metaphorical way, although these can also be Spencerian as well.

Note

1 Settled hunter–gatherers typically create communities near water—oceans, lakes, and rivers—and thus can fish. They also begin to domesticate animals and sometimes plants. These populations typically grow larger, thereby forcing the emergence of differences of power, or the first political systems.

8

Durkheimian Selection
The Social Ecology of Religious Evolution

[It] is inevitable that organs similar to one another come into contact,
embark upon a struggle and try to substitute themselves for one another.
Émile Durkheim (1893[1997]: 211–212) on the causes
of societal differentiation or "social speciation"

Basics of Organizational Ecology

The third selection process driving the evolution of religion is ecological. Religious organizations or cult structures can always be conceptualized as populations of such structures seeking resources within various types of resource niches. Religious cult structures vary along a number of dimensions: beliefs about the nature of the supernatural, divisions of labor within cult structures that vary along such dimensions as size and degree of hierarchical organization, leadership within and across the cult structures of a particular religion, ritual practices directed at the supernatural within and outside of cult structures, as well as other demographic characteristics, such as the socio-economic status of their members. When looked at from an ecological perspective, religious cult structures compete for a variety of resources within the broader niche created by those seeking commitments to religious beliefs, rituals, and community. Important sub-niches within the overall niche in which cult structures compete for members include: members from varying demographic and socio-economic backgrounds; material and financial resources from donations and dues on members; political resources from those with power in the community and at the societal level; ideological resources that can make the beliefs more attractive to potential members; organizational resources such as technologies; resources for marketing religious beliefs and rituals; human resources as volunteers and professional incumbents in the division of labor of the cult structure; and virtually any other resource that can be used to sustain cult structures and, if desired, expand their community, beliefs, and ritual practices.

In contrast, the Darwinian imagery applied to superorganisms that was presented in Figure 2.5 on p. 37 undergirds Durkheim's and all contemporary analyses of the ecology of corporate units in differentiated societies revealing markets, quasi-markets, law, and relatively stable polity. In Figure 8.1,

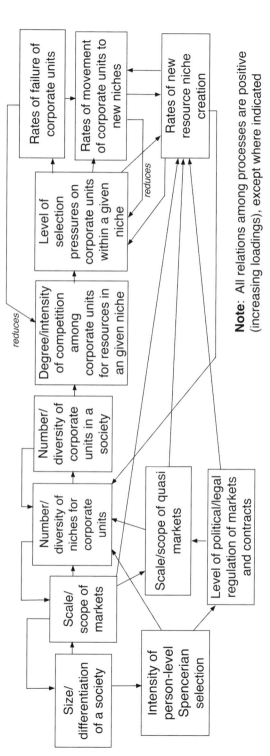

Note: All relations among processes are positive (increasing loadings), except where indicated

Figure 8.1 Elaboration of Durkheimian Selection Model

we draw out the Darwinian imagery in Durkheim's model and add variables that affect the selection dynamics that can be drawn from organizational ecology.

In organizational ecology (e.g., Hannan and Freeman 1977, 1989; Hannan and Carroll 1992; Hannan, Polos, and Carroll 2007), populations of organizations are defined as organizations that exist within the same resource niche. Organizations that enter a niche are considered successful, or "fit," when they can secure resources and become templates or models for other organizations subsequently entering the niche. As new organizations enter the niche, the density among organizations increases; with increases in density, competition for resources escalates. As a niche reaches its carrying capacity, selection intensifies, with those organizations unable to secure sufficient resources dying off or, as Durkheim (1893: 266) emphasized, using their capacities for agency and, thus, moving to another existing niche or even creating a new niche. The typical life cycle of organizations entering a new resource niche is for there to be a dramatic overshoot of the capacity of the niche to support all organizations with the result that, as competition and selection increase exponentially, unfit organizations die out. Thus, once organizations are initially successful in a niche, populations of organizations in this niche grow rapidly but, as the carrying capacity of the niche is reached and then surpassed, a large die-off of unfit organizations leads to a very rapid decline in the overall number of organizations in the niche. Just as the initial growth in the number of organizations overshoots the carrying capacity of the niche, so the die-off undershoots its carrying capacity, with the result that, after unfit organizations have died off, the number of organizations that can be supported is far below its carrying capacity. One consequence of this undershoot is a second upward swing in the population of organizations but, this time, organizations are more mindful of the limited nature of resources in the niche. Hence, the new growth is neither as fast nor as steep as the initial growth of the population of organizations during the early days of niche exploitation.

Organizations can adopt a variety of strategies to survive in a resource niche. One is to specialize in a sub-niche within the larger niche by remaining relatively small and focused, and most importantly, these organizations are able to adjust rapidly to cycles and fluctuations in the type and level of resources available. Specialists tend to evolve in niches where there are frequent changes in the total resources available. The opposite strategy is to become a large organization in a niche, exploiting all of the sub-niches within it. This strategy works best when the cycles of fluctuation are steep and of longer duration; with the ability to exploit all sub-niches, larger organizations can ride out long downturns much better than smaller specialists because they can keep a flow of at least some resources from the niche moving into the organization. When cult structures organize for more violent forms of competition, however, they initiate more Marxian selection processes (see Chapter 10); and while elements of Durkheimian selection persist, the overall nature of selection shifts to destroying the institutional systems (e.g., polity, law, and markets) that constrain Durkheimian selection.

Unlike Marxian selection, the Durkheimian selection now theorized by contemporary organizational ecology assumes that organizations are making goods or providing services in markets, which *institutionalize the competition* among organizations in various niches. This institutionalization typically comes from polity and law as institutional domains, as well as from market mechanisms. For organizations that are not in an explicit economic market, however, some conceptual adjustment needs to be made, and this is the case with religious organizations. For example, a society may have only one dominant religion legitimating centers of power and, in return, is protected and subsidized by the power of polity, as is the case in Denmark or Italy. At times, this domination is so great that the only way an alternative religion can emerge is to seek power, turning ecological competition into a religious movement and Marxian selection (see Chapter 10). However, as we emphasized in Chapter 2, in societies where there is competition among cult structures, they are often in *quasi-markets* with market demands generated by various economic and demographic subpopulations seeking religious involvements.

In these quasi-markets, where money is somewhat secondary to recruiting memberships (who then donate or pay dues to the organizations that recruit them), cults compete for members and other resources that allow the cult structure to sustain itself. There is not an explicit market or pricing mechanism in the competition among cult structures, but the ability of a cult to sustain itself by recruiting members becomes a good proxy for fitness, and indeed, money from worshipers is typically exchanged for piety/sacredness/salvation that is bestowed on members by cult structures in exchange for their commitment to beliefs, willingness to engage in rituals, and of course, to contribute money, time, and energy to sustain the cult structure. Those cult structures that can survive over long periods of time and gain members can therefore be defined as the most fit because they not only gain members who contribute material resources, they also typically have been successful in gathering other types of resources. The more resources a cult structure can secure *vis-à-vis* the competition, the more likely it is to be able to sustain itself and, indeed, attract members to its community of believers and ritual practices directed at the supernatural.

Like any organization in a dense niche with increasing competition, cult structures specialize in how they are organized and the kinds of beliefs and rituals that they employ to attract and keep members, and thereby secure additional resources. In societies like the United States, where there are many different types of denominations of Christians, the organizations of various denominations compete over how evangelical they are, along with other considerations such as conservative or liberal social and political beliefs and demographics of their members (by age, ethnicity, social class, levels of education, etc.). In the United States, for example (see later discussion), more evangelical cults sustain themselves better than traditional protestant cult structures (e.g., Presbyterians, Methodists, Episcopalians), but all religious organizations are, to a small and persistently increasing degree, losing out in competition with non-religious organizations and the moral order that they establish (McCaffree 2017; Zuckerman 2016). In other societies, different patterns prevail; these patterns are affected by beliefs and rituals, recruiting abilities of organizations, political connections, and increasingly in the world today, how willing organizations are to use violence to achieve political ends as they recruit members who can also become quasi-militaristic forces, thus increasing the level of Marxian selection on the world scene.

In order to recruit members, cult structures must offer a set of beliefs about the supernatural, ritual practices, a community of believers, and an organizational structure that individuals find appealing. Much like more purely economic organizations, religious cults tend to pursue somewhat different strategies, with some being large and others specialized within the same basic niche composed of persons seeking religion. In order to be successful in the competition, cults must develop belief systems that, as noted earlier, resonate with members' own moral beliefs and their person-level psychological needs (installed by Darwinian selection in the human genome). They must also engage in ritual activities that correspond to potential members' comfort levels in arousing emotions and invocation of the supernatural forces. Additionally, they must have leaders in the division of labor of cult structures that can emotionally reach potential members. In societies without a state-sponsored religion, the number of religious organizations in competition can be quite large, especially in societies where markets and quasi-markets are well institutionalized and where the population is diverse by ethnicity, social class, levels of education, regional variations, levels and types of urbanization, immigration rates, and other forces that increase the diversity of potential members in the general resource niche composed of all those seeking to join a community of worshipers. Moreover, in democratic societies, the resource niche for religion can be quite large and differentiated, unless one cult structure dominates and is supported by the state. Rapid social change that increases individuals' level of anxiety is also likely to see new cult structures entering a religious niche for those seeking religion. Indeed, as is emphasized in Figure 7.1 on p. 151, person-level needs (e.g., for anxiety reduction, efficacy, verification of self, fairness in exchange) create a large set of potential resource niches, especially if quasi-markets are well institutionalized and supported by polity and law.

McPherson and colleagues (McPherson 1983a, 1988; McPherson and Ranger-Moore 1991; McPherson and Rotolo 1996) have applied organizational ecology models to voluntary associations and sodalities, such as service clubs. The more general model as it has unfolded is useful in examining religious organizations. These possess some of the properties of service clubs in that individuals voluntarily join them, although religious cults are often forced upon people by virtue of their families' religious affiliation, by the state, or some other powerful party. Still, the general model can be useful in examining the ecology of religion. McPherson and Ranger-Moore (1991) have a general conception of a society as a distribution of persons and perhaps families in what they term *Blau-space* in honor of the sociologist, Peter M. Blau (1977, 1994). Individuals in a society are almost always categorized by what Blau termed "parameters," which can be *nominal* and discrete (e.g., ethnicity, gender) by virtue of the fact that a person is either in or not in a particular category, or *graduated* (e.g., level of income, amount of education), in which parameters vary by degree, although graduated parameters are often converted into nominal categories (i.e., rich, poor, educated, uneducated). A society as a whole, therefore, is a space in which individuals are distributed into categories that are often differentially evaluated (rich are more valued than the poor, as are the more educated compared to uneducated). Of course, any given individual can belong to many different categories, as is the case of a rich male, who is highly educated, and who reveals a distinctive ethnicity/race.

Religious affiliation can also be a nominal parameter, as is evident by Jewish, Christian, and Islamic factions. Each of the categories in Blau-space can be visualized as a potential resource niche in which religious cult structures recruit members. Even religious points in Blau-space can involve competition for members, as is the case when Christian cults—Catholics vs. Protestants, or factions or denominations within each—compete with each other, or when a growing religion like Islam recruits members from potentially diverse cult structures as regular members or as members of extreme cults like ISIS. Alternatively, cults may specialize and seek particular points in Blau-space: white-suburban-affluent points to a mega-church, poor ethnic minorities to a storefront Protestant church in the ethnic ghetto, working-class persons to Catholic churches in urban areas, angry youth in urban or rural areas to branches of Islam, and so on.

Figure 8.2 represents an adaptation of McPherson's ecological model. As populations grow, they differentiate, creating more niches in Blau-space. Like all organizational ecological processes, the success of organizations increases the number of corporate units entering any given niche, which, in turn, increases density, competition, and organizational failings. For example, as mega-churches increased and caused density in the resource niche of affluent, mostly white, lifestyle oriented Christians in the United States, some of these churches began to fail, as was so dramatically illustrated by one of the founding organizational forms, the Crystal Cathedral in Garden Grove, California backed up by its media outlet "the hour of power." Others sustained themselves by recruiting from new places or nodes in Blau-space, thus decreasing homogeneity among members of a corporate unit. All of these mega-churches in the United States have cut significantly into traditional protestant denominations because of their more dramatic rituals and staging of religious rituals, forcing some churches to consolidate and/or recruit new categories of persons and families in Blau-space.

These person-level need-states and the emotions surrounding them can serve not only as resource niches but can also become the driving force for social movements in general and religious movements in particular. People who have experienced negative emotions and have grievances against the existing system of institutional domains, particularly the economic and political, and who have faired poorly in the stratification system distributing resources unequally, can become part of the more general mobilization in social movement or even revolutionary organizations seeking change. Thus, as is so evident in many parts of the world today, religious social movements form around grievances generated by people's emotions, typically negative emotions that can be mobilized for conflict. Often these religious social movements seek not only to dominate within the religious institutional domain but also to dominate other institutional domains as well. The competition evident within the ecology of religious organizations can thus escalate to conflict, often violent, over which religious cults and beliefs are to dominate within a society; since such conflicts are always highly moralized, they do not lead to moral compromises but, instead, to moralized violence. We thus need to add to any view of the ecology of religious organizations an additional set of generalizations that are part of a larger social movement for change in the institutional structure and culture of a society. For this reason, we have isolated two additional types

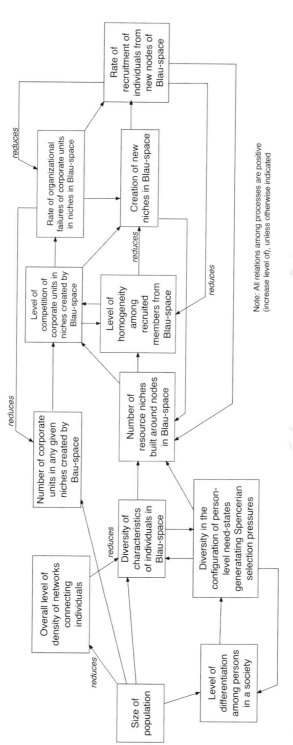

Figure 8.2 Adaptation of McPherson/Ranger-Moore Model of the Ecology of Blau-space

Note: All relations among processes are positive (increase level of), unless otherwise indicated

of sociocultural selection—Spencerian Type-2 and Marxian selection—to be examined in the next chapters.

Robert Wuthnow's Ecological Analysis of Cultural Ideologies

Three decades ago, Robert Wuthnow (1987) sought to generalize a theory about dynamics among religious denominations to a new level of abstraction, where emphasis is on the evolution of "moral orders," with religion being one of the more prominent of such orders. In developing this theory, Wuthnow develops a theory of Durkheimian selection by borrowing from the human ecology models, especially models of organizational ecology.

A moral order persists because the organizations in which particular ideologies develop are able to secure resources in competition with other organizations engaged in the same activity. Success or "fitness" of an organization and its moral order are related to (a) the flexibility of moral codes, (b) the nature of rituals used to dramatize these codes and, thereby, to reinforce commitments to a particular ideology, (c) the institutional environments in which variations in moral codes are generated, and (d) the level of resource mobilization by, and competition among, organizations engaged in producing these variations in moral codes.

Moral Orders and Ideological Production

A moral order is composed of moral codes that define commitments to a particular course of behavior, which can be viewed as divided into three distinctive components or "dualities": (1) moral objects vs. real programs, (2) core self vs. enacted roles, and (3) inevitable constraints vs. intentional actions. These dichotomies of a moral order become enshrined in ideologies or evaluative beliefs about what is right, proper, and good. While religion is one of the most prominent of organizations generating moral orders through sets of religious beliefs and rituals, it is not the only such organization in complex societies. Indeed, all social movement organizations, whether religious, political, or economic, are positing an ideology signaling a particular kind of moral order. Similarly, corporate units in almost all institutional domains—kinship, economy, polity, law, science, education, etc.—reveal ideologies framing a moral order for corporate units within these institutional domains and often for the entire institutional domain. These moral orders point to and dramatize collective values of the society as a whole, and in so doing generate more specific ideologies that reveal moral codes revealing the three dualities noted previously. Let us begin with the key properties of these moral codes.

The Structure of Ideologies and the Moral Order

(1) Moral Objects vs. Real Programs

The ideologies defining a successful moral order distinguishes among (a) "objects of commitment" and (b) activities or "real programs" in which the commitments are realized. There is, of course, a connection between the objects of commitment and the behaviors that individuals emit to demonstrate this commitment, but at the same time, there is some autonomy between (a) and (b). A moral order can only be effective when it connects objects of commitment and real programs to demonstrate and reinforce this commitment, while at the same time not welding the two tightly together. For instance, commitment to a particular set of religious beliefs and the symbols marking these beliefs is realized by sets of ritual activities signifying adherence to these beliefs, thereby demonstrating commitment, but there is a flexibility in how these programs play out and a certain degree of separation between the two. Only in this way can a moral order evidence the flexibility to persist over time under changing conditions.

(2) Core Self vs. Enacted Roles

Moral codes, Wuthnow argues, must distinguish between (a) a person's real or "core self" about who they are and (b) the various types of "roles" that they must play in complex societies. Moral codes allow persons to evaluate self and moral worth of their behaviors, but at the same time these codes allow individuals to see "the real me" as distinct from the roles that one is often forced to play and the roles that can compromise this sense of self. In this way, individuals can sustain or verify their core sense of self as a moral self, even as they must play roles that are not wholly consistent with this sense of self. For example, people can be "forgiven" if some activities do not fully support their moral self, as long as they also play roles and engage in rituals reinforcing religious beliefs that partially define the real and moral self. Without this flexibility, individuals would be confined to a limited number of roles to demonstrate their piety, or they would constantly feel guilt and shame for having to play certain roles in complex divisions of labor.

(3) Inevitable Constraints vs. Intentional Actions

Moral codes must distinguish between (a) those forces that are out of people's control and (b) those that they can control. Moral codes thus emphasize those behaviors and actions that people can control, evaluating such behaviors in terms of their conformity to the dictates of an ideology, while forgiving or suspending evaluations of those actions that are not under individuals' voluntary control. Without this distinction, it would be difficult to know what kinds of behaviors of individuals are to be subject to moral evaluations. If all behaviors are subject to moral evaluations, individuals would feel constantly guilty for acts not under their control, thereby making a moral order impossible to live in, particularly in complex societies where individuals must engage in a wide variety of actions in roles and positions of organizations or corporate units within diverse institutional contexts.

Wuthnow emphasizes that these elements of a moral order produce binary oppositions that facilitate individuals' commitments to a particular ideology, such as a set of religious beliefs, while at the same time enabling them to engage in actions that are required within the institutional systems of a society. Thus, by (a) enabling individuals to connect objects of worship marking religious beliefs with real programs of behaviors that can be separated by other programs of behavior in non-religious domains, (b) allowing persons to retain a core self and moral self as they must engage in actions that do not fully live up to these senses of self, and (c) by separating behaviors that are not under volitional control of persons, the ideology of a religious moral order gives individuals flexibility and allows them to avoid the demoralization, guilt, shame, and other negative emotions that would come without this flexibility. It is this flexibility in how individuals are evaluated from the perspective of moral codes that enables a moral order to sustain itself, especially in societies where there is a great deal of competition in moral orders within religion as well as between religion and organizational systems in other institutional domains.

From the perspective of Type-1 Spencerian selection, religious cults that develop flexibility in their codes and ritual practices to meet them are more likely to have integrative consequences for a society because individuals will maintain their commitments to societal values by virtue of ritualized behaviors directed at totems marking the ideologies drawn from these values. In this way, institutional commitments become commitments to the society in which these develop. Moreover, allowing individuals to verify their core self, and indeed, to moralize this sense of self, even as persons must play roles not totally in-sync with this self, fulfills the most important need-state that individuals possess. At the same time, the need for a sense of efficacy and anxiety reduction is also met, thereby providing a basis for further commitment to institutional systems.

The Nature of Ritual

Rituals directed at moral objects allow individuals to dramatize collective values and commitments to ideologies incorporating these values. They heighten emotions and facilitate definitions of one's true self as moral, one's actions as moral, and one's moral actions as under their control. In so doing, very fundamental need-states of individuals can be realized, such as the need to verify self, to feel some sense of efficacy, to be part of an important collectivity, to feel that self, roles, and moral commitments are congruent and consistent, and to reduce uncertainty, especially in a complex social world. These are, as referenced in Figure 7.1 on p. 151, very much like most of the need-states that have driven Type-1 Spencerian selection. Thus, moral orders, including religious orders, that allow individuals to meet these fundamental human need-states are more likely to attract adherents to moral codes and the rituals that demonstrate commitment to these codes than those religions that are too rigid and inflexible. In the long run, such religions will generally "lose out" in the dynamics of Durkheimian selection, especially in societies revealing institutional systems that constantly produce ideological variations.

Wuthnow's theory is most applicable to more differentiated societies allowing some choices in not only religious commitments but also commitments in other institutional domains. Indeed, the model of organizational ecology works best in societies that institutionalize competition in markets and quasi-markets, such as those that allow individuals to choose their religious affiliations among competing cult structures. In Wuthnow's model, then, meeting basic and fundamental need-states of individuals, while also providing some sense of embeddedness in and commitment to ideologies and societal values, can be marketed by cult structures in a variety of ways. Those cults that can present themselves as able to meet needs for self-verification, efficacy, and anxiety reduction, coupled with a sense of contributing to the overall integration of society, will gain members over those that cannot as effectively market their package of cult structure, ideologies, and rituals directed at these ideologies.

Institutional Context, Ideological Variation, and Selection among Moral Orders

Moral orders in highly structured, if not repressive, societies that do not change or reveal much innovation can often sustain inflexible moral orders because they do not generate much ideological variation. Even with less flexibility where there is little competition from other moral orders and cults, a dominant moral order will not, in the long run, sustain legitimacy or endure, if ideological codes do not facilitate the ordering of moral objects/real programs, self/roles, inevitable constraints/intentional control of acts. If these codes cannot consistently inspire individuals to engage in communicative acts and, most importantly, collective and individual rituals to objects symbolizing the moral order, the stability and legitimacy of a moral order will be problematic. Indeed, the Reformation that introduced Protestantism into the Catholic moral order in Europe is an example of what can occur; once Protestant denominations proliferated, they were in a state of Durkheimian selection not only with Catholicism but with each other as well.

Moral orders will change with the evolution of a society's institutional systems, and, indeed, such change inevitably leads to the production of new ideological variations. Societies where change causes the production of new ideological variations generally reveal markets and quasi-markets for distributing resources, including symbolic resources. Moreover, they often evidence some degree of political democracy or at least tolerance of some differences; and they have laws limiting the powers of political and religious actors. Yet, even when these conditions are not fully realized, religious revolts can emerge—e.g., as noted earlier, the Protestant Reformation—when they order *objects/real programs*, *self/roles*, and *constraints/options* that allow individuals to meet fundamental human needs in response to constant Spencerian selection pressures that always push on sociocultural formations. Furthermore, if effective and emotion-arousing rituals can dramatize these more flexible codes, if individuals can engage in communicative acts in support of these codes, and if codes reduce risks, anxieties, ambiguity, and unpredictability in life, then individuals will be attracted to such moral orders, even under high degrees of political constraint and control by state-sponsored religions.

The level of ideological production, however, will dramatically increase under certain conditions, suggested previously: a high degree of heterogeneity among individuals and social units (i.e., high levels of sociocultural differentiation), diversity of resources and their distribution, rate and degree of change (from any source) of institutional systems and their legitimating ideologies, the number of symbolic codes, the weakness in connections among symbolic codes in various institutional domains, and the inability or disinclination of political authors to repress ideological production. As these conditions become more manifest in a society, the rate of Durkheimian selection among all organizations in all institutional domains will increase, and even in the religious domain where ideologies are conservative, this type of selection will increase among various religious cult structures. The likelihood that new ideological variations in general will survive and become institutionalized depends upon the capacity of an ideological variant to (a) secure a resource base (money, communication networks, rituals, organizational footings, and leadership), (b) establish clear goals and pursue them, (c) articulate ideological variants that enshrine general societal values and legitimate existing political authority, and (d) remain flexible, which, in turn, is related to the number of symbolic codes in its ideology and the weakness/looseness of connections among these codes.

When these ecological dynamics of Durkheimian selection are applied to religion, as a central moral order in all societies, a general theory of religious evolution emerges from Wuthnow's more general analysis of moral orders. This theory is highly compatible with our effort to outline various selection forces involved in religious evolution. At the very least, Wuthnow highlights the psychological dimensions of Spencerian selection, Type-1, outlined in Chapter 7. Thus, the effectiveness of religions under conditions of Durkheimian selection is very much related to its success in meeting the need-states of humans for verification of self, efficacy, security, and other such fundamental needs. Just as religions, when they first evolved in human societies, met these needs, so these same needs *constantly put selection pressure on* populations and their institutional systems. At the same time, and increasingly so as societies grew and became more complex, these fundamental psychological needs continued to exert selection pressures even as more macro-level selection pressures regularized production and reproduction, while using power and culture to regulate and control conflict, including religious competition under the conditions of increasing Durkheimian selection.

Illustrative Examples of Durkheimian Selection among Religious Cult Structures

Hopi Indians

The Hopi Indians in northeastern Arizona are a good example of former hunter–gatherer groups that migrated to the Black Mesa complex at the southwestern edge of the Colorado Plateau and evolved into an early horticultural society. Evidence of this evolutionary transition is clear in the extensive archaeological record, the many clan migration myths, and in both recent as well as the current social organization. The archaeological record documents that groups of people migrated into the region, established pueblo settlements, and then moved on. This pattern was found in the whole of the southwestern United States. One of the more spectacular examples is Mesa Verde complex of pueblos in Colorado, which were abandoned by 1285. Various theories ranging from draught to epidemics and/ or hostile attacks have been posited without much supporting evidence, however.

Durkheimian selection processes kick in when groups of people converge on a particular area and compete for limited resources. In the case of the Hopis, the limited but rich alluvial soil in the arid valleys below the mesas and the formerly rich fauna quickly became matters of social management and conflict. Hopi clan migration narratives are an integral part of their key myth about the emergence of humankind from a world below this world (Geertz 1984, 1994: 70ff.). Upon emerging, the various clans wandered into the wilderness, met with particular animals and supernatural creatures with whom they established totemic relations, and dealt with other human groups. According to these traditions, they would stop for brief periods of time, planting crops to carry with them, but otherwise maintaining a hunter–gatherer lifestyle (Voth 1903: 22). Many petroglyphs in the southwest regions indicate that people worshipped a Mother of the Game, known in Hopi as Tiikuywuuti, "Woman with protruding child" (McCreery and Malotki 1994: 138–142). The latter appears in the Snake Clan migration narrative, where one of the members of the clan was left behind in the desert during a protracted childbirth. Upon returning to find out her fate, the clan members found that she had transformed into a powerful creature covered in blood who was able to confer prowess to Hopi hunters (Voth 1903: 352–353). Even today, Hopi farmers meet her in their dreams and gain luck (Geertz 2007).

The recorded traditions of the various clans are rich in details, but more important for us here is the recorded procedure of gaining access to the Hopi villages and lands. Mennonite missionary H.R. Voth recorded the following incident in a Third Mesa narrative:

> When a clan arrived, usually one of the new arrivals would go to the village and ask the village chief for permission to settle in the village. He usually asked whether they understood anything to produce rain and good crops, and if they had any cult, they would refer to it and say, "Yes, this or this we have, and when we assemble for this ceremony, or when we have this dance, it will rain. With this we have traveled, and with this we have taken care of our children." . . . When a new clan arrived, the village chief would tell them: "Very well, you participate in our cult and help us with the ceremonies," and then he would give them their fields according to the way they came. And that way their fields were all distributed.
>
> (Voth 1905: 24)

Thus, according to Hopi traditions, the various clans arrived and gradual accretion occurred leading to the complex ceremonial and social organization of the Hopis. At the turn of the 19th century, there was a very large number of clans hierarchically organized in 12 exogamic phratries. The weak ties between clans were strengthened through marriage and membership in secret societies or sodalities that performed the yearly cycle of ceremonies. Fields, sacred places, water holes, and eagles' nests were distributed on the basis of clan accretion and village decision.

It is not known when the organizational structure fell in place, but the archaeological records indicate that in many instances, villages broke up, were abandoned, some were destroyed, and competing groups either died out or moved elsewhere. Although attempts to connect specific archaeological sites to Hopi oral traditions are mixed, the oral traditions tend to concur in general with the archaeological evidence. One example concerns the abandoned village called Sitkyatki, an extensive prehistoric ruin some 2 miles northeast of the present village of Walpi, First Mesa. The site is highly interesting because although the village was covered by sand long ago, archaeologists found a lot of beautiful pottery known as Jeddito yellow ware (Fewkes 1896). Modern researchers have failed to reach an exact date of abandonment, but Ekkehart Malotki argued that it was abandoned before the Spanish arrival sometime between 1500 A.D. and 1600 A.D. (Malotki 1993: 119). Early archaeologists and ethnologists have variously argued that the village was abandoned due to land disputes with a neighboring village, disagreements over control of water resources, and linguistic differences. The ten oral narratives published so far also give a variety of reasons. Several mention a race to the death between two male rivals over a female. Others mention that the village chief caused the destruction of the village because he felt that the villagers were turning evil (Malotki 1993: 120). Rivalries, jealousies, and witchcraft are common causes of village dissolutions in Hopi oral narratives (Malotki and Gary 2001; Geertz 2011). By far, the most common assumption among Hopis is that the village chiefs and other leaders deliberately plan village destructions. This assumption was termed "the Tiingavi Hypothesis" by anthropologist Gordon V. Krutz, based on the Hopi term tiingavi, "religious intent" (Krutz 1973: 85). The term is used when leaders announce the date of an upcoming religious ceremony, but is used here as a term covering deliberate plots by leaders to fulfill clan prophecies concerning the end of the world. This hypothesis has been explored in greater detail by anthropologist Peter M. Whiteley and scholar of religion Armin W. Geertz (Whiteley 1988; Geertz 1994).

By far the best example of Durkheimian selection is the split of the village of Oraibi in 1906. The split is one of the most intensively studied social and political events in Hopi history. Ostensibly due to factional differences concerning American governmental interference, the two factions engaged in a pushing contest during which the hostile faction lost. They were subsequently forced to leave the village and move on. During the next years, the split of Oraibi led to the foundation of three new villages and the enlargement of a fourth existing village. This situation reduced Oraibi to a ghost town by the 1930s, with less than 10 percent of its former populace (Whiteley 2008, vol. 1: 5). Peter Whiteley has shown that none of the proposed causes could sufficiently explain the split. It was evidently not because of overpopulation, drought, wash backup, or Navajo and Mormon encroachment, but was the result of complex material, social, ideological, and agential factors (Whiteley 2008, vol. 1: 830). Interestingly, the result was that the village of Hotevilla, founded by the hostile faction in 1907, survived as the only village on Third Mesa that had the clans and secret societies necessary to maintain the full annual cycle of ceremonies and, thus, maintain political power and social stability. Thus, the losers became the winners until they, too, either died or were marginalized by the villagers who were tired of factional disputes and social unrest.

Early Christ-Religion as an Example of Durkheimian Selection

In the previous chapter we dealt with the emergence of Axial age forms of religion. The term Axial age—coined by Karl Jaspers in 1946 but dating back to the German historian Ernst von Lassaulx (1854) and presumably Hegel's *Vorlesungen über die Philosophie der Geschichte* (1821), in which he spoke about a "hinge" (German "Angel") around which world history is turning (Hegel 1986)—is contested and often criticized for reflecting Protestant self-affirmation. (For the historical background of the term, see Joas 2014, who also points to Abraham Hyacinthe Anquetil-Duperron [1731–1805]; for Anquetil-Duperron, see Metzler 1991.) That may well be, but it does not reduce the value of the term or its theoretical implications in as much as it is capable of shedding light on a decisive transition in cultural history. The burden of proof lies not in unravelling the ideological background of the term, important as it is, but in providing an alternative explanation that can account for the empirical data.

The transition from archaic to Axial age types of religion did not happen overnight. It was a process that lasted several centuries, which is why it makes good sense to distinguish between Axial age forms of religion and axiality. Whereas the former happened during the first Axial age period, that is the 6th to the 3rd century BCE, axiality is defined as those Axial age type features that occurred in subsequent centuries. Early Christ-religion and formative Islam are significant examples of the latter: a fact already noted in Nietzsche's subtle observation in his preface to *Beyond Good and Evil* (1886) that Christianity can be conceived of as "Platonism for the people." Although Nietzsche vehemently opposed this type of religion for its world-renouncing aspects, he was right in his assessment of early Christ-religion as Platonism for the masses. Perhaps more precisely, formative Christ-religion is better categorized as religious axiality disseminated to considerably wider masses compared to the original Axial age types of religion, a form of religious democratization.

We used examples from early Christ-religion to illustrate Spencerian Type-1 selection. In this section, we shall also see Durkheimian selection at play in early Christ-religion; it is clearly evident in the context of early Christ-religion and the mystery cults. First, however, we must address several problems.

In numerous scholarly as well as popular writings on the emergence of early Christianity, as it is called in these writings, there is a strong tendency to take the religious "victory" of Christianity for granted. Almost deterministically or mechanically, it is assumed that Christianity had to come out as the conqueror of paganism and the victoress of Antiquity, thereby, paving the way for the subsequent development and in particular prefiguring of modern European history. This approach, however, does not provide a historically accurate description determined as it ultimately is by religious confessional interests in documenting the supremacy of Christianity. During its first centuries of existence as a trajectory within Judaism, there was nothing predestined or inevitable in what eventually became the religious hegemony of Christianity during the 5th and 6th centuries. The game was entirely open in the competition between, for instance, mystery cults and early Christ-religion during the first centuries. Yet, in retrospect, it makes sense to see this development in light of Durkheimian selection with the important ramification that historically the process was not a direct, inescapable continuity from early forms of Christ-religion to Constantine's transformation of Christ-religion into a legitimate religion, thus facilitating an institutionally sanctioned form of doctrinal homogeneity (325 CE), and Theodosius the First's subsequent declaration of Nicean Christianity as the religion of the Empire (380 CE).

From the end of the 19th century, the Graeco-Roman mystery cults became popular in the history of scholarship on early Christ-religion as a religio-historical foil in descriptions of its success. The mystery cults were conceived of as particularly pertinent with respect to early Christ-religion's rituals that were claimed to have been taken over from initiation rituals (baptism) and communal banquets (the Lord's Supper) in the mystery cults. Often this led to historically skewed accounts of the mystery cults that portrayed them as deficient forms of early Christ-religion. The influence from the mystery cults was a way of emphasizing the novel and genuine character of "Christianity" by claiming, on the one hand, that it did not originate in Jewish "efforts of self-justification," nor did it, on the other hand, derive from the mystery cults. Recourse to the Biblical background secured the latter argument.

Recent research on the mystery cults, however, has made it abundantly clear that they were far more traditional in the type of religion that they manifested. Furthermore, older scholarship considered them to be far more homogeneous than they were (cf. Smith 1990; Bowden 2010). They were not the "personal salvation religions" claimed by previous scholarship.

That said, however, it is true that early Christ-religion evolved in an environment in which the mystery cults attracted considerable attention. Germane to our purpose are the Isis cult and Mithraism, which strictly speaking did not constitute mystery cults, but came close to them. Similar to Christ-religion, both of these cults were found all across the Roman Empire. From Christian writers of the late 2nd and 3rd century as well as their Graeco-Roman counterparts, we know that they saw Christ-religion and the mystery cults as serious competitors.

Mystery religions and the early Christ-religion shared numerous features. In different ways, these forms of religion allowed followers and supporters to contribute financially to their spread by sponsoring meals, setting up shrines, altars, paying for priests, etc. To the best of our knowledge, however, early Christ-religion was not as confined to particular social segments as most of the mystery cults, which were favored by, for instance, soldiers, elite women, specific ethnic groups, etc. Although distinct and, therefore, particular by virtue of its worldview, Christ-religion, in principle, reached out to all social segments of the Empire: "There can be neither Jew nor Greek, there can be neither slave nor freeman, there can be neither male nor female—for you are all one in Christ Jesus," as Paul famously argued (Galatians 3:28).

To this we may add another important feature of Christ-religion which may account for its ultimate success in terms of dissemination. From its earliest period on, Christ-religion constituted a "provisional welfare state" for those such as orphans, widows, the elderly, the poor, the ill, etc., who generally did not fare well in the Empire. We see this already in one of the earliest texts that we have, namely Paul's Second Letter to the Corinthians from around 52 CE. Here he sets up a collection for the benefit of "God's holy ones" presumably referring to the Christ-adherents of Jerusalem (cf. 2 Cor 8:4; 9:12). The collection is not only meant to serve the poor but also to bind the different communities together and subtly increase their dependence upon Paul as the initiator of the contribution. Paul also urges his different communities to compete with each other and surpass the other communities with their contribution (Petersen 2018a):

> Next, brothers, we will tell you of the grace of God which has been granted to the churches of Macedonia, and how, throughout continual ordeals of hardship, their unfailing joy and their intense poverty have overflowed in a wealth of generosity on their part. I can testify that it

was of their own accord that they made their gift, which was not merely as far as their resources would allow, but well beyond their resources; and they had kept imploring us most insistently for the privilege of a share in the fellowship of service to God's holy people—it was not something that we expected of them, but it began by their offering themselves to the Lord and to us at the prompting of the will of God.

(2 Cor 8:1–5)

As if this were not enough, Paul uses Christ's sacrificial death as an authoritative model to be emulated by the Corinthians:

You are well aware of the generosity which our Lord Jesus Christ had, that, although he was rich, he became poor for your sake, so that you should become rich through his poverty. I will give you my considered opinion in the matter; this will be the right course for you as you were the first, a year ago, not only to take any action but also even to conceive the project. Now, then, complete the action as well, so that the fulfilment may—so far as your resources permit—be proportionate to your enthusiasm for the project. As long as the enthusiasm is there, the basis on which it is acceptable is what someone has, not what someone does not have.

(8:9–12)

There is no doubt about what Paul expects from his Corinthian recipients. The example clearly demonstrates how Durkheimian selection mechanisms are brought to bear on the dissemination of early Christ-religion. It shows the efficacy of Durkheimian selection in the growth, preservation, and spread of particular cultures and groups. An alternative economic system is set up with system-internal values regulating and enforcing it. Leaders fill out the role of securing the autonomy of this new religious niche.

Undoubtedly, there are many factors that need to be taken into account when it ultimately came to Christianity's independence as an autonomous and, with respect to Judaism, independent religion during the late 4th and 5th century (Reed and Becker 2003; Boyarin 2004; Petersen 2005). When we compare the spread of early Christ-religion with the mystery cults, however, the ability of early Christ-religion to fill out the niche of economic support in conjunction with a religious worldview is obvious. Surely, this element of constituting a "provisional welfare system" must have been an important factor in what eventually led to Christianity's religious hegemony. One last example will suffice to make the point.

At the turn of the 3rd century, the Christian theologian, Tertullian, in numerous writings uses this element of financial support to marginalized groups in his rhetorical effort to recruit more Christ-followers. In his Apology from 197 CE, Tertullian emphasizes the irreproachable ethos and virtuous life of Christ-followers over and against pagan accusations. In chapter 39 of the work, Tertullian makes it clear that there is nothing abominable taking place at Christ-religious gatherings. He also underlines how Christ-adherents constitute an ideal society:

> The tried men of our elders preside over us, obtaining that honor not by purchase, but by established character. There is no buying and selling of any sort in the things of God. Though we have our treasure-chest, it is not made up of purchase-money, as of cult (*religio*) that has its price. On the monthly day, if he likes, each puts in a small donation; but only if it be his pleasure, and only if he be able: for there is no compulsion; all is voluntary. These gifts are, as it were, piety's deposit fund. For they are not taken thence and spent on feasts, and drinking-bouts, and eating-houses, but to support and bury poor people, to supply the wants of boys and girls destitute of means and parents, and of old persons confined now to the house; such, too, as have suffered shipwreck; and if there happen to be any in the mines, or banished to the islands, or shut up in the prisons, for nothing but their fidelity to the cause of God's Church, they become the nurslings of their confession. But it is mainly the deeds of a love so noble that lead many of us to put a brand upon us. *See*, they say, *how they love one another*, for themselves [that is, the pagans—the present authors] are animated by mutual hatred; how they are ready even to die for one another, for they themselves will sooner put to death.
>
> (39:5–7; ANF translation, amended)

Even if we do not take Tertullian's contention that there is no compulsion at face value, the statement is nevertheless extraordinary. Although Tertullian's portrayal of early Christ-religion due to the circumstances of the Apology may be rosy, it is a fact that this type of religion found its own particular niche in setting up a provisional welfare system, thereby minimizing social inequity and moving beyond many traditional ethnic and social boundaries. In competition with the mystery cults, early Christ-religion came to out-compete the former not least due to the alternative and attractive economic system it established. We see this as a striking example of Durkheimian selection. Numerous moral, altruistic values cherished in early Christ-religion may also be found in a number of Graeco-Roman philosophical currents. Yet, the philosophical schools never succeeded in setting up such moral altruistic systems in practice. Additionally, the schools always remained an elite phenomenon. Thus, this aspect contributed greatly to Christianity's eventual religious hegemony in the late Roman Empire and subsequent further spread.

Competition and Change in Memberships of Religious Cult Structures in the United States

For more than 20 years, the trends in "secularization" in Europe and the Western world more generally have been compared to American exceptionalism. The argument has been that while church memberships continue to decline as individuals seek other than religious moral orders, religion in the United States remains strong and vibrant and, thus, has resisted this European pattern of secularization. The trend in most of the West is to drop individual and family affiliations with a specific church, but sustain a belief in the supernatural, followed by a decline in beliefs about the gods of a specific pantheon, although often a sense of "spirituality" persists. Such trends can be interpreted as an outcome of Durkheimian selection in which more secular moral orders over the last century are increasingly being chosen in preference to affiliation with particular cult structures and, finally, with their ideologies and conceptions about the pantheons of the supernatural realm (i.e., a belief in God).

The United States was seen as an exception to this trend because of the prominence of evangelical religions and mega-churches, high rates of stated beliefs by the public in "God," and generally moderate degrees of attendance in church services. The Christian moral order seemed to be doing very well in competition with other non-Christian affiliations and, more importantly, with secular moral orders in other institutional domains. The broader changes began a generational shift of Americans, perhaps as what Michael Hout and Claude Fischer term "the sixties effect," away from orthodox Christian religiosity, church attendance, and daily prayer (McCaffree 2017: 3). Over the last several decades, it has not been acknowledged that there are interesting effects from Durkheimian competition and selection within the domain of religion in the U.S. and between religion and other institutional domains that also posit a moral order. One trend in the United States was the rise of the Religious Right, which supported the conservative politics of the Republican party. Despite all of the success, at least for a while, of Right Wing Politics fueled by growing memberships in evangelical religious cults, this "Faustian bargain," as McCaffree (2017) termed it, has backfired in both the political and religious domains. Liberal democrats were elected in eight of the last 12 years of the presidency (before Trump's election in 2016) and, most interestingly, the rate of non-affiliation with religious cults began to increase from 8 percent to 15 percent in the 1960s and, by 2015, jump again to 23 percent (PEW Foundation 2015).

The gains and losses of Christian cult structures in the US are revealing. For example, about 24 percent of Americans identify as evangelical Protestants, but this figure masks the fact that 8.3 percent will at some point no longer identify with evangelicalism. Thus, many envangelicals leave this form of worship, but at the same time, a somewhat larger number of 9.8 percent begin to identify with it. Thus, it is always the *net loss* of those born and raised in a religion and those coming into a religion from another cult that is critical. The percentage of evangelicals, therefore, has increased from 24 percent to slightly over 25 percent overall because of the 1 percent net increase of those joining from other religions over those leaving. Mainline traditional Protestant denominations have declined from the 19 percent of individuals claiming it as their childhood religion to only 14.7 percent as 10.4 percent left and were replaced by only 6.1 percent from other religions, creating the approximately 4 percent drop in religious affiliation within traditional Protestant cult structures. Catholicism in the US has decreased from being the childhood religion of 31.7 percent of Americans to 20.8 percent of the population that are now affiliated with the Roman Catholic Church because almost 13 percent left to be replaced by only 2 percent from other religions. Other non-Christian religions such as Judaism, Islam, Buddhism, Hinduism, and other world religions have remained at more or less the same levels of participation overall, having increased about 1.2 percent from early childhood religions to current religions (PEW Foundation 2014: 3). The most dramatic increase is among unaffiliated, which was 9.2 percent of the childhood non-affiliation of their parents to almost 23 percent, 4.3 percent of the population defecting to a religious affiliation (approximately half) but replaced by 18 percent who had chosen to leave a childhood religious group.

The data are relatively clear (see PEW Foundation 2015, and McCaffree 2017 for more details): a pattern of secularization like that in the rest of the West, especially Western Europe and Canada, is starting to take hold in the United States. Religion in general is beginning to lose members to moral orders in other institutional domains as a result of Durkheimian selection among religious cults and between religious organizations and those in other institutional domains. While there remains a certain stigma of being not religious, especially if people proclaim themselves to be "atheists," being non-affiliated with any church is the first step to becoming non-religious. There are large differences by regions in the US, with the West and North more unaffiliated than the South, as well as ethnicity/race, with whites being less affiliated than African Americans (whose Protestant religious cults were the organizational basis of the Civil Rights movement in the 1960s) and Latinos (many of whom are immigrants from the Catholic Americas) are more likely to be affiliated than non-Hispanic whites. Yet, a prediction would be that rates of non-affiliation will increase in even these ethnic subcultures in the US.

Because the United States is highly differentiated with many different types of corporate units in diverse institutional domains creating ideologies that embody American cultural values, there are many moral orders to choose from, and, given the mobility of Americans from their natal communities and even from their ethnic roots, change in affiliations will increase. Moreover, the United States has highly dynamic markets and quasi-markets by which individuals affiliate with corporate units; due to the range of variants in ideologies and underlying moral orders, we expect that Durkheimian selection will continue to push Americans toward secularism, even as a large and substantial subpopulation remains highly committed to evangelical religious culture structures. Thus, secularization will in the immediate term also produce polarization of the religious and non-religious, often making for a clash of moral orders.

Conclusion

Under conditions of Durkheimian selection, religious cult structures are very much driven by efforts to meet need-states of individuals, as these were outlined in the last chapter. The moral codes of religious beliefs, the nature of the powers of the supernatural realm, and the types of ritual by which appeals to the supernatural realm are made and by which cultural codings are affirmed vary among religions, and, moreover, different configurations of these basic elements of religion may appeal to somewhat different subpopulations in a society. However, all of these elements of religions must address fundamental need-states that are evident in the neuroanatomy of humans as evolved apes. Thus, cult structures reducing sources of anxiety, fostering a sense of personal efficacy, increasing acts of self control, and providing for a sense of self verification are likely to be more successful than others, depending upon the demographic characteristics of target members.

The level of competition among religious culture structures will be related to the diversity of potential members of these structures, especially with respect to varying levels of economic inequality, categoric-unit memberships (class, ethnicity), differential evaluations of these memberships and their unequal treatment, and the level and ways in which universal need-states are aroused within subpopulations differentiated by categoric-unit memberships. Under these general conditions, it becomes more likely that there will be more sub-niches in a society that, in turn, creates opportunities for diverse religious cult structures to make their appeals. Such appeals begin with increased production of new ideological variants in the system of moral codes in a society, a good portion of which will be religious and tied to particular cult structures; under these conditions, existing cult structures and perhaps new structures will begin to compete for resources. Variations in ideological production will further increase, as noted by Wuthnow (1987), by rates of broader institutional change within societies and inflexibility in the religious codes of existing religions. If competition is allowed by the political system (rather than repressed), then quasi-competitive markets for religion can emerge and set into motion the same dynamics among cult structures as economic actors in purely economic markets. Moreover, as long as violence is not employed as a strategy, such markets can create considerable diversity within and between particular religious markets by somewhat different beliefs about the supernatural, organizational features of their respective cult structures, and their ritual practices. If, however, cult structures or polity initiate violence and persecution of some cult structures, then the potential for Marxian selection increases.

Both Durkheimian and, as we will see, Marxian selection are similar in at least this sense. The "most fit" religious cult structures will be those that can secure material resources (especially money but also territory and other material resources), networks of communication (particularly for recruiting members), organizational footings, templates, and alliances (especially with sources of political power inside or outside a society), leadership, and emotion-arousing rituals and moral codes that drive commitments to culture structures. If selection is more Durkheimian, then ideologies are diverse, encompassing and, hence, flexible. If these ideologies lead to the development of more emotion-arousing rituals, then these new ideologies and rituals will enable existing or new cult structures to be successful in competition. In contrast, if the selection becomes more Marxian, then more demonstrative and tightly woven religious ideologies, coupled with not only emotion-arousing rituals but also rituals that arouse individuals to incur the costs of conflict and violence, are likely to prove more fit. Moreover, if a religion can be successful in generating a sense of complimentary opposition, seeing other religions as evil and dangerous, then those religions that can organize solidarities among members around this opposition are likely to be more successful under conditions of Marxian selection to be analyzed in Chapter 10.

In the next chapter, we examine Type-2 Spencerian selection, which is generally associated with geopolitics and, to a lesser extent, geo-economics. As societies engage in warfare, the winner in a conflict will generally regulate in some fashion those conquered. To varying degrees, they will use strategies of regulation that revolve around, at one pole, coercion and often the imposition of their culture, especially language and religious ideologies on those under their domination and, at the other pole, co-optation where indigenous institutional systems and culture are left largely intact but subject to taxation and other forms of securing resources for the victor in warfare. When co-optation occurs, Durkheimian selection can increase, as was so evident in the Roman Empire where the polytheistic systems of the Romans was not imposed, perhaps because it was too complex, but ironically, other cult structures were allowed to secure resources and ultimately out-compete the complex religious system of the Romans. Even as Christianity was repressed and persecuted in what is now Palestine/Israel, it was able to use the Roman infrastructure to find converts to its monotheistic message that resonated with the need-states of the commercial middle class, as outlined for Spencerian selection Type-1 in the previous chapter. Thus, following the distributive infrastructure—roads, canals, ports, and market systems—Christianity was able to secure converts to the point that it became the state religion. As we will see in the next chapter, Spencerian selection Type-2 has been a powerful force in religious evolution, but this evolution has also involved both Durkheimian and Type-1 selection when the coercive force of a hegemony is more relaxed and relies on co-optive strategies rather than blunt coercion.

9

Type-2 Spencerian Selection
The Geopolitics of Religious Evolution

We must not let our feelings blind us to the proofs that inter-social conflicts have furthered the development of evolution . . . Moreover, dislikes of governments of certain kinds must not prevent us from seeing their fitness *to their circumstances.*"

Herbert Spencer on "Political Institutions," in
The Principles of Sociology (1879: 231)

As was emphasized in Chapter 2, Herbert Spencer's (1874–1896) sociology often applied his famous phrase—"survival of the fittest"—to analyze inter-societal warfare. More-fit societies generally win wars against the less fit; and as they do so, they often incorporate the conquered population into their institutional systems, including their religious systems. The result is that the size and complexity of societies increased over the long-course of societal evolution, although Spencer argued that markets in industrial societies could now replace warfare as the driving force of future societal evolution, thereby generating new incentives for innovation in production. Spencer's important insight in his geopolitical and geo-economic analysis is that religion often evolves with political evolution because polity depends upon religion for legitimation of its conquests, for regulating and controlling conquered populations, and for managing inequalities that inevitably increase as power is consolidated and used in conquests of other populations. Thus, geopolitical warfare among societies is often a form of selection among superorganisms and their constituent institutional systems, especially polity and religion.

Warfare, Conquest, and Geopolitical Formations

Since Spencer's time, a large literature on geopolitics and geo-economics has accumulated, often under the label "world-systems analysis" (e.g., Wallerstein 1974, 1984, 1989; Chase-Dunn 1998; Chase-Dunn 2001; Chase-Dunn and Hall 1997; Arrighi 1994; Arrighi and Silver 1999; Frank 1978). Both geopolitical and geo-economic systems have existed even among hunter–gatherer populations, particularly settled hunter–gatherers (Chase-Dunn and Lero 2014; Chase-Dunn and Mann 1998; Ember 1978), but with horticulture and then agrarian societal formations, such systems became ever-more common. A geopolitical system is built up by warfare or even threats of warfare, with one society coming to dominate another. With conquest or even political co-optation by virtue of Type-2 Spencerian selection comes a host of Type-1 Spencerian selection problems that affect the evolution of religions. It is necessary, then, to specify some of the conditions leading to warfare and conquest, as Type-2 Spencerian selection pushes religious evolution directly and indirectly via its effects on Type-1 selection pressures.

Warfare and Conquest as a Selection Process

Warfare can be conceptualized as an ecological process in which one superorganism seeks to occupy the resource niche(s) of another, typically their sovereign geographical space and the resources, both biophysical and sociocultural, contained in this space. To win a war and gain access to the resources of another society or societies, it is necessary to mobilize resources that can increase the fitness of a war-making society *vis-à-vis* its potential target(s); and out of the conflict between societies, superorganisms evolve—typically becoming larger and more complex, while revealing considerable inequality in the distribution of valued resources. The rather large literature on geopolitics specifies the key conditions that set off geopolitical mobilization of societies for warfare (see Turner 2010a for a review). Figure 9.1 adds more dynamics in play than the simplified model of Type-2 Spencerian selection presented in Chapter 2.

Conditions of Geopolitical Mobilization

The potential for geopolitical mobilization increases when a society can consolidate the bases of power—coercive, administrative, symbolic (ideological), and (material) incentive—to control and manipulate individual and corporate actors in a society. This mobilization is most likely to occur with population growth as it generates Type-1 Spencerian selection pressures for regulation through the consolidation of power and for increased production resulting in increased material wealth to finance political (and religious) activities. As the size and scale of polity grows, so does the potential for geopolitical mobilization, but not without a strong symbolic base of power provided by religious beliefs and rituals that legitimate polity and its capacity to extract resources from a population and the inequalities that inevitably emerge from such resource extraction. When religion cannot provide this critical base of symbolic power, the potential for geopolitical mobilization decreases. Indeed, without legitimation by religion, societies have often disintegrated or become targets for conquest by a better-organized polity of another society.

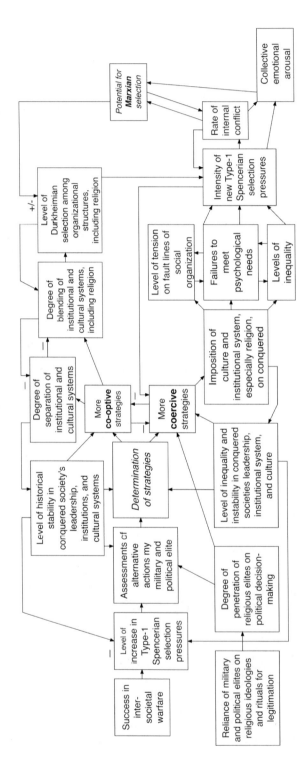

Figure 9.1 Key Dynamics of Type-2 Spencerian Selection

Political mobilization under any other conditions will increase with what Chase-Dunn (2001) and Carneiro (1970, 1973) have termed "circumscription" by other societies that box in a society that has depleted its resources and set off environmental degradation. Equally often, surrounding populations set off environmental degradation, forcing a society to move against its neighbors in search of new resource bases. Indeed, much early warfare among horticulturalists was the result of resource depletion among contiguous populations, forcing some populations to move and secure resources elsewhere. As a society marches to secure resources under conditions of circumscription, it soon confronts other societies that control needed resources.

When neighboring societies become defined as a threat, whether for environmental disruption or threats of aggressive movements, the likelihood of warfare increases. This sense of threat is compounded, when there has been a history of (a) economic competition among societies or key actors in the economies of societies; (b) political competition, especially over perceptions of military might; (c) past conflicts that have kept societies mobilized for war; and (d) differences in [i] values and beliefs, [ii] ethnicity, and [iii] religion.

These historical conditions are often magnified by efforts of political leadership in societies to deflect attention away from grievances of their own population over domestic inequality. Therefore, increasing inequality, hardening of class boundaries, and lowered rates of upward mobility across classes will often lead polity to strategically manufacture a sense of threat, sometimes an "internal threat" against stigmatized categories of persons, as was the case of Jews in Nazi Germany, but equally often an "external threat" posed by other societies. In either or both cases, as was illustrated by Nazi Germany, threats can be expressed to justify the consolidation and centralization of power. When religious elites and their use of rituals and beliefs support polity in these actions, then the extension of power will be more effective, even as it increases inequalities.

Even without real or pumped up external threats, polities will often engage in conflict with other societies if they perceive that they have a productive and military advantage. In making such calculations, actors in polity will also calculate their "marchland advantage" to determine if they are sufficiently protected by geographical/ecological barriers (oceans, mountain, deserts, etc.) when they march out to war (something that Nazi Germany did not do and, hence, had to fight a war on all fronts). Polities often start wars without making accurate assessments of their productive, military, and marchland liabilities because of their perception that their symbolic bases of power are weakening from inequalities but are potentially salvageable by success in war and mobilization of religious cults and their leaders to provide backing for warfare, although a loss of a war will erode a polity's prestige in their local world system (Weber 1922) or even initiate a revolution because of grievances over inequalities (Skocpol 1977). Because leaders in polity frequently miscalculate their advantages over their neighbors, warfare backfires and makes them vulnerable to conquest by another marching society. Even if initial calculations are born out by military success, the very nature of empire formations causes, first of all, the marchland advantage to decrease as more and more enemies accumulate on the margins of the empire as it advances. Second, the logical loads of controlling territory and distributing resources to coercive and administrative infrastructures inevitably increase as a marching polity moves further from its original home base (Collins 1984), as was dramatically demonstrated by the collapse of the Soviet Union in 1990s or by the very far-flung British empire a century earlier. Empires tend not to last very long because of these realities of empire formation, although the Roman Empire represents a notable exception to this generalization primarily, we suspect, because it did not seek to tightly control and regulate its conquered territories (see Turchin 2003, 2006, as well as Turchin and Nefedov 2009, for sophisticated modeling and historical examples of these and other dynamics affecting empire formation).

Winning Wars and Controlling Territory

Wars are generally won by larger and more productive societies with polities that can mobilize large coercive forces, have logistical capacities for administration, communication, and transportation, and, most importantly, that evidence a domestic base of symbolic power, which has often been provided by religious cult structures, beliefs, and rituals. Winning battles and even a war are only effective to the degree that the polity of one society can control the larger territory and its indigenous population. Maintaining coercive and administrative control is very costly, as noted previously, with the result that coercive empires built around domination by military force and tight administration rarely lasts very long, especially if the empire is large and loses its marchland advantages and must face enemies along most of its borders. Empires that recruit conquered populations and corporate units from their institutional systems will generally last longer, especially if they can integrate cultural beliefs, and, even more so, religious beliefs. Moreover, if an empire can avoid a showdown war with another advancing empire, it has a better chance of enduring for a time. However, to the extent that the conquered are exploited, they must be coercively controlled, which, in the end, will erode the economic, symbolic, and coercive bases of power.

Thus, the stability of an empire is affected by such conditions as (Collins 1986; Turner 2017): (a) the size of the territory held; (b) the size and diversity of the population to be controlled; (c) the number of "enemies" along the borders of the empire; (d) the logistical problems in moving materials, people, troops, and information about an empire; (e) the level of production of the consolidated populations in an empire; (f) the political stability of the home base from which an empire originated, and most importantly; (g) the capacity to maintain a symbolic base of power legitimating the activities of political leaders and the inequalities that always accompany the consolidation of power and resource extraction to maintain power.

To the extent that (g) is provided through adoption of some beliefs and rituals of the indigenous population, and indoctrination of conquered populations into a common religion, an empire can endure for longer periods of time. Yet, empires can also be prolonged perhaps even longer when they allow the indigenous religion to persist, exchanging religious "freedom" for acceptance of the new political system (as the Roman Empire did, and even the short-lived British empire did to some degree) that allows not only religious but other institutional systems to persist in more or less their pre-conquest form. But even as indigenous religions are left largely intact, the religion from the conquering society may still spread across the larger empire on both economic and political networks, often blending with indigenous religions over the long run, and thereby causing religion to evolve, or perhaps even phasing out an indigenous religion by a combination of Type-2 Spencerian and Durkheimian selection, thereby accelerating religious evolution and, potentially, religious and political conflict between colonizers and the colonized.

Thus, because religion is so central to a people's daily lives, particularly in traditional and historical societies, but as is obvious today, in contemporary ones as well, warfare and shifting political boundaries almost always cause religions to move across territories and, like gene flow in Darwinian evolution, evolve within and among human superorganisms. At times, as was evident in the Christian Crusades of the 10th and 11th centuries, religions can mobilize fractured or still evolving societal-level governments (in the case of Western Europe, the evolution of European societies from the feudal estates that provided some integration during the Middle Ages; and along with this political mobilization, religion moves across territories with the coercive and administrative forces that it has promoted into action). As religion migrates on these networks, it can itself evolve or cause evolution among indigenous religions, or once again, it can set off another wave of religious and political conflict by virtue of Type-2 Spencerian selection or even Marxian selection.

Illustrative Examples on the Evolution of Religion by Type-2 Spencerian Selection

Mesoamerican Empires and Ceremonial Centers

In the following, we have chosen examples from an archaic religion and from axial and post-axial religions. In Bellah's terminology (1964, 2011a), archaic religions are found in Africa, the Pacific Islands, the Americas, India, China, and of course the ancient Mediterranean and Middle East. These religions were intrinsic to large urban populations based on agriculture. They constituted the predominant type of religion in the ancient world such as we know it from Vedic religion in India, ancient Chinese religion, classical Greek and Roman religion, Egyptian and Israelite religion, etc. The main identifying feature of archaic religions is an organized cult structure with professional priesthoods, dramatic processions, sacrifice, and worship focused on temple institutions. Archaic societies are hierarchical with a king, who in many societies is thought to be divine or of divine lineage, noble families, and the priests. Cultic activities are carried out by specialized priests, and there are often a variety of cults with each having their own deity, personnel, and rituals. In archaic contexts, there is a clear two-class system whereby commoners are more or less passive spectators of the cosmic drama unfolding through ritual pageantry and acted out by the elite in concert with a clearly defined divine pantheon, frequently under the protection and demands of a Big God who is often embodied or impersonated by the king.

Although the religious symbol system is highly differentiated, the worldview is still monistic in the sense that nature, society, and the supernatural are all part of a single cosmos (Bellah 2005: 70). At the same time, however, there is a clear-cut distinction between humans and divine beings in the sense that ordinary humans will never attain the status of divine beings. In fact, the basic rationale of the temple and sacrificial system is that of upholding the ontological balance between the divine and the human. Through sacrifice, humans "pay back" to the gods what they have ultimately received from the celestial world. In this sense, the sacrificial system serves to emphasise the gods as contractual lords over humans as contractual servants. This fundamental distinction lies at the core of the temple and sacrificial system, which functions not only to make the asymmetrical relationship between the two patently clear but also to retain the ontological balance as unequivocal.

Spencerian Type-2 selection is widespread throughout human history in various indigenous as well as urban populations. Examples of indigenous populations with imperialistic ambitions are found in the Americas, Africa, and the Pacific Islands. Some, such as the expansion of the Aztec Empire and the Pacific Island cultures, consist of competition over trade networks and valuable resources. Others, such as the many empires in Africa, based their power on competition over natural resources. Still others, such as European empires, based their power on the exploitation of indigenous human and natural resources. In the Americas, Europeans vied for territory, natural resources, and political influence at home. In all these cases, religious beliefs and practices were the constant companions of polity, sometimes curbing, but always legitimizing military, economic, and political hegemony.

A highly useful political instrument in the rise of empires was human sacrifice, a practice found in indigenous cultures, early civilizations, and empires. But why is human sacrifice widespread, and, to what selection pressures is human sacrifice an adaptive response? Psychologist Joseph Watts and his team tested the social control hypothesis by applying Bayesian phylogenetic methods to 93 traditional Austronesian cultures (Watts et al. 2016). The social control hypothesis claims that human sacrifice is used to legitimate polity and class systems and, at the same time, it stabilizes stratification—a hypothesis that restates Spencer's conception of Type-1 selection. The results of their analysis support the hypothesis. Human sacrifice, it seems, "stabilizes social stratification once stratification has arisen, and promotes a shift to strictly inherited class systems" (Watts et al. 2016: 228).

Thus, the increase in population density and competition for resources, as well as the need for protection, leads to urban social systems and the rise of social elites. The inequalities of such systems and their legitimation are promoted and stabilized, among other things, by human sacrifice. This is possible, it is argued, because "it minimizes the potential of retaliation by eliminating the victim, and shifts the agents believed to be ultimately responsible to the realm of the supernatural" (Watts et al. 2016: 231)—thereby representing an adaptive response to Type-2 Spencerian selection pressures. In a separate study (Watts et al. 2015), they show that broad supernatural punishment (and not moralizing high gods, as Norenzayan has argued [Norenzayan 2013; see also Geertz 2014]) precedes the evolution of political complexity in Austronesia. In an earlier and broader cross-cultural study using the Standard Cross-Cultural Sample (SCCS) (Murdock and White 1969), anthropologist Michael Winkelman came to the similar conclusion that human sacrifice correlated significantly with population pressures, war for land and resources, and ideological legitimation (Winkelman 1998).

This is certainly the case in the Mesoamerican empires. All of the societies in the region shared a similar worldview: hieroglyphic writing;

monumental pyramids; 260-day calendars; common myths and religious elements such as gods, priesthoods, and ritual societies; captive sacrifice; self-inflicted ritual bloodletting; ritual ballgames etc. (Schele and Miller 1986; Carrasco 1990: 29–30). Despite these commonalities, the Classic Lowland Maya consisted of aggressive, rivaling city-states, constantly at war with one another, often taking prominent captives and torturing them to death (Coe 1986: 3). None, however, gained ascendency over the others. As Schele and Miller note, "Blood was the mortar of ancient Maya ritual life" (Schele and Miller 1986: 14). Prisoners of war supplied the need for state blood sacrifices to nourish the gods and sustain the universe (Schele and Miller 1986: 301). These bloodletting rituals were conceived of as actually giving birth to the gods in corporeal form as they were personified by the divine king, who would wear their costumes during state ritual events (Schele and Miller 1986: 302).

Maya art and writing recorded events of war and sacrifice as well as the bloodlines of the various kings buried in monumental pyramids. The kings and nobility also practiced bloodletting during important events such as the birth of a male heir, marriage ceremonies, or the dedication of monuments and buildings. Noble and royal bloodlines were claimed to stretch back to divine origins, and, thus, bloodletting rituals were manifestations of these divine bloodlines (Schele and Miller 1986: 175). The blood of high-ranking captives was also a central element in state ritual as well as in the ballgame, played in ceremonial precincts, that victims were forced to participate in, after which the losers were decapitated. The game was a reenactment of the Hero Twins who instituted the game to the annoyance of the gods of the Underworld. The gods defeated them, however, by deception, and the Twins were sacrificed. Subsequently, one of the decapitated heads spat at the daughter of an Underworld lord and impregnated her. Her twins grew up and took up the ballgame of their father. They succeeded in defeating the evil designs of the Underworld gods, but were sacrificed in the end and transformed into the sun and moon or, in other traditions, the sun and Venus (Schele and Miller 1986: 243–245).

Older research had assumed that the Maya were not as blood-thirsty as the Aztecs, but recent research has shown that this was not the case. The Aztecs were Nahuatl-speaking invaders from the north who succeeded after a century of struggle in defeating the warring Chichimec city-states of the collapsed Toltec empire. They subsequently took on the local cultural, technological, and agricultural practices. Together with two other city-states (Acolhuas of Texcoco and the Tepanecs of Tlacopan), the so-called Triple Alliance—established in 1428—gained control over the Valley of Mexico, and the Aztecs came to rule over an impressive empire (Carrasco 1990: 46; Smith 1986: 73). By 1502, during the rule of Moctezuma II, their last king, they had control over most of Mexico as well as some Mayan and Zapotecan areas, until their defeat by the Spanish in 1519 (Guerra 1971: 13). Through control of trade routes and large-scale military campaigns as well as important alliances with city-states and provinces, the Aztecs established one of the most impressive empires in history (Carrasco 1990: 46). Besides the glorification of war and warriors, Aztec culture produced mural paintings, literature, philosophy, poetry, rhetoric, beautifully painted manuscripts, astronomy, a calendrical system, magnificent structures and temples, music, dance, and much more (Carrasco 1990: 78–85). Their social system was hierarchical, like the Maya, but they had an elected monarchy with nobility and priestly classes, and a highly developed administrative system—they kept for instance highly detailed tax records and recorded events in beautiful codices with pictographs and rebus writing.

The capital city of Tenochtitlan, originally established in 1325, was the symbol and embodiment of the empire. It was the largest city in pre-Columbian America, covering an area of 1,350 hectares with approximately 200,000 inhabitants (Smith 2005: 412). It was the center of the world, organized in four quarters around a massive ceremonial center (thus symbolizing the five cardinal directions). It was divided by four large causeways that received all of the roads of central Mesoamerica (Carrasco 1990: 47). The city boasted palaces, 25 pyramids with temples on top, a civic center, a large market place, and much more (Guerra 1971: 15). This stratified society consisted of the elite on the one hand—the king and nobles and a highly developed priesthood that controlled not only the state cult but also the educational system—and the commoners on the other (Nicholson 1971: 436; Smith 1986).

According to historian of religion David Carrasco, Aztec religion rested on four important elements: warfare, order controlled in the capital, fear of cosmic instability, and relations with the gods (Carrasco 1990: 45). Their worldview observed sharp "alternations between order and disorder, cosmic life, and cosmic death ... [which] was marked on both the celestial and terrestrial levels by combats, sacrifice, and rebellion as well as by harmony, cooperation, and stability" (Carrasco 1990: 47). This worldview was legitimated in the myth of the suns, representing four prior ages and the current fifth age. The central deity was Huitzilopochtli, the sun, which was reborn every day and sustained by human blood (Carrasco 1999). As Francisco Guerra noted, "Their rituals included sacrifices of prisoners or other victims, extraction of their hearts which were offered to the god, and anthropophagy, including over 20,000 victims yearly at Tenochtitlan" (Guerra 1971: 14). War was a necessary source of sacrificial victims whose hearts and blood were "debt-payment" (*nextlaoaliztli*) necessary in rejuvenating the gods and the "Giver of Life" with their energy (Carrasco 1990: 49).

The ceremonial events were deliberately used for political purposes to justify conquests and legitimate the political order thereby imposed. The much debated "Flowery Wars," which were staged battles between the warriors of the Triple Alliance and the warriors of the Tlaxcalan-Pueblan Valley Kingdoms to the east, were used "to reestablish or disrupt the borders and balance of power between competing city-states" (Carrasco 1990: 49). Drawing on the world-systems theory of Immanuel Wallerstein, anthropologists Richard Blanton and Gary Feinman have shown that the Triple Alliance system was an example of the manipulation of "flows of material, energy, and people at a macro-regional (what he [Wallerstein] calls a 'world-system') scale through the establishment of ties of superordinance/dependency" to gain wealth and power (Blanton and Feinman 1984: 674). Furthermore, anthropologist Michael E. Smith has also argued that the main integrative factor of the Alliance was the "collusion between rulers of the core states and the nobility of the provinces, who gained economic rewards for their participation in the tribute empire" (Smith 1986: 70; see also Almazán 1999). Smith has shown that crucial to the success of the Triple Alliance was the fact that they allowed the rulers of conquered provinces to continue their own tribute systems, only requiring a quota for the Alliance—underscoring that the central polity of the empire could take a more co-optive strategy of domination. Thus, besides "marriage alliances, redistributive ceremonies, and long-distance trade connections . . . the most important incentive that the . . . [conquered] nobility gained from the empire was Mexican support for their rule and legitimacy" (Smith 1986: 81).

The whole system of stratification involved the control of information flow through ritual and propaganda. The large-scale ceremonies, attended by allies and enemies alike, were not just displays of human sacrifice; they also included "sumptuous feasting, gift giving, and royal distribution to the gathered nobility" (Smith 1986: 75). Knowing that the subject rulers and others were in fact related to the emperor in one way or another gives the impression that the sacrifices were a form of religious entertainment for the nobles "along with the dances, speeches, processions, and other theatrical ceremonies" (Smith 1986: 75). The sacrifices may have terrified and impressed the commoners, but strengthened ties between the elites—thereby meeting Type-1 Spencerian selection pressures for regulation and integration of an empire, but also responding to Type-2 Spencerian selection pressures through the use of religious rituals to stabilize the geopolitical and geo-economic systems established by conquest.

Thus, human sacrifice was an integral part of an exceedingly complex social, economic, political, military, religious, and ecological system. The leadership took care of the populace but used the system to increase their own power and wealth thus increasing inequality in the distribution of valued resources. This is one of the reasons, Carrasco argues, that the Aztecs had "an extraordinary focus on elite human beings" (Carrasco 1990: 22). The large-scale pageantry at the ceremonial sites communicated "the structure and dynamics of the universe," which can be summed up in the three major elements of world-making, world-centering, and world-renewing: "the ceremonial center and celestial event (worldmaking), human creativity and sacrifice in the hands of the elite (worldcentering), and the commitment to rejuvenation (worldrenewing)" (Carrasco 1990: 23).

Religion and Warfare as a Strong Feature of Axiality

In Chapters 7 and 8, we have discussed the emergence of Axial age religion. At this point, it is necessary to explain precisely the main features of these types of religion in order to understand how the close relationship between religion, violence, and war became intensified with the emergence of Axial age religion.

There are 12 features shared by these admittedly very different movements that make it not only justifiable but also reasonable to include them under the same theoretical category.

1. Axial age religions reflect a form of "thinking about thinking." Contrary to archaic forms of religion, Axial age religions are characterized by increasing self-reflexivity often formulated in second-order concepts and expressed in the ability to understand one's own thinking and practice from an assumed external perspective.
2. This form of self-reflexivity is closely related to a foundational epistemology expressed in spatial categories, whereby differences between opposing views are projected onto a vertical axis and expressed as a contrast between the heavenly over and against the mundane perspective. This dualistic spatial staging is similarly often projected onto an axis of depth that implies a congruent disparity between interiority and exteriority, soul and body.
3. There is not necessarily a transition from polytheism towards henotheism or monotheism, but generally there is a noticeable reduction of the divine pantheon of archaic types of religion.
4. Axial age religions acknowledge the existence of rivalling worldviews, but these are denigrated in order to substantiate one's own truth.

5. They are distinguished from archaic ones by loosening or even abolishing the ontological differences between gods and humans. Therefore, they encourage adherents to imitate the godhead to such an extent that eventually the followers are thought to transcend the ontological difference between divine and human.

6. They place considerable emphasis on the element of *askēsis* understood in the basic Greek sense of training. By engaging in various forms of self-exercises, the practitioners in different axial religions undergo different forms of privations relating to what they consider false values. At the same time as they have abandoned previous values, they strive to inculcate the principles of their new worldview by embodying them.

7. Axial types of religion exemplify a shift in emphasis from the ritual observances of traditional religious sacrifices to various forms of inner attitudes as a prerequisite for proper cultic observance. This is sometimes called the displacement of ritual by a moral stance. It is not traditional cult *per se* that is criticized. What is called for is a moral attitude reflecting the new worldview as a presupposition for observing rituals in the proper manner.

8. Axial age religions often evolve a universal egalitarian ethic.

9. The emergence of this form of religion characteristically occurs in a situation of considerable social competition involving religious entrepreneurs' dissociation from the ruling elite—whether political or religious or both—and defiance against traditional kinship structures and political power as well as a plea for greater equality and social justice.

10. They typically evolve in socio-cultural conditions of increased density in populations in tandem with enhanced urbanization on a considerably larger scale compared to the urban conditions of archaic forms of religion. In fact, one may argue that whereas archaic religions are intrinsically connected to urbanity, Axial age religions are inherently related to imperial or "cosmic" cultures.

11. By virtue of their defiance of ethnic religions and the emphasis they place on partaking in universal truth, Axial age religions develop—in principle—as trans-ethnic types of religion, thereby confronting or making traditional religious boundaries superfluous or irrelevant.

12. Although Axial age religions generally evolve as an elite phenomenon, over centuries some of them develop into far greater movements spreading to areas distant from their original locations (Petersen 2013, 2017).

There is a huge difference between archaic religions with occasional ruptures of violence and institutionalized forms of aggression, as in human sacrifices, and violence in religious axiality. In the latter, violence is turned into an aggressive, zealous attempt at turning everybody else into adherents of the religion in question. That is the cultural and religious novelty in Axial age religions.

Jan Assmann is famous for what he calls the "Mosaic difference" and the "price of monotheism," by which he refers to the tendency of monotheistic religions to malign and eradicate rivalling worldviews (Assmann 2003). It should be noted, however, that this tendency is not solely restricted to Israelite religion. It is, as we have argued, a basic feature of all Axial age religions as well as those religions that followed and were strongly characterized by axiality. In fact, it is an even more noticeable feature in the post-Axial types of religion, since the Axial age religions proper did not have the institutional and societal backing needed for disseminating their worldview through warfare. As mentioned, they were exclusively an elite phenomenon. This, however, changed with the emergence of religions of axiality, when the originally relatively reduced elite members became replaced with the dissemination of axiality to far greater segments of the population. Examples of this are found in the numerous instances in which Christianity was violently imposed on other people, the spread of Islam by warfare, and the Chinese dissemination of Buddhism and Confucianism by way of the Korean kingdom Baekje on the Korean peninsula during the mid-6th century CE to Japan. Less violently, but nonetheless characterized by the same zeal to impose one's worldview on other people, is missionization. As is well-known from, for example, the history of Christianity, missionization often went hand in hand with gun power: either you convert or you die. This dimension of religions of axiality has left an appalling and horrendous track of blood in its wake.

Hunter–gatherer religions or archaic religions were not engaged in imposing their respective religions on other people. Greek religion was for Greeks only. Ndembu religion for Ndembus only, and so forth. This changed, in principle, with the emergence of Axial age religions and in the practices of religions of axiality, especially so at times and in places in which religions of axiality had the needed military, political, and social mechanisms that would allow them to spread their message by force.

There are two aspects here. The first pertains to what we from an external perspective view as intra-group impositions, whereas the second relates to inter-group enforcement of one's religion. The history of Christianity and Islam provide copious evidence of both. Roman Catholics have striven to enforce Catholicism on people adhering to Orthodox Christianity and vice-versa. The same phenomenon has been at play in the history of Western Europe during which Protestants of various denominations have fought against Catholics and Catholics against Protestants to impose their particular forms of Christianity. The religious wars of Britain are a telling example, as is the Thirty Years' War of Western and Central Europe. Parallel wars have been fought throughout the history of Islam with the most prominent fronts drawn between the Sunnis and Shias.

Parallel to intra-group violence over religion are inter-group wars in which an empire or nation seeks to enforce its religion upon the people of another nation or empire by forcing them to convert. Christian attempts of forced conversion of Jews and Muslims are unequivocal as are the reverse examples of Muslim efforts to force Christians and Jews to convert to Islam. Once again, however, it is crucial to emphasize that this is not a phenomenon solely found in monotheistic religions. We already noted the historical situation in which China, due to the cultural and territorial extension of the Han dynasty through the Korean kingdom of Baekje, imposed Buddhism and especially Confucianism upon Japan.

Ultimately, what we claim is that although religion and violence have been intrinsically connected since hunting and gathering, just as religion has constantly functioned as a driver of cultural evolution and as a stabilizing factor in securing social cohesion, something novel happened with the emergence of Axial age religions and especially so with the appearance of the post-Axial religions or religions of axiality. With the emergence of missionization as a core feature of post-Axial religions and the concomitant need to eradicate rivalling truth claims originating in the conviction of possessing the absolute truth, forced conversion became a stock phenomenon in the history of especially Christianity and Islam. The felt need to annihilate competing worldviews and by all means to disseminate one's own onto other people often in close conjunction with the expansion of empires tellingly demonstrates Spencerian Type-2 selection.

Inherent Limitations of the Movement of Religion across Societies

Some religions are more "portable" than others because of the inherent nature of beliefs about the supernatural, ritual practices directed at the supernatural, cult structures and their organization, and communities of worshipers. If we look at the two largest religions in the world today—Christianity and Islam—that have moved across the globe, they have beliefs that allow all who adhere to beliefs and practice rituals potential access to the supernatural realm. Moreover, all who take up the beliefs of Islam or Christianity become members of a cult structure; the beliefs themselves are relatively simple because there is only one god and a comparatively clear set of moral codes (and in Islam, a system of law).

The ritual practices of both religions are comparatively simple to practice, and they can be practiced by individuals alone, with periodic mediation of important calendrical rituals by religious specialists attached to cult structures; the cult structures themselves, while highly bureaucratic, are open and receptive at the membership level. Since Islam, Christianity, and Judaism all come from the same root-religion, it is instructive to ask why Judaism from the Talmudic period and onwards has not spread as fast and far as Islam and Christianity. One answer is the amount of work required to be a member of the cult structure: mandatory learning of texts to be displayed in a public ritual (Petersen 2017b). Another is the pressures for ethnic endogamy, with Jews required to marry Jews in more traditional branches, and while more liberal sects allow for intermarriage, early brands of Judaism generally did not, thus making it more difficult for the religion to move to new populations (instead, historically Jews themselves have been mobile, adhering to their beliefs and rituals; and because of discrimination against them as ethnic minorities in many societies, they have not had the power and perhaps not even the inclination to seek new members). This latter answer is closely related to what we think is the ultimate reason for Judaism's limited spread to other ethnic groups. It was during the Talmudic period that saw the emergence of Yerushalmi and Bavli (4th–6th century) that Rabbinic Judaism evolved into Judaism *par excellence*. This development is unthinkable without the development of Christ-religion into an independent, autonomous religion with regard to Judaism, that is, Christianity (cf. Boyarin 2010; Becker and Reed 2003). In fact, we may account for this development in terms of Durkheimian selection. One trajectory of ancient Judaism, Christ-religion, came to fill the niche of an Axial trans-ethnic Judaism preoccupied with dissemination of itself to "all pagans" (cf. Matthew 28: 19f.). What eventually became the other grand Judaism, Rabbinic Judaism, filled a niche more in line with classical Israelite religion and late Second Temple Judaism in general and its subsequent development in Mishnaic Judaism. Since proselyte baptism always constituted an option in Rabbinic Judaism, it is obviously wrong to identify it with a form of religion restricted to kinship and ethnicity only. That said, however, Judaism's predominantly ethnic kinship-founded type of religion can only be appreciated and understood when we grasp how Judaism and Christianity developed in close relationship to each other and eventually came to fill out two very different religious niches. Moreover, many religions are tied to place, local communities and regions. For example, religions such as Hinduism, while quite large because of the large population served and at one time mobile, are now more difficult to transport across societal boundaries because the beliefs are complex, as are the rituals, and membership is tied to specific territories with little effort to expand to new societies.

Thus, geopolitics and even geo-economics cannot always make religions more mobile; religions are often tied to territories and ethnic identities, while their beliefs and rituals are too complex or require too much study. Although Christians can engage in much Bible study as do Muslims in similar efforts to understand the Quran, these are not hard requirements for membership in many cult structures, *per se*, although the fundamentalist wing of these religions requires a great deal of study as a means for isolating recruits. Still, even with emphasis on textual studies, the required rituals are relatively simple and can be performed anywhere by an individual. While the requirement to pray to Mecca five times each day may seem like a burden, it is done relatively easily at any location. Moreover, by engaging in prayer so frequently, commitments to the belief systems of Islam are built up and encourage efforts to bring others into the fold.

The Spanish Conquest of the Americas

Perhaps the best example of a response to Type-2 Spencerian pressures began in 1519 with the conquest of the Aztecs and the imposition of a new empire upon the old one that had been built up through inter-city conflicts and consolidations of ever-larger territories by a series of indigenous hegemonists of North, Central, and South America. The Spanish, in the end, took the coercive route to responding to Type-2 Spencerian selection pressures by imposing Catholicism and forcing linguistic changes that are still evident throughout the Americas, especially Central and South America, much of the Caribbean, and portions of North America (e.g., Mexico but at one time what is now central and southern California and southern Texas, Arizona, and New Mexico).

Why and how did the importation of the culture of Spain (and Portugal as well) occur? Religion was at the center of this form of coercive domination by Spain over "its" territories. Before the Spanish conquest of the Aztecs and Incas, Christopher Columbus' "Voyage of Discovery," in 1492, was always intended, or soon after the "discovery," to involve the colonization and extraction of whatever economic resources could be found, accompanied by missionary activity to pacify the indigenous populations. Pope Alexander VI bestowed "colonial rights" over the newly discovered lands to both Spain and Portugal, documenting that the Roman Catholic Church was always involved in political decisions about how to dominate the newly conquered territories. The objective of Spanish imperialism was to control large territories that would extend Spanish culture and language, while increasing Spanish wealth and geopolitical power *vis-à-vis* other European powers. These goals could best be achieved by the mission activity of the Catholic Church.

Hernán Cortés emphasized that the "Indians" needed to be subordinate to the Spanish throne and the "mysteries of Christ." The Catholic Church had already ruled that war could only be made on populations that rejected the Gospel, and so the war itself could be legitimated in light of this doctrine of the Church. This doctrine also legitimated the plan to convert the indigenous population of the Americas to Christianity and thus make them no longer subject to further war—which in reality and over the long run turned out to be a somewhat empty debating point. Still, Spencerian Type-1 selection pressures—to regulate the larger conquered population—set into motion Spencerian Type-2 selection where Catholicism was ordained to be more "fit" than the religions of the indigenous "Indians" in the Americas.

Cortes requested that "spiritually minded" priests be sent to "new Spain" who were practical and capable of converting the native populations. This request set into motion the first Franciscan priests (the most famous being Father Junipero Serra, who was recently canonized as a Saint), followed by priests from the Jesuits and other Catholic orders.

The basic approach of the Church and local Spanish governmental officials was to pull natives from the hinterlands into more concentrated assemblies in order to convert them to Catholicism, or at least try to do so (which was the basic requirement of the Church), but with conversion to Catholicism, the missionaries could pull many natives away from the slavery imposed by some conquistadors (because "fellow" Catholics cannot be used as slaves), even though the Spanish, much like colonists in what became the United States, still tended to see Native Americans as biologically inferior (as, in the most benign characterization, as "child-like," which is remarkable in light of the grandeur of Aztec civilization witnessed by the Spanish). In North America, the mission system scattered over the southern part of the United States, and most extensively up the California coast to San Francisco. In South America, Reductions, or mini city-states were created by Jesuits, spreading across Argentina, Bolivia, and Uruguay, and to Brazil controlled by the Portuguese.

The strategy was to use coercive threats and material incentives to pull individuals in, giving them "work," and educating them into Christianity. The missions and Reductions were not only economic and educational sites, but they were also locales for various garrisons and concentrations of coercive power. These communities of activity were successful in at least getting the indigenous populations around them to appear to be converted, but often they were not, and more often, they began to create a more polytheistic reconciliation of Christian monotheism with their local religious icons. Indeed, to this day, the further one goes from urban areas in Latin America, the more the remnants of the first American religions and languages can be found.

Nonetheless, the strategy employed was certainly coercive, following the labels in Figure 9.1, and it worked for a time in pacifying the populations of the Americas. Also, an equally powerful force of pacification was European diseases that killed off at least a third of the indigenous population, and even more in locations such as Florida. A smaller population is generally easier to control, and so, as is often the case, an army's germs can be as deadly as their armaments. Other dynamics outlined in Figure 9.1, however, emphasized that coercive strategies are difficult to sustain over long periods of time, although the Spanish empire could exist for a longer than the normal time because of the differences in level of development between conquerors and conquered and, of course, because of the devastation of disease. Eventually, inequalities that produced tensions around fault lines of any pattern of social organization, coupled with failures to meet the key psychological needs of all humans, led to conflicts between the descendants of the conquered and their conquerors by the middle of the 18th century, and earlier in many locales. These conflicts would eventually intensify to full revolutions in some societies over the next two centuries, and the problems of stability linger in much of Latin America today.

This big fault line of tension building up to conflict sometimes obscures the internal conflict among the dominant factions in the Americas. There were significant disagreements between religious and political personnel, as well as considerable disagreement among the members of the religious orders that were at the center of the conversion of the natives. There was, in some ways, a pattern of Durkheimian selection in the competition among religious orders, as well as the "converts" to Christianity who still clandestinely worshiped their local gods. Indeed, North American Christianity has such remnants of indigenous religions in such strange practices as associating rabbits and eggs with celebrations of Christ's resurrection, and more "pagan" rituals and holidays such as Halloween (in the US) and "Day of the Dead" in Mexico, coupled with the strange juxtaposition of iconic symbols from mostly-dead local religions with symbols of the Virgin Mary.

Yet, the outcome is still a dramatic realization that Type-2 Spencerian selection several hundred years ago converted a large portion of the world's population to Christianity, although in some areas Catholicism is losing members in a Durkheimian competition with alternative moral orders; and moreover, in other remote areas, Catholicism has never taken and is not likely to take hold. Like all forms of coercion and imposition of ideologies (like Christianity), to resolve Type-1 Spencerian selection problems, the use of coercion and imposition of new ideologies as a strategy for Type-2 Spencerian selection creates a new round of Spencerian Type-1 selection pressures, often accompanied by Durkheimian selection pressures. The result is instability in a society's political system, but less so in the religious system that was once imposed. Even efforts to secularize in a kind of "New

Age" ideology have not been highly successful in Latin America. Thus, what was transplanted with no real rivals (except the remnants of now "dead" religions), Type-2 selection driving religious evolution tends to endure, especially if internal Durkheimian competition is limited. Thus, religion, once institutionalized in the context of destroying its rivals, tends to persist, even as the political system constantly undergoes rounds of coups, revolts, and other destabilizing processes.

A Note on Geo-Economic Formations

Geo-eonomic systems often emerge out of geopolitical systems, or vice versa, when an existing geo-economic system is usurped by an expanding geopolitical empire. In either case, networks of trade and exchange almost always bring movement of religious cult structures, beliefs, and rituals from one society to another. When a geo-economic hegemon relies upon relatively unregulated markets to distribute resources among populations spread across the societies of this geo-economic system, religion can also be marketed and hence be subject to quasi-competitive market forces, often in accordance with the principles of Durkheimian selection examined in Chapter 8. For example, Christianity moved across the Roman Empire, as outlined in the last chapter, along the trade routes and networks of merchants, even as a dominating political system existed. Indeed, in organizing the early Christ-movement less than two decades after Jesus' death, Paul explicitly mobilized resources—symbolic and organizational—to attract individuals and families of the merchant middle classes to this niche in what was termed *Blau-space* in the previous chapter. Thus, the level of dynamism of markets within a geopolitical formation can also accelerate the evolution of religion as cult structures seek resource niches within conquered populations. To the extent that the geo-economic system dominates geopolitical formations, this movement and evolution of religion will be more pronounced and rapid. Geo-economic systems provide networks driven by market exchange relations along with religious ideas and rituals, and the cult structures organizing these can travel relatively unfettered unless they threaten indigenous systems of power and/or an in-place religion.

Yet, even with restrictions imposed by existing systems of power and religion, markets *per se* create holes and gaps in these systems; thereby, they provide conduits by which new ideas can travel, even if in a more clandestine manner. Such was surely the case for the movement of Christian beliefs in the early days; this movement was so successful that the Roman Empire eventually became Christian. In more recent centuries, as capitalism and democracy have spread across more societies, religious ideas can travel by means of geo-economic networks with less fear of persecution. For example, the significant increase in rates of migration of skilled technology workers from Middle Eastern countries during the late 1970s to the United States brought a new type of Arab and, in the case of immigrants from Iran, Persian populations to the United States, although Islam had already come to the United States and appealed to some members of the US African-origin population (indeed, the largest Islamic subpopulation in the United States is still Black Muslims). Similarly, much earlier at the turn into the 20th century, open markets had brought persecuted Christian Arabs, who were mostly small-scale traders from what is now Lebanon and Syria, to the United States during the wave of migrations from the Middle East. Of course, the formation of the European Union, mostly an economic formation opening up indigenous markets and, at the same time, lowering some national barriers, allowed for the spread of Muslims across Europe over the last 30 years. This capacity to migrate along networks created by labor markets is, however, now being seriously tested by the flood of refugees from the war-torn Middle East.

Conclusion

It is clear that religion and warfare are connected, whether as a cause and/ or effect of warfare. For much of human history, religion was the dominant ideology and worldview of most societies; as polity consolidated and centralized power as societies began to grow, religion served to legitimate this growth of power and the inequalities that concentrated power in a society always generates. Thus, religion allowed polity to respond to Type-1 Spencerian selection pressures examined in Chapter 7, but also set the stage for the use of religion to legitimate polity as it conquered other societies and, if necessary, to change the religious ideologies and worldviews of those conquered. True, religious elites were often part of the political impetus for external conquest—as was certainly the case with the movement of Spain and Catholicism into the Americas. Whether as part of the planning for warfare and conquest or as a reliable tool for legitimating political activities once conquest has been initiated, religion and polity have remained connected.

There have been many variations on the degree to which the religion of conquering states has been imposed upon the conquered, and when religion is part of the impetus for conquest—as has been the case with Islam and Christianity at many points in world history—the coercive strategy of imposing a religion on those conquered is employed, thereby setting off

Spencerian Type-2 dynamics. When, however, the motivations and impetus for conquest are not tied to religion but to geo-economics and, to a lesser extent, geopolitics, more co-optive strategies can be employed, as was evident with the Roman conquests, in some conquests by even the highly militaristic Aztec polity, and as was the case for much of the British Empire in places such as India, where the indigenous religion and its association with political control was too well entrenched to be displaced without creating a new level of Spencerian Type-1 selection pressures on controlling the newly conquered population. When the co-optive route of domination is taken (i.e., pay tribute to a hegemonist who leaves most of the indigenous institutional systems and their cultures intact), religion is not as central to addressing Type-1 Spencerian selection. Dealing with Type-1 pressures is more likely to revolve around law, tax formulas, compounding of local power bases with the coercive and administrative bases of power of the hegemonist, and exchanges (typically unequal) between the dominated and the dominant.

When the institutional systems and cultures of those conquered are diverse, and themselves subject to past warfare, as was the case in much of the Americas, conquest uses religion as the centerpiece of a coercive strategy of destroying indigenous religions, cultures, and institutions—as was evident with the Spanish (and their versions of the mission system) and with patterns of earlier conquest (before the Spanish) in central America by various city states that became empires with elaborate ceremonial centers (and eventually conquered by the Spanish).

Karl Marx may well be turning over in his grave in seeing what we are calling Marxian selection in the next chapter as another type of connection between religion and political-economic conflicts within and between societies. For Marx, religion was an obfuscation that needed to be eliminated in order for the subjugated to realize their true class interests in revolutionary conflict. The reality, however, has turned out to be much different than Marx could have foreseen. Much conflict in human societies today revolves around religious cults, believers, and rituals because religion is often the basis of unequal distributions of resources and patterns of religious/ethnic discrimination in much of the world. Because religion moralizes actions, religious conflicts tend to be particularly intense and violent because they are over more than material resources. They are also over beliefs and rituals by which people verify themselves as moral persons, and such moralization of people's worldviews is less subject to compromise. Thus, Marx was correct in much of his argument that inequalities in economic and social positions in society are a source of tension and resource mobilization for conflict against oppressors, but because class and other position in a society are often conflated with religion, it is religion that serves as the basis for mobilization of conflict, which assures that the conflicts will be intense and that they will often spill over to neighboring societies and, indeed, potentially spread across multiple societies. Marxian theory predicted something that never really occurred: a revolt by the proletariat in a capitalist society; but his theory, when hitched up with religious dynamics, can predict when violent conflict will occur in *any* society.

10
Marxian Selection
The Dynamics of Religious Conflict

[C]ollective action stirs the lava of a volcanic eruptions: collective action is
about power and politics; it inevitably raises questions or right and wrong,
justice and injustice, hope and hopelessness . . .

Charles Tilly (1978)

The competition and selection among cult organizations can often be part of a larger social movement in a society, where the cult is used to push a more encompassing political and moral agenda. Such was the case in the United States with the Civil Rights movement for over a century, but especially in the 1960s when the movement gained real traction by relying heavily on religious organizations in the American South for much of its recruiting and organizational base. At other times, a religion itself becomes a social movement, seeking to expand its political power to press for what can often become a revolutionary agenda. The literature on social movements is vast within sociology and political science, but the basic dynamics that have been outlined in this large literature can be tailored to analyzing the evolution of religion as it becomes a force seeking to change institutional systems as part of a larger agenda to consolidate political power and to control the actions of individuals and corporate units within some, or even all, institutional domains.

All of the world religions have spread across geographical regions that were not always the same society, at least initially. At times, this diffusion of a religion can involve Durkheimian more than Marxian selection as, for example, was the initial spread of Christianity across the Roman Empire on Roman roads and commercial networks of the merchant classes. At other times, as was examined in Chapter 9, religions spread as a byproduct of political conquests of other populations and societies through Spencerian Type-2 selection, as was clearly evident with Catholicism in the Americas. Colonization almost always leads to some displacement of the indigenous religion by the conquering power, but the degree and extent of religious displacement can vary, as was the case in the British colonization of India or much of the initial conquests of the Roman empire, where most of the dominant religions of the conquered populations persisted, compared to the Spanish colonization of the new world, where active efforts to replace indigenous religions with Catholicism were conducted. If the religion of a conquering power does not use violence or even the administrative power of the colonizing society, then the clash of religions is more Durkheimian but, equally often, the clash is supported by the coercive powers of the conquering society and its imposition of a legal system and varying degrees of political control. Even seemingly more Durkheimian dynamics, such as the founding of the mission organizational system in California where Catholicism was preached, were Spencerian Type-2, or even Marxian, because of the use of Spanish power to force conversions to Catholicism.

Dynamics of Marxian Selection

Figure 2.6 on p. 43 in Chapter 2 outlines in model form the key dynamics of Marxian selection. In this chapter, our goal is to examine these in more detail, as a series of unfolding processes over time, as it applies to religious evolution. Driving all Marxian selection is *emotional arousal* among a subpopulation and *its mobilization for conflict*, sometimes led by polity but equally often by religious leaders who emerge in competition among several religious cult structures and who then begin to mobilize subpopulations for coercive conflict against those who dominate, often members of rival sects that have controlled the polity.

Emotional Arousal and Mobilization for Conflict

As emphasized in the last chapter, like any organization that is building up its structure and culture, a social movement organization (SMO) seeks resources of various kinds, such as material (money and capital), demographic (categories of people in Blau-space), technological (knowledge about how to organize and manipulate environments), organizational (networks, allies, and templates for building structures), and cultural (ideologies for recruiting and legitimating organizational activities). The success of an SMO depends upon how many of all these basic kinds of resources can be secured, but success of SMO also rests on the capacity of its leaders to arouse and tap into the emotional energy of particular subpopulations in a society who have grievances that arouse syndromes of negative emotions that, reciprocally, feed back to increase grievances in what can become a constantly escalating cycle.

The energy behind a social movement is ultimately the micro-level negative emotional arousal of persons (Turner 2008, 2014; Goodwin et al. 2001, 2004; Goodwin and Jasper 2006). Emotions are aroused by conditions that individuals see as problematic and often unjust in the institutional systems of a society as these systems distribute resources, such as money, political power, educational credentials, honor and prestige, and even positive emotions as a valued resource unequally and thereby create a system of stratification (Turner 1984, 2014). Also important is the positive emotional energy that individuals experience when organizing against their perceived oppressors. Thus, the full polarity of emotions is almost always evident in the mobilization of individuals by social movement organizations.

In general, the more particular categories (ethnic, class, religious) of persons have been denied access to resource-bestowing corporate units, the greater will be their negative emotional arousal and sense of grievance and injustice. And, the larger the number of such persons in a society is, the more potential does a social movement, once started, have in changing the structure and culture of a society, particularly when a population is highly stratified. Again, many of the need-states (verification of self, profitable exchanges, sense of efficacy, etc.) that individuals seek to meet in normal interactions can, when they go unmet, increase negative emotional arousal; and the more interactions with others in corporate units degrade their status, roles, and cultures, as well as their sense of self, efficacy, and other needs, the more intense this arousal will be. What may originally start out as anxiety, and perhaps even shame, can soon turn into diffuse anger and violence. Thus, anger and, indeed, very violent first-order elaborations of anger like *vengeance* (anger at enemies, mixed with happiness at doing harm to these perceived enemies) can assure that conflict will become violent. Once again, the same forces that allow individuals to bond to each other can work, in stratified societies, to mobilize individuals to wage war against others and to change the fundamental nature of the institutional systems that have degraded and denied them. As people's sense of grievance suddenly escalates in response to events that often seem important only in retrospect, the relative deprivations of persons can also suddenly escalate; and people's diffuse and somewhat *generalized beliefs* about the causes of their distress push their emotions to a much higher level of intensity (Smelser 1963).

Deprivations, Emotions, and Attributions

As this sense of deprivation increases, individuals begin, individually and collectively, to make attributions with respect to whom and what bears responsibility for their anger and sense of deprivation. As noted in Chapter 5, negative emotions tend to have a *distal bias*, with individuals making external attributions to particular leaders and, equally important, to the institutional structures of a society as they generate inequalities (Lawler 2001; Turner 2002). Generalized beliefs can increasingly become focused through *frames*, often articulated by charismatic leaders, that specify particular targets for individuals' sense of deprivation. At times these frames can even focus on members of other categoric units (ethnic and religious being the most common), thereby raising the anger and injustice to very high levels—often preparing people to commit extreme violence such as genocide and violent oppression of religious enemies. Indeed, the more members of categoric units are blamed for others' deprivations, the more likely is the ensuing conflict by an SMO to be violent; and such is particularly likely to be the case when people have repressed their sense of shame and humiliation at the hands of these "categories of others" to the point that their diffuse anger begins to circle around dangerous emotions like needs for *vengeance*. SMOs can tap into this anger and recruit members who will eventually become the corporate unit's arm of violence; and often the SMOs that engage in this kind of recruitment are religious. Indeed, the more one religious cult can claim that another cult structure is filled with hated members of other categoric units (ethnic and/or religious), the more a religious movement can justify the use of extreme violence.

The Spread of Violence and Institutional Change

However, once violence occurs, it will often be extended beyond persecution of members of other religious communities and include a broader agenda of taking state power and controlling key institutional domains. At other times, attributions target non-religious targets, such as political leaders and the institutional arrangements that these leaders have supported; and here, even if the conflict is mobilized by religious organizations, it targets the centers of power. Yet, if revolt against these centers of power is successful, the new consolidation of power will be built around religious beliefs, as happened in the Iranian Revolution of the late 1970s and as the current movement of ISIS across the Middle East seeks to do (see later discussion of ISIS).

As SMOs are successful in recruiting members to their cause, framing activities by leaders become ever-more focused on particular moral issues and sources that are seen to be responsible for their grievances. Organizational leaders articulate a unifying ideology, often drawn from religious beliefs, if cult structures are organizing into SMOs, that challenge the authority of those in power, and typically all other cult structures organizing worship of the supernatural. These challenges are highly moralized, which means that they further escalate emotions to the point that compromises over moral issues are no longer possible, thereby assuring violence.

Resources and Recruiting

As SMOs recruit members, they employ a number of strategies, including (Turner 2013): (a) use of movement ideologies to verify the identities, especially core and social identities, of those recruited; (b) use of cells and subgroups to increase the sense of group inclusion and solidarity among movement members; (c) providing status locations and roles in the SMO that are rewarding and meaningful to members; (d) using interaction rituals at the group level to jack up emotions (see Figure 6.1 on p. 132); (e) using religious rituals to retain commitments to the larger belief system of the religiously oriented SMO; and (f) recruiting, often through the internet and social media, (i) younger members who are more willing to take risks and engage in violence to realize (ii) their moral/religious beliefs that are (iii) symbolized with totems and toward which (iv) rituals are enacted. Even if an SMO is not religious, it will engage in these recruiting practices, and if the SMO is religious, symbols marking the sacred and supernatural, coupled with ritualized appeals to the supernatural, will further moralize beliefs and arouse ever-more intense emotions.

Social movements of any sort are most likely to occur in what can be described as a liminal zone between, at one pole, (a) a system of political democracy where an open system of politics makes social movements less necessary and, at the other pole, (b) a system of coercive repression that makes movements unlikely to form or to be successful. It is typically in societies that repress dissent but do not have complete coercive and administrative control of the population and that do not respond politically to accumulating grievances that social movements are most likely to turn violent when mobilized. Violence will be most intense when the movement is organized around categoric-unit memberships, particularly religious and ethnic categories of persons or both, in which one set of categoric-unit members is mobilized to destroy the perceived oppression, now and in the past, of another set of categoric-unit members. It is for this reason that religious social movements, driven by emotions about perceived grievances against members of demonized categoric-units, become highly violent—another consequence of Darwinian natural selection making an evolved ape so emotional and capable of remembering and re-evoking past affronts to members of their religious affiliation in the distant past, often centuries after perceived religious oppression.

Movement Success

Social movements are successful under a number of basic conditions. First, if the political system is weak, even a coercive system, the arousal of emotions, particularly under the rubric of a religious cause, generates extreme violence that can simply overwhelm polity and other religious cults in a society. Second, the level of negative emotional energy, particularly long-endured shame at the hands of perceived enemies, particularly categoric-units composed of members of another religious cult structure, will have large effects on how successful a movement will be. Third, qualifying this generalization is the relative size of the subpopulations being mobilized. The larger the size of the emotionally aroused subpopulation vis-à-vis its antagonists, the more likely the mobilization is to be successful. Fourth, access to means of coercion is also critical, especially if a movement is protracted over time and settles into true warfare (as a form of civil war) as opposed to shorter-term riots and revolutionary violence. Often, particularly in the case of religious movements that turn violent, external client states and related cult structures support those engaged in violence, as is clearly the case with ISIS in the second decade of the 20th century. Equally often, the opposing side of SMO mobilization by a religious cult also has external client states or cult structures that support them with armaments and other material resources for the use of violence, thus assuring that the conflict will escalate and the aftermath of warfare will lead to oppression by the winning side, thereby setting up the potential for a new round of grievances and emotional arousal down the road for yet another religious conflict conforming to the dynamics of Marxian selection outlined in Figure 2.6 on p. 43 and Figure 10.1.

The relation of populations to the ecology and demography of territory can also become an important variable in conflict. Large subpopulations fighting in small territories assure much violence and killing, whereas smaller subpopulations invading the territories of another subpopulation in a larger territory can prolong conflict, particularly if the two sides are more or less equally matched in their respective capacities for warfare. When conflict is fought in urban centers, then it becomes extremely violent as factions fight over neighborhoods and, in the process, physically destroy the urban infrastructure.

Violent Religious Movements as Ecological Processes

Herbert Spencer's (1851) famous phrase, "survival of the fittest," had what became a Darwinian ring, but as we have emphasized, he increasingly used this phrase to denote warfare between societies, with the larger, more technologically advanced and productive society generally winning wars, and thus ratcheting up the overall complexity of societies in the world. But, religious movements that turn violent within and between societies tend to do just the opposite and tend to reduce complexity because they involve extreme orthodoxy in religious beliefs and imposition of these beliefs to all institutional realms or domains, thereby reducing complexity of culture and imposing structural arrangements that revolve around coercive domination. Warfare can be considered an ecological process, just one involving very

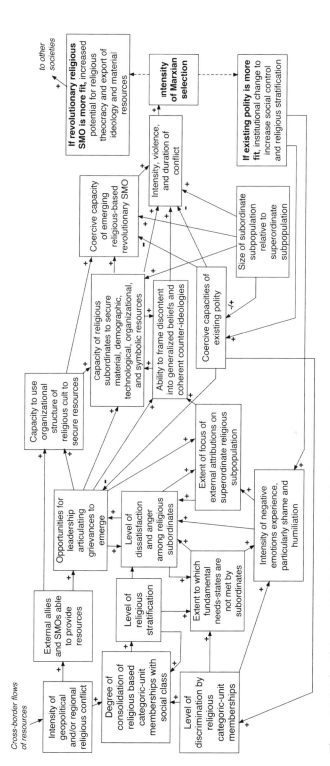

Figure 10.1 The Elaborated Model of Marxian Selection Dynamics

extreme competition among larger social units. Religious warfare begins as competition between or among cult structures, escalates into warfare and violence, and then into acts of oppression aimed at vanquishing the conquered within a delimited area, perhaps just one society or a region of societies. The goal of the conflict is social control of the population in this territory and its conversion to the winning religious cult system. Normally, organizations do not engage in such destructive and oppressive conduct, unless the organizations are armies of a political regime. Religious and ethnic movements can, however, become very much like state warfare when they have access to recruits, material resources, and most importantly, war-making technologies of client states or, as is the case today in the world, an active arms market. These conflicts typically evidence much more intensity and violence because participants have long-term hostilities, often fueled by shame and past humiliations at the hands of an enemy, and beliefs in the justice of their cause legitimated by highly moralized religious codes and rituals, which most armies cannot match. Indeed, a state would probably not want its entire army so emotionally mobilized, only its elite and strategically used special-forces units. A "religious war" is often a collective fight to the death, and only an animal with very intense emotions coupled with a large neocortex could engage in such battles; and so, the very forces that made religion possible are also the forces that make religious conflict so destructive.

Figure 10.1 seeks to incorporate this discussion into a more robust model of Marxian selection dynamics than was presented in Figure 2.6, which was only intended to introduce the idea of Marxian analysis being seen as a kind of selection process. In Figure 10.1 we have focused on religion when it becomes the basis for discrimination against one religion by another or others, thus setting up a stratification system based on membership in religious-based categoric-units arranged in a system of domination. Often religion is tied to ethnicity, which makes the system of stratification doubly volatile. Indeed, when religion is the basis of super-subordination, many of the dynamics that inhibit class-based Marxian selection actually work to increase the intensity of conflict and selection. Thus, most of the arrows in the figure are positive because once the religious stratification system begins to mobilize as a revolutionary SMO, the dynamics are difficult to arrest, unless the polity has enormous coercive power. If polity does not have such power, mobilization for conflict will continue. In democratic societies, however, this kind of mobilization is unlikely to occur because there will be less stratification based upon religion, and the most common dynamic will probably be Durkheimian selection. But, when Marxian dynamics are initiated, the conflict will often draw resources from outside of a society, and if religious SMOs prove to be more fit than polity, the new polity will become more theocratic and, moreover, will export resources to other societies and thus set into motion more Marxian selection on a regional and perhaps even global scale. So, again, the irony is that Marxian selection dynamics are more likely to be set into motion when class and religion are consolidated (i.e., memberships in different religious cults is correlated with high, middle, and low positions in the class structure.)

Illustrative Examples of Marxian Selection and the Evolution of Religions

War in Sri Lanka

Because of popular perceptions of Buddhism, it is difficult for many to understand the behavior of Buddhist groups in Sri Lanka in their violence against the Tamil minority, armed conflict with the Tamil Tigers, and the persecution and violence against Muslim and Christian minorities. Major news commentators and internet publications struggle to understand how a religion claiming to be canonically pacifistic and non-violent (*ahimsa*), even to the point of being vegetarians to avoid killing other sentient beings, could possibly condone organizations such as the Bodu Bala Sena (BBS—Buddhist Power Force) that systematically incites mobs to demolish mosques, burn homes, kill innocent victims, provides an ideology for governmental policies against minorities, and persecutes pacifist Buddhists (Ridge 2007; Hays 2014; Isaacs 2014; Mohan 2015; Haviland 2015; Jerryson 2015; Jimenez 2015). Scholars have equally struggled to explain these developments (see for instance Bond 1988; Dharmadasa 1992; Gombrich and Obeyesekere 1988; Bartholomeusz 2002). The fundamental issue is whether Buddhists can be violent even though they adhere to Buddhist doctrine or whether violent Buddhists are simply not "true" Buddhists. If we think about it, the same argument concerning other religions is often offered. As anthropologist Henry Munson, among many others, has pointed out: "Religion kills" because it arouses emotions and moralizes ideologies that legitimate violence (Munson 2005: 223). Scholar of religion Michael K. Jerryson argues correctly that religious traditions are "quintessentially social in nature" and thus subject to all positive and negative human elements. Buddhism is no exception, he points out, "Within the various Buddhist traditions . . . there is a long history of violence. Since the inception of Buddhist traditions 2,500 years ago, there have been numerous individual and structural cases of prolonged Buddhist violence" (Jerryson 2010: 3). Sociologist Charles Selengut in his *Sacred Fury* has equally argued that "all religions have themes both of forgiveness and peacemaking as well as demands for retribution and violence against their enemies" (Selengut 2003: 12).

Sri Lankan Buddhism itself was the victim of Marxian selection pressures. It is hardly surprising that the current situation is a convoluted result of colonialism in Sri Lanka. The Portuguese, having arrived on the island in 1517, spent a century subduing and definitively colonizing the island in 1619. Then the Dutch, having signed a treaty in 1638 with Rajasinghe II, booted the Portuguese out by 1656, but remained in the areas they conquered, despite treaty stipulations. England took control of the island beginning in 1796 and ended Sri Lanka's independence in 1815. The British followed their usual principles of colonization: the introduction of a capitalistic system, the establishment of transportation and communication infrastructures, the development of printing facilities and a school system under missionary control, and the implementation of a plantation economy—first with coffee and subsequently with tea—and, finally, the encouragement of English-educated indigenous collaborators, giving rise to a middle class using the new social mobility to circumvent family, caste, and ethnic dividing lines and thus, acquiring enormous wealth (Roberts 1997: 1011). All of these initiatives, however, were accompanied by the all too common denigration of indigenous culture. As anthropologist Michael Roberts has shown, they were treated with humiliating subordination that encouraged Type-2 Spencerian selection in which missionaries sought to impose Christianity:

> The British rulers exuded an overwhelming self-conviction in the superiority of their civilization and looked down on the various "native races" in British Ceylon as ignorant, barbarous, and effeminate. The missionaries and their evangelical supporters in the early and mid-nineteenth century persistently vilified the Buddhist and Hindu religions as "pagan," "idolatrous," and full of superstition.
>
> (Roberts 1997: 1008)

Towards the end of the 19th century, Ceylonese nationalism arose together with Sinhala nationalistic tendencies in an attempt to regain self-respect. One of the catalysts of this movement was Anagarika Dharmapala (1864–1933), who joined forces with Theosophists, Henry Steel Olcott and Helena Blavatsky, in reforming and reviving Ceylonese Buddhism. This has been termed "Protestant Buddhism" by anthropologist Gananath Obeyesekere (Gombrich and Obeyesekere 1988: 215). Roberts, among others, has shown that Dharmapala broke with Theosophy in 1902 after having actually studied Buddhist texts. "My Pali studies," Dharmapala wrote, "have opened my eyes and I find the erroneous doctrines of Theosophy and all other *isms* injurious for the growth of the human mind" (quoted in Roberts 1997: 1014). What influenced Dharmapala was the 6th-century text called *Mahavamsa* (Great Chronicle), written by Theravada monks. It claimed that the Buddha himself had visited Sri Lanka three times and named it *sihadipa* (island of the Sinhalese) and *dhammadipa* (island ennobled to protect and propagate Buddhism). As DeVotta and Stone have shown, "the vast majority of Sinhalese accept its pro-Buddhist and pro-Sinhalese accounts as indisputable history" (DeVotta and Stone 2008: 34). Dharmapala promoted a glorified version of virtuous Sinhalese Buddhist kings, an enlightened society, and a moral population. Such a reign, he argued, "could be reinstituted, although that required both laymen and *bhikkhus* to regain their rightful status in society" (DeVotta and Stone 2008: 35).

Political scientist Neil DeVota has argued that Dharmapala's rhetoric consisted of not only praising Buddhism and Sinhalese culture but also blaming the British and Christians, instilling the fear that Buddhism was threatened, and encouraging revitalization (DeVotta 2001: 78). He targeted significant "Others" through racist rhetoric: black Africans, British Christians, Muslims, and Hindus: "Buddha is the unifier of Asia. Muhammad was a brigand and a plunderer. Christians are immoral hypocrites" (Sept. 1913, quoted in Roberts 1997: 1024). "Of all the destructive religions Mohammedanism is the worst. Then comes Christianity and Brahmanism. Christianity, Zoroastrianism and Brahmanism; Brahmanism was partially successful in destroying Buddhism" (May 1903, quoted in Roberts 1997: 1024). This rhetoric led to clashes during the 1920s and 1930s with Hindu Tamils, among others. It made matters worse that the Tamils also considered Sri Lanka to be their rightful homeland (Bartholomeusz 1999: 216).

In 1946, a Buddhist monk (*bhikkhu*), Walpola Rahula, published an important work, *Bhiksuvage Urumaya* (The Heritage of the Bhikkhu), which not only embraced Dharmapala but also transformed the role of the reclusive monk into that of a political activist. He argued with reference to the *Mahavamsa* that monks have always made political contributions and even engaged in military activity. War was legitimate "if waged to liberate and protect nation and religion" (DeVotta and Stone 2008: 35). Thus the "political *bhikku*" that he promulgated had profound influence on later developments (DeVotta and Stone 2008: 35; Seneviratne 1999). After independence in 1948, a climate of Sinhala-Buddhist "chauvinism, indeed even fundamentalism that continues to the present has linked ideas of a Buddhist homeland to Sri Lanka and the Sinhala people" (Bartholomeusz

1999: 216–17), thus instilling the idea that no other ethnic or religious groups had claims to the "'sacred' Buddhist island" (Bartholomeusz 1999: 216).

During the early 1950s a radical Buddhist monk political party, the Eksath Bhikku Peramuna (EBP—United Monks Front) was established by Mapitigama Buddharakkhita (1921–67). They entered the national elections in 1956 during which the United National Party and its right-wing, English-educated leadership was defeated (Roberts 199: 1006). The EBP had great influence on later groups (Matthews 1988–89: 622 n.4) and actively supported the new Prime Minister Solomon Bandaranaike who institutionalized the "Sinhala only" policy. In 1958, the first anti-Tamil pogrom occurred (Vaitheespara 2007: 60). Although the EBP supported the "Bandaranaike revolution," they were nevertheless implicated in his assassination in 1959 by the monk Talduwe Somarama for being too accommodating of the Tamils (Matthews 1988–89, 622 n.4; Jimenez 2015). Violence, disenfranchisement, and persecution against the Tamils continued until the 1983 slaughter of thousands of Tamils in and around Colombo (Bartholomeusz 1999: 216). During that same year, the parliament enacted the Sixth Amendment to the constitution making all separatist activities unconstitutional and thus denying Tamils normal democratic process (Hennayake 1989: 402). Thus began the civil war between the Liberation Tigers of Tamil Eelam (LTTE) and the Sinhala-Buddhist government, which lasted from 1983 until 2009 and killed an estimated 70,000 people.

Much of the above can be understood in terms of Marxian selection. We will, however, mention two brief examples of this that stand out much more clearly during the 2000s. But a few words about Spencerian Type-2 selection pressures must be said, which have contributed significantly to later Marxian selection pressures. Political scientist Matthew Isaacs, at Brandeis University, in his insightful analysis has argued that during the 1950s, the State no longer gave material support to the Buddhist *sangha* (Buddhist clergy). There are around 30,000 monks divided into numerous sects, which earlier were regulated by a high council. The various sects thus became dependent on lay worshippers, which undermined the Buddhist hierarchy and simultaneously increased resource competition between the various sects. The end result was that representatives from poorer temples embraced a more radical message that increased radicalism and activism by monks, especially since the 1970s (Isaacs 2014). Thus, Marxian pressures kicked in. The two examples will show how a highly influential Buddhist monk political party incited extreme violence against religious minorities as well as pacifist Buddhists while various governments tacitly stood by, and how recent governments have attempted to seize control of Buddhist and Sinhalese identity from extremist groups.

The first example begins with the establishment of the Jathika Hela Urumaya (National Heritage Party) by Buddhist monks just two months prior to the 2004 elections. They ran over 260 candidates and won nine seats in the 225-member parliament (DeVotta and Stone 2008: 32). Their platform consisted, among other things, of preserving Sri Lanka's "unitary status" (in other words, no accession of provinces to the Tamils), "force the Norwegian facilitators out of the country, . . . and institute a *dharmarajya* (righteous state)" (DeVotta and Stone 2008: 32). They pushed for bloody military campaigns against the LTTE. Some Buddhist monks began attacking Hindu temples, Christian churches, and Muslim mosques. In 2012, the splinter group Bodu Bala Sena (BBS—Buddhist Power Force) was founded by monks Kirama Wimalajothi and Galagoda Aththe Gnanasara in Colombo. Their platform called for "a united legal system, affirmative action for Buddhist studies students in universities, the use of Buddhist monks as government school teachers, and a definition of Sri Lanka as a definitively Buddhist, Sinhalese nation" (Hays 2014). The latter was in reference to the fact that the Constitution of the First Republic of Sri Lanka from 1972 only allows Buddhism a "foremost place" (DeVotta and Stone 2008: 43). Their activities consisted of staging large-scale protests against Muslims especially, but also colleges, churches, blasphemers, and pacifist or liberal Buddhists. Muslims were accused of trying to outbreed and eventually outnumber Buddhists, as well as missionizing, extremism, and receiving support from Middle Eastern powers, and Christians were accused of converting Buddhists (Hays 2014). These protests have led to riots; destruction of mosques, churches, homes, and business establishments; murder and violence against targeted individuals. In June 2014, after an anti-Muslim rally led by BBS monks, Muslims in three towns located in the center of the Buddhist resurgence were assaulted; more than 50 were wounded and four killed, and Molotov cocktails were used to burn and loot homes and businesses (Hays 2014). Think tanks like the Terrorism Research and Analysis Consortium (TRAC) have called for designating the BBS as a terrorist organization.

The second example concerns governmental attempts to curb extremist groups and take control of Buddhist and Sinhalese identity. Popular support for the BBS and other similar organizations has been waning since 2014, and the government has issued statements urging the BBS to avoid conflicts (Hays 2014). Gnanasara was even arrested in 2015 but later freed on bail. More interestingly, however, is how the government is attempting to take control. A curious example is the governmental restriction on Western tourists with Buddha tattoos. In 2013 a British tourist, Antony Ratcliffe, was detained at the Bandaranaike International Airport and later deported because of his Buddha tattoo. He is reported to have said, "As soon as he saw it, the chief officer went crazy. You could see it on his face, he looked really angry and said I would have to go back to London" (Speri 2014). A year later, another British tourist, Naomi Michelle Coleman, was detained at the airport for the same reason. A police spokesman told reporters, significantly, that she was arrested "for hurting others' religious feelings" (Speri 2014).

More seriously, however, it seems that the Sri Lankan government is attempting to rewrite history, according to Rohini Mohan in *The New York Times* (2015):

> More perniciously, a nostalgia for Buddhist supremacy is now widespread. Today, a revisionist version of history is celebrated in films, books, TV programs and state-run newspapers. In the Tamil-dominated north, and in the east, where most of the country's Muslims live, national monuments have been erected to honor Buddhist kings. Government offices frequently announce 'rediscoveries' of long-lost Buddhist temples and Buddha statues are placed in areas sacred to Muslims or Tamils. In the Kanniya hot springs in the east, a sign in Sinhalese and English explains that the site—considered among Tamils to be linked to a Hindu myth—had been part of an ancient Buddhist monastery. In Kuragala in the central hills, the culture ministry built a Buddhist stupa at a Sufi Muslim cave, declaring it an ancient monastery site. These claims are not based on new archeological findings; the Sri Lankan government is simply rewriting history with a more politically expedient narrative.
>
> (Mohan 2015)

We cannot guess what the future will bring, but Marxian selection pressures, perhaps the most dangerous and destructive of all—epidemics and natural catastrophes excepted—can be changed through revolution and/or international pressures. The Sinhalese, however, have enormous respect for Buddhist monks—the saffron robes function as emotional totems. As long as the "fearless monk" marching to the "battlefront" (Abeysekara 2001: 5) continues to be romanticized by citizens, leaders, and the government, and if minorities fight back, there will be no end to hostilities in the near future.

Islamic State

Marxian selection pressures may be seen both in the context of ideology and religion as the previous example vividly demonstrates. The struggle for Basque independence in Northern Spain exemplifies these selection pressures at work in the realm of politics. Often, however, Marxian selection pressures articulated in terms of politics latch on to religion, thereby creating an even more powerful and enduring symbolic world by which they come to be expressed. The fight for sovereignty in Northern Ireland, for instance, prominently testifies to politics and religion as a powerful cocktail in terms of Marxian selection pressures. A current and presently attention-drawing example is found in the Middle East in various Islamistic organizations engaging in ruthless conflicts with each other, with foreign troops, and, occasionally, with local populations. In addition to the previous example from Sri Lanka, we will round off this chapter by examining one contemporary and particularly prominent Islamistic organization, namely ISIS or IS as another example of Marxian selection pressures.

In the wake of Samuel Huntington's famous *The Clash of Civilizations*, it has been common to interpret atrocities committed by various Islamistic organizations in terms of a "war against the West" and against perceived Western values such as democracy, equality, freedom of the press, etc. This is, of course, a rhetorically effective weapon in such conflicts. When cases of Islamistic organizations, however, are seen in light of Marxian selection pressures, contemporary hostilities in the Middle East, North Africa, South Asia, and occasionally—manifested in terrorist attacks—in Europe and North America appear to be crucial elements of regional power struggles in the Middle East and North Africa. The conflicts and rivalries of these extremist organizations are prompted by a steadily growing and inevitable process of modernization, as it threatens traditional beliefs which are further threatened by the global economy and political reality. IS's and similar Islamistic groups' violent attempts to establish a Middle Eastern world-wide caliphate should be seen in this light. As much as terrorist attacks on European and North American soil are meant to terrify Western populations and thereby also attract new recruits, they are predominantly acting within the framework of regional Middle Eastern competition for status recognition and increased military and cultural power.

Since its appearance in 1999 as *Jama'at al-Tawhid wal-Jihad* and its subsequent rise during the Iraqi insurgence following the Allied invasion of Iraq in 2003 in pledged alliance with *al-Qaeda*, IS (*Islamic State*—also known by the names of *ISIL* [*The Islamic State of Iraq and the Levant*], *ISIS* [*Islamic State of Iraq and Syria*], and by its Arabic acronym *Daesh*) has become a major player in Middle Eastern and North African politics. It is involved in religious, cultural, political, military, and terrorist activities in North Africa (notably Libya and Nigeria), South Asia (Pakistan), Europe and North America (through terrorist attacks), but has its main base in Syria and Iraq. The group took on the name of IS subsequent to its proclamation of a worldwide caliphate in 2014 with Abu Bakr al-Baghdadi as caliph and Al-Raqqah as the capital city. Superficially, the establishment of the caliphate may be seen as a restoration of an ancient Islamic form of government similar to the more famous Caliphates of Bagdhad, Damascus, and Istanbul. In fact, however, it constitutes a tiny, fairly homogeneous "nation" of Sunni Muslims in Syria comparable to the emergence of other nationalist states in the Middle East. It was especially set up to protect a "minority group" of Sunni Muslims in Syria. Although Sunni Muslims by all evidence constitute the majority of the population in Syria, Sunnis were severely suppressed during the ruling Ba'ath regime and felt threatened not only by this but also by the proximity of Shia Islam domination in Iran. IS represents a Salafi jihadist militant group that adheres to a fundamentalist Wahhabi interpretation of Sunni Islam. In Iraq and Syria, IS has primarily engaged in war against rivalling interpretations of Islam represented by Iranian supported Shia Islamic groups who, among other things, fight for the protection of the Shia sacred shrine of Sayyida Zainab (a daughter of the Rashid caliph and first Shia imam, Ali, and his wife Fatimah) located 6 miles southeast of Damascus, by the Ba'ath regime and by less severe representatives of Sunni Islam.

IS embodies all the characteristics of a social movement organization seeking material, demographic, technological, organizational, and cultural resources. Only if IS, like any other SMO, is capable of attracting and gaining these various resources, will it be and remain successful. It is especially for this reason that IS engages in terrorist attacks around the globe in order to increase their reputation among adherents and potential supporters in the Middle East, North Africa, and Europe as well as North America. Although relatively small in number, the European and North American citizens who have travelled to Syria and Afghanistan to fight for IS are a telling example. The rhetoric exhibited in sermons, speeches, video footage, etc. by leaders of IS patently demonstrates how the success of an SMO also depends on the capacity of its leaders to arouse and tap into the emotional energy of a group of people (Sunni Muslims), thereby enforcing social cohesion within the SMO and mobilizing its members to act against perceived foes such as Shia Muslims, representatives of the detested Ba'ath regime, and perceived ambassadors of the West. Sunni Muslims are depicted as victims of various forms of suppression and injustice from which they must liberate themselves in order to vindicate and succeed in establishing the true Islamic caliphate.

When interpreted from this perspective, the success of any act of war, aggression, or violent action by or on behalf of IS is an indexical token of the truth of IS's worldview and, thus, a self-fulfilling prophecy. IS communications notably illustrate how putting the blame on others for deprivations experienced by Sunni Muslims constitutes a powerful instrument in arousing feelings and inducing followers to violent actions against the assumed instigators. In fact, IS's famous use of violence—most abhorrently expressed in video footage of beheadings—demonstrates our previous assertion that religious SMOs justify the use of extreme aggression in cases in which their members have become filled with hatred against representatives of other categoric-units such as Shia Muslims, exponents of Ba'ath politics, or representatives of the "West." Opponents and antagonists of IS are shamed, castigated, and de-humanized, thereby strengthening the rhetoric and underlying emotions necessary to mobilize actions against adversaries or representatives of rivalling worldviews. Without further ado, then, in the present era, IS constitutes one of the clearest examples of an extremely violent religious movement predominantly engaged in intra-Muslim struggles but using inter-conflicts to attract attention to the regional intra-rivalries. The movement embodies a stringent religious orthodoxy, which its leaders zealously strive to impress upon its members and, at the same time, to impose on all institutional realms. IS unabashedly pursues a program of full control over the entire population within its territory, transforming them into loyal adepts of its worldview. In their adamant and fanatic pursuit of this goal, IS shuns no means, whatever the costs in terms of extreme violence and loss of human lives may be. The conflicts pursued by IS exemplify extreme intensity and violence due to long-term hostilities fueled as it has been in the past by perceived shame and humiliation at the hands of their enemies. As such, IS represents a singular case of Marxian selection pressures involving the type of reduction in complexity of culture which we previously referred to. It conspicuously testifies to a structural arrangement revolving around coercive domination.

Conclusion

The evolution of human societies from simple to more complex forms has always involved warfare, but religious violence has also been involved in both the evolution and de-evolution of complexity. Religion emerged under Darwinian selection as the neuroanatomy of evolving hominins was rewired to make the ancestors of humans ever-more emotional and, then, with this expanded emotional palette, more intelligent and able to engage in religious behavior. Religion became institutionalized because of Spencerian selection pressures (Type 1); and religion continued to evolve through a combination of Spencerian (Types 1 and 2), Durkheimian, and Marxian selection dynamics. If Durkheimian dynamics cause too much death of unfit organizational forms, including religious cult structures, or domination by coercive forms of social control by a religious cult, these selection processes will almost always escalate Spencerian selection pressures because extreme Durkheimian selection and Marxian selection generate perpetual problems of social control along the regulatory fault line of all sociocultural formations. They can also generate additional problems along the other fault lines: production, reproduction, and distribution. Therefore, even as religion becomes institutionalized under Spencerian (Type 1 or Type 2) selection processes and, thereby, has resolved for a time the emergence of new selection pressures, the subsequent evolution of religion has often been driven by both Durkheimian and Marxian selection pressures, both of which can rekindle Spencerian selection. For example, whatever the fate of the current warfare in the Middle East, regulation of whatever type of society or inter-societal system that emerges from this warfare is bound to generate extreme Spencerian selection pressures from regulation as a basic fault line of human organization. Coercion will be the initial response of the victorious parties, but coercion only generates grievances and negative emotions that set into motion new forms of Marxian selection that, in turn, escalate Spencerian selection.

Religion has thus been *both* an integrative and a disintegrative force in human societies because it arouses emotions, moralizes ideologies, and promotes both intolerance and discrimination, while at the same time providing a critical mechanism for the integration of both simple and complex societies. Such is the outcome of Darwinian selection by making an evolved ape both emotional and intelligent—perhaps too much so, because the verdict on whether or not humans will survive for another millennia is certainly unclear at the end of the second decade of the 21st century.

Epilogue

*We did not come from nowhere. We are
embedded in a very deep biological and
cosmological history. That history does not
determine us, because organisms from the
very beginning, and increasingly with each
new capacity, have influenced their own fate.
But our remarkable freedom . . . is embedded in
a cosmological and biological matrix that
influences everything we do.*
            Robert N. Bellah (2011: 83) in *Evolution in Human History*

We have recounted the extraordinary story of a species perhaps on the edge
of extinction. A species that through incremental changes in its emotional
centers succeeded in surviving the savanna and beyond by creating social
systems more or less designed to meet its creature needs and emotional
drives. Although it may sound self-contradictory, it is a story of blind *and*
teleological selection. The juxtaposition of blind and teleological selection
is the result of different types of selective processes at play in hominin evolution. The dazzling increase in emotional nuances so necessary for strong
social bonding gave purpose to the lives of these creatures, and that purpose *changed the rules of selection*. The irony, we have shown, is that once
social systems come into play, they take on their own blind processes, and
as pressures increase in terms of population growth, resource distribution,
production, regulation, and reproduction, we end up with social institutions that, after the long reign of hunting and gathering societies, now favor
the emotional needs of only an elite few. *Homo sapiens*' history is that of a
species muddling its way through system after system, sometimes design-
ing, but mostly not, ways to keep us off the edge. And now, as we reach a
stage of reasonable social stability and security, we are nevertheless at the
edge not only because of continued selective pressures but also because of
the ecological catastrophe that our emotional need-states and sociocultural systems have caused.

This extraordinary tale can only be understood scientifically through the combined use of a plurality of methods and theories. Many in the human and social sciences have argued that evolutionary theory has no explanatory role in sociocultural analyses. In the natural sciences, many claim that the only legitimate evolutionary processes are biological ones. But, we hope to have shown that both camps are both right and wrong.

Within sociology, W.G. Runciman (1983–87 [2009]) has been a persistent advocate of theorizing about selection processes. And, like any sociologist, the unit of selection is more than the human body but, instead, what he terms "syntax," which is close to our use of the phrase "sociocultural formations," although it probably emphasizes more fidelity between culture and social structure than we consider warranted. In these pages we have sought to follow at least the spirit of Runciman's and other social scientists' lead to connect the analysis of selection on both biological and sociocultural phenotypes. There obviously can be little doubt that selection has been at work on human phenotypes, including their behavioral propensities, and the underlying genotype generating these phenotypes. The same is true of organizational phenotypes or sociocultural formations such as groups, organizations, communities, institutional systems, societies, and inter-societal systems, although the cultural codings—values, beliefs, ideologies, norms, and other symbol systems—that accompany these sociocultural formations do not have the same direct effects on these social phenotypes as do genes on biological phenotypes.

However, and this point is critical, the units in sociocultural phenotypes, beginning with humans as biological organisms and moving through all of the superorganisms that humans can construct, are teleological. They can be, and often are, goal-directed; and furthermore, their capacities for agency actively change sociocultural formations and the very environments to which they must adapt. These additional features of sociocultural systems require that we differentiate between and conceptualize different types of selection from the type of natural selection emphasized in biology.

So, an important goal of the book has been to lay out several types of selection dynamics that are different from those conceptualized in biology. They are different because the units under selection are different from biological bodies *per se*. Non-biological, sociocultural selection does not, however, obviate the importance of analysis of what we have termed Darwinian selection. Indeed, a good portion of this book is devoted to Darwinian natural selection because a view of how humans acquired their basic behavioral, cognitive, and emotional capacities and propensities is not only crucial but also adds greatly to any sociological explanation. For example, using the data on primates and employing cladistic analysis has enabled us to explain in some considerable detail why humans are naturally prone to be religious and to engage in ritual behaviors. Similarly, engaging in comparative neuroanatomy on ape and human brains has enabled us to understand what natural selection has been doing to the neurology of hominins over the last 5 to 7 million years—a development that eventually made humans religious. Religion was not in any real sense "selected for" but, rather, it is a byproduct of paramount selection pressures on hominins in order to make them more social and thus more capable of forming permanent groups. Most early hominins could not survive on or near the African savanna over the last 5 to 7 million years, although some like Australopithecines probably began to briefly forage in more open country. Yet, as the forests of Africa continued to recede during the Pleistocene with global cooling, the more immediate hominin ancestors of *Homo sapiens,* such as *Homo habilis* and *Homo erectus*, were able to move out onto open-country habitats and, in the end, move out of Africa. This migration was possible because blind natural selection hit upon a solution to the low-sociality and low-levels of group formation among all extant species of apes today, and in the distant past.

Yet, underlying the biology, especially the neurology that made religion possible, is only part of the explanation of the evolution of religion; and the same is true for all institutional systems that humans have created. These institutional systems, composed of corporate units organizing people's activities, are also a product of selection, but a different kind of selection, revealing at least the forms that we have emphasized—Spencerian selection (Type-1 and Type-2), Durkheimian selection, and Marxian selection. We are not arguing that these are the only types of sociocultural selection, but we maintain that they are critical to understanding the evolution of religion. Behaviors, even biologically driven behaviors, cannot explain how these behaviors became institutionalized and how these institutional systems evolved over historical time. For that, we need more sociological explanations, but such explanations are, as we have tried to demonstrate, best built upon some basic knowledge about the biology and neurology of hominins as they evolved along the hominin clade that led to *Homo sapiens.*

Some will, undoubtedly, criticize us for deviating from the confines imposed by blind Darwinian selection working on phenotypes highly constrained by underlying genetic codes. Yet, sociocultural selection is neither entirely blind nor is it tightly regulated by cultural codings; and so, even the rough analogy between organisms and superorganisms soon breaks down and, as a result, requires that we look at selection dynamics in human superorganisms in a new light. We have sought to focus on religion because, first, it is one of the oldest human institutional systems and clearly it has a biological basis—even more so than does the first human institutional system: the nuclear family—and second, because it continues to evolve in a highly dynamic way.

Thus, we have illustrated, obviously in only an evocative sense, the four types of selection by providing instructive examples of each type of selection during religious evolution at different times and places. These illustrations are not necessarily definitive; instead, they provide a *sense for the relevance* of sociocultural models of selection in the analysis of institutional evolution. Emphasis on selection is not, of course, the only explanation of religious evolution, but it is nonetheless a useful one that adds to the power of social science explanations. So, to our critics, we would ask the opposite question: how far will high-fidelity models of Darwinian selection take us in explaining the complex, fluid, and multilevel dynamics of sociocultural systems when each part or component of these systems is teleological and can remake itself through acts of agency?

In the case of religion, we have demonstrated how useful a Darwinian approach can be in understanding why religion would emerge in the first place, but in trying to explain the subsequent institutionalization of behavioral propensities installed by Darwinian natural selection and the further evolution of these institutional systems over the last 300,000 years, we need other selection models. This is exactly what we have tried to provide.

From our perspective, most social phenomena require both explanations at the biological level and at the sociocultural level. An evolutionary perspective forces this coupling of biological and sociological on explanations; and that is why we have taken an evolutionary approach because *both* organic and human superorganic evolution have been *driven by selection forces*. To proclaim that there is only one type of selection is to confine analysis unnecessarily to the organismic level; to allow for additional types of selection to operate enables us to explain the evolution of human superorganisms in ways that are not possible by biology alone. As Durkheim was among the first to truly perceive, humans are *homines duplices*, because they possess a biology that generates individualism but must live in societies that must constrain such individualism. For Durkheim, there is always a tension between the human organism and the superorganisms in which they live.

Since religion has exerted a key role in human evolution—positively as well as negatively—by enhancing hominin possibilities for social bonding and groupishness, we have focused on the origins of religion and its subsequent evolution in order to examine crucial selection mechanisms in human evolution. Neither biological nor cultural evolutionary theories alone can account for this development. What is needed is a truly bio-socio-cultural evolutionary approach based on an acknowledgement of different selection mechanisms. In the wake of Durkheim and Robert Bellah, we have attempted to outline the biological and cultural origins of religion and the interplay between the two. We believe that such an approach is called for if we wish to understand and explain the evolution of modern humans. Religion has been an obvious case on which to apply such an approach. We confidently leave it to our readers to assess the merits of our pluriform methodology.

Bibliography

Abeysekara, Ananda. 2001. "The Saffron Army, Violence, Terror(ism): Buddhism, Identity, and Difference in Sri Lanka." *Numen* 48 (1): 1–46.

Abrutyn, Seth. 2014a. "Religious Autonomy and Religious Entrepreneurship: An Evolutionary-Institutionalist's Take on the Axial Age." *Comparative Sociology* 13 (2): 105–134.

———. 2014b. *Revisiting Institutionalism in Sociology: Putting the "Institution" Back in Institutional Analysis*. New York: Routledge.

———. 2015a. "Pollution-Purification Rituals, Collective Memory, and Religious Evolution: How Cultural Trauma Shaped Ancient Israel." *American Journal of Cultural Sociology* 3 (1): 123–155.

———. 2015b. "The Institutional Evolution of Religion: Innovation and Entrepreneurship in Ancient Israel." *Religion* 45 (4): 505–531.

Adophs, R. 2003. "Cognitive Neuroscience of Human Social Behaviour." *National Review of Neuroscience* 4: 165–178.

Alcock, John. 2001. *The Triumph of Sociobiology*. New York: Oxford University Press.

Allen, M.J. 1998. "Effervescence and the Origins of Human Society." Pp. 149–161 in *On Durkheim's Elementary Forms of the Religious Life*, edited by N.J. Allen, W.S.F. Pickering, and W. Watts Miller. London: Routledge.

Al-Masari. S., A. Al-Sobhi. Nadhra, J. Matari, Wilson, and P. Gingerich. 2010. "New Oligocene Primate from Saudi Arabia and the Divergence of Apes and Old World Monkeys." *Nature* 466: 36–365.

Almazán, Marco A. 1999. "The Aztec States-Society: Roots of Civil Society and Social Capital." *American Academy of Political and Social Science* 565: 162–175.

Anderson, J.R., and G.G. Gallup, Jr. 1999. "Self-recognition in Non-human Primates: Past and Future Challenges." Pp. 175–194 in *Animal Models of Human Emotion and Cognition*, edited by M. Haug and R.E. Whalen. Washington DC: American Psychological Association.

Andrews, Peter. 1981. "Species Diversity and Diet in Monkeys and Apes during the Miocene." Pp. 25–61 in *Aspects of Human Evolution*, edited by C.B. Stringer. London: Routledge.

———. 1989. "Palaeoecology and Laetoli." *Journal of Human Evolution* 18: 173–181.

———. 1996. "Palaeoecology and Hominoid Palaeoenvironments." *Biological Review* 71: 257–300.

———. 2007. "The Biogeography of Hominid Evolution." *Journal of Biogeography* 34: 381–382.

Andrews, Peter and J. Kelley. 2007. "Middle Miocene Dispersals of Apes." *Folia Primatological* 78: 328–343.

Andriani, Pierpaolo and Gino Cattani. 2016. "Exaptation as Source of Creativity, Innovation, and Diversity: Introduction to the Special Section." *Industrial and Corporate Change* 25 (1): 115–131.

Antón, Susan, Richard Potts, and Leslie Aiello. 2014. "Evolution of Early Homo: An Integrated Biological Perspective." *Science* 345: 45.

Arbib, Michael A. 2011. "From Mirror Neurons to Complex Imitation in the Evolution Of Language and Tool Use." *Annual Review of Anthropology* 40: 257–273.

Arrighi, G. 1994. *The Long Twentieth Century*. London: Verso.

Arrighi, G. and B. Silver. 1999. *Chaos and Governance in the Modern World System: Comparing Hegemonic Transitions*. Minneapolis, MN: University of Minnesota Press.

Assmann, Jan. 2003. *Die mosaische Unterscheidung oder der Preis des Monotheismus*. Munich: Carl Hanser Verlag.

Atmoko, Sri, Ian Singleton, Maria van Noordwijk, Carel van Schaik, and Tatang Setia. 2008. "Male–male relationships in Orangutans." Pp. 230–243 in *Orangutans: Geographic Variation in Behavioral Ecology and Conservation*, edited by S. A. Wich, S. S. U. Atmoko, T. M. Setia, and C. P. van Schaik. Oxford: Oxford University Press.

Axelrod, Robert. 1984. *The Evolution of Cooperation*. New York: Basic Books.

Bachhofen, Johann J. [1861] 1931. "Das Mutterecht." In *The Making of Man: An Outlines of Anthropology*, edited by R. Manheim. New York: Modern Library.

Baizer, Joan S., James F. Baker, Kristin Haas, and Raquel Lima. 2007. "Neurochemical Organization of the Nucleus *Paramedinaus Dorsalis* in the Human." *Brain Research* 1176: 45–52.

Baldwin, P. J. 1979. *The Natural History of the Chimpanzee (Pan troglodytes verus) at Mt. Assirik, Senegal*. Ph.D Thesis, University of Stirling, Scotland.

Baldwin, P. W., C. McGrew, and C. Tutin. 1982. "Wide-ranging Chimpanzees at Mt. Assirik, Senegal." *International Journal of Primatology* 3: 367–385.

Barger, Nicole, Lisa Stefanacci, and Katerina Semendeferi. 2007. "A Comparative Volumetiric Analysis of the Amygdaloid Complex and Basolateral Division of the Human and Ape Brain." *American Journal of Physical Anthropology* 134: 392–403.

Barger, Nicole, Kari L. Hanson, Kate Teffer, Natealie M. Schedker-Ahmed, and Katernia Semendeferi. 2014. "Evidence for Evolutionary Specialization in Human Limbic Structures." *Frontiers in Human Neurosciences* 8 (article 277): 1–17. http://dx.doi.org/10.3389/fnhum.2014.00277

Barger, Nicole, Lisa Stefanacci, Cynthia Schumann, Chet C. Sherwood, Jacopo Annese, John M. Allman, Joseph A. Buckwalter, Patrick R. Hof, and Katerina Semendeferi. 2012. "Neuronal Populations in the Basolateral Nuclei of the Amygdala Are Differentially Increased in Humans Compared with Apes: A Stereological Study." *Journal of Comparative Neurology* 520: 3035–3054.

Bartholomeusz, Tessa J. 1999. "Mothers of Buddhas, Mothers of Nations: Kumaranatunga and Her Meteoric Rise to Power in Sri Lanka." *Feminist Studies* 25 (1): 211–225.

——. 2002. *In Defense of Dharma: Just-War Ideology in Buddhist Sri Lanka*. London: Routledge Curzon.

Barton, Robert A. 1998. "Visual Specialization and Brain Evolution in Primates." *Proceedings of the Royal Society, London, B. Biological Sciences* 265: 1933–1937.

Barton, Robert A. and Chris Venditti. 2012. "Human Frontal Lobes Are Not Relatively Large." *Proceedings of the National Academy of Sciences* 110 (22): 9001–9006.

Becker, Adam H. and Annette Yoshiko Reed (Eds.). 2003. *The Ways That Never Parted: Jews and Christians in Late Antiquity and Early Middle Ages*. Tübingen: Mohr-Siebeck.

Beckoff, Marc and Jessica Pierce. 2009. *Wild Justice: The Moral Lives of Animals*. Chicago, IL: University of Chicago Press.

Begun, D. 2002. "European Hominoids." Pp. 339–368 in *The Primate Fossil Record*, edited by W. Harwig. Cambridge: Cambridge University Press.

Begun, David R. and Laszlo Kordos. 2009. "Cranial Evidence of the Evolution of Intelligence in Fossil Apes." Pp. 260–279 in *Evolution of Thought: Evolutionary Origins of Great Ape Intelligence*, edited by A. E. Russon and D. R. Begun. New York: Cambridge University Press.

Belin, Pascal. 2006. "Voice Processing in Human and Non-Human Primates." *Philosophical Transactions of the Royal Society* 361: 2091–2107.

Bellah, Robert N. 1964. "Religious Evolution." *American Sociological Review* 29 (3): 358–374.

——. 2005. "What Is Axial about the Axial Age?" *Archives Européennes de Sociologie* 46 (1): 69–89.

——. 2011a. *Religion in Human Evolution: From the Palaeolithic to the Axial Age*. Cambridge, MA: Harvard University Press.

——. 2011b. "Nothing Is Ever Lost. An Interview with Robert Bellah," interview with Robert N. Bellah by Nathan Schneider posted on the *Immanent Frame. Secularism, religion, and the public sphere* 14.09.2011 (accessed January 21, 2016).

Bennur, Sharath, Joji Tsunada, Yale E. Cohen, and Robert C. Liu. 2013. "Understanding the Neurophysiological Basis of Auditory Abilities for Social Communication: A Perspective on the Value of Ethological Paradigms." *Hearing Research* 305: 3–9.

Beran, M. J., L. M. Hopper, F. B. M. de Waal, K. Sayers, and S. F. Bronsnan. 2016. "Chimpanzee Food Preference, Associative Learning, and the Origins of Cooking." *Learning and Behavior* 44 (2): 103–108.

Berger, Joseph. 1988. "Directions in Expectation States Research." Pp. 450–474 in *Status Generalization: New Theory and Research*, edited by M. J. Webster and M. Foschi. Stanford, CA: Stanford University Press.

Berger, Joseph and Morris Zelditch. 1985. *Status, Rewards, and Influence*. San Francisco: Jossey-Bass.

Berger, Joseph, Bernard P. Cohen, and Morris Zelditch, Jr. 1972. "Status Characteristics and Social Interaction." *American Sociological Review* 37: 241–255.

Berger, Joseph, M. Hamit Fisek, Robert Z. Norman, and Morris Zelditch, Jr. 1977. *Status Characteristics and Social Interaction: An Expectation-States Approach*. New York: Elsevier.

Berger, Joseph, Robert Z. Norman, James W. Balkwell, and Roy F. Smith. 1992. "Status Inconsistency in Task Situations: A Test of Four Status Processing Principles." *American Sociological Review* 57: 843–855.

Bickerton, Derek. 2003. "Symbol and Structure: A Comprehensive Framework for Language Evolution." Pp. 77–93 in *Language Evolution: The States of the Art*, edited by M. S. Christiansen and S. Kirby. Oxford: Oxford University Press.

Biddle, Bruce J. and Edwin Biddle. 1966. *Role Theory: Concepts and Research*. New York: Wiley.

Bienvenu, Thibaut, Franck Guy, Walter Coudyzer, Emmanuel Glissen, Georges Roudaldes, Patrick Vignaud, and Micel Brunet. 2011. "Assessing Endocranial Variations in Great Apes and Humans Using 3D Data from Virtual Endocasts." *American Journal of Physical Anthropology* 145: 231–246.

Biesele, Megan. 1993. *Women Like Meat: The Folklore and Foraging Ideology of the Kalahari Ju/'hoan*. Bloomington, IN: Indiana University Press.

Biesele, Megan and Kxao Royal-/O/OO. 2010. "Ju/'Hoansi." Pp. 205–209 in *The Cambridge Encyclopedia of Hunters and Gatherers*, edited by Richard B. Lee and Richard Daly. Cambridge: Cambridge University Press.

Blanton, Richard and Gary Feinman. 1984. "The Mesoamerican World System." *American Anthropologist* 86: 673–682.

Blau, Peter M. 1977. *Inequality and Heterogeneity: A Primitive Theory of Social Structure.* New York: The Free Press.

Bloch, Jonathan, Mary Silcox, Doug Boyer and Eric Sargis. 2007. "New Paleocene Skeletons and the Relationship of Plesiadapiforms to Crown-Clade Primates." *The National Academy of Sciences of the USA* 104: 1159–1164.

——. 1994. *Structural Context of Opportunities.* Chicago, IL: University of Chicago Press.

Blute, Marion. 2010. *Darwinian Sociocultural Evolution: Solutions to Dilemmas in Cultural and Social Theory.* Cambridge: Cambridge University Press.

Boehm, Christopher. 2013. *Moral Origins: The Evolution of Virtue, Altruism, and Shame.* New York: Basic Books.

Boesch, Christophe and Hedwige Boesch-Achermann. 2000. *The Chimpanzees of the Taï Forest.* Oxford: Oxford University Press.

Bond, George D. 1988. *The Buddhist Revival in Sri Lanka: Religious Tradition, Reinterpretation, and Response.* Delhi: Motilal Banaarsidass Publishers Private Ltd.

Book Symposium. 2015. "Big Gods by Ara Norenzayan." *Religion, Brain, and Behavior* 5: 266–342.

Borgatti, Stephen, Martin Everett, and Jeffrey Johnson. 2013. *Analyzing Social Networks.* Los Angeles: Sage.

Bowden, H. 2010. *Mystery Cults of the Ancient World.* Princeton, NJ: Princeton University Press.

Boyarin, Daniel. 2010. *Borderlines. The Partition of Judaeo-Christianity.* Philadelphia, PA: University of Pennsylvania Press.

Boyd, Robert and Peter J. Richerson, 1983. *Culture and the Evolutionary Process.* Chicago: Chicago University Press.

——. 1992. "How Microevolutionary Processes Give Rise to History." Pp. 179–208 in *History and Evolution*, edited by M. H. Nitecki and D. V. Nitecki. Albany, NY: State University of New York Press.

——. 2005. *The Origin and Evolution of Cultures.* New York: Oxford University Press.

Boyer, Pascal. 2001. *Religion Explained: The Evolutionary Origins of Religious Thought.* New York: Basic Books.

Bradley, B. 2008. "Reconstructing Phylogenies and Phenotpes: A Molecular View of Human Evolution." *Journal of Anatomy* 212: 337–353.

Bradley, B., M. Robbins, E. Williamson, H. Steklis, N. Steklis, N. Eckhardt, C. Boesch, and L. Vigilant. 2005. "Mountain Gorilla Tug-of-War: Silverbacks Have Limited Control over Reproduction in Multimale Groups." *Proceedings of the National Academy of Sciences* 102: 9418–9423.

Breggin, Peter R. 2015. "The Biological Evolution of Guilt, Shame, and Anxiety: A New Theory of Negative Emotions." *Medical Hypotheses* 85 (1): 17–24.

Brosnan, Sarah F. 2006. "Nonhuman Species Reactions to Inequity and Their Implications for Fairness." *Journal of Social Justice* 19: 153–185.

Brosnan, Sarah F. and Frans B. M. de Waal. 2003. "Animal Behaviour: Fair Refusal by Capuchin Monkeys." *Nature* 428: 128–140.

——. 2014. "Evolution of Responses to (Un)Fairness." *Science* 346 (6207): 125776–1–5.

Brosnan, Sarah F., Hillary C. Schiff, and Frans B. M. de Waal. 2005. "Tolerance for Inequity May Increase with Social Closeness in Chimpanzees." *Proceedings of the Royal Society of London* 272: 253–258.

Brothers, L. 1990. "The Social Brain: Project for Integrating Primate Behavior and Neurophysiology in a New Domain." *Concepts Neuroscience* 1: 27–51.

Bruck, Jason. 2014. "Decades-Long Social Memory in Bottlenose Dolphins." *Proceedings of the Royal Society B* 280 (1768): 1–6.

Bruner, Emiliano, Luca Bondioli, Afredo Coopa, David Frayer, Ralph Holloway, Yosief Libsekal, Tsegai Medin, Lorenzo Rook, and Roberto Macchiarelli. 2016. "The Endocasts of the One-Million-Year-Old Human Cranium from Buia (UA31) Danakil Eritrea." *American Journal of Physical Anthropology* 160 (3): 458–468.

Bub, Daniel. 2008. "Reflections on Language and Evolution of the Brain." *Cortex* 22: 206–217.

Burghardt, Gordon M. 2005. *The Genesis of Animal Play: Testing the Limits.* Cambridge, MA: MIT Press.

Burke, Peter J. and Jan E. Stets. 2009. *Identity Theory.* New York: Oxford University Press.

Butler, A.G. 1994. "The Evolution of the Dorsal Pallium in the Telencephalon of Amniotes: Cladistic Analysis and a New Hypotheses." *Brain Research Review* 19: 66–101.

Caldwell M.C., and D.K. Caldwell. 1966. "Epimeletic (Care-giving) Behavior in Cetacea." Pp. 755–789 in *Whales, Dolphins, and Porpoises,* edited by K.K. Norris. Berkeley, CA: University of California Press.

Call, Josep and Michael Tomasello. 2007. *The Gestural Communication of Apes and Monkeys.* New Jersey: Lawrence Erlbaum Associates.

———. 2008. "Do Chimpanzees Have a Theory of Mind: 30 Years Later." *Trends in Cognitive Science* 12: 187–192.

Callaway, Ewen. 2017. "Oldest *Homo sapiens* Fossil Claim Rewrites of Our Species' History." www.nature.com/news/oldest-homo-sapiens-claim-rewrites-our-species-history-1.22114.

Camerer, Colin F. 2013. "Experimental, Cultural, and Neural Evidence of Deliberate Prosociality." *Trends in Cognitive Science* (March) 17: 106–110.

Campbell, Christina, Agustín Fuentes, Katherine MacKinnon, Simon Bearder, and Rebecca Stumpf. 2011. *Primates in Perspective.* New York: Oxford University Press.

Carneiro, Robert L. 1967. "On the Relationship of Size of Population and Complexity of Social Organization." *Southwestern Journal of Anthropology* 23: 234–243.

———. 1970. "A Theory on the Origin of the State." *Science* 169: 733–738.

———. 1973. "Structure, Function, and Equilibrium in the Evolutionism of Herbert Spencer." *Journal of Anthropological Research* 29 (2): 77–95.

———. 2015. "Spencer's Conception of Evolution and Its Application to the Political Development of Societies." Pp. 215–228 in *Handbook on Evolution and Society: Toward an Evolutionary Social Science,* edited by J.H. Turner, R. Machalek, and A. Maryanski. New York: Routledge/Paradigm.

Carrasco, Davíd. 1990. *Religions of Mesoamerica: Cosmovision and Ceremonial Centers.* San Francisco, CA: Harper.

———. 1999. *City of Sacrifice: The Aztec Empire and the Role of Violence in Civilization.* Boston, MA: Beacon Press.

Carter, Rita. 2008. *Multiplicity: The New Science of Personality, Identity, and the Self.* New York, Boston and London: Little, Brown and Company.

Cerling, Thure, Jonathan Wynn, Samuel Andanje, Michael Biard, David Korir, Naomi Levin, William Mace, Anthony Macharia, Jay Quade, and Christopher Remien. 2011. "Woody Cover and Hominin Environments in the Past 6 Million Years." *Nature* 476: 51–56.

Chase-Dunn, Christopher. 1998. *Global Formation: Structures of the World Economy.* Lanham, MD: Rowaman and Littlefield.

———. 2001. "World Systems Theorizing." Pp. 589–612 in *Handbook of Sociological Theory,* edited by J.H. Turner. New York: Kluwer Academic/Plenum Publishers.

Chase-Dunn, Christopher and P. Crimes. 1995. "World Systems Analysis." *Annual Review of Sociology* 21: 387–417.

Chase-Dunn, Christopher and Thomas D. Hall. 1997. *Rise and Demise: Comparing World Systems*. Boulder, CO: Westview.

Chase-Dunn, Christopher and K.M. Mann. 1998. *The Wintu and Their Neighbors: A Very Small World System in Northern California*. Tucson, AZ: University of Arizona Press.

Chase-Dunn, Christopher and Bruce Lerro. 2014. *Social Change: Globalization from the Stone Age to the Present*. Colorado: Paradigm Publishers.

Chatterjee, Helen, Simon YW Ho, Ian Barnes and Colin Groves. 2009. "Estimating the Phylogeny and Divergence Times of Primates Using a Supermatrix Approach." BMC *Evolutionary Biology* 9: 259.

Cheney, D.R. Seyfarth, and B. Smuts. 1986. "Social Relationships and Social Cognition in Non-Human Primates." *Science* 234: 1361–1366.

Clark, Amy. 2012. "Embodied, Embedded, and Extended Cognition." Pp. 275–292 in *The Cambridge Handbook of Cognitive Science*, edited by K. Frankish and W. Ramsey. Cambridge: Cambridge University Press.

Clark, Candace. 1987. "Sympathy Biography and Sympathy Margin." *American Journal of Sociology* 93: 290–321.

——. 1990. *Misery Loves Company: Sympathy in Everyday Life*. Chicago, IL: University of Chicago Press.

Clark, Jason A. 2013. "Intersections between Development and Evolution in the Classification of Emotions." *Developmental Psychobiology* 55 (1): 67–75.

Clowry, Gavin. 2014. "Seeking Clues in Brain Development to Explain the Extraordinary Evolution of Language in Humans." *Language Sciences* 46: 220–231.

Coe, Michael D. 1986. "Preface." Pp. 1–4 in *The Blood of Kings: Dynasty and Ritual in Maya Art*, edited by Linda Schele and Mary Ellen Miller. New York: George Braziller, Inc.

Collins, Randall. 1975. *Conflict Sociology: Toward an Explanatory Science*. San Diego, CA: Academic Press.

——. 1986. *Weberian Sociological Theory*. Cambridge: Cambridge University Press.

——. 2004. *Interaction Ritual Chains*. Princeton, NJ: Princeton University Press.

Colomy, Paul. 1998. "Neofunctionalism and Neoinstitutionalism: Human Agency and Interest in Institutional Change." *Sociological Forum* 13: 265–300.

Conroy, Glenn and Herman Pontzer. 2012. *Reconstructing Human Origins: A Modern Synthesis*. New York: W.W. Norton and Company.

Cooley, C.H. 1902 [1964]. *Human Nature and the Social Order*. New York: Schocken Books.

Copeland, Sandi, M. Sponheimer, D. de Ruiter, J. Lee-Thorp, D. Codron, P. le Roux, V. Grimes, and M. Richards. 2011. "Strontium Isotope Evidence for Landscape Use by Early Hominins." *Nature* 474: 76–78.

Cords, Marina. 2012. "The Behavior, Ecology, and Social Evolution of Cercopithecine Monkeys." Pp. 91–112 in *The Evolution of Primate Societies*, edited by J. Mitani, J. Call, P. Kappeler, R. Palombit, and J. Silk. Chicago, IL: University of Chicago Press.

Corruccini, R.S. and R.L. Ciochon. 1983. "Overview of Ape and Human Ancestry: Phyletic Relationships of Miocene and Later Hominoidea." Pp. 3–19 in *Interpretations of Ape and Human Ancestry*, edited by S. Corruccini and R.L. Ciochon. New York: Plenum Press.

Cosmides, Leda. 1989. "The Logic of Social Exchange: Has Natural Selection Shaped How Humans Reason?" *Cognition* 31: 187–276.

Cosmides, Leda and John Tooby. 1992. "Cognitive Adaptations for Social Exchange." Pp. 163–228 in *The Adapted Mind: Evolutionary Psychology and the Generation of*

Culture, edited by J. H. Barkow, L. Cosmides, and J. Tooby. New York: Oxford University Press.

Damasio, Antonio. 1994. *Descartes' Error: Emotion, Reason, and the Human Brain.* New York: G. P. Putman.

———. 2000. *The Feeling of What Happens: Body, Emotion and the Making of Consciousness.* London: Heinemann.

Damasio, Antonio and Norman Geschwind. 1984. "The Neural Basis of Language." *Annual Review of Neuroscience* 7: 127–147.

Darwin, Charles. 1859 [1958]. *On The Origins of Species, By Means of Natural Selection.* New York: New American Library.

———. 1872. *The Expression of the Emotions in Man and Animals.* London: John Murray.

———. 1871 [1875]. *The Descent of Man and Selection in Relation to Sex.* New York: D. Appleton and Co.

Dawkins, Richard. 1976. *The Selfish Gene.* Oxford: Oxford University Press.

———. 2006. *The God Delusion.* New York: Houghton Mifflin.

Deacon, Terrance W. 1997a. "What Makes the Human Brain Different?" *Annual Review of Anthropology* 26: 189–193.

———. 1997b. *The Symbolic Species: The Co-Evolution of Language and the Human Brain.* London: Allen Lane The Penguin Press.

———. 2009. "Relaxed Selection and the Role of Epigenesis in the Evolution of Language." Pp. 740–760 in *Oxford Handbook of Developmental Behavioral Neuroscience*, edited by Mark Blumberg, John Freeman, and Scott Robinson. New York: Oxford University Press.

Dean, Christopher and Meave Leakey. 2004. "Enamel and Dentine Development and the Life History Profile of *Victoriapithecus macinnesi* from Maboko Island, Kenya." *Annals of Anatomy* 28: 405–414.

Dembo, Mana, Davorka Radovčić, Heather Garvin, Myra Laiard, and Lauren Schroeder. 2016. "The Evolutionary Relationships and Age of Homo Naledi: An Assessment Using Dated Bayesian Phylogenetic Methods." *Journal of Human Evolution* 97: 17–26.

DeVotta, Niel. 2001. "The Utilisation of Religio-Linguistic Identities by the Sinhalese and Bengalis: Towards General Explanation." *Commonwealth and Comparative Politics* 39 (1): 66–95.

DeVotta, Neil and Jason Stone. 2008. "Jathika Hela Urumaya and Ethno-Religious Politics in Sri Lanka." *Pacific Affairs* 81 (1): 31–51.

Dharmadasa, K. N. O. 1992. *Language, Religion, and Ethnic Assertiveness: The Growth of Sinhalese Nationalism in Sri Lanka.* Ann Arbor, MI: University of Michigan Press.

Dimberg, Ulf and Monika Thunberg. 1998. "Rapid Reactions to Emotional Facial Expressions." *Scandinavian Journal of Psychology* 39: 39–45.

Dobzhansky, Theodosius. 1973. "Nothing in Biology Makes Sense Except in Light of Evolution." *The American Biology Teacher* 35 (3): 125–129.

Donald, Merlin. 1991. *Origins of the Modern Minds: Three Stages of Evolution of Culture and Cognition.* Cambridge, MA: Harvard University Press.

———. 2001. *A Mind So Rare: The Evolution of Human Consciousness.* New York: Norton.

Duchin, Linda. 1990. "The Evolution of Articulate Speech: Comparative Anatomy of the Oral Cavity in Pan and Homo." *Journal of Human Evolution* 19: 687–697.

Dugas-Ford, Jennifer and Clifton W. Ragsdale. 2015. "Levels of Homology and the Problem of Neocortex." *Annual Review of Neuroscience* 38: 351–68.

Dunbar, Robin. 1984. *Grooming, Gossip and the Evolution of Language.* London: Faber and Faber.

Dunn, Mathew. 2016. *Reviving the Organismic Analogy in Sociology: Human Society as a Social Organism*. Ph.D dissertation, U.C. Riverside.

Durham, William H. 1991. *Coevolution: Genes, Culture, and Human Diversity*. Stanford, CA: Stanford University Press.

Durham, William H. and Arthur P. Wolf (Eds.). 2004. *Inbreeding, Incest, and the Incest Taboo*. Stanford, CA: Stanford University Press.

Durkheim, Émile. 1893 [1997]. *The Division of Labor in Society*. New York: Free Press.

———. 1895 [1982]. *The Rules of Sociological Method and Selected Texts On Sociology and Its Method*. New York: The Free Press.

———. 1912 [1995]. *The Elementary Forms of the Religious Life*. New York: The Free Press.

Durkheim, Émile and Marcel Mauss. 1903 [1963]. *Primitive Classification*. Chicago, IL: University of Chicago Press.

Dussel, Enrique. 1981. *A History of the Church in Latin America*. Wm. B. Eerdmans Publishing.

Eibl-Eibesfeldt, Irenäus. 1996. *Love and Hate: The Natural History of Behavior Patterns*. New York: Aldine de Gruyter.

Eccles, John C. 1989. *Evolution of the Brain: Creation of Self*. London: Routledge.

Eisenstadt, S.N. 1964. "Social Change, Differentiation and Evolution." *American Sociological Review* 29: 375–386.

Ekman, Paul. 1984. "Expression and the Nature of Emotion." Pp. 319–343 in *Approaches to Emotion*, edited by K. Scherer and P. Ekman. Hillsdale, NJ: Lawrence Erlbaum.

Ember, Carol R. 1978. "Myths about Hunter-Gatherers." *Ethnology* 17: 439–448.

Emde, Robert N. 1962. "Level of Meaning for Infant Emotions: A Biosocial View." Pp. 1–37 in *Development of Cognition, Affect and Social Relations*, edited by W.A. Collins. Hillsdale, NJ: Lawrence Erlbaum.

Enard, W.M. 1978. "Myths about Hunter-Gatherers." *Ethnology* 17: 439–448.

Enard, Wolfgang, Molly Przeworski, Simon E. Fisher, Cecilia S.L. Lai, Victor Wiebe, Takashi Kitano, Anthony P. Monaco, and Svante Paabo. 2002a. "Molecular Evolution of FOXP2, A Gene Involved in Speech and Language." *Nature* 418: 869–872.

Enard, Wolfgang, Philipp Khaitovich, Joachim Klose, Sebastian Zollner, Florian Heissig, Patrick Giavalisco, Kay Nieselt-Struwe, Elaine Muchmore, Ajit Varki, Rivka Ravid, Gaby M. Doxiadis, Ronald E. Bonttrop, and Svante Paabo. 2002b. "Intra-and Inter-specific Variation in Primate Gene Expression Patterns." *Science* 296: 340–342.

Fahy, Geraldine, Michael Richards, Julia Riedel, Jean-Jacques Hublin, and Christophe Boesch. 2013. "Stable Isotope Evidence of Meat Eating and Hunting Specialization in Adult Male Chimpanzees." *Proceedings of the National Academy of Sciences* 110: 5829–5833.

Falk, Dean. 2000. *Primate Diversity*. New York: W.W. Norton.

———. 2007. *The Evolution of Broca's Area*, IBRO History of Neuroscience (www.ibro.info/ Pub/Pub_Main_Display.asp?LC_Docs_ID=3145).

———. 2011. *The Fossil Chronicles: How Two Controversial Discoveries Changed Our Views of Human Evolution*. Berkeley, CA: University of California Press.

Fashing, P. (2011). "African Colobine Monkeys." Pp. 203–228 in *Primates in Perspective*, edited by C. Campbell, A. Fuentes, K. Mackinnon, S. Bearder, and R. Stumpf. New York: Oxford University Press.

Fedurek, Pawel, Zarin P. Machanda, Anne M. Schel, and Katie E. Slocombe. 2013. "Pant Hoot Chorusing and Social Bonds in Male Chimpanzees." *Animal Behavior* 86: 189–196.

Ferrari, Pier Francesco and Giacomo Rizzolatti (Eds.). 2015. *New Frontiers in Mirror Neuron Research*. Oxford: Oxford University Press.

Fewkes, Jesse W. 1896. "The Prehistoric Culture of Tusayan." *American Anthropologist* 9 (5): 151–173.

Fisher, R. A. 1930. *The Genetical Theory of Natural Selection*. Oxford: Clarendon.

Fisher, Simon E. and Gary F. Marcus. 2006. "The Eloquent Ape: Gene, Brains, and The Evolution of Language." *Nature Reviews/Genetics* 7: 9–20.

Fiske, Alan Page. 1991. *Structures of Social Life: The Four Elementary Forms of Human Relations: Communal Sharing, Authority Ranking, Equality Matching, Market Pricing*. New York: Free Press.

Fitch, W. Tecumseh, Bart de Boer, Neil Mathur, and Asif A. Ghanzantar. 2016. "Monkey Vocal Tracts are Speech-Ready." *Sciences Advances* 2: 1–7.

Fleagle, John. 2013. *Primate Adaptation and Evolution*. Amsterdam: Elsevier.

Foley Robert A., Lahr M.M. 1992. "Beyond Out of Africa: Reassessing the Origins of Homo Sapiens." *Journal of Human Evolution* 22: 523–529.

——. 1997. "Mode 3 Technologies and the Evolution of Modern Humans." *Cambridge Archeological Journal* 7: 3–36.

Forey, P. L. et al. 1992. *Cladistics: A Practical Course in Systematics*. Oxford: Clarendon Press.

Forey, P. L., Humphries, C. J., Vane-Wright, R. I. E. 1994. *Systematics Association Special Volume, No. 50. Systematics and Conservation Evaluation; Symposium*. London, June 17–20, 1992. Oxford: Oxford University Press.

Fortelius, M. and A. Hokkanen. 2001. "The Trophic Context of Hominoid Occurrence in the Later Miocene of Western Eurasia: A Primate-Free View." Pp. 19–47 in *Hominoid Evolution and Climatic Change In Europe*, edited by L. de Bonnis, G. Koufos, and P. Andrews. Cambridge: Cambridge University Press.

Fox, Robin. 1980. *The Red Lamp of Incest*. New York: Lyle Stuart.

Frank, André Gunder. 1975. *On Capitalist Underdevelopment*. Oxford: Oxford University Press.

——. 1978. *World Accumulation, 1492–1789*. New York: Monthly Review Press.

——. 1979. *Dependent Accumulation*. New York: Monthly Review Press.

——. 1980. *Crisis in World Economy*. New York: Holmes and Meier.

——. 1998. *Reorient: Global Economy in the Asian Age*. Berkeley, CA: University of California Press.

Franks, David D. 2010. *Neurosociology: The Nexus between Neuroscience and Social Psychology*. New York: Springer.

Franks, David D. and Jonathan H. Turner. 2012. *Handbook of Neurosociology*. New York: Springer.

Gallup, Gordon G., Jr. 1970. "Chimpanzees: Self-Recognition." *Science* 167: 88–87.

——. 1979. *Self-Recognition in Chimpanzees and Man: A Developmental and Comparative Perspective*. New York: Plenum Press.

——. 1980. "Chimpanzees and Self-awareness." Pp. 223–243 in *Species Identity and Attachment: A Phylogenetic Evaluation*, edited by M. A. Roy. New York: Garland Press.

——. 1982. "Self-Awareness and the Emergence of Mind in Primates." *American Journal of Primatology* 2: 237–248.

Gallup, Gordon, Steven Platek and Kristina Spaulding. 2014. "The Nature of Self-Recognition Revisited." *Trends in Cognitive Science* 18: 57–58.

Gardner, R. L. 1896. *Gorillas and Chimpanzees*. London: Osgood, McLaine and Co.

Garfinkel, Harold. 1967. *Studies in Ethnomethodology*. Englewood Cliffs, NJ: Prentice-Hall.

Garstang, Michael. 2015. *Elephant Sense and Sensibility.* London: Academic Press/Elsevier.

Gazzaniga, Michael S. and Charlotte S. Smylie. 1990. "Hemisphere Mechanisms Controlling Voluntary and Spontaneous Mechanisms." *Annual Review of Neurology* 13: 536–540.

Gebo, Daniel. 2004. "A Shrew-Sized Origin for Primates." *Yearbook of Physical Anthropology* 47: 40–62.

Gebo, Daniel, N. Malit and I. Nengo. 1997. "New Proconsuloid Postcranials from the Early Miocene." *Primates* 50: 311–319.

Gebo, D. L. Maclatchy, R. Riryo, A. Deino, J. Kingston, and D. Pilbeam. 1997. "A Hominoid Genus from the Early Miocene of Uganda." *Science* 276: 401–404.

Geertz, Armin W. 1984. "A Reed Pierced the Sky: Hopi Indian Cosmography on Third Mesa, Arizona." *Numen* 31 (2): 216–241.

———. 1994. *The Invention of Prophecy: Continuity and Meaning in Hopi Indian Religion.* Berkeley, CA: University of California Press.

———. 1999. "Definition as Analytical Strategy in the Study of Religion." *Historical Reflections/Reflexions Historiques* 25 (3): 445–475.

———. 2007. "Tsu'ngyam Tradition: Men, Women and Snakes in Hopi Theology." Pp. 103–118 in *Schlangenritual: Der Transfer der Wissensformen vom Tsu'ti'kive der Hopi bis zu Aby Warburgs Kreuzlinger Vortrag,* edited by C. Bender, T. Hensel, and E. Schüttpelz. Berlin: Akademie Verlag.

———. 2011. "Hopi Indian Witchcraft and Healing: On Good, Evil, and Gossip." *American Indian Quarterly* 35 (3): 372–393.

———. 2013. "Whence Religion? How the Brain Constructs the World and What This Might Tell Us about the Origins of Religion, Cognition and Culture." Pp. 17–70 in *Origins of Religion, Cognition, and Culture,* edited by Armin W. Geertz. Durham: Acumen Publishing Limited.

———. 2014. "Do Big Gods Cause Anything?" *Religion* 44 (4): 609–613.

———. 2016. "Conceptions of Religion in the Cognitive Science of Religion." Pp. 127–139 in *Contemporary Views on Comparative Religion in Celebration of Tim Jensen's 65th Birthday,* edited by P. Antes, A. W. Geertz, and M. Rothstein. Sheffield: Equinox Publishing Ltd.

Gergely, Gyorgy and Gergely Csibra. 2006. "Sylvia's Recipe: The Role of Imitation and Pedagogy." Pp. 229–255 in *The Transmission of Cultural Knowledge,* edited by N. J. Enfield and S. C. Levinson. Oxford: Berg Press.

Geschwind, Norman 1965a. "Disconnection Syndromes in Animals and Man, Part I." *Brain* 88: 237–294.

———. 1965b. "Disconnection Syndromes in Animals and Man, Part II." *Brain* 88: 585–644.

———. 1965c. "Disconnection Syndromes in Animals and Man." *Brain* 88: 237–285.

———. 1985. "Implications for Evolution, Genetics, and Clinical Syndromes." Pp. 247–278 in *Cerebral Lateralization in Non-Human Species,* edited by S. D. Glick. Orlando, FL: Academic.

Geschwind, Norman and Antonio Damasio. 1984. "The Neural Basis of Language." *Annual Review of Neuroscience* 7: 127–147.

Gibbons, Ann. 2013. "Stunning Skull Gives a Fresh Portrait of Early Humans." *Science* 342: 297–298.

Gillespie-Lynch, K., P.M. Greenfield, Y. Feng, S. Savage-Rumbaugh and H. Lyn. 2013. "A Cross-Species Study of Gesture and Its Role in Symbolic Development: Implications for the Gestural Theory of Language Evolution." *Frontiers in Psychology* 4: 160.

Glazko, G.V. and M. Nei. 2003. "Estimation of Divergence Times for Major Lineages of Primate Species." *Molecular Biology and Evolution* (Supplement) 20: 424–434.

Goffman, Erving. 1959. *The Presentation of Self in Everyday Life*. New York: Penguin.

——. 1963. *Behavior in Public Places*. New York: Free Press.

——. 1967. *Interaction Ritual*. Garden City, NY: Anchor Books.

——. 1971. *Relations in Public*. New York: Basic Books.

——. 1974. *Frame Analysis: An Essay on the Organization of Experience*. New York: Harper and Row.

——. 1981. *Forms of Talk*. Philadelphia, PA: University of Pennsylvania Press.

——. 1983. "The Interaction Order." *American Sociological Review* 48: 1–17.

Goldschmidt, Walter. 1966. *Comparative Functionalism*. Berkeley, CA: University of California Press.

Gombrich, Richard F. and Gananath Obeyesekere. 1988. *Buddhism Transformed: Religious Change in Sri Lanka*. Princeton, NJ: Princeton Univesity Press.

Goodall, A. and C. Groves. 1977. "The Conservation of Eastern Gorillas." Pp. 599–637 in *Primate Conservation*, edited by Prince Rainier III of Monaco and G. Bourne. New York: Academic Press.

Goodall, Jane. 1986. *The Chimpanzees of Combe: Patterns of Behavior*. Cambridge, MA: Belknap Press.

——. 1990. *Through a Window: 30 Years Observing the Gombe Chimpanzees*. London: Weidenfeld & Nicolson.

——. 2005. "Do Chimpanzees Have Souls: Possible Precursors of Religious Behavior in Animals." Pp. 274–279 in *Spiritual Information: 100 Perspectives on Science and Religion*, edited by C.L. Harper. Philadelphia and London: Templeton Foundation Press.

Goodwin, Jeff and James M. Jasper. 2004. *Rethinking Social Movements: Structure, Culture, and Emotion*. Lanham, MD: Rowman & Littlefield.

——. 2006. "Emotions and Social Movements." Pp. 612–636 in *Handbook of The Sociology of Emotions*, edited by Jan E. Stets and Jonathan H. Turner. New York: Springer.

Goodwin, Jeff, James M. Jasper, and Francesca Polletta. 2001. *Passionate Politics: Emotions and Social Movements*. Chicago, IL: University of Chicago Press.

Gould, Stephen J. 2002. *The Structure of Evolutionary Theory*. Cambridge, MA: Harvard University Press.

Granovetter, Mark. 1973. "The Strength of Weak Ties." *American Journal of Sociology* 78: 1360–1380.

Gregory, W. 1916. "Studies on the Evolution of Primates." *Bulletin of the American Museum of Natural History* 35: 239–255.

Guatelli–Steinberg, D.D., D.J. Reid, A. Biship, and C.S. Larsen. 2005. "Anterior Tooth Growth Periods in Neanderthals Were Comparable to Those of Modern Humans." *Proceedings of the National Academy of Science* 102: 14186–14202.

Guenther, Mathias. 1999. *Tricksters and Trancers: Bushman Religion and Society*. Bloomington and Indianapolis: Indiana University Press.

Guerra, Francisco. 1971. *The Pre-Columbian Mind: A Study into the Aberrant Nature of Sexual Drives, Drugs Affecting Behaviour, and the Attitude towards Life and Death, with a Survey of Psychotherapy, in Pre-Columbian America*. London: Seminar Press.

Guttelmann, David, Josep Call, and Michael Tomasello. 2009. "Do Great Apes Use Emotional Expressions to Infer Desires?" *Developmental Science* 12 (5): 688–698.

Hackett, Troy A. 2011. "Information Flow in the Auditory Cortical Network." *Hearing Research* 271: 133–146.

Hamilton, William D. 1964. "The Genetical Evolution of Social Behaviour" I and II. *Journal of Theoretical Biology* 7: 1–16, 17–52.

Hannan, Michael T. and John Freeman. 1977. "The Population Ecology of Organizations." *American Journal of Sociology* 82: 929–964.

———. 1989. *Organizational Ecology.* Cambridge, MA: Harvard University Press.

Hannan, Michael T. and G.R. Carroll. 1992. *Dynamics of Organizational Populations: Density, Legitimation and Competition.* New York: Oxford University Press.

Hannan, Michael T., L. Polos, and G R. Carroll. 2007. *Logics of Organization Theory: Audiences, Code, and Ecologies.* Princeton, NJ: Princeton University Press.

Harcourt Alexander H. and Kelly J. Stewart. 2007. "Gorilla Society: What We Know and Don't Know." *Evolutionary Sociology* 16: 147–158.

Hare, B. 2011. "From Hominoid to Hominid Mind: What Changed and Why." *Annual Reviews of Anthropology* 40: 293–309.

Hare, Brian, Josep Call, and Michael Tomasello. 2001. "Do Chimpanzees Know What Conspecifics Know?" *Animal Behavior* 61: 139–151.

———. 2006. "Chimpanzees Deceive a Human Competitor by Hiding." *Cognition* 101: 495–514.

Harrison, N.A., M.A. Gray, P.J. Gianaros, and H.D. Gritchley. 2010. "The Embodiment of Emotional Feelings in the Brain." *Journal of Neuroscience* 38: 1287–1284.

Hart, Benjamin L., Lynette A. Hart, Noa Pinter-Wollman. 2008. "Large Brains and Cognition: Where Do Elephants Fit In?" *Neuroscience and Biobehavioral Reviews* 32: 86–98.

Harwig, Walter. 2011. "Primate Evolution." Pp. 19–31 in *Primates in Perspective*, edited by C. Campbell, A. Fuentes, K. MacKinnon, M. Panger, and S. Bearder. New York: Oxford University Press.

Hassig, Ross. 1988. *Aztec Warfare: Imperial Expansion and Political Control.* Norman, OK: University of Oklahoma Press.

———. 2005. *War and Society in Ancient Mesoamerica.* Berkeley, CA: University of California Press.

Haun, D.B.M. and J. Call. 2009. "Great Apes' Capacities to Recognize Relational Similarity." *Cognition* 110: 147–159.

Haviland, Charles. 2015. "The Darker Side of Buddhism." *BBC News Magazine* May 30, 2015. www.bbc.com/news/magazine-32929855 (accessed August 5, 2016).

Hays, Catherine. 1951. *The Ape in Our House.* New York: Harper.

Hays, Mark. 2014. "Meet the Violent Buddhists Starting Riots in Sri Lanka." _*Vice News* June 30, 2014. www.vice.com/read/meet-the-violent-buddhists-starting-riots-and-killing-muslims-in-sri-lanka (accessed August 5, 2016).

Hechter, Michael. 1987. *Principles of Group Solidarity.* Berkeley, CA: University of California Press.

Hegel, Georg Wilhelm Friedrich. 1986. *Werke in 20 Bänden. Vorlesungen über die Philosophie der Geschichte. Werke 12*, Eva Moldenhauer and Karl Markus Michel (Eds.) Frankfurt: Suhrkamp.

Hennayake, Shantha K. 1989. "The Peace Accord and the Tamils in Sri Lanka." *Asian Survey* 29 (4): 401–415.

Henrich, Joseph. 2016. *The Secret of Our Success: How Culture Is Driving Human Evolution, Domesticating Our Species, and Making Us Smarter.* Princeton, NJ: Princeton University Press.

Herbinger, Ilka, Christophe Boesch, and Martmut Rothe. 2001. "Territory Characteristics among Three Neighboring Chimpanzee Communities in the Tai National Park, Cote d'Ivoire." *International Journal of Primatology* 22 (2): 143–166.

Herculano-Houzel, Suzana. 2012. "The Remarkable, Yet Not Extraordinary, Human Brain as a Scaled-up Primate Brain and Its Associated Cost." *Proceedings of the National Academy of Sciences* 109, suppl. 1: 10661–10668.

Herculano-Houzel, S. and J.H. Kaas J.H. 2011. "Gorilla and Orangutan Brains Conform to the Primate Cellular Scaling Rules: Implications for Human Evolution." *Brain Behavior Evolution* 77: 33–44.

Herman, Louis. 2012. "Body and Self in Dolphins." *Consciousness and Cognition* 21: 526–545.

Hernandez-Aguilar, R.A., J. Moore, and T.R. Pikering. 2007. "Savanna Chimpanzees Use Tools to Harvest the Underground Storage Organs of Plants." *Proceedings of the Natural Academy of Sciences* 104: 19210–19213.

Heyes, C.M. 1994. "Social Learning in Animals: Categories and Mechanisms." *Biological Reviews* 69: 207–231.

Hjalmar S. Kühl, Ammie K. Kalan, and Christophe Boesch. 2016. "Chimpanzee Accumulative Stone Throwing." *Scientific Reports* 6, Article number: 22219.

Hochschild, Arlie R. 1979. "Emotion Work, Feeling Rules and Social Structure." *American Journal of Sociology* 85: 551–575.

———. 1983. *The Managed Heart: Commercialization of Human Feeling*. Berkeley, CA: University of California Press.

Hoover, K. 2010. "Smell with Inspiration: The Evolutionary Significance of Olfaction." *Yearbook of Physical Anthropology* 53: 63–74.

Horowitz, Alan C. 2003. "Do Chimps Ape? Or Apes Human? Imitation and Intension in Humans (Homo sapiens) and Other Animals." *Journal of Comparative Psychology* 117: 325–336.

Huizinga, Johan. 1938 [1955]. *Homo Ludens: A Study of the Play-Element in Culture*. Boston: Beacon Press.

Hunt, K.D. and W.C. McGrew. 2002. "Chimpanzees in Dry Areas of Assirik, Snegal, and Semliki Whildlife Reserve, Uganda." Pp. 35–51 in *Great Apes Societies*, edited by W.C. McGrew, L. Marchant, and T. Nisida. Cambridge: Cambridge University Press.

Huxley, Thomas. 1863. *Evidence as to Man's Place in Nature*. New York: D. Appleton and Company.

Iannaccone, Laurence R. and William Sims Bainbridge. 2009. "Economics of Religion." Pp. 461–475 in *The Routledge Companion to the Study of Religion*, edited by John Hinnells. London: Routledge.

Isaacs, Matthew. 2014. "Why Are Buddhist Monks Promoting Violence in Sri Lanka?" *Political Violence @ a Glance* July 1, 2014. https://politicalviolenceataglance.org/2014/07/01/why-are-buddhist-monks-promoting-violence-in-sri-lanka/ (accessed August 5, 2016).

Israfil, H., S.M. Zehr, A.R. Mootnick, M. Ruvolo, and M.E. Steiper. 2011. "Unresolved Molecular Phylogenies of Gibbons and Siamangs based on Mitochondrial, Y-linked Loci, and X Linked Loci Indicate a Rapid Miocene Radiations or Sudden Variance Event." *Molecular Phylogenetics and Evolution* 58(3): 447–455.

Itakura, Shoji. 1996. "An Exploratory Study of Gaze-Monitoring in Non-Human Primates." *Japanese Psychological Research* 38: 174–180.

Izard, Carroll E. 1992/1977. *Human Emotions*. New York: Plenum Press.

Jablonka, Eva, and Marion J. Lamb 2005. *Evolution in Four Dimensions: Genetic, Epigenetic, Behavioral, and Symbolic Variation in the History of Life*. Boston, MA: MIT Press.

Jackendoff, Ray. 2002. *Foundations of Language: Brain, Meaning, Grammar, Evolution*. Oxford: Oxford University Press.

Jarvis, M.J. and G. Ettlinger. 1977. "Cross-Modal Recognition in Chimpanzees and Monkeys." *Neuropsychologia* 15: 499–506.

Jasper, James M. and Lynn Owens. 2014. "Social Movements and Emotions." Pp. 495–510 in *Handbook of The Sociology of Emotions*, edited by Jan E. Stets and Jonathan H. Turner. New York: Springer.

Jeffers, R. and Lehiste, I. 1979. *Principles and Methods for Historical Linguistics.* Cambridge, MA: MIT Press.

Jensen, Jeppe Sinding. 2014. *What Is Religion?* London: Routledge.

Jerryson, Michael K. 2010a. "Introduction." Pp. 3–16 in *Buddhist Warfare*, edited by Michael K. Jerryson and Mark Juergensmeyer. Oxford: Oxford University Press.

——. 2010b. "Monks with Guns: Buddhists Aren't Immune to Anger, Fear, or Violence." *Religion Dispatches* January 12, 2010. http://religiondispatches.org/monks-with-guns-discovering-buddhist-violence/ (accessed August 9, 2016).

——. 2015. "The Rise of Militant Monks." *Lion's Roar* August 23, 2015. www.lionsroar.com/the-rise-of-militant-monks/ (accessed August 5, 2016).

Jimenez, Larry. 2015. "10 Rogue Buddhists Who Went Overboard with Violence." *Listverse* April 20, 2015. http://listverse.com/2015/04/20/10-rogue-buddhists-who-went-over board-with-violence (accessed August 5, 2016).

Joas, Hans. 2014. *Was ist die Achsenzeit? Eine wissenschaftliche Debatte als Diskurs über Transzendenz.* Basel: Schwabe.

Johnson, Allen W. and Timothy Earle. 2000. *The Evolution of Human Societies: From Foraging Group to Agrarian State.* Stanford, CA: Stanford University Press.

Johnson, D.D.P. 2005. "God's Punishment and Public Goods: A Test of the Supernatural Punishment Hypothesis in 186 World Cultures." *Human Nature* 16: 410–446.

——. 2009. "Darwinian Selection in Asymmetric Warfare: The Natural Advantage of Insurgents and Terrorists." *Journal of the Washington Academy of Sciences* 95: 89–112.

——. 2016. *Payback: God's Punishment and the Evolution of Cooperation.* New York: Oxford University Press.

Johnson, D.D.P. and J.M. Bering. 2006. "Hand of God, Mind of Man: Punishment and Cognition in the Evolution of Cooperation." *Evolutionary Psychology* 4: 219–233.

Johnson, D.D.P. and O. Kruger. 2004. "The Good of Wrath: Supernatural Punishment and the Evolution of Cooperation." *Political Theology* 5: 159–176.

Johnson, D.D.P., H. Lenfesty, and J.P. Schloss. 2014. "The Elephant in the Room: Religious Truth Claims, Evolution and Human Nature." *Philosophy, Theology and the Sciences* 1: 200–231.

Johnson Hodge, Caroline. 2007. *If Sons, Then Heirs: A Study of Kinship and Ethnicity in the Letters of Paul.* Oxford: Oxford University Press.

Johnstone, Brick. A. Bodling, D. Cohen, S.E. Christ, and A. Wegrzyn. 2012. "Right Parietal Lobe-Related 'Selflessness' as the Neuropyschological Basis of Spiritual Transcendence." *The International Journal for the Psychology of Religion* 22: 267–284.

Jolly, Allison. 1985. *The Evolution of Primate Behavior.* New York: Macmillan.

Kagaya, M.N. Ogihara, and M. Nakastsukasa. 2010. "'Is the Clavicle of Apes Long.' An Investigation of Clavicular Length in Relation to Body Mass and Upper Thoracic Width." *International Journal of Primatology* 31: 209–217.

Kaminski, Juliane, Josep Call, and Michael Tomasello. 2008. "Chimpanzees Know What Others Know, but Not What They Believe." *Cognition* 109: 224–234.

Kaneko, Takaaki and Masaki Tomonaga. 2011. "The Perception of Self-Agency in Chimpanzees (*Pan troglodytes*)." *Proceedings of the Royal Society* 278 (1725): 3694–3702.

Kari, Suzanne Kraus and Barbara Canlon. 2012. "Neuronal Connectivity and Interactions between the Auditory and Limbic Systems. Effects of Noise and Tinnitus." *Hearing Research* 288 (1–2): 34–46.

Karten, Harvey J. 1997. "Evolutionary Developmental Biology Meets the Brain: The Origins of the Mammalian Cortex." *Proceedings of the American National Academy of Sciences* 94 (7): 2800–2804.

Katz, Richard. 1982a. *Boiling Energy*. Cambridge, MA: Harvard University Press.

———. 1982b. "Accepting 'Boiling Energy': The Experience of !Kia-Healing among the !Kung." *Ethos* 10 (4): 344–368.

Kay, P. and P. Ungar. 1997. "Dental Evidence for Diet in Some Miocene Catarrhines with Comments on the Effects of Phylogeny on the Interpretation Adaptation." Pp. 131–150 in *Function, Phylogeny, and Fossils: Miocene Hominoid Evolution and Adaptations*, edited by D. Begun, C. Ward, and M. Rose. New York: Plenum.

Keenan, Julian, Paul Mark A Wheeler, and Michael Ewers. 2003. "The Neural Correlates of Self-awareness and Self-recognition." Pp. 166–179 in *The Self in Neuroscience and Psychiatry*, edited by T. Kircher and A. David. Cambridge: Cambridge University Press.

Keller, Gerta and John A. Barron. 1987. "Paleodepth Distribution of Neocene Deep-Sea Hiatuses." *Paleoceangraphy* 2 (6): 697–713.

Keller, Helen. 1904. *The World I Live In*. London: Hodder and Stoughton.

Kelley, Jay. 2004. "Life History Evoluton in Miocene and Extant Apes." Pp. 223–248 in *Human Evolution Through Developmental Change*, edited by Nancy Menugh-Purrus and Kenneth J. McNamara. Baltimore, MD: Johns Hopkins University Press.

Kelley, Jay, and T. M. Smith. 2003. "Age at First Molar Emergence in Early Miocene *Afropithecus turkanensis* and Life-History Evolution in the *Hominoidea*." *Journal of Human Evolution* 44: 307–329.

Kemp, T. S. 2005. *The Origin and Evolution of Mammals*. Oxford: Oxford University Press.

Kemper, Theodore D. 1987. "How Many Emotions Are There? Wedding the Social and the Autonomic Components." *American Journal of Sociology* 93: 263–289.

Kemper, Theodore D. and Randall Collins. 1990. "Dimensions of Microinteraction." *American Journal of Sociology* 96: 32–68.

Kenneth, R., Scott H. Johnson-Frey, and Scott T. Grafton. 2004. "Functional Imaging of Face and Hand Imitation: Towards a Motor Theory of Empathy." *NeuroImage* 21: 601–607.

Kirk, C. 2006. "Visual Influences on Primate Encephalization." *Journal of Human Evolution* 51: 76–90.

Kitchen, A., De. Denton, and L. Brent. 1996. "Self-recognition and Abstraction Abilities in the Common Chimpanzee Studied with Distorting Mirrors." *Proceeding of National Academy of Sciences* 93 (14): 7405–7408.

Knott, Cheryl, Lydia Beaudrot, Tamaini Snaith, Sarah White, Hartmut Tschauner, and George Planansky. 2008. "Female–Female Competition in Bornean Orangutans." *International Journal of Primatology* 29: 975–997.

Krogman, Wilton. 1951 "The Scars of Human Evolution." *Scientific American* 185 (6): 54–57.

Krubitzer, L. and J. Kaas. 2005. "The Evolution of Neocortex in Mammals: How Is Phenotypic Diversity Generated." *Current Opinion in Neurobiology* 15: 444–453.

Krutz, Gordon V. 1979. "The Native's Point of View as an Important Factor in Understanding the Dynamics of the Oraibi Split." *Ethnohistory* 20 (1): 77–89.

Kühl, Hjalmar S. et al. 2016. "Chimpanzee Accumulative Stone Throwing." *Nature Scientific Reports* 6: 22219: 1–8.

Kummer, Hans. 1971. *Primate Societies*. Chicago: Aldine & Atherton.

Lahnakoski, Juha M., Enrico Glerean, Iiro P. Jääskeläinen, Jukka Hyönä, Ritta Hari, Mikko Sams, and Lauri Nummenmaa. 2014. "Synchronous Brain Activity across Individuals Underlies Shared Psychological Perspectives." *NueroImage* 100: 316–324.

Langergraber, K. E. Schubert, C. Rowney. R. W. Wrangham, V. Reynolds, K. Hunt, and I. Vigilant. 2007. "Genetic Differentiation and the Evolution of Cooperation in Chimpanzees and Humans." *Proceedings of the Royal Society of London B* 278: 2546–2542.

Langergraber, Kevin E., Christophe Boesch, Eiji Inoue, Miho Inoue-Murayama, John C. Mitani, Toshisada Nishida, Anne Pusey, Vernon Reynolds, Grit Schubert, Richard W. Wrangham, Emily Wroblewski, and Linda Vigilant. 2011. "Genetic and 'Cultural' Similarity in Wild Chimpanzees." *Proceedings of the Royal Society* 278: 408–416.

Lawler, Edward J. 2001. "An Affect Theory of Social Exchange." *American Journal of Sociology* 107: 321–352.

Lawler, Edward J., Shane Thye, and Jeongkoo Yoon. 2009. *Social Commitments in a Depersonalized World*. New York: Russell Sage.

LeDoux, Joseph E. 1996. *The Emotional Brain: The Mysterious Underpinnings of Emotional Life*. New York: Simon and Schuster.

Lee, Richard B. 1979. *The !Kung San: Men, Women and Work in a Foraging Society*. Cambridge: Cambridge University Press.

Lee, Richard B. and Richard Daly (Eds.). 1999. *The Cambridge Encyclopedia of Hunters and Gatherers*. Cambridge: Cambridge University Press.

Lee, Richard and Irven DeVore. 1968. *Man the Hunter*. Chicago: Aldine.

Lents, Nathan H. 2016. *Not So Different: Finding Human Nature in Animals*. New York: Columbia University Press.

León-Portilla, Miguel. 1992. *The Broken Spear*. Boston: Beacon Press.

Lewis-Williams, J. D. 1990. *Discovering Southern African Rock Art*. Cape Town: David Philip.

Lieberman, Philip. 2006. *Toward an Evolutionary Biology of Language*. Cambridge, MA: Harvard University Press.

———. 2007. "The Evolution of Human Speech: Its Anatomical and Neural Basis." *Current Anthropology* 48: 39–66.

Loewenstein, George, Scott Rick, and Jonathan D. Cohen. 2008. "Neuroeconomics." *Annual Review of Psychology* 59: 647–672.

Lowie, Robert H. 1966/1948. *Social Organization*. New York: Holt, Rinehart, and Winston.

Luhmann, Niklas. 1982. *The Differentiation of Society*. New York: Columbia University Press.

Lukas, D. V. Reynolds, C. Boesch and L. Vigilant. 2005. "To What Extent Does Living in a Group Mean Living with Kin?" *Molecular Ecology* 14: 2181–2196.

Luncz, Lydia V., Roger Mundry, and Christophe Boesch. 2012. "Evidence for Cultural Differences between Neighboring Chimpanzee Communities." *Current Biology* 22: 922–926.

Lycett, Stephen J., Mark Collard, and William C. McGrew. 2010. "Are Behavioral Differences among Wild Chimpanzees Communities Genetic or Cultural? An Assessment of Using Tool-Use Data and Phylogenetic Methods." *American Journal of Physical Anthropology* 142: 461–467.

Maas, P. 1958. *Textual Criticism*. Oxford: Oxford University Press.

Machalek, Richard. 1992. "Why Are Large Societies So Rare?" *Advances in Human Ecology* 1: 33–64.

Mackinnon, John. 1974. "The Behaviour and Ecology of Wild Orangutans (*Pongo Pygmaeus*)." *Animal Behaviour* 22: 3–74.

Maclatchy, L. 2004. "The Oldest Ape." *Evolutionary Anthropology* 13: 90–103.

Maclatchy, L., Rossie, J., and Kingston, J. 2015. "The Ecological Niche of the Morotopithecus, with Implications for Hominoid Evolution." A paper presented at the 84th Annual Meeting of the American Association of Physical Anthropology.

Malinowski, Bronislaw. 1944. *A Scientific Theory of Culture and Other Essays*. London, Oxford: Oxford University Press.

Malotki, Ekkehart. 1993. *Hopi Ruin Legends: Kiqötutuwutsi*. Lincoln, NE: University of Nebraska Press.

Malotki, Ekkehart and Ken Gary. 2001. *Hopi Stories of Witchcraft, Shamanism, and Magic*. Lincoln, NE: University of Nebraska Press.

Marshall, Douglas A. 2017. "Moral Origins of God: Darwin, Durkheim, and the Homo Duplex Theory of Theogenesis." *Frontiers of Evolutionary Sociology and Biosociology*. In press, www.frontiersin.org.

Marx, Karl. 1845–46 [1972]. "The German Ideology." Pp. 146–202 in *The Marx-Engels Reader*, edited by Robert C. Tucker. New York: W.W. Norton & Company.

Marx, Karl and Fredrich Engels. 1848 [1971]. *The Communist Manifesto*. New York: International Publishers.

Mary-Rousselière, Guy. 1984. "Iglulik." Pp. 431–446 in *Arctic*, edited by D. Damas. *Handbook of North American Indians*, volume 5. Washington DC: Smithsonian Institution.

Maryanski, Alexandra. 1986. "African Ape Social Structure: A Comparative Analysis." Ph.D. Dissertation, University of California, Irvine.

———. 1987. "African Ape Social Structure: Is There Strength in Weak Ties?" *Social Networks* 9: 191–215.

———. 1992. "The Last Ancestor: An Ecological-Network Model on the Origins of Human Sociality." *Advances in Human Ecology* 2: 1–32.

———. 1993. "The Elementary Forms of the First Proto-Human Society: An Ecological/Social Network Approach." *Advances in Human Evolution* 2: 215–241.

———. 1995. "African Ape Social Networks: A Blueprint for Reconstructing Early Hominid Social Structure." Pp. 67–90 in *Archaeology of Human Ancestry*, edited by J. Steele and S. Shennan. London: Routledge.

———. 1996. "Was Speech an Evolutionary Afterthought?" Pp. 79–102 in *Communicating Meaning: The Evolution and Development of Language*, edited by B. Velichikovsky and D. Rumbaugh. Mahwah, NJ: Erlbaum.

———. 1997. "The Origin of Speech and Its Implications for Optimal Size of Human Groups." *Critical Review* 12: 233–249.

———. 2013. "The Secret of the Hominin Mind: An Evolutionary Story." Pp. 257–287 in *Handbook of Neurosociology*, edited by D. Franks and J.H. Turner. New York: Springer.

Maryanski, Alexandra and Jonathan H. Turner. 1992. *The Social Cage: Human Nature and the Evolution of Society*. Stanford, CA: Stanford University Press.

Maryanski, Alexandra, Peter Molnar, Ullica Segerstrale, and Borris M. Velichikovsky. 1997. "The Social and Biological Foundations of Human Communication." Pp. 181–200 in *Human by Nature*, edited by P. Weingart, S. Mitchell, P. Richerson, and S. Maasen. Mahwah, NJ: Erlbaum.

Massey, Douglas. 2002. "A Brief History of Human Society: The Origin and Role of Emotion in Social Life." *American Sociological Review* 67: 1–29.

Matsuzawa, Tetsuro. 2009. "The Chimpanzee Mind: In Search of the Evolutionary Roots of the Human Mind." *Animal Cognition* 12, suppl. 1: S1–9.

Matsuzawa, Tetsuro, Tatyana Humle, and Yukimaru Sugiyama. 2011. *The Chimpanzees of Bossou and Nimba*. New York: Springer of Japan.

Matthews, Bruce. 1988–1989. "Sinhala Cultural and Buddhist Patriotic Organizations in Contemporary Sri Lanka." *Pacific Affairs* 61 (4): 620–632.

Maynard Smith, John 1982. *Evolution and the Theory of Games*. Cambridge: Cambridge University Press.

Mayr, Ernst. 2001. *What Evolution Is*. New York: Basic Books.

McCaffree, Kevin. 2017. *The Secular Landscape: The Decline of Religion in America*. New York: Palgrave Macmillan.

McCreery, Patricia and Ekkehart Malotki. 1994. *Tapamveni: The Rock Art Galleries of Petrified Forest and Beyond*. Petrified Forest: Petrified Forest Museum Association.

McGrew, William. C. 1981. "The Female Chimpanzee as a Human Evolutionary Prototype." Pp. 35–73 in *Woman the Gatherer*, edited by Frances Dahlberg. New Haven, CT: Yale University Press.

———. 1983. "Animal Foods in the Diets of Wild Chimpanzees (*Pan troglodytes*): Why Cross Cultural Variation?" *Journal of Ethology* 1: 46–61.

———. 1992. *Chimpanzee Material Culture: Implications for Human Evolution*. Cambridge: Cambridge University Press.

———. 2010. "In Search of the Last Common Ancestor: New Findings on Wild Chimpanzees." *Philosophical Transactions of the Royal Society* 365: 3265–3267.

McGrew, W.C., P.J. Baldwin, and G.E.G. Tutin. 1981. "Chimpanzees in Hot, Dry, and Open Habitat: Mt. Assirik, Senegal, West Africa." *Journal of Human Evolution* 10: 227–244.

McLennan, John F. 1896. *Studies in Ancient History*. London: Macmillan Co.

McNeill, William H. 1997. *Keeping Together in Time: Dance and Drill in Human History*. Cambridge, MA: Harvard University Press.

McPherson, J. Miller. 1981. "A Dynamic Model of Voluntary Affiliation." *Social Forces* 59: 705–728.

———. 1983a. "An Ecology of Affiliation." *American Sociological Review* 48: 519–532.

———. 1983b. "The Size of Voluntary Organizations." *Social Forces* 61: 1044–1064.

———. 1983c. "Ecological Theory." Pp. 263–89 in *Handbook of Social Theory*, edited by G. Ritzer. Newbury Park, CA: Sage.

———. 1988. "A Theory of Voluntary Organization." Pp. 42–76 in *Community Organizations*, edited by C. Milofsky. New York: Oxford University Press.

McPherson, J. Miller and J. Ranger-Moore. 1991. "Evolution on a Dancing Landscape: Organizations and Networks in Dynamic Blau Space." *Social Forces* 70 (1): 19–42.

McPherson, Miller and T. Rotolo. 1996. "Testing a Dynamic Model of Social Composition: Diversity and Change in Voluntary Groups." *American Sociological Review* 61: 179–202.

Mead, George Herbert. 1934. *Mind, Self, and Society*. Chicago, IL: University of Chicago Press.

———. 1938. *Philosophy of the Act*. Chicago, IL: University of Chicago Press.

Meltzoff, A.N. 2002. "Imitation as a Mechanism of Social Cognition: Origins of Empathy, Theory of Mind, and the Representation of Action." Pp. 6–25 in *Handbook of Childhood Cognitive Development*, edited by U. Goswami. Oxford: Blackwell Publishers.

Menzel, E.W. 1971. "Communication about the Environment in a Group of Young Chimpanzees." *Folia Primatologica* 15: 220–232.

Merker, Bjorn H., Guy S. Madison, and Patricia Eckerdal 2009. "On the Role and Origin of Isochrony in Human Rhythmic Entrainment." *Cortex* 45 (1): 4–17.

Metzler, Dieter. 1991. "A.H. Anquetil-Duperron (1731–1805) und das Konzept der Achsenzeit." Pp. 123–133 in *Achaemenid History, VII*, edited by H. Sancisi-Weerdenburg and J.W. Drijvers. Leiden: Brill.

Miller, L. E. and A. Treves. 2011. "Predation on Primates: Past Studies, Current Challenges, and Directions for the Future." Pp. 535–547 in *Primates in Perspective*, edited by C. J. Campbell, A. Fuentes, K. C. Mackinnon, M. Panger, and S. K. Bearder. Oxford: Oxford University Press.

Mitani, J. C. and K. L. Brandt. 1994. "Social Factors Influence the Acoustic Variability in the Long-distance Calls of Male Chimpanzees." *Ethology* 96: 233–255.

Mitani, J. C. and J. Gros-Louis. 1998. "Chorusing and the Call Convergence in Chimpanzees: Tests of Three Hypotheses." *Behaviour* 45: 1041–1064.

Mitani, J. C., Merriwether, D. A., and Zhang, C. 2000. "Male Affiliation, Cooperation and Kinship in Wild Chimpanzees." *Animal Behavior* 59: 885–893.

Mitani, J. C. and T. Nishida. 1993. "Context and Correlates of Long-distant Calling by Male Chimpanzees." *Animal Behavior* 45: 735–746.

Mitani, J. C. and P. S. Rodman. 1979. "Territoriality: The Relation of Ranging Patterns and Home Range Size to Defendability, with an Analysis of Territoriality among Primate Species." *Behavioral Ecology and Sociobiology* 5: 541–551.

Mitani, J. C. and D. P. Watts. 2004. "Why Do Chimpanzees Share Meat?" *Animal Behavior* 61: 915–924.

——. 2005. "Correlates of Territorial Boundary Patrol Behavior in Wild Chimpanzees." *Animal Behavior* 70: 1079–1086.

Mitchell, P. 2011a. "Acquiring a Theory of Mind" In *An Introduction to Developmental Psychology*, Second Edition, edited by A. Slater and G. Bremner. Oxford: Blackwell.

——. 2011b. "Inferences about Guessing and Knowing by Chimpanzees (*Pan troglodytes*)." *Journal of Comparative Psychology* 104 (3): 203–210.

Mizusaki, Beatriz E. P., Armen Stepanyants, Dimitri B. Chklovskii, and Jesper Sjostrom. 2016. "Neocortex: A Lean Mean Memory Storage Machine." *Nature Neuroscience* 19 (5): 643–644.

Mohan, Rohini. 2015. "Sri Lanka's Violent Buddhists." *The New York Times* January 2, 2015. www.nytimes.com/2015/01/03/opinion/sri-lankas-violent-buddhists.html?=1 (accessed August 5, 2016).

Moore, Deborah L., Kevin E. Bangergraber, and Linda Vigilant. 2015. "Genetic Analyses Suggest Male Philopatry and Territoriality in Savanna-Woodland Chimpanzees (*Pan troglodytes schweinfurthii*) of Ugalla, Tanzania." *International Journal of Primatology* 36: 377–397.

Morgan, Lewis Henry. [1871] 1997. *Systems of Consanguinity and Affinity of the Human Family*. Lincoln, NE: University of Nebraska Press.

Muller, M. N. and J. C. Mitani. 2005. "Conflict and Cooperation in Wild Chimpanzees." *Advances in the Study of Behavior* 35: 275–331.

Munson, Henry. 2005. "Religion and Violence." *Religion* 35 (4): 223–246.

Murdock, George P. 1949. *Social Structure*. New York: Macmillan and Co.

Murdock, G. P., and D. White. 1969. "Standard Cross-Cultural Sample." *Ethnology* 8: 329–369.

Napier, J. 1963. "Brachiators and Brachiators." Pp. 183–195 in *The Primates: Symposia of the Zoological Society of London*, edited by J. Napier and N. A. Barniat. London: Zoological Society of London.

Nargolwalla M. C., D. R. Begun, M. C. Dean, D. J. Reid, and L. Kordos. 2005. "Dental Development and Life History in *Anapithecus hernyaki*." *Journal of Human Evolution* 49: 99–121.

Newton, P. N., Dunbar, R. I. M., 1994. "Colobine Monkey Society." Pp. 311–346 in *Colobine Monkeys: Their Ecology, Behaviour and Evolution*, edited by A. Davies and J. Oates. Cambridge: Cambridge University Press.

Nicholson, Henry B. 1971. "Religion in Pre-Hispanic Central Mexico." Pp. 395–446 in *Archaeology of Northern Mesoamerica, Part One* (*Handbook of Middle American Indians*, volume 10), edited by Gordon F. Ekholm and Ignacio Bernal. Austin, TX: University of Texas Press.

Nishida. T. 1990. *The Chimpanzees of the Mahale Mountains: Sexual and Life History Strategies*. Tokyo: University of Tokyo Press.

Norenzayan, Ara. 2013. *Big Gods: How Religion Changed Conflict and Cooperation*. Princeton, NJ: Princeton University Press.

Norenzayan, A. and and A. F. Shariff. 2008. "The Origin and Evolution of Religious Prosociality." *Science* 322: 58–62.

Nummenmaa, Lauri, Enrico Glerean, Mikko Viinikainen, Iiro P. Jääskeläinen, Riitta Hari, and Mikko Sams. 2012. "Emotions Promote Social Interaction and Synchronizing Brain Activity across Individuals." *Proceedings of the National Academy of Sciences* 109 (24): 9599–9604.

Nummenmaa, Lauri, Heini Saarimäki, Enrico Glerean, Athanasios Gotsopoulos, Iiro P. Jääskeläinen, Riitta Hari, and Mikko Sams. 2014. "Emotional Speech Synchronizes Brains across Listeners and Engages Large-scale Dynamic Brain Networks." *NeuroImage* 102: 498–509.

Obhi, Sukhvinder S. and Natalie Sebanz. 2011. "Moving Together: Toward Understanding the Mechanisms of Joint Action." *Experimental Brain Research* 211: 329–336.

Okamoto, Sanae, Masaki Tomonaga, Kiyoshi Ishii, Nobuyuki Kawai, Masayuki Tanaka, and Tetsuro Matsuzawa 2002. "An Infant Chimpanzee (*Pan troglodytes*) Follows Human Gaze." *Animal Cognition* 5: 107–114.

Okasha, Samir. 2006. *Evolution and Levels of Selection*. Oxford: Oxford University Press.

Olsen, Mancur. 1967 [1971]. *The Logic of Collective Action*. Cambridge, MA: Harvard University Press.

Osgood, Charles E. 1966. "Dimensionality of the Semantic Space for Communication via Facial Expressions." *Scandinavian Journal of Psychology* 7: 1–30.

Panksepp, Jaak. 1982. "Toward a General Psychobiological Theory of Emotions." *Behavioral and Brain Sciences* 5: 407–467.

Pannese, Alessia, Didier Grandjean, and Sacha Fruhholz. 2015. "Subcortical Processing of Auditory Communication." *Hearing Research* 328: 67–77.

Parr, Lisa A., Bridget M. Waller, and Jennifer Fugate. 2005. "Emotional Communication in Primates: Implications for Neurobiology." *Current Opinion in Neurobiology* 15: 716–720.

Parsons, Talcott. 1951. *The Social System*. New York: Free Press.

Passingham, Richard E. 1973. "Anatomical Differences between the Neocortex of Man and the Other Primates." *Brain Behavioral Evolution* 7: 337–359.

——. 1975. "Changes in the Size and Organisation of the Brain in Man and His Ancestors." *Brain and Behavior Evolution* 11: 73–90.

——. 1982. *The Human Primate*. Oxford: Freeman.

Petersen, Anders Klostergaard. 2005. "At the End of the Road: Reflections on a Popular Scholarly Metaphor." Pp. 45–72 in *Papers from the Seventh Nordic New Testament Conference in Stavanger* 2003, edited by Jostein Ådna. Tübingen: Mohr Siebeck.

——. 2012. "Finding a Basis for Interpreting New Testament Ethos from a Greco-Roman Philosophical Perspective." Pp. 53–81 in *Early Christian Ethics in Jewish and Hellenistic Contexts*, edited by Jan Willem van Henten and Joseph Verheyden. Leiden and Boston: Brill.

——. 2013. "Attaining Divine Perfection through Different Forms of Imitation." *Numen* 60 (1): 7–38.

———. 2017. "Plato's Philosophy – Why Not Just Platonic Religion?" Pp. 9–36 in *Religio-Philosophical Discourses in the Mediterranean World: From Plato, through Jesus, to Late Antiquity*, edited by Anders Klostergaard Petersen and George van Kooten. Leiden and Boston: Brill.

———. 2018a. *Testing Trust. Observing Obligation: A Biocultural Evolutionary Approach to 2 Corinthians with Special Focus on Chapters 8–9*. Forthcoming.

———. 2018b. "The Relationship between Text and Ritual," in *Oxford Handbook of Early Christian Rituals*, edited by Risto Uro, Rikard Roitto, and Richard E. De Maris. Oxford: Oxford University Press.

Petkov, Christopher I. and Benjamin Wilson. 2008. "On The Pursuit of the Brain Network for Proto-syntactic Learning in Non-Human Primates: Conceptual Issues and Neurobiological Hypotheses." *Philosophical Transactions of the Royal Society* 367: 2077–2088.

Pew Foundation Poll. 2014. "How Americans Feel About Religious Groups." www.pewforum.org (accessed March 18, 2017).

———. 2015. "U.S. Public Becoming Less Religious." www.pewforum.org (accessed March 18, 2017).

Pew Research Center. 2015. "The Changing Religious Composition of the U.S." www.pewforum.org/2015/0512/chapter-1-the-changing-religious-composition-of-the-U.S/ (accessed March 18, 2017).

Phelps, E. A. and J. E. Le Doux. 2005. "Contributions of the Amygdala to Emotion Processing: From Animal Models to Human Behavior." *Neuron* 48: 175–187.

Pilbeam, D and N. Young. 2004. "Hominoid Evolution: Synthesizing Disparate Data." *Comptes Rendus Palevol* 3: 305–321.

Pinker, Steven. 2002. *The Blank Slate: The Modern Denial of Human Nature*. New York: Viking.

———. 2012. "The False Allure of Group Selection." http://edge.org/conversation/the-false-allure-of-group-selection (accessed March 18, 2017).

Platvoet, Jan G. 1999. "At War with God: Ju/'Hoan Curing Dances." *Journal of Religion in Africa* 29 (1): 2–61.

Platvoet, Jan G. and Arie L. Molendijk. Eds. 1999. *The Pragmatics of Defining Religion: Contexts, Concepts and Contests*. Leiden, Boston, Köln: E. J. Brill.

Plotnik, Joshua, Frans de Waal, Diana Reiss. 2006. "Self-recognition Among Asian Elephants." *Proceedings of the National Academy of Sciences* 103 (45): 17053–17057.

Plutchik, Robert. 1980. *Emotion: A Psychoevolutionary Synthesis*. New York: Harper and Row.

———. 2002. *Emotions and Life: Perspectives from Psychology, Biology, and Evolution*. Washington, DC: American Psychological Association.

Povinelli, Daniel J. 2000. *Folk Physics for Apes: The Chimpanzee's Theory of How the World Works*. Oxford: Oxford University Press.

Povinelli, Daniel J. and Timothy J. Eddy. 1997. "Specificity of Gaze-following in Young Chimpanzees." *British Journal of Developmental Psychology* 15: 213–222.

Povinelli, Daniel J. and Jennifer Vonk. 2003. "Chimpanzee Minds: Suspiciously Human?" *Trends in Cognitive Sciences* 7: 157–160.

Povinelli, D.J., K. E. Nelson, and S. T. Boysen. 1990. "Inferences about Guessing and Knowing by Chimpanzees (*Pan troglodytes*)." *Journal of Comparative Psychology* 104: 203–210.

Povinelli, D.J., A. Rulf, K. Landau, and D. Bierschwale. 1993. "Self-recognition in Chimpanzees (*Pan troglodytes*): Distribution, Ontogeny, and Patterns of Emergence." *Journal of Comparative Psychology* 107: 347–372.

Prado-Martinez, Javier, et al. 2013. "Great Ape Genetic Diversity and Population History." *Nature* 499 (7459): 471–475.

Premack, David and Guy Woodruff. 1978. "Does the Chimpanzee Have a Theory of Mind?" *Behavior and Brain Science* 1: 515–526.

Prescott, William H. 2000. *History of the Conquest of Mexico and History of the Conquest of Peru.* Mineola, NY: Dover.

———. 2005. *History of the Conquest of Peru.* Mineola, NY: Dover.

Pruetz, Jill. 2006. "Feeding Ecology of Savanna Chimpanzees (*Pan troglodytes verus*)." Pp. 161–182 in *Feeding Ecology of Great Apes and Other Primates,* edited by G. Boesch, G. Hohmann, and M. Robbins. Cambridge: Cambridge University Press.

Pruetz, J.D. and P. Bertolani. 2007. "Savanna Chimpanzees (*Pan troglodytes verus*) Hunt with Tools." *Current Biology* 17: 1–6.

———. 2009. "Chimpanzee (*Pan troglodytes verus*) Behavioral Responses to Stresses Associated with Living in a Savanna-mosaic Environment: Implications for Hominin Adaptations to Open Habitats." *Paleoanthropology* 2009: 252–262.

Pruetz, Jill and Thomas C. LaDuke. 2010. "Reaction to Fire by Savanna Chimpanzees (*Pan troglodytes verus*) at Fongoli, Senegal." *American Journal of Physical Anthropology* 141: 646–650.

Pruetz, J.E. and S. Lindshield. 2012. "Food and Tool Sharing among Savanna Chimpanzees." *Primates* 53: 133–145.

Prüfer, Kay et al. 2012. "The Bonobo Genome Compared with the Chimpanzee and Human Genomes." *Nature* 486: 527.

Pusey. A.E. 1980. "Inbreeding Avoidance in Chimpanzees." *Animal Behavior* 28: 543–552.

———. 2005. "Inbreeding Avoidance in Primates." In *Inbreeding, Incest, and the Incest Taboo,* edited by A.P. Wolf and W.H. Durham. Stanford, CA: Stanford University Press.

Pusey, Anne E. and Craig Packer. 1987. "The Evolution of Sex-biased Dispersal in Lions." *Journal of Behaviour* 101: 275–310.

Raaum, R., Kirstin, L., Sterner, N., Noviello, C., Stewart, C., and Disotell, T. 2005. "Catarrhine Primate Divergence Dates Estimated from Complete Mitochondrial Genomes: Concordance with Fossil and DNA Evidence." *Journal of Human Evolution* 48: 237–257.

Radcliffe-Brown, A.R. 1952. *Structure and Function in Primitive Society.* New York: Free Press.

Raghanti, Mary Ann, Cheryl D. Simpson, Jennifer L. Marchiewicz, Joseph M. Erwin, Patrick R. Hof, and Chet C. Sherwood. 2008. "Differences in Cortical Serotonergic Innervation among Humans, Chimpanzees, and Macaque Monkeys: A Comparative Study." *Cerebral Cortex* 18: 584–597.

Rakic, P. and D. Kormack. 2001. "Neocortical Expansion and Elaboration During Primate Evolution: A View from Neuroembryology." Pp. 30–56 in *Evolutionary Anatomy of the Primate Cerebral Cortex,* edited by K.R. Gibson and D. Falk. Cambridge: Cambridge University Press.

———. 2007. "The Development and Evolutionary Expansion of the Cerebral Cortex in Primates." Pp. 243–59 in *Evolution of Nervous Systems: A Comprehensive Reference, Volume* 4, edited by J. Kaas and T. Preuss. Amsterdam: Elsevier.

Rasmussen, Knud. 1929. *Intellectual Culture of the Iglulik Eskimos* (Report of the Fifth Thule Expedition 1921–24, vol. VII, no. 1). Copenhagen: Gyldendalske Boghandel, Nordisk Forlag.

Rauschecker, Josef P. and Sophie K. Scott. 2016. "Pathways and Streams in the Auditory Cortex." Pp. 287–298 in *Neurobiology of Language,* edited by G.S. Hickok and S.C. Small. New York: Elsevier.

Reed, Annette Yoshiko and Adam H. Becker. 2003. "Introduction: Traditional Models and New Directions." Pp. 1–33 in *The Ways That Never Parted: Jews and Christians in Late Antiquity and the Early Middle Ages*, edited by Adam H. Becker and Annette Yoshiko Reed. Tübingen: Mohr-Siebeck.

Reiss, Diana and Lori Marino. 2001. "Mirror Self-recognition in the Bottlenose Dolphin: A Case of Cognitive Convergence." *Proceedings of the National Academy of Sciences* 98: 5937–5942.

Reynolds, Vernon. 1967. *The Apes: The Gorilla, Chimpanzee, Orangutan, and Gibbon: Their History and Their World*. New York: E. Dutton.

Rhine, Raymond J. and Alexandra Maryanski. 1996. "A Twenty-One year History of a Dominant StumpTail Matriline." Pp. 473–500 in *Evolution and Ecology of Macaque Societies*, edited by J. Fa and D. Linburg. Cambridge: Cambridge University Press.

Rice, Patricia and Norah Moloney. 2005. *Biological Anthropology and Prehistory: Exploring Our Human Ancestry*. Boston: Pearson.

Richerson, Peter J. and Robert Boyd. 2005. *Not by Genes Alone: How Culture Transformed Human Evolution*. Chicago: Chicago University Press.

Richter, Daniel, Rainer Grun, Renaud Joannes-Boyau, et al. 2017. "The Age of the Hominin Fossils from Jebel Irhoud, Morocco, and the Origins of the Middle Stone Age." *Nature*, volume 546, June 8.

Ridge, Mian. 2007. "Sri Lanka's Buddhist Monks Are Intent on War." *The Telegraph* June 17, 2007. www.telegraph.co.uk/news/worldnews/1554817/Sri-Lankas-Buddhist-monks-are-intent-on-war.html (accessed August 5, 2016).

Ridley, Mark. 1996. *Evolution*. Malden, MA: Blackwell Sciences.

Rilling, James K. 2014a. "Comparative Primate Neuroimaging: Insights into Human Brain Evolution." *Trends in Cognitive Sciences* 18 (1): 46–55.

——. 2014b. "Comparative Primate Neurobiology and the Evolution of the Brain Language Systems." *Current Opinion in Neurobiology* 28: 10–14.

Rizzolatti, Giacomo and Gorrado Sinigalia. 2008. *Mirrors in the Brain: How Our Minds Share Actions, Emotions, and Experience*. Oxford: Oxford University Press.

Rizzolattti, Giacomo, Luciano Fadiga, Leonardo Fogassi, and Vittorio Gallese. 2002. "From Mirror Neurons to Imitation: Facts and Speculations." Pp. 247–266 in *The Imitative Mind: Development, Evolution and Brain Bases*, edited by W. Prinz and A. N. Meltzoff. Cambridge: Cambridge University Press.

Robbins, Martha. 2011. "Gorillas: Diversity in Ecology and Behavior." Pp. 326–339 in *Primates in Perspective*, edited by C. Campbell, A. Fuenter, K. MacKinnon, S. Bearder and R. Stumpf. New York: Oxford University Press.

Roberts, Michael. 1997. "For Humanity. For the Sinhalese. Dharmapala as Crusading Bosat." *The Journal of Asian Studies* 56 (4): 1006–1032.

Rosenbaum, S., A.A. Maldonado-Chaparro, and T.S. Stoinski. 2016. "Group Structure Predicts Variation in Proximity Relationships between Male-Female and Male-Infant Pairs of Mountain Gorillas (*Gorilla Beringei beringei*)." *Primates* 57: 17–28.

Rueschemeyer, Dietrich. 1986. *Power and the Division of Labour*. Stanford, CA: Stanford University Press.

Ruff, Christopher B., M. Loring Burgess, Richard A. Ketcham, and John Kappelman. 2016. "Limb Bone Structural Proportions and Locomotor Behavior in A.L. 288–1 ("Lucy")." *PLOS ONE* 11 (11): e0166095.

Rugg, Harold Ordway. 1916. *The Experimental Determination of Mental Discipline in School Studies*. Baltimore, MD: Warwick and York.

Rumbaugh, M. Duane. 2013. *With Apes in Mind: Emergence, Communication and Competence*. Distributed by Amazon.com.

——. 2015. "A Salience Theory of Learning and Behavior and Rights of Apes." Pp. 514–536 in *Handbook on Evolution and Society: Toward an Evolutionary Social Science*, edited by J. H. Turner, R. Machalek, and A. Maryanski. New York: Routledge/Paradigm.

Rumbaugh, Duane and E. Sue Savage-Rumbaugh. 1990. "Chimpanzees: Competencies for Language and Numbers." Pp. 409–441 in *Comparative Perception: Complex Signals, Volume 2*, edited by W. Stebbins and M. Berkley. New York: Wiley and Sons.

Rumbaugh, Duane M. and D. A. Washburn. 2003. *Intelligence of Apes and Other Rational Beings*. New Haven, CT: Yale University Press.

Runciman, W. G. 1983–1997. *A Treatise on Social Theory, Volume 1–3*. Cambridge: Cambridge University Press.

——. 2009. *The Theory of Cultural and Social Selection*. Cambridge: Cambridge University Press.

——. 2015. "Evolutionary Sociology." Pp. 194–214 in *Handbook of Evolution and Society: Toward an Evolutionary Social Science*, edited by J. H. Turner, R. Machalek, and A. R. Maryanski. Boulder, CO: Paradigm/New York: Routledge.

Russon, Anne. 2009. "Orangutans." *Current Biology* 19: 295–297.

Sachs, Harvey. 1972. "An Initial Investigation of the Usability of Conversational Data for Doing Sociology." Pp. 31–74 in *Studies on Conversation, 2 Volumes*, edited by D. Sudnow. New York: Free Press.

Sachs, Harvey, Emanuel Schefloff, and Gail Jefferson. 1974. "A Simple Systematics for the Analysis of Turn Taking in Conversation." *Language* 50: 696–697.

Sanderson, Stephen K. 2001. *The Evolution of Human Sociality. A Darwinian Conflict Perpective*. Lanham, MD: Rowman and Littlefield.

Sargis, E. J. 2004. "New Views on Tree Shrews: The Role of Tupaiids in Primate Supraordinal Relationships." *Evolutionary Anthropology* 13: 56–66.

Savage-Rumbaugh, Sue E. and Roger Lewin. 1994. *Kanzi: The Ape at the Brink of the Human Mind*. New York: John Wiley and Sons.

Savage-Rumbaugh, Sue E., Duane Rumbaugh, and Sally Boysen. 1978. "Symbolic Communication Between Two Chimpanzees." *Science, New Series* 201 (4356): 641–644.

Savage-Rumbaugh, Sue E., Jeannine Murphy, Rose A. Seveik, Karen E. Brakke, Shelly L. Williams, and Duane M. Rumbaugh. 1993. *Language Comprehension in the Ape and Child*. Chicago: University of Chicago Press.

Savage-Rumbaugh, Sue E., Rose A. Seveik, and William D. Hopkins. 1988. "Symbolic Cross-Model Transfer in Two Species." *Child Development* 59: 617–625.

Saxe, Rebecca, and N. Kanwisher. 2003. "People Thinking about Thinking People: The Role of the Temporo-Parietal Junction in 'Theory of Mind.'" *NeuroImage* 19: 1835–1842.

Saxe, Rebecca, Laura E. Schulz, and Yuhong V. Jiang. 2006. "Reading Minds Versus Following Rules: Dissociating Theory of Mind and Executive Control in the Brain." *Social Neuroscience* 1: 284–298.

Schaller, George. 1962. *The Ecology and Behavior of the Mountain Gorilla*. Ph.D. dissertation, University of Wisconsin.

Scheff, Thomas. 1988. "Shame and Conformity: The Deference-Emotion System." *American Sociological Review* 5: 395–406.

Schele, Linda and Mary Ellen Miller. 1986. *The Blood of Kings: Dynasty and Ritual in Maya Art*. New York: George Braziller, Inc.

Schenker, Natalie Marie. 2007. *Comparative Analysis of Broca's Area in Hominoids*. Ph.D. Dissertation, University of California, San Diego.

Schenker, Natalie M., Anne-Marie Desgouttes, and Katernia Semendeferi. 2005. "Neural Connectivity and Cortical Substrates in Hominoids." *Journal of Human Evolution* 49: 547–569.

Schenker, Natalie M., William D. Hopkins, Muhammad A. Spocter, Amy R. Garrison, Cheryl D. Stimpson, Joseph M. Erwin, Patrick R. Hof, and Chet C. Sherwood. 2010. "Broca's Area Homologue in Chimpanzees (*Pan troglodytes*): Probabilistic Mapping, Asymmetry, and Comparison to Humans." *Cerebral Cortex* 20 (3): 730–742.

Schniedewind, William M. 2004. *How the Bible Became a Book: The Textualization of Ancient Israel.* Cambridge: Cambridge University Press.

Schutz, Alfred. 1932 [1967]. *The Phenomenology of the Social World.* Evanston, IL: Northwestern University Press.

Selengut, Charles. 2003. *Sacred Fury: Understanding Religious Violence.* Walnut Creek, CA: Altamira Press.

Semendeferi, Katerina and Hanna Damasio. 2000. "The Brain and Its Main Anatomical Subdivisons in Living Hominoids Using Magnetic Resonance Imaging." *Journal of Human Evolution* 38: 317–332.

Semendeferi, Katerina, A. Lu, Natalie Schenker, and Hanna Damasio. 2002. "Humans and Great Apes Share a Large Frontal Cortex." *Nature Neuroscience* 5: 272–276.

Semendeferi, Katerina, E. Armstrong, A. Schleicher, K. Zilles, and G. W. Van Hoesen. 2001. "Prefrontal Cortex in Humans and Apes: A Comparative Study of Area 10." *American Journal of Physical Anthropology* 114 (3): 224–241.

Seneviratne, H. L. 1999. *The Work of Kings: The New Buddhism in Sri Lanka.* Chicago: University of Chicago Press.

Setia, Tatang Mitra, Roberto Delgado, S. Suci Utami Atmoko, Ian Singleton and Carel P. Van Schaik. 2008. "Social Organization and Male-Male Relationships." Pp. 245–253 in *Orangutans: Geographical Variation in Behavioral Ecology and Conservation.* Oxford: Oxford University Press.

Shackleton, N. J. 1987. "Oxygen Isotopes, Ice Volume and Sea Level." *Quaternary Science Reviews* 6: 183–190.

Shariff, A. F. and A. Norenzayan. 2007. "God Is Watching You: Priming God Concepts Increases Prosocial Behavior in an Anonymous Economic Game." *Psychological Science* 18: 803–809.

Sherwood, Chet. C. 2007. "The Evolution of Neuron Types and Cortical Histology in Apes and Humans." Pp. 355–378 in *Evolution of Nervous Systems 4: The Evolution of Primate Nervous Systems,* edited by T. M. Preuss and J. H. Kaas. Oxford: Academic Press.

Sherwood, Chet C., Ralph L. Holloway, Katerina Semendeferi, and Patrick R. Hof. 2005. "Is Prefrontal White Matter Enlargement a Human Evolutionary Specialization?" *Nature Neuroscience* 8: 537–538.

Sherwood, Chet C., Francys Subiaul, and Tadeusz W. Zawidzki. 2008. "A Natural History of the Human Mind: Tracing Evolutionary Changes in Brain and Cognition." *Journal of Anatomy* 212: 426–454.

Shi, Peng, Margaret A. Bakewell, and Jianzhi Zhang. 2006. "Did Brain-specific Genes Evolve Faster in Humans than in Chimpanzees?" *Trends in Genetics* 22 (11): 608–613.

Simons, E. L. 1993. "New Endocasts of Aegyptopithecus: Oldest Well-Known Preserved Record of the Brain in in Anthropoidea." *American Journal of Science* 293A: 383–390.

Singer, T., F. Seymour, J. O'Doherty, H. Kaube, R. J. Dolan, and C. D. Frith. 2004. "Empathy for Pain Involves the Affective but Not Sensory Components of Pain." *Science* 303 (5661): 1157–1162.

Skocpol, Teda. 1979. *States and Social Revolutions: A Comparative Analysis of France, Russia, and China*. New York: Cambridge University Press.

Skyrms, Brian 1996. *Evolution of the Social Contract*. Cambridge: Cambridge University Press.

———. 2004. *The Stag Hunt and the Evolution of Social Structure*. Cambridge: Cambridge University Press.

Smelser, Neil J. 1963. *Theory of Collective Behavior*. New York: Free Press.

Smith, Jonathan Z. 1990. *Drudgery Divine: On the Comparison of Early Christianities and the Religions of Late Antiquity*. Chicago, IL: Chicago University Press.

———. 1998. "Religion, Religions, Religious." Pp. 269–284 in *Critical Terms for Religious Studies*, edited by Mark C. Taylor. Chicago and London: University of Chicago Press.

Smith, Michael E. 1986. "The Role of Social Stratification in the Aztec Empire: A View from the Provinces." *American Anthropologist* 88: 70–91.

———. 2005. "City Size in Late Postclassic Mesoamerica." *Journal of Urban History* 31 (4): 403–434.

Snow, David A., and Sarah A. Soule. 2010. *A Primer on Social Movements*. New York: W.W. Horton & Company.

Sober, Elliott and Wilson, David S. 1998. *Unto Others. The Evolution and Psychology of Unselfish Behavior*. Cambridge, MA: Harvard University Press.

Spencer, Herbert. 1851 [1988]. *Social Statics: Or, the Conditions Essential to Human Happiness Specified, and the First of Them Developed*. New York: Appleton-Century-Crofts.

———. 1874–96 [1899]. *The Principles of Sociology*. New York: Appleton-Century-Crofts.

Speri, Alice. 2014. "Your Buddha Tattoo Is Hurting Sri Lanka's Feelings and Will Get You Deported." *Vice News* April 22, 2014. https://news.vice.com/article/your-buddha-tattoo-is-hurting-sri-lankas-feelings-and-will-get-you-deported (accessed August 13, 2016).

Spocter, Muhammad A., William D. Hopkins, Amy R. Garrison, Amy L. Bauernfeind, Cheryl D. Stimpson, Patrick R. Hof, and Chet C. Sherwood. 2010. "Wernicke's Area Homologue in Chimpanzees (*Pan troglodytes*) and Its Relation to the Appearance of Modern Human Language." *Proceedings of the Royal Society* B doi:10.1098/rspb.2010.0011: 1–10.

Stanford, C.B. 1990. *The Hunting Apes: Meat Eating and the Origins of Human Behavior*. Princeton, NJ: Princeton University Press.

Stanford, Craig, John Allen and Susan Antón. 2013. *Biological Anthropology*: Boston: Pearson.

Stark, Rodney, and William Sims Bainbridge. 1996. *A Theory of Religion*. New Brunswick, NJ: Rutgers University Press.

Stebbins, G. Ledyard. 1969. *The Basis of Progressive Evolution*. Chapel Hill, NC: University of North Carolina Press.

Stephan, Heinz. 1983. "Evolutionary Trends in Limbic Structures." *Neuroscience and Biobehavioral Reviews* 7: 367–374.

Stephan, Heinz and O.J. Andy. 1969. "Quantitative Comparative Neuroanatomy of Primates: An Attempt at Phylogenetic Interpretation." *Annals of the New York Academy of Science* 167: 370–387.

———. 1977. "Quantitative Comparison of the Amygdala in Insectivores and Primates." *Acta Antomica* 98: 130–153.

Stephan, Heinz, Georg Baron, and Heiko Frahm. 1986. "Comparative Size of Brains and Brain Components." Pp. 1–37 in *Comparative Primate Biology, Volume 4*, edited by H. Steklis and J. Erwin. New York: Alan R. Liss.

Stephen, Heinz, Heiko Frahm, and Georg Baron. 1981. "New and Revised Data on Volumes of Brain Structures in Insectivores and Primates." *Folia Primatoligica* 35: 1–29.

Sterck, E. 2012. "The Behavioral Ecology of Colobine Monkeys." Pp. 65–90 in *The Evolution of Primate Societies*, edited by J. Mitani, J. Call, P. Kappeler, R. Palomit. Chicago: University of Chicago Press.

Stevens, J. H. Vervaecke, H. De Vries, and L. Elsacker. 2006. "Social Structures in *Pan Paniscus*: Testing the Female Bonding Hypothesis." *Primates* 47: 210–217.

Stevens, N. J., E. R. Seiffert, P.M. O'Conner, E. M. Roberts, M.D. Scmitz, C. Krause, E. Gorscak, S. Ngasala, T.L. Hieronymus and J. Temu. 2013. "Paleontological Evidence for an Oligocene Divergence Between Old World Monkeys and Apes." *Nature* 497: 611–614.

Steward, Julian. 1955 [1972]. *Theory of Culture Change*. Champaign, IL: University of Illinois Press.

Stringer, Chris and Julia Galway-Witham. 2017. "On the Origins of Our Species." Nature.com/newsletters.

Stumpf, R.M., E. Thompson, M. Muller, and R. Wrangham. 2009. "The Context of Dispersal in Kanyawara Chimpanzees." *Behaviour* 146: 629–656.

Subiaul, Francys. 2007. "The Imitation Faculty in Monkeys: Evaluating Its Features, Distribution, and Evolution." *Journal of Anthropological Science* 85: 35–62.

Suddendorf, Thomas and Emma Collier-Baker. 2009. "The Evolution of Primate Visual Self-recognition: Evidence of Absence in Lesser Apes." *Proceedings of the Royal Society* 276: 1671–1677.

Summers-Effler, Erika. 2010. *Laughing Saints and Righteous Heroes: Emotional Rhythms in Social Movement Groups*. Chicago, IL: University of Chicago Press.

Swanson, Guy E. 1964. *The Birth of the Gods: The Origin of Primitive Beliefs*. Ann Arbor, MI: University of Michigan Press.

Taglialatela, J.P., Jamie L. Russell, Jennifer A. Schaeffer, and William D. Hopkins. 2008. "Communicative Signaling Activates 'Broca's' Homolog in Chimpanzees." *Current Biology* 18: 343–348.

——. 2009. "Visualizing Vocal Perception in Chimpanzee Brain." *Cerebral Cortex* 19: 1151–1157.

——. 2011. "Chimpanzee Vocal Signaling Points to a Multimodal Origin of Human Language." *PLoS ONE* 6(4): e18852.

Talkington, William J., Jared P. Taglialatela, and James W. Lewis. 2013. "Using Naturalistic Utterances to Investigate Vocal Communication Processing and Development in Human and Non-human Primates." *Hearing Research* 305: 74–85.

Tanaka, Jiro. 1969. "The Ecology of Social Structure of Central Kalahari Bushmen." *Kyoto University African Studies* 3: 1–26.

Tanaka, Jiro and Kazuyoshi Sugawara. 2010. "/Gui and //Gana." Pp. 195–199 in *The Cambridge Encyclopedia of Hunters and Gatherers*, edited by Richard B. Lee and Richard Daly. Cambridge: Cambridge University Press.

Temerin, Alis and John Cant. 1983. "The Evolutionary Divergence of Old World Monkeys and Apes." *The American Naturalist* 122: 335–351.

Thierry Bernard. 2011. "The Macaques." Pp. 229–241 in *Primates in Perspective*, edited by C. Campbell, A. Fuentes, K. MacKinnon, S. Bearder and R. Stumpf. New York: Oxford University Press.

Tilly, Charles. 1978. *From Mobilization to Revolution*. New York: McGraw-Hill.

Tilly, Charles, Louise Tilly, and Richard Tilly. 1975. *The Rebellious Century 1830–1930*. Cambridge, MA: Harvard University Press.

Todorov, Tzvetan. 1999. *The Conquest of America: The Question of the Other*. Norman, OK: University of Oklahoma Press.

Tomasello, Michael and Josep Call. 1997. *Primate Cognition*. Oxford: Oxford University Press.

——. 2007. "Ape Gestures and the Origins of Langauge." Pp. 221–239 in *The Gestural Communication of Apes and Monkeys*, edited by J. Call and M. Tomasello. Mahwah, NJ: Lawrance Erlbaum.

Tomasello, Michael, Brian Hare, and Tara Fogleman. 2001. "The Ontogeny of Gaze Following in Chimpanzees, *Pan troglodytes*, and Rhesus Macaques, *Macaca mulatta*." *Animal Behavior* 61: 335–343.

Tomasello, Michael, Josep Call, Katherine Nagell, Raquel Olguin, and Malinda Carpenter. 1994. "The Learning and Use of Gestual Signals by Young Chimpanzees: A Transgenerational Study." *Primates* 35: 137–154.

Tomonaga, Michael. 1999. "Attending to the Others' Attention in Macaques' Joint Attention or Not?" *Primate Research* 15: 425.

Tooby, John and Leda Cosmides 1992. "The Psychological Foundations of Culture." Pp. 19–136 in *The Adapted Mind: Evolutionary Psychology and the Generation of Culture*, edited by Jerome H. Barkow, Leda Cosmides, and John Tooby. Oxford: Oxford University Press.

Trivers, Robert L. 1971. "The Evolution of Reciprocal Altruism." *Quarterly Review of Biology* 46: 35–57.

——. 2005. "Reciprocal Altruism: 30 Years Later." Pp. 67–83 in *Cooperation in Primates and Humans: Mechanisms of Evolution*, edited by P.M. Kappeler and C.P. van Schaik. New York: Springer.

Tsai, Jessica Chia-Chin, Natalie Sebanz and Günther Knoblich. 2011. "The GROOP Effect: Groups Mimic Group Actions." *Cognition* 118: 135–140.

Turchin, Peter. 2003. *Historical Dynamics: Why States Rise and Fall*. Princeton, NJ: Princeton University Press.

——. 2006. *War and Peace and War: The Life Cycles of Imperial Nations*. New York: Pi Pres.

——. 2016. *Ultrasociety: How 10,000 Years of War Made Humans the Greatest Cooperators on Earth*. Chaplin, CT: Beresta Books.

Turchin, Peter and Sergey A. Nefedov. 2009. *Secular Cycles*. Princeton, NJ: Princeton University Press.

Turner, J.H. 1972. *Patterns of Social Organization: A Survey of Social Institutions*. New York: McGraw-Hill.

——. 1987. "Toward a Sociological Theory of Motivation." *American Sociological Review* 52: 15–27.

——. 1988. *A Theory of Social Interaction*. Stanford, CA: Stanford University Press.

——. 1995. *Macrodynamics: Toward a Theory on the Organization of Human Populations*. New Brunswick: Rutgers University Press.

——. 1996a. "The Evolution of Emotions in Humans: A Darwinian-Durkheimian Analysis." *Journal for the Theory of Social Behaviour* 26: 1–34.

——. 1996b. "Cognition, Emotion, and Interaction in the Big-Brained Primate." *Contemporary Studies in Sociology* 13: 297–318.

——. 1997a. *The Institutional Order*. New York: Longman.

——. 1997b. "The Evolution of Emotions: The Nonverbal Basis of Human Social Organization." Pp. 211–228 in *Nonverbal Communication: Where Nature Meets Culture*, edited by Ullica Segerstrale and Peter Molnar. Hillsdale, NJ: Erlbaum.

——. 1998. "The Evolution of Moral Systems." *Critical Review* 11: 211–232.

———. 1999a. "The Neurology of Emotions: Implications for Sociological Theories of Inter-personal Behavior." *Social Perspectives on Emotion* 5: 81–108.

———. 1999b. "Toward a General Sociological Theory of Emotions." *Journal for the Theory of Social Behaviour* 29: 133–162.

———. 1999c. "The Neurology of Emotions: Implications for Sociological Theories of Inter-personal Behavior." Pp. 83–96 in *The Sociology of Emotions*, edited by D. Franks and C. Smith. Greenwich, CT: JAI Press.

———. 2000. *On the Origins of Human Emotions: A Sociological Inquiry into the Evolution of Human Affect.* Stanford, CA: Stanford University Press.

———. 2002. *Face to Face: Toward a Theory of Interpersonal Behavior.* Palo Alto, CA: Stanford University Press.

———. 2003. *Human Institutions: A New Theory of Societal Evolution.* Boulder, CO: Rowan and Littlefield.

———. 2007a. *Human Emotions: A Sociological Theory.* London: Routledge.

———. 2007b. "Justice and Emotions." *Social Justice Research* 20: 312–335.

———. 2010ba. *Theoretical Principles of Sociology, Volume 1 on Macrodynamics.* New York: Springer.

———. 2010b. *Theoretical Principles of Sociology, Volume 2 on Microdynamics.* New York: Springer.

———. 2010c. "Natural Selection and The Evolution of Morality in Human Societies." Pp. 125–146 in *Handbook of The Sociology of Morality*, edited by S. Hitlin and S. Vaisey. New York: Springer.

———. 2013. *Theoretical Principles of Sociology, Volume 3 on Mesodynamics.* New York: Springer.

———. 2014a. "The Evolution of Affect, Sociality, Altruism and Prosocial Behavior in Humans." Pp. 275–301 in *Altruism, Morality, and Social Solidarity: Envisioning a Field*, edited by V. Jeffries and L. Nichols. London: Palgrave.

———. 2014b. "The Evolution of Emotions in Humans." Pp. 11–36 in *Handbook of the Sociology of Emotions, Volume 2*, edited by J.E. Stets and J.H. Turner. New York: Springer.

———. 2014c. "The Biology and Evolution of Morality." Pp. 134–145 in *The Science of Moral-ity: Disciplinary and Interdisciplinary Approaches Now and in the Future*, edited by S. Hitlin and J. Stets. Washington, DC: National Science Foundation/American Socio-logical Association.

———. 2017. "Principles of Inter-societal Dynamics." *Journal of World Systems Research*, in press.

Turner, Jonathan H. and Seth Abrutyn. 2017. "Returning the 'Social' to Evolutionary Sociol-ogy: Reconsidering Spencer, Durkheim, and Marx's Models of 'Natural' Selection." *Sociological Perspectives*, in press.

Turner, Jonathan H. and Alexandra Maryanski. 2005. *Incest: Origins of the Taboo.* Boulder, CO: Paradigm Press.

———. 2008. *On The Origins of Societies by Natural Selection.* Boulder, CO: Paradigm Press.

———. 2015. "Evolutionary Sociology: A Cross-Species Strategy for Discovering Human Nature." Pp. 546–571 in *Handbook of Evolution and Society: Toward an Evolutionary Social Science*, edited by J.H. Turner, R. Machalek, and A.R. Maryanski. Boulder, CO: Paradigm/New York: Routledge.

Turner, Jonathan H. and Jan E. Stets. 2005. *The Sociology of Emotions.* New York: Cambridge University Press.

———. 2006. Turner, Jonathan H. and Jan E. Stets. "The Moral Emotions." Pp. 544–568 in *Handbook of The Sociology of Emotions*, edited by J.E. Stets and J.H. Turner. New York: Springer.

Turner, Ralph H. 1962. "Role-taking: Processes versus Conformity." Pp. 20–40 in *Human Behavior and Social Processes*, edited by A. Rose. Boston: Houghton Mifflin.

Turner, Jonathan H., Richard Machalek, and Alexandra Maryanski (Eds.). 2015. *Handbook of Evolution and Society: Toward an Evolutionary Social Science*. Boulder, CO: Paradigm/ New York: Routledge.

Tutin, W., W.C. McGrew, and P.J. Baldwin. 1982. "Responses of Wild Chimpanzees to Potential Predators." Pp. 136–141 in *Primate Behavior and Sociobiology*, edited by B. Chiarelli and R. Corruccini. Berlin: Springer-Verlag.

Vaitheespara, Ravi. 2007. "Sanmugathasan, the Unrepentent Left and the Ethnic Crisis in Sri Lanka." *Economic and Political Weekly* 42 (43): 58–65.

Varki, Ajit. 2007. "Genomic Comparisons of Humans and Chimpanzees." *Annual Review of Anthropology* 36: 191–209.

Varki, Ajit and David L. Nelson. 2007. "Genomic Comparison of Humans and Chimpanzees." *Annual Review of Anthropology* 36: 191–209.

Vigliocco, Gabriella, Stavaroula-Thaleia Kousta, Pasqule Anthony Della Rosa, David P. Vinson, Marco Tettamanti, Joseph T. Devlin, and Steano R. Capppa. 2014. "The Neural Representation of Abstract Words: The Role of Emotions." *Cerebral Cortex* 24: 1767–1777.

Voth, H.R. 1903. "The Snake Legend." Pp. 349–353 in *The Oraibi Summer Snake Ceremony*, by H.R. Voth (Field Columbian Museum Publication 83, Anthropological Series III. (4): 263–358). Chicago: Field Columbian Museum.

———. *The Traditions of the Hopi* (Field Columbian Museum Publication 96, Anthropological Series Vol. VIII). Chicago: Field Columbian Museum.

de Waal, Frans B.M. 1989. "Food Sharing and Reciprocal Obligations among Chimpanzees." *Journal of Human Evolution* 18: 433–459.

———. 1991. "The Chimpanzee's Sense of Social Regularity and Its Relation to the Human Sense of Justice." *American Behavioral Scientist* 34: 335–349.

———. 1996. *Good Natured: The Origins of Right and Wrong in Humans and Other Animals*. Cambridge, MA: Harvard University Press.

———. 2009. *The Age of Empathy: Nature's Lessons for a Kinder Society*. New York: Three Rivers Press.

———. 2013. *The Bonobo and the Atheist: In Search of Humanism among the Primates*. New York: W.W. Norton.

———. 2016. *Are We Smart Enough to Know How Smart Animals Are?* New York: W.W. Norton.

de Waal, Frans B.M., and Sarah F. Brosnan. 2006. "Simple and Complex Reciprocity in Primates." Pp. 85–106 in *Cooperation in Primates and Humans: Mechanisms and Evolution*, edited by P. Kappeler and C.P. van Schaik. Berlin: Springer-Verlag.

Wallace, Anthony F.C. 1966. *Religion in Anthropological View*. New York: Random House.

Wallerstein, Immanuel M. 1974. *The Modern World System: Capitalist Agriculture and the Origins of the European World Economy in the Sixteenth Century*. New York: Academic Press.

———. 1984. *The Politics of the World Economy: The States, the Movements and Civilizations*. Cambridge: Cambridge University Press.

———. 1989. *The Modern World System III: The Second Era of Great Expansion of the Capitalist World-Economy, 1730–1840s*. New York: Academic Press.

Watts, D.P. and J.C. Mitani. 2001. "Boundary Patrols and Intergroup Encounters in Wild Chimpanzees." *Behaviour* 138: 299–327.

——. 2002. "Hunting Behavior of Chimpanzees at Ngogo, Kibale National Park, Uganda." *International Journal of Primatology* 23: 1–28.

Watts, Joseph, Simon J. Greenhill, Quentin D. Atkinson, Thomas E. Currie, Joseph Bulbulia, and Russell D. Gray. 2015. "Broad Supernatural Punishment but Not Moralizing High Gods Precede the Evolution of Political Complexity in Austronesia." *Proceedings of the Royal Society B* 282(2014.2556): 1–7.

Watts, Joseph, Oliver Sheehan, Quentin D. Atkinson, Joseph Bulbulia, and Russell D. Gray. 2016. "Ritual Human Sacrifice Promoted and Sustained the Evolution of Stratified Societies." *Nature* 532: 228–234.

Weber, Bruce H. and David J. Depew. Eds. 2003 *Evolution and Learning: The Baldwin Effect Reconsidered*. Cambridge, MA, and London: MIT Press.

Weber, Max. 1922 [1968]. *Economy and Society: An Outline of Interpretive Society*, edited by G. Roth and C. Wittich. Berkeley and Los Angeles: University of California Press.

Weiner, Bernard. 1986. *An Attribution Theory of Motivation and Emotion*. New York: Springer.

Wellman, Barry and S. O. Berkowitz. 1988. *Social Structures: A Network Approach*. New York: Cambridge University Press.

Wells, Spencer. 2002. *The Journey of Man: A Genetic Odyssey*. Princeton, NJ, and Oxford: Princeton University Press.

Westergaard, G. C and C.W. Hyatt. 1994. "The Responses of Bonobos (*Pan pansicus*) to Their Mirror Images: Evidence of Self-recognition." *Human Evolution* 9: 273–279.

White, F.J. 1989. "Ecological Correlates of Pygmy Chimpanzee Social Structure." Pp. 154–164 in *Comparative Socioecology*, edited by V. Standen and R.A. Foley. Oxford: Blackwell.

Whitehead, Hal and Luke Rendell. 2015. *The Cultural Lives of Whales and Dolphins*. Chicago, IL: University of Chicago Press.

Whiteley, Peter M. 1988. *Deliberate Acts: Changing Hopi Culture through the Oraibi Split*. Tucson, AZ: University of Arizona Press.

——. 2008. *The Orayvi Split: A Hopi Transformation*. Vol. 1, *Structure and History*. Vol. 2, *The Documentary Record*. New York: American Museum of Natural History.

Whiten, Andrew. 2011. "The Scope of Culture in Chimpanzees, Humans, and Ancestral Apes." *Philosophical Transactions of the Royal Society* 366: 997–1007.

Whiten, Andrew., J. Goodall, W.C. McGrew, T. Nishida, V. Reyonolds, Y. Suglyama, C.E.G. Tutin, R.W. Wrangham, and C. Boesch. 1999. "Cultures in Chimpanzees." *Nature* 399: 682–685.

Whiten, A. and T. Suddendorf. 2007. "Great Ape Cognition and the Evolutionary Roots of Human Imagination." Pp. 31–60 in *Imaginative Minds*, edited by I. Roth. Oxford: Oxford University Press.

Williams, George, C. 1966. *Adaptation and Natural Selection. A Critique of Some Evolutionary Thought*. Princeton, NJ: Princeton University Press.

Wilson, David Sloan. 1975. "A Theory of Group Selection." *Proceedings of the National Academy of Sciences* 72: 143–146.

——. 2002. *Darwin's Cathedral. Evolution, Religion, and the Nature of Society*. Chicago: Chicago University Press.

Wilson, David Sloan and Edward O. Wilson. 2007. "Rethinking the Theoretical Foundations of Sociobiology." *The Quarterly Review of Biology* 82 (4): 327–348.

Wilson, Edward O. 1975. *Sociobiology: The New Synthesis*. Cambridge, MA: Harvard University Press.

——. 1978. *On Human Nature*. Cambridge, MA: Harvard University Press.

——. 1998. *Consilience: The Unity of Knowledge*. London: Little, Brown.

Winkelman, Michael. 1998. "Aztec Human Sacrifice: Cross-Cultural Assessments of the Ecological Hypothesis." *Ethnology* 37 (3): 285–298.

Wolpoff, Milford H. 1999. *Paleoanthropology*. Boston: McGraw-Hill.

Wuthnow, Robert. 1987. *Meaning and The Moral Order: Explorations in Cultural Analysis*. Berkeley, CA: University of California Press.

Yang H., P.D. Jeffrey, J.J. Miller, E. Kinnucan, Y. Sun, N.H. Thomas, P. Zheng Chen, W.H. Lee, and N.P. Pavletich. 2002. "BRCA2 Function in DNA Binding and Recombination from a BRCA2-DSS1-ssDN NPA Structure." *Science* 297(5588): 1837–1848.

Young, Nathan. 2003. "A Reassessment of Living Hominoid Postcranial Variability: Implications for Ape Evolution." *Journal of Human Evolution* 45: 441–464.

Young, Nathan, Terrence Capellini, Neil Roach and Zeresenay Alemseged. 2015. "Fossil Hominin Shoulders Support An African Ape-like Last Common Ancestor of Humans and Chimpanzees." *Proceedings of the National Academy of Sciences* 112: 11829–11834.

Zalmout, Lyad, W. Sanders, L. MacLatchy, G.g Gunnell, Y. Al-Mufarreh, M. Ali, A. Nasser, A. Al-Masari, S. Al-Sobhi, A. Nadhra, A.l Matari, J. Wilson, and P. Gingerich. 2010. "New Oligocene Primate from Saudi Arabia and the Divergence of Apes and Old World Monkeys." *Nature* 466: 360–365.

Zimmer, Carl. 2016. "Monkeys Could Talk, but They Don't Have the Brains for It." www.nytimes.com/2016/12/09/science/monkeys-speech.html (accessed March 18, 2017).

Zolikoffer, Christoph P.E. and Marcia Silva Ponce de Leon. 2013. "Pandora's Growing Box: Inferring the Evoluton and Development of Hominin Brains from Endocasts." *Evolutionary Anthropology* 22: 20–33.

Zuckerman, Phil. 2016. *The Nonreligious: Understanding Secular People and Societies*. New York: Oxford University Press.

Index

adaptive problems in society 25–30, 150, 159
Aegytopithecus 52–3
African Americans 198–9
afterlife, the 158
agency 12, 38, 62, 149–50
Alexander VI, Pope 218
amniotes 21–2
amygdala, the 83–5, 154
ancestor worship 144
Andrews, Peter 50
anger 22, 90, 227
anthropoids 52
anxiety and anxiety-reduction 143, 153–8, 169, 186
apes 54–63, 68–71, 94, 99; behavioral capacities and propensities of 107–23
archaic religions 214–15
askēsis 174
Assmann, Jan 215
attribution theory 118–19
Australopithecines 75–9, 82–3, 245
autism 85
Axial age religions 170–3, 192, 213–16
Aztec civilization 210–12, 218–22

al-Baghdadi, Abu Bakr 240
Bandaranaike, Solomon 236
bands 127, 139, 143–7, 163–4
Barger, Nicole 85
Bartholomeusz, Tessa J. 235–6
behavioral capacities 30, 128–9
Bellah, Robert N. 12, 135, 170, 243, 247
Blanton, Richard 212
Blau, Peter M. (and *Blau-space*) 140, 181, 221
Blavatsky, Helena 234
body language 124
bonding 84–6, 91, 96–8, 115–16, 123, 131, 134–6, 142–4, 153, 159, 164, 227, 243, 246; between mother and infant 96–7
Brahmanism 235

brain, the, evolution of 47–8
British Empire 206–7, 223, 225
Broca's area 93–5, 133, 155
Buddharakkhita, Mapitigama 236
Buddhism 163–70, 215–16, 233–7
Bushmen 163–9

Call, Josep 63, 119
Carneiro, Robert L. 205
"carnivals" 110–14
Carrasco, David 211–13
Chase-Dunn, Christopher 205
chimpanzees 65–71, 75, 86, 93, 98–102, 107, 110–23, 134, 137–41, 145
China 216
Christ-religion, early form of 170–4, 192–6, 217
Christianity 192–201, 215–22, 225, 234–7
Ciochon, R.L. 50
"circumscription" 205
Civil Rights movement 225
civil war 46
cladistic analysis 60–72, 76, 79, 138, 244–5; of the social structure of the LCA 63–72
class conflict 40–1
Coleman, Naomi Michelle 238
Collier-Baker, Emma 6
Collins, Randall 109, 112, 126, 131–2, 161
colobines 56
colonialism and colonization 31–2, 225, 234
Columbus, Christopher 218
communities of worshipers 130, 216
community, sense of 4–6, 71, 75, 109, 122
community as the basic social unit 101–2
"community complex" concept 5, 102, 130, 134, 142, 153, 158–61
competition for resources 16–17, 33–4, 38, 209
conflict in society 41, 223; *see also* religious conflict
Confucianism 215–16